Strategic Operations Management

This indispensable text offers students a high quality treatment of strategic operations management. It provides the reader with a clear understanding of the importance and nature of operations strategy by determining exactly which core competencies, resources, technologies and key management activities underpin an operations strategy. The book demonstrates how various 'building blocks' can be combined and customized into unique operations strategies. When these strategies are correctly implemented, they provide sustainable competitive advantage and allow firms to provide a diverse range of services and goods in their increasingly demanding, complex and dynamic marketplaces and spaces.

Strategic Operations Management contains chapters that cover customizing operations strategies for retail, manufacturing, services and SMEs, as well as sections on e-business and complexity theory in relation to operations theory.

Features offered include:

- extended case studies including several from Europe, North America and Asia;
- case vignettes;
- learning objectives;
- key terms;
- chapter introductions to aid reader accessibility;
- 'time out' boxes to prompt the reader to review what has been learnt;
- 'critical reflection' boxes that analyse theories and models.

Robert H. Lowson is the Director of the Strategic Operations Management Centre at the University of East Anglia, Norwich, UK, and regularly visits universities throughout Europe and North America. He is a Leverhulme Trust Research Fellow and works as a consultant in a number of sectors. Dr Lowson has published widely on operations strategy and general management issues.

Strategic Operations Management

The new competitive advantage

Robert H. Lowson

London *and* New York

First published 2002
by Routledge
11 New Fetter Lane, London EC4P 4EE

Simultaneously published in the USA and Canada
by Routledge
29 West 35th Street, New York, NY 10001

Routledge is an imprint of the Taylor & Francis Group

© 2002 Robert H. Lowson

Typeset in Perpetua and Bell Gothic by Florence Production Ltd, Stoodleigh, Devon
Printed and bound in Great Britain by T.J. International Ltd, Padstow, Cornwall

British Library Cataloguing in Publication Data
A catalogue record for this book is available from the British Library

Library of Congress Cataloging in Publication Data
A catalogue record for this book is available from the Library of Congress

ISBN 0–415–25654–2 (hbk)
ISBN 0–415–25655–0 (pbk)

To Freda and Tom

Contents

Figures

Tables

Case studies

Preface

INTRODUCTION

From our international research and teaching at the Strategic Operations Management Centre (SOMC) at the University of East Anglia, it has become clear that the strategic issues involved in operations management are assuming greater importance in many commercial sectors, both public and private. The world is changing. The consumer is spoiled. Diversity is rampant, and we have moved away from the supply side of business to a 'pull' world. Consumer demand is approaching the chaotic in its insatiable appetite for diverse, individualized services and goods that are provided by flexible and responsive organizations. To understand this shift, management theorists have developed a whole galaxy of operations strategies. For many firms competing in increasingly complex and dynamic sectors, the correct choice, implementation and evolution of such a strategy can provide considerable competitive advantage.

As the title of this book suggests, operations strategy holds the key to competitive advantage for many organizations. Indeed, it is increasingly recognized as a significant contributor to the effective strategic management of firms both large and small, domestic or international and both profit and non-profit making. Further, despite its historical evolution from a manufacturing or production setting, the service sector and even quasi-governmental institutions now recognize its ubiquitous value and worth.

The study of operations management is one of the oldest business disciplines, but operations strategy, as a subject, is a relatively new phenomenon. This has a major implication: as with any new and unfolding discipline, much of what is reported in this book is heavily research-orientated, both empirical and conceptual. This is important: considerable management literature exists offering glib eulogies without substance or advocation and description without any attempt at order, quantification or practical implementation. Worse, many approaches reported have suggested almost catholic applicability. It stretches credibility to accept, as many suggest, that all these remedies can offer profound utopian benefits to every firm and every industry: a universal panacea no matter what the ill! The complexity of our organizations and their contingent, embedded nature in their business and wider environments, makes such claims naive and even misleading.

Yet very little is known about operations strategies, their building blocks and their individual power if properly deployed, despite their receiving extensive coverage in management literature. Too often, unfortunately, we have been offered accolades without substance. Despite attracting folklore status, even their strongest supporters are often unable to discern between fact and fiction as they peddle catholic benefits. Further, there is a conspicuous absence of 'how-to' information; the kind needed for practical implementation. One of the principal aims of this text is to explode a few myths.

First, the book is intended to help students of business and management, both under-graduate and postgraduate, to discover exactly what components underpin an operational strategy. The text provides the reader with a clear understanding of the importance and nature of operations strategy. Further, we demonstrate how this knowledge, when combined with the correct strategic implementation, allows firms to provide a diverse range of services and goods in their increasingly demanding, complex and dynamic marketplaces or marketspaces. The text will also appeal to the practising manager who may wish to explore how conceptual and theoretical perspectives can be employed in a practical setting.

Second, we believe that the teaching of operations management in Europe, North America and Asia is assuming a more strategic perspective in a significant shift away from the traditional treatment of the subject. Service and manufacturing organizations are now operating in fast-moving arenas. Future and potential managers (in the form of the under-graduate and postgraduate student population) need to appreciate the degree of complexity involved in such competition and the key contemporary issues they are likely to face upon joining an organization. The teaching of operations management is a growth area that is assuming greater importance in business schools and schools of management. Employers are seeking to recruit more students equipped with knowledge of this discipline at a strategic level. It is now clear that strategic operations management, in its ability to equip firms with the wherewithal to supply the value that consumers demand, provides the key foundation of all business success.

Finally, the book offers axioms firmly rooted in current empirical research. The author has led a five-year international research study in operations strategy and management. This work gathered data from leading international retailers, manufacturers and service providers. Their best-practice examples will be used for case study material in the text (see p. xvi). The research also enables the publication to appeal to North American as well as European audiences.

OUTLINE STRUCTURE

From the outset, the objectives of this text were to offer a well-structured and balanced account of current research. In addition, it was felt vital to construct a book that promoted analysis and understanding and built upon practical applications in diverse consumer sectors – good theory will help good practice, but understanding theory without understanding practice can be dangerous. The book is, therefore, structured in three distinct parts.

Part I, *understanding*, comprises an introduction to operations management (chapter 1) and offers various frameworks for the academic analysis of the subject (chapter 2). Finally, chapter 3 concludes this section by providing a full review of strategic management at the various levels within the organization. Here, the alternate and opposing schools of thought are debated and operations strategy introduced. These chapters provide a bedrock of knowledge as we underline the growing importance of operations at a strategic level. We describe the genealogy of strategic operations management, and its increasing contribution to competitive advantage by providing a fast, accurate and flexible response to demand complexity.

Part II offers further *analysis* and the beginnings of *synthesis*. This is the heart of the book. It supplies a unique understanding of operations strategy (chapter 4) by offering, and attempted possibly for the first time, an academic taxonomy, both at generic and applied levels. The aim is to posit a solid, research-based classification from which future research can proceed. The essence of operations strategy is discussed in chapter 5. Here, we introduce the notion of strategic building blocks from which the final strategy is derived. Using this understanding, chapter 6 gives a review of strategy deployment and implementation. In this chapter, we describe how the various building blocks are combined or fused into a unique strategy capable of sustained competitive advantage. Chapter 7 continues the theme of composition by explaining how certain tactical factors and contingency issues will also influence the shape of the strategy – as well as acting as key management levers. We return to the competitive dimensions of the operations strategy in chapter 8 by explaining in detail how it will contribute to competitive edge. Finally, chapters 9 and 10 offer a slight digression. Having gained an appreciation of the nature and role of the operations strategy we return to its *raison d'être*: understanding and satisfying demand complexity (chapter 9) and the latest research initiatives, such as the influences of complexity theory (chapter 10).

Part III deals with practical *applications*. The basic aim of the section is to translate strategy into action using a number of discrete domains. This is an important perspective. Far too little consideration has been given to the essential differences between organizations. As mentioned earlier, it is often assumed that one particular approach or strategy will work equally well in every firm or sector. We beg to differ. The fundamental philosophy of Part III adheres to the dictum that each operations strategy will be, to a degree, unique. That said, for the purposes of this text we are forced to generalize, but do so with this principle in mind. In chapter 11, the retail and manufacturing applications of the operations strategy are examined using the strategic building blocks established earlier. The service sector and small and medium-sized enterprises (SMEs) are the focus of chapter 12. It was felt necessary to include, and dedicate quite a large section of the text to these two organizational communities, given the importance of their current standing in many economies and the sparseness of the operational management literature devoted to their activities. We also note the modern movements towards international trade and the evolution of advanced supply networks in chapter 13. We asseverate that these managerial approaches exemplify the benefits and contribution accruing from a properly deployed and implemented operations strategy. Finally, chapter 14 explores two modern, yet little understood applications of an operations strategy: e-business and strategic coordination. The former, as an enabling technology and method of conducting business, is likely to remain an influential field of study; while the latter speculates upon a new and tentative role for an operations strategy.

A guide for the reader

This text has tried to respond to the demand for more research and publication in the study of operations strategy while keeping the work manageable; using a combination of in-depth coverage combined with examples and tasks. This note offers some practical advice to enable the reader to get the most from the material.

USING STRATEGIC OPERATIONS MANAGEMENT

There are three guiding principles that will benefit students and managers alike:

1   Ensure that the concepts, frameworks and theories are properly understood through analysis and synthesis;
2   Apply the theoretical elements to practical applications, either in the book or from your own experience;
3   Remember that this text offers a number of perspectives, but there will always be counter claims. Reading more widely (from the references given) and considering counter arguments as a part of an academic critique, will firmly establish a learning ethos.

Aims of the book

The book is intended as a core text and compulsory reading for students of operations strategy and management at both undergraduate (B.Sc.) and postgraduate level (M.Sc. and MBA). It has been derived from research, teaching and work experience over the past fifteen years. However, it also proposes a new direction as well as offering students a comprehensive study of strategic operations management.

Pedagogic features of the text

- A *chapter map* to guide the reader through the work, and highlighting the interconnections between the three parts and their chapters is provided at the beginning of the text on p. 2.

- *Learning objectives* are included at the beginning of each chapter showing the likely achievements and acting as a reflective mechanism by which to check progress.
- *Case vignettes* appear throughout each chapter in order to 'ground' important concepts in a more practical setting.
- *Time out boxes* are also extensively used and have accompanying questions. These ensure the reader understands the theory/practice connection.
- *Critical reflection* commentaries offer alternative academic perspectives that may not be mainstream, but encourage the reader to be aware of differing viewpoints.
- *Chapter conclusions* recap and review the main points raised.
- *Discussion questions, work assignments and exam questions* are also suggested in order to test learning of both concepts and applications. They are also useful as team or group exercises.
- *A case study* ends most chapters helping to consolidate learning of the major themes. There are also suggested discussion questions to accompany each case.
- *A commentary* is provided prior to each part of the book to explain the connections between the issues in various chapters.
- *Recommended key readings* are listed at the end of most chapters. These are intended to help the reader conduct research and read widely.

Teaching and learning resources

The *Strategic Operations Management* web site can be viewed at:
   http://www.routledge.com/textbooks/0415256550

Foreword

The increasingly volatile market conditions that now face many firms around the world are bringing new challenges to operations management. There is now a recognition that operational efficiency and effectiveness are critical to gaining and retaining competitive advantage. Survival in these global markets demands far higher levels of agility and responsiveness that was ever the case in the past. yesterday's model of how to manage operations is now being questioned. New solutions are required as well as a wider view of what constitutes operations strategy and management.

Robert Lowson's book breaks new ground in its review of the way in which value is created and differentiation achieved through superior operations strategies. Using appropriate examples and case studies the book brings to life the new ideas that are being adopted by leading organizations. The insights that it provides will guide managers and students in their search for understanding of the concepts and tools that underpin excellence in operations strategies.

Martin Christopher
Professor of Marketing and Logistics and
Chair of the Centre for Logistics and Transportation
Cranfield School of Management

Acknowledgements

There are at present only a few books concerning operations strategy. Many are limited in their scope to the consideration of purely manufacturing aspects (despite their undisputed worth). Others remain conceptual. This offering is intended to be extensively research-led. Many concepts may be controversial and open to critique but that is the nature of the beast. Nevertheless, it is hoped that a significant first step has been made towards a greater understanding of a young and unfolding discipline: one based upon creative thought and empirical scientific study, rather than mere evangelical description. To do this, however, has required a contribution from a vast number of people who have made this book possible.

To this end, gratitude, and more, is necessary and expressed to all those that have given so much to this project. In particular: to Helen for her friendship and support over the years and to Katie and Charlie for showing they care. To Lizzy for her unconditional love and for introducing me to the furrier species, and to Alan Hunter of North Carolina State University for his continued efforts in attempting to teach me how to think. To Nicola Burgess at UEA, who shows exceptional creativity and potential and contributed much. To Tracey George, with her wonderful organizational ability to discern the 'wood from the trees'. Last, but not least, to Ian Brodie of UEA and the Open University, for his friendship and inspiration.

Finally, there are many friends, colleagues and students both at UEA and Cardiff University who have given time and thought and who deserve my sincerest recognition and gratitude. My thanks to you all.

Bob Lowson
June 2002

Understanding

Owl hasn't exactly got Brain, but he Knows Things.

A.A. Milne (1973)

The first part of this book is devoted to understanding. In the immortal words of A.A. Milne, understanding and knowledge are vital to the development of an academic critique. In this first section, we aim to provide the reader with a full appreciation of operations management and its importance for the modern organization. Thereafter, in chapter 2, the reader is provided with three important frameworks. These give differing academic perspectives, each an important, although contrasting, contribution to the analysis of any operational situation.

Part I concludes with an examination of business strategy, and in particular the different approaches and viewpoints currently evident in the corporate strategy debate.

The understanding of these perspectives allows us to locate the role of operations strategy within a strategic hierarchy and genealogy, and to demonstrate its contribution to competitive advantage for any organization.

CHAPTER MAP

Before embarking upon the first chapter, the following 'chapter map' describes the locus of each particular part of the book, the chapters involved and their interconnection. It is suggested that the reader refer back to this as and when necessary throughout the text.

CHAPTER MAP

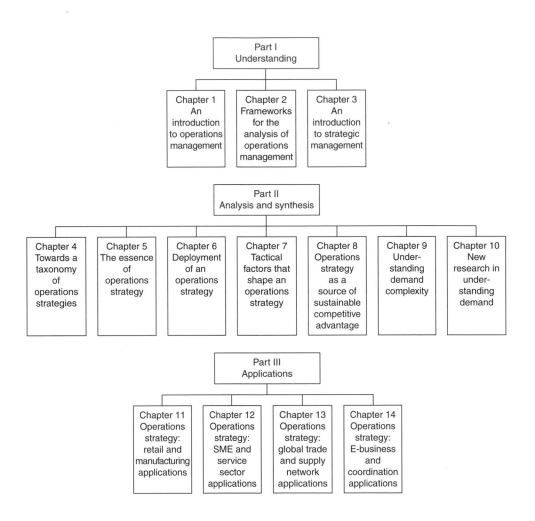

Chapter 1

An introduction to operations management

This first chapter is an introduction to operations management. It provides both new and experienced students with some key and basic concepts that they will carry with them throughout the rest of the book.

LEARNING OBJECTIVES

After considering this chapter, the reader will be able to:

- Appreciate the importance of operational management for all firms, whether they offer services or manufacture tangible goods
- Identify operational activities both from a narrow and broad perspective using the three definitions provided
- Be able to locate modern operations management perspectives and have an understanding of their historical evolution and the various important trends
- Explain the main differences between, and classifications of, products and services
- Understand the various types of operation that are used and the strong link between them and the demands upon the organization for flexibility
- Understand the main theoretical frameworks used to study operational management as well as appreciating their advantages and disadvantages

> ### KEY TERMS
>
> - Operations management
> - Supply and demand
> - Product and service combinations and 'servitization'
> - Consumer demand, variety, diversity, flexibility, responsiveness and operational types

INTRODUCTION

The value that is added by both operations management and operations strategy is fundamental to most organizations. Operational activities are central to the provision of services and/or goods. Every organization provides a product and service combination. A meal in a restaurant, a visit to the hospital, buying a pair of Levi 501s, making a pair of Levi 501s, Woodstock Festival, insuring an automobile, staying in an hotel, going to the cinema, even the workings of a prison; all have operations activities and their management is central to the successful provision of goods and services. Even Government departments can draw heavily upon operational initiatives and strategies when they talk about supply chain management, lean supply, just in time and total quality management.

This first chapter sets the scene for the rest of the book. It aims to offer the reader an insight into the importance of operations management and gives a firm platform for the study of operations strategy. Those with a comprehensive understanding of the main tenets of operations management might like to skim through this first section and then move directly to chapter 2.

THE CONTRIBUTION OF OPERATIONS MANAGEMENT

Operations management has its origins in the study of 'production' or 'manufacturing management'. These terms still very much apply to manufacturing organizations that will have distinct operational activities that convert say, beans and rich tomato sauce into cans of baked beans to be sold by a retailer. Thus, we can initially think of operations management as being part of a distinct function producing a product and service combination, just as we have marketing and accounting functions in many organizations. Our first definition of operations management is therefore:

Definition 1
The design, operation and improvement of the systems that create and deliver the firm's primary product and service combinations.

Every organization that offers goods or services has an operations activity. As far as the organization structure is concerned, some firms will have a discrete operations function. This might be called a manufacturing department, an operations system, or have no identifiable name at all. However, like marketing and accounting, it is a fundamental function of the firm with professionally trained operations or production managers responsible for conversion of resources into the required product and service combinations. In some organizations such managers will have different titles, a store manager for a retailer, administrative managers within a hospital or distribution managers in a logistics company. This first definition tends to be rather narrow as it applies to core conversion processes (mostly manufacturing). We need therefore to widen the definition of operations management to a second level:

Definition 2
The design, operation and improvement of the internal and external systems, resources and technologies that create and deliver the firm's primary product and service combinations.

This definition expands the operations management concept beyond just internal production or manufacturing. Now it will encompass other activities such as purchasing, distribution, product and process design, etc. Further, there will also be external managerial responsibilities at a supply network level, covering a number of interconnections between external firms.

Increasingly, however, modern economies are built around services and experiences, and here operations management is no less important. As Slack *et al.* (2001) point out, there should be a broader viewpoint that will take into account all activities throughout the firm that have any connection with delivery of a service on a day-to-day, 'make it happen' basis. This brings us to the third definition of operations management:

Definition 3
The design, operation and improvement of the internal and external systems, resources and technologies that create product and service combinations in any type of organization.

This definition has subtly changed from the second. It now includes both manufacturing and non-manufacturing firms (the service sector – whether profit or non-profit making) and more importantly, covers operational activities and systems throughout the organization, whether performed by an individual, group, unit or department. For example, a marketing or sales function can also be viewed as an operational activity – this also gives us the notion of internal consumers and suppliers. All activities in an organization will create a product and service combination (the latter might include information) supplied to either an internal or external consumer. Similarly, other internal/external suppliers will also support these activities. We can now see that the broad definition of operations management covers the main activities throughout a firm and its supply network contributing to the delivery of a product and service. These activities and their various interfaces can best be viewed as a number of consumer/supplier linkages.

5

Now, if one accepts the above definitions, it becomes clear that operations has a strategic contribution to make in supporting the needs of customers and consumers: the purpose of this book. We now examine the nature of operations management in more depth and expand on the need for an operations strategy; partly, an integrating system between these operational activities and the wider business strategy.

TIME OUT BOX I

Traditionally, economic activity is described in stages:
- Primary (extractive)
- Secondary (goods producing)
- Tertiary (domestic services)
- Quarternary (trade and commerce services)
- Quinary (refining and extending human capacities)

To which we can now add:
- Experience

Can you provide examples for each of these, demonstrating the main operational activity?

THE STUDY OF OPERATIONS MANAGEMENT

We now build on the contribution of operations management to an organization. In particular, more detail is given regarding the development of the subject, the types of operation and product and service combinations, and the main frameworks that can be used to analyse operational activities.

The history of operations strategy and management

The study of operations management and operations strategy is a relatively new discipline, when compared with many of the social and natural sciences. However, as Meredith and Amaoaka-Gyampah (1990) remark, when it comes to the study of organizations, business and management, 'We in the field of operations management consider our field to be one of the oldest in business schools pre-dating the emergence of finance and accounting by decades'. Despite some amazing production feats in ancient civilizations and early modern epochs – the building achievements of the Romans, the pyramids of Egypt and the Great Wall of China – operations management as a discipline is more usually associated with the production of consumer goods. As we can see in Table 1.1, the growth of the subject and its major influences can be traced back to the late eighteenth and early nineteenth centuries. The table shows only the major operations-related concepts during this time (some of which are not always original ideas!).

Table 1.1 *The historical growth of operations management and strategy*

Period	Concept	Originator and/or influence
Industrial Revolution during late eighteenth and early nineteenth centuries	Factory management and the change from craft working to centralized, mechanically powered factory systems	Developed during the onset of the Industrial Revolution in the period when factories were created
1769	Steam engine	James Watt
1776	Division of labour. Worker specialization and the breaking down of the production process into small tasks performed by different workers. Also encourages specialized machinery	Adam Smith, *Wealth of Nations*
1790s	Interchangeable parts. A move to volume production with standardized parts rather than customized one-at-a-time operation. Led to the need for system of measurement and inspection, standard production methods and supervisory quality checking	Eli Whitney
Scientific management 1910s–1920s	Principles of scientific management	
1911	The best methods of performing each job based on observation, measurement and analysis. Standardization of practices and economic incentives	Frederick W. Taylor
1911	Industrial psychology. Time and motion studies – the efficiency experts	Frank and Lillian Gilbreth
1912	Activity scheduling methods and charts	Henry Gantt
1913	Application of scientific management. The moving assembly line and high volume, mass production	Henry Ford
Quality controls 1930s	Sampling and inspection. Statistical control methods	Walter Shewart
Human relations movement 1930s–1960s	Importance of worker motivation	
1930s	Hawthorne Studies. Worker motivation and technical aspects of work affected productivity	Elton Mayo

continued

Table 1.1 *continued*

Period	Concept	Originator and/or influence
1940s	Motivation theories – hierarchy of needs	Abraham Maslow
1950s	Motivation theories – hygiene factors	Frederick Herzberg
1960s	Motivation theories – theory X and Y	Douglas MGregor
Management science 1940s–1960s	Early computerization and cybernetics	Norbert Wiener, John von Neumann, Gregory Bateson
1940s	Multidisciplinary team approaches to complex systems problems. Linear programming (simplex method)	Various operations research groups. George Dantzig
1950s–1960s	Extensive development of operations research tools (simulation, waiting-line theory, mathematical programming, project scheduling techniques Programme Evaluation and Review Technique (PERT) and Critical Path Analysis (CPA)	Many researchers in Europe and the US
1951	Digital computer	Remington Rand
1960s	MRP	Joseph Orlicky, IBM
Quality revolution 1970s–1990s	Service quality and production quality in a total quality management ethos	
1970s	Mass production in the service sector	McDonald's Restaurants
1980s–1990s	Total Quality Management (TQM) and Total Quality Control (TQC)	W. Edwards Deming Joseph Juran
Manufacturing strategy paradigm 1970s–1990s	Manufacturing as a competitive weapon	
1970s–1990s	The influence of just in time (JIT) and other Japanese manufacturing methods: Kanban, Poka-yokes, empowerment, flexible manufacturing systems, etc. Lean Production	Taiichi Ohno and the Toyota Production System
1980s	Operational contribution to competitive strategy	Wickham Skinner Hayes and Wheelwright

Era / Period	Development	Attribution
1980s	Computer-integrated Manufacturing (CIM) and personal computers	
1980s–1990s	Supply chain management	Various consultants and companies
1990s	Operations strategies are applied to all organizations (not just manufacturing)	
1990s	Business process re-engineering	Hammer and Champney
Information revolution 1980s–2000s		
1970s	Electronic Data Interchange (EDI), Electronic Funds Transfer (EFT) and Electronic Point of Sale (EPoS)	Numerous individuals and companies
1990s	Internet, WWW, electronic enterprise; Learning organization	
Globalization 1990s–2000s		
1990s–2000s	Worldwide markets and operations; Electronic commerce and electronic enterprises	
Information and consumer revolution 2000s–	Agility, flexibility and responsiveness; Time as a competitive weapon; Supplier network management; Mass customization; E-commerce and V-business, E-tailing and E-operations; Customizing operations strategies by demand behaviour	Lowson
The next era?????		

We can see the large number of influences and significant events, many of them overlapping, upon the discipline of operations management.

TIME OUT BOX II

Forecasting, especially longer term, proves increasingly difficult for organizations. Sometimes we can extrapolate trends, but the future is not always a continuation of the past. Two questions:

1   What operational trends might continue into the next 2–3 decades?
2   What methods can organizations use to attempt to understand future influences, particularly external ones?

Types of product

When discussing a definition of operations management, we used the term 'product and service combinations'. This is an important point. The type of product and/or service has important implications for operations management, as we shall see in chapter 3, on operations strategy. Types of product and/or service and their different behaviours drive many activities and strategies in an organization. In addition, for the study of operations management, there are clear distinctions between goods and services (although these will in future become increasingly blurred). For example:

■   Services are mostly intangible (an insurance package, a flight between two cities, advice from a lawyer, etc.);
■   Services are normally produced and consumed simultaneously (a visit to the doctor, a haircut), there is no inventory involved;
■   Services are often unique and one-off (each medical operation is different, financial packages such as pensions and investments are individualized);
■   Services have a high consumer interaction, and this involves uniqueness (try having your hair styled or your teeth polished without being there!);
■   Services are often difficult to define and are dynamic. Services are inconsistent and change rapidly (each meal in a restaurant is subtly different and unique, the service on your car or the visit to the doctor is different every time, a motor vehicle insurance policy may look the same but it changes as your car matures);
■   Services often have a large knowledge-base and are hard to automate (education, medicine and legal services for example);
■   Services are widely dispersed; they are brought to the clients/consumers at their home or a central purchasing point (a retailer for example).

In Table 1.2 we detail some more distinctions.

Table 1.2 *Some possible differences between services and goods*

Service attributes	Goods attributes
Tend to be intangible	Tend to be tangible
Reselling is unusual	Products can be resold
Most services cannot be stored as an inventory	Inventories can be built and the product stored
Many aspects of quality are hard to measure	Most aspects of quality are measurable
Selling is a crucial part of the service	Sales are at a distance (temporally) from the production
The provider rather than the product is transportable	Product can be transported
Site of service is important for customer contact	Site of facility has cost implications, rather than customer
Services are often difficult to automate	Production processes can be automated
Response time is shorter as customer is part of the process – markets are thus often local	Longer response time due to separation of production from consumption or sale – markets are global
Labour intensive	Capital intensive
Generally, smaller facilities needed	Generally, larger facilities

The astute reader will note the use of the term 'possible' in Table 1.2. It is true to say that most goods will contain service elements and some services contain tangible goods. We can think about this in terms of a continuum as in Fig. 1.1.

Services (and in chapter 12 we discuss the various types), now constitute the largest economic sector in many western economies. For example, as a percentage of gross domestic product (GDP), services have risen from 48 per cent to 69 per cent in the UK and 60 per cent to 75 per cent in the USA (*The Economist*, 1999). In addition, the service element (often in the form of information – the information content) of most tangible products is becoming more important, hence our reference to product and service combinations. As Vandermerwe and Rada (1988) suggest:

> More and more corporations throughout the world are adding value to their core corporate offerings through services. The trend pervading almost all industries, is consumer demand-driven, and perceived by corporations as sharpening their competitive edges.
>
> Modern corporations are increasingly offering fuller market packages or 'bundles' of consumer-focused combinations of goods, services, support, self-service, and knowledge. But services are beginning to dominate.
>
> The movement is termed the 'servitization of business' . . . and is clearly a powerful new feature of total market strategy being adopted by the best companies. It is leading to new relationships between them and their consumers.

11

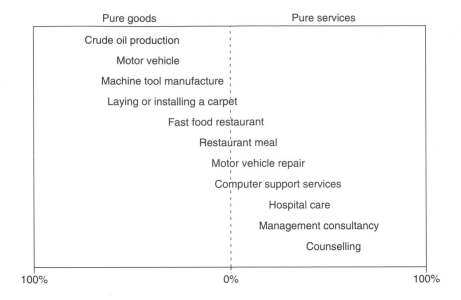

Figure 1.1 The goods–services continuum

CASE VIGNETTE **DULUX PAINTS**

Dulux paints (part of Imperial Chemicals Industries plc) no longer manufacture and sell paint for room decoration; their value added product is now atmosphere. You can buy, for example, Heritage Colours. These can be Georgian, Art Deco and Edwardian, Victorian, etc. to evoke a period atmosphere in a home of any age. Historical research has revealed the types of paint used, its effect, and its composition – Dulux tries to faithfully recreate these. In addition, free information helplines and a web site can be contacted for inquiries about stockists, the products, advice on product specifications, advice on creating themes and schemes, a local decorator service, and even recommended reading about restoration of period properties, the paint makers and historical figures responsible for particular interior designs.

TIME OUT BOX III

Seeking an example of 'serivitization', we examined what many people would naturally think of as a tangible purchase: the motor vehicle. If buying from Vauxhall motors, these are the options under the 'Vauxhall Experience':

- *Finance*. Hire purchase, lease purchase, personal leasing and choices 1, 2, 3.
- *Masterfit*. While-you-wait, book-in-advance servicing, with advance quotations, twelve month warranty, courtesy car and special viewing areas to watch repairs.

- *Accident support*. Free roadside recovery and repair.
- *Insurance coverage*.
- *Safeguard*. A protection scheme for all faults over 1, 2 or 3 years.
- *Mobility*. Special help for drivers with disabilities.
- *A car*!

According to Vauxhall Motors: 'The package reflects consumer desires for life-time satisfaction and support.'

Can you provide other examples of more tangible goods that have increasingly important service elements?

In later chapters we return to the importance of product and service combinations for organizations and their strategies. We now turn to the nature of operations. Just as organizations produce products and services they also use different types of operations.

Types of operation and the flexibility needed

Organizations undertake many diverse activities in providing different types of product and service. Often they will have numerous suppliers and customers. Our point is that modern organizations are complex entities and there will be many different types of operation, both in individual firms as well as across different industries. Clearly types of operation will vary across different sectors. Aluminium smelting is markedly different to a call centre or dealing with insurance claims. We need to think about the various operational types generically and how we can offer a taxonomy of operational forms.

TIME OUT BOX IV

What is the difference between a taxonomy and a typology?

One way of classifying the different types of operation witnessed in any organization is to equate them to the activities undertaken and the degree of flexibility sought. Activities, as we have seen, can take place within a distinct operational function, throughout the whole organization and encompass other organizations in a supply and demand network. Likewise, the degrees of flexibility can be viewed at different levels.

Before going further, we need to spend a little time thinking about the concept of flexibility. It is a subject to which we will return throughout the book and one that is exercising the minds of many managers in today's organizations. Flexibility can be examined from the viewpoint of three particular issues: the stimuli for greater variety, the various classifications of flexibility, and the measurement of flexibility.

The stimuli for greater flexibility

Flexibility in operational systems is as a response to the need for variety and its attendant uncertainty. The former can be viewed as being demand driven, while the latter are a supply dilemma.

CONSUMER DEMAND FOR VARIETY

In the last four decades consumer tastes have altered radically. Consumer demand in many sectors for both goods and services is displaying piecemeal, disjointed and unsystematic tendencies and thus becoming increasingly difficult to satisfy. Consumer purchases are more than ever a reflection of a lifestyle or fashion statement rather than the satisfaction of a basic need, and this is only the beginning. To this has to be added the complexity of instantaneous, electronic, worldwide communication, and an information explosion that has served to educate the average shopper beyond any level seen to date. To meet these changing demand patterns, organizations are having to react more speedily, while at the same time avoiding the penalties associated with increasingly volatile demand. In the fashion-clothing sector, this drive for variety has reached almost chaotic proportions as we can see in the following case.

CASE VIGNETTE **ARCADIA GROUP**

According to the Operations Director of Arcadia, a leading UK clothing retailer:

> Consumer demand is today more fragmented. The consumer is more discerning about quality and choice and with an increasing fashion influence: no single style or fashion has dominated for any length of time. The importance of increased consumer purchasing power and a search for individuality has added to the multi-dimensionality that consumer goods and services organizations have to contend with. Traditional seasons overlap as summer/winter clothes are demanded throughout the year. Style changes, once predictable and linked to formal changeover times, are now fluid and constantly changing; replaced at the slightest hint of fashion preference. "Basics", those staid garments without seasonality and volatility, now are subject to even shorter seasons.

Empirical research data also confirms some of these trends. In a 1999/2000 survey of UK retailers and manufacturers in fast-moving consumer goods (FMCG) industries was conducted by the Strategic Operations Management Research Centre at the University of East Anglia. Eighty-five per cent of retail respondents agreed that 'for sale' seasons were becoming much shorter. In addition, 93 per cent of respondents to the survey witnessed a trend towards greater product volatility, fashion influence, difference and customization over the last three years. Similar questions were posed to a separate survey of manufacturers. Here, 81 per cent agreed that seasons were much shorter, 87 per cent saw more volatility in style introductions, and 93 per cent believed unique and customized goods to be of increasing importance (Lowson *et al.*, 1999).

These changes in the business environment are bringing about unprecedented reconfiguration of consumer demand, as witnessed by many organizations supplying product and service combinations. In turn, these forces are being passed along supply and demand systems. Unfortunately, the further away from the point of sale, and indication of demand preference, the harder it becomes to react in an effective and efficient manner. Recourse to long term forecasting becomes virtually useless as complexity and dynamism continue to grow. This brings us to the second problematical area when considering the driving forces for variety, the inherent uncertainty that this brings.

DEMAND UNCERTAINTY

If we accept the picture of increasing variety in both goods and services and the search for ways to customize products at an individual level, we can see that many industries are characterized by difficult trading conditions. Unfortunately, modern organizations are ill-equipped to deal with such uncertainty. First a short history lesson.

At the beginning of the twentieth century, manufacturing, for example, was characterized by an emphasis on mass-markets, high volume, and the use of interchangeable parts. When the principles of scientific management, as promulgated by Frederick Taylor and his disciples, were also adopted, it produced a new era of industrial power that was eagerly exploited by the likes of Henry Ford, Isaac Singer and Andrew Carnegie.

The dogma was clear. For utmost efficiency in any factory: divide work into the smallest possible components; assign the tasks to specialists; appoint managers to supervise and make decisions, leaving workers free to concentrate on manual tasks; reduce variation to a minimum; standardize all inputs and outputs to reduce defects; exercise control through a rigid hierarchy which channels communication in the form of exception reports upward and directives downward; measure performance by cost, scale, experience, and length of production run; and employ forecasting systems in order to anticipate any possible changes.

In 1974, Wickham Skinner proposed the idea that manufacturers have to learn to focus their plants (or even departments within plants) on a limited range of technologies, volumes, markets and products, and that strategies, tactics, and services should all be arranged to support that focus. The maxim was that a factory that succeeds in focusing its activities will outperform one that does not. Costs would be lower than in unfocused operations due to experience curve and scale benefits; consequently focus provides competitive advantage (Skinner, 1974).

There are, however, always trade-offs with such an approach; for example, low cost and flexibility are inappropriate bedfellows. If the market demands greater variety and diversification, the focused factory comes under considerable strain, often alleviated only at the expense of high inventory levels.

As we reached the 1980s, it soon became apparent that organizations operating in this manner were unable to cope with one particular demand: variety. Fundamental and radical new methods of organization and management were needed once the demand for diversity reached a critical level. We are still searching for these new approaches (many of which we now call operations strategies) and this is the subject of this book.

We will return to these ideas later. Those interested in the debate regarding flexibility as a response to uncertainty are recommended to consider an early research paper: Swamidass and Newell (1987).

The next factor we need to consider is the changes that these stimuli have engendered in organizational structure.

THE ORGANIZATIONS RESPONSE TO CHANGING CONSUMER DEMAND

Today's commercial environment requires businesses to seek greater product and process variation (flexibility) through agility and responsiveness; a possible rejection of the Fordist principles of mass manufacturing, and a move towards mass customization (see Piore and Sabel, 1984 and Pine *et al.*, 1993).

CASE VIGNETTE **MASS CUSTOMIZATION**

The aim of mass customization is to provide varied and often individually customized products at the low cost of standardized, mass-produced goods. As Pine *et al.* (1993) comment:

> Mass customization calls for flexibility and quick responsiveness. In an ever-changing environment, people, processes, units and technology reconfigure to give consumers exactly what they want. Managers co-ordinate independent, capable individuals, and an efficient linkage system is crucial. Result: low-cost, high quality, customized goods and services.

However, this Holy Grail of mass customization can only be attained once an entire supply network[1] with all various firms, is integrated and data openly shared allowing visibility at all stages. A supply/demand system that is fully visible provides the basis for flexibility and responsiveness to real-time demand.

How close are we to achieving such a situation? Figure 1.2 shows the evolution of such a supply/demand system. The first stage, I, depicts the situation for most goods and services sectors at the turn of the last century. The participants considered themselves as separate and autonomous industries with no influence, reliance or interconnection with each other. The second stage, II, shows the effect of interdependence and the supply chain is born. But industries remain manufacturing- and product-driven. In stage III we see the current situation (theoretically); with Electronic Data Interchange (EDI) beginning to form an interface between industries in a pipeline responding to a consumer pull.

In the light of the changing business environment described above, a fourth more radical and advanced stage is needed for successful competition and the necessary flexibility.

....

1 Supply/demand networks or systems are our preferred terminology to describe what is often known as the 'supply chain'. We feel that the terms 'system' or 'network' demonstrate a complex flow of information and products, both up and downstream, whereas a 'chain' only really represents a linear sequence of activities. This is covered in more detail in chapter 13.

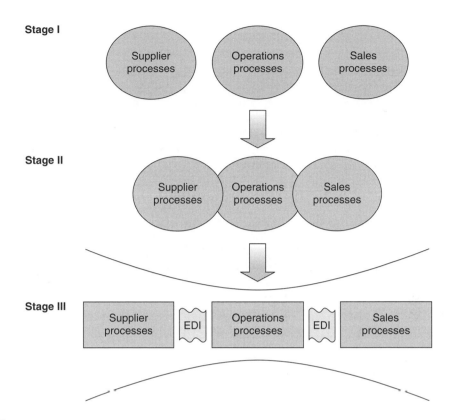

Figure 1.2 *Supply system evolution*
Source: adapted from Lowson et al. *(1999)*

Figure 1.3 shows stage IV, what we term the 'cluster of value'. This is a future vision. The consumer group is the nucleus of activity, dictating and driving all demand preferences for variety. The entities circling (sales processes, operations processes, supplier processes) are all closely linked and responding by providing value in the exact format required. Consumer groups are constantly changing over time and organizations are involved in many different simultaneous clusters of value at any given point. This type of structure and interaction is necessary in response to growing demand variety, including the move to mass customization of services and goods.

The classification of flexibility

Operational flexibility and the activities that comprise it can be witnessed at three levels in an organization, no matter whether providing a service or a good:

1   At an inter- and intra-organizational level. A strategic choice: both the firm and its supply and demand systems are concerned with the ability to offer a particular level of flexibility in its product and service combinations.

Stage IV

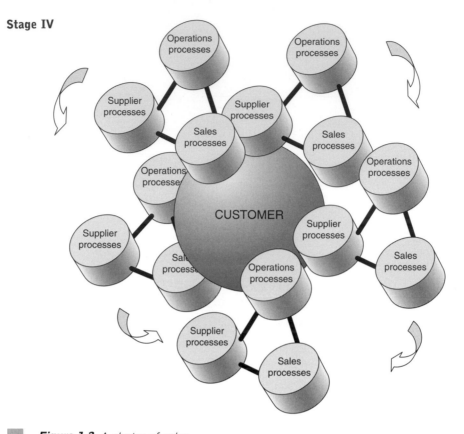

Figure 1.3 *A cluster of value*

2   At an operations level. Whether in a distinct operations function or throughout the organization, a concern for whether the operations activities are capable of sufficient product and service flexibility.
3   At an individual, resource, process and structure level. Are our human resources (whether as individuals or in teams or groups), other resources (machinery, etc.), our processes (stages or activities necessary to complete a task) and structure (how the system is organized and governed) sufficiently flexible to match the variety of tasks required to support levels 1 and 2?

The strategic nature of flexibility applies at a total supply and demand system and organizational level (1 and 2 above). Thus, we can conceptually think of flexibility as being both an external and internal response to the value demanded by the customer.

EXTERNAL RESPONSE TO CUSTOMER VALUE DEMANDS
1   Product and service combination flexibility. The ability to introduce and modify products and service combinations according to demand variety.
2   Mix flexibility. An ability to change the range of product and service combinations being produced over a given time period.

3   Volume flexibility. Being able to change the level of an operations output over time.
4   Logistics flexibility. An ability to provide the flexibility that determines when and where and how a product or service is provided.
5   Monetary flexibility. A flexibility over when, where, and how payment is made for the necessary goods and services (including interests rates, instalments, etc.).
6   Contact flexibility. The degree of direct contact with customers and the influence this has upon value and customer satisfaction.

Flexibility requires a firm's internal and external boundaries to be redrawn. Atkinson (1984), using the flexible firm model, debated the implications for manpower, work and employment. He identifies three types of flexibility to which we add a further two below.

INTERNAL RESPONSE TO CUSTOMER VALUE DEMANDS
1   Functional flexibility. Redeployment of workers as the product and production tasks require.
2   Numerical flexibility. The capacity to make changes in employment levels to match demand.
3   Financial flexibility. Pay and other employment costs reflecting the objectives of numerical and functional flexibility.

To these we can add:

4   Temporal flexibility. Flexibility in timing work arrangements to match demand needs.
5   Technological flexibility. The flexibility of process technology to be used for multiple purposes.

  Given the importance of flexibility, it seems advisable that an organization devises methods to ascertain the levels it requires. However, flexibility is a concept that is difficult to quantify and operationalize – to a degree, each business must assess its individual impact in terms of the general benefits and costs it brings.

Types of operations revisited

Having given consideration to the variety of demands placed on an organization and the consequent flexibility necessary for modern operations, we now return to generic types of operations possible. This can be done by expanding upon the various types of flexibility encountered and addressing the two flexibility classifications: external and internal response to customer value demands.

EXTERNAL RESPONSE TO CUSTOMER VALUE DEMANDS
■   Product and service combination flexibility;
■   Mix flexibility;
■   Volume flexibility;
■   Logistics flexibility;

- Monetary flexibility;
- Contact flexibility.

INTERNAL RESPONSE TO CUSTOMER VALUE DEMANDS
- Functional flexibility;
- Numerical flexibility;
- Financial flexibility;
- Technological flexibility;
- Temporal flexibility.

The types of operation needed in each of the above instances and the environmental influences necessitating their adoption can be seen in Tables 1.3 and 1.4.

As we can see, the various flexibility categories will have a direct impact upon the types of operation involved and their organization. Those firms specializing in highly customized customer flexibility will also have high internal flexibility and will be complex in nature, with much variety and change. An acute understanding of demand and their environment is important as their markets are also likely to be complex, competitive and fast moving – in short this type of business will often be described as organic and highly contingent upon its environment (Burns and Stalker, 1961). In addition, the styles of operation and organization will also vary between the organizational subunits. Hence the degree of differentiation in operations will alter according to the nature of the industry and its environment. An appropriate degree of integration will also be required to tie these differentiated operational activities together (Lawrence and Lorsch, 1967). Conversely, industries and sectors requiring lower levels of flexibility are likely to be populated by firms with more standardized, routine operations producing product and service combinations that offer little change. Demand over time is steady and easier to forecast. Firms can specialize in higher volume operations to take advantage of economies of scale and experience curve benefits. More mechanistic in nature, these businesses will utilize regimented and stereotypical operations that will change little across the whole organization.

TIME OUT BOX V

What are the implications for the Kentucky Fried Chicken operation if its consumers suddenly decide they want individual meals that are unique, high quality, with lots of variety and variation and served by waiters at the table?

CONCLUSION

In chapter 1 we have described the contribution of operations management to the study of business, management and organizational theory. Definitions have been provided that will, hopefully, help the reader to gain a clear impression of the discipline. The chapter has also

Table 1.3 *A typology of operations: an external response to customer value demands*

Types of flexibility*	External demands and forces	Operational examples	Ramifications for operations
Product and service combination flexibility	High levels ■ Rapidly changing nature of demand ■ Short product life cycles Low levels ■ Static product demand ■ Standardized goods and services	High levels ■ Fashion clothing retailer ■ Food retailer ■ Specialized services (legal, medical, etc.) Low levels ■ Utility services ■ Process manufacturing (oil, chemicals, etc.)	High levels ■ Understanding complex demand ■ Highly flexible, customized operations ■ High consumer contact ■ Rapid product development/modification ■ Importance of innovations and change ■ Scope and variety more important than scale Low levels ■ Little change ■ Routine regular, standardized products and activities ■ Little product development/modification ■ Scale needed to reduce cost
Mix flexibility	High levels ■ Rapidly changing types of demand for mixed product offerings ■ Products demanded in combinations ■ High substitution of one good for another Low levels ■ Demand for single product type ■ Little product substitution	High levels ■ Electronic goods with hardware/software combinations ■ Emergency services ■ Gourmet foods and restaurants ■ Department stores Low levels ■ Bakery (single type of good sold) ■ Auto tyre replacement services ■ Window cleaning	High levels ■ Understanding complex demand ■ Parallel operations necessary to produce the variety needed ■ High levels of inventory often required ■ Flexible workforce and technology ■ Ability to change output flexibly Low levels ■ Standardization and task specialization ■ Well defined operations
Volume flexibility	High levels ■ Large peaks and troughs in demand	High levels ■ Ice cream and soft drinks ■ Restaurant services ■ Mass entertainment events	High levels ■ Flexibility of operations, technology and people ■ Ability to alter capacity and type of operation

continued

Table 1.3 continued

Types of flexibility*	External demands and forces	Operational examples	Ramifications for operations
Volume flexibility	Low levels ■ Regular and repeatable operations with little change to demand volume	Low levels ■ Fast food restaurants ■ Manufacture of socks ■ Public transport systems	Low levels ■ Operational repetition ■ Little change in capacity or operation
Logistics flexibility	High levels ■ Specialized and personalized delivery services ■ Just in Time delivery services ■ Vendor managed inventory Low levels ■ Consumer travels to collect goods ■ Consumer desires/needs to be present for product/service provision	High levels ■ Home delivery logistic systems ■ Delivery of components to another manufacturer in exact quantities and when needed ■ Management of a customer's inventory for them Low levels ■ Retail shop ■ Hairdressers, dentist, doctor, etc.	High levels ■ Physical flexibility needed in distribution systems ■ Often necessitates outsourcing to logistical expert Low levels ■ Little flexibility in either demand or supply side as this is provided by consumer
Monetary flexibility	High levels ■ Payments flexibility for credit, instalments, charge-back, payment as consumed, etc. Low levels ■ Payment on purchase or on delivery	High levels ■ This type of flexibility increasingly witnessed for expensive purchases (cars, houses, holidays) Low levels ■ Traditional retail transaction	High levels ■ Financial flexibility requires a firm to restructure its accountancy systems and its relationships with finance providers Low levels ■ Payment made at point of consumption
Consumer contact flexibility	High levels ■ How much time operational personnel spend with consumer ■ Waiting time is crucial ■ Often, higher variety Low levels ■ Time lag between production and consumption	High levels ■ Fast food restaurant ■ Medical services Low levels ■ Process manufacturing ■ Distance learning ■ Internet banking	High levels ■ High control levels needed for efficiency and effectiveness ■ Quality is immediately apparent ■ Consumer contact skills needed Low levels ■ Quality defects not immediately apparent ■ Low consumer contact ■ Standardized goods ■ Lower labour costs

* External response to consumer value demands. In this section, external demands for flexibility prompt changes in product and service combinations.

Table 1.4 A typology of operations: an internal response to customer value demands

Types of flexibility*	External demands and forces	Operational examples	Ramifications for operations type
Functional flexibility	High levels in any of the above categories	■ Manufacturer of consumer goods with large peaks and troughs in demand (ice cream, soft drinks) ■ Processing plants with seasonal influences (sugar beet processing) ■ Many automotive firms require that managers and clerical staff be prepared to work on production lines if necessary ■ Skilled engineering workers on oil or gas platforms must undertake semi-skilled or unskilled work if there is no available craft work	■ The firm uses a small core group of workers who are given job security in return for task and role flexibility as required by products and production
Numerical flexibility		■ Seasonal service sectors such as holiday resorts	■ Surrounding the core workers are short-term, part-time, job sharing, temporary workers who can be used to change the workforce numbers in line with demand levels
Financial flexibility		■ Pay rates and structures will reflect individual performance and demand levels	■ Pay and other employment costs reflect the state of supply and demand in the external labour market and support the objectives of functional and numerical flexibility
Temporal flexibility		■ 24-hour retailing ■ Bank opening at weekends and evenings	■ Scheduling of work attendance to meet fluctuations in demand
Technological flexibility		■ A farm tractor ■ Transportation technology ■ Cooking equipment	■ Product, process and information technology tends to be multi-purpose – applied and adapted to a number of uses

* Internal response to consumer value demands. In this section, external demands for flexibility prompt internal changes in organization.

discussed the types of product and service combinations now supplied by most commercial organizations. In addition, a link was made between operations and flexibility often required in a modern enterprise. Chapter 2 continues to examine the role of operations management by offering key frameworks necessary for further, more detailed, analytical study.

CASE STUDY – OPERATIONS STRATEGY IN ACTION

Clipper Navigation Inc. – an introduction to operations management (www.victoriaclipper.com)

Victoria Clippers are some of the world's quickest catamarans; in fact, the Victoria Clipper IV's turbojet service makes it the fastest passenger ferry in North America. The speed of the clipper ships during the 71-mile voyage between Victoria (the capital of Vancouver Island on the north-west coast of Canada) and Seattle is 25 to 45 knots (about 28 to 53 miles per hour), enabling them to complete the journey in two to three hours.

These unique Clipper Ferries operate between Seattle, the San Juan Islands, Victoria and Vancouver. The service is renowned for not only its speed, but also its comfort, reliability, frequency and low cost. It makes perfect sense for holidaymakers who can leave the car behind in the gridlock that is sometimes Seattle, and island hop between the beautiful islands. It is also the favoured route of many business travellers and commuters who either live on the many islands or travel between Vancouver City and Seattle. What better way might there be to arrive at work? Sitting on a 'float plane' in the comfort of the vast viewing areas (on the sundeck or inside) watching Orca whales and bald eagles circling the stunning vegetation of the many coves and islands. With towering trees and snow-capped mount Rainier as a backdrop, as an attendant serves you in your seat. It is a unique travel experience. And all this for less than a rail commuter would pay to travel from the Home Counties to London.

Because so little of these aluminium alloy catamarans lies below the water line, they are remarkably easy to handle and provide both a fast and smooth ride. These are also large ships. The latest Clipper IV carries 350 passengers and is 132 feet from stem to stern with a cruising range of 346 nautical miles. There are 12 ferries in the fleet and they sail four times a day between Seattle, Vancouver and Victoria. In addition there are departures twice a day from each of these cities that stop off at the various islands and other coastal towns.

Coordination of these services is vital. All the departures of Clippers ferries have to be closely coordinated with all the booking services and reservations for both pedestrian and car passengers. Many of the ferry sailing's link up with local motor coach companies, small seaplane services, helijet flights and Amtrak Railways that will drive on and off and take passengers to destinations further afield such as Portland in Oregon, the Canadian Rockies and the Whistler Ski Resort.

Operations management is a key concern for Clipper Navigation. As their Vice-President for Operations, Tom Morris remarks:

The coordination and management of these interconnected operations is vital to us. But it is not just a matter of internal operations, the success of our services relies heavily upon our partners, both horizontal and vertical.

ANSWERS TO TIME OUT BOXES

Time out box I

Economic activities can be classified as:

- Primary or extractive – these are concerned with agriculture, mining, fishing and forestry. The main operational activity involves transforming natural resources to produce a product.
- Secondary or goods producing – manufacturing and processing activities that transform raw materials and components into finished goods.
- Tertiary or domestic services – restaurants, hotels, barber and beauty shops, laundry and dry cleaning, maintenance and repair for example. Here the transformation involves the delivery of a product and service combination.
- Quaternary (trade and commerce services) – transportation, retailing, communication, finance and insurance, real estate, governmental, etc. Again, the delivery of services is the main transformation.
- Quinary (refining and extending human capacities) – health, education, research, recreation, arts. Transforming and satisfying human self-actualization needs.
- Experience (the experience economy providing entertainment, education, aestheticism and escapism). The transaction provides an experience in which value is created through engaging and connecting with the consumer in a memorable way. It is the basis of operation for Starbucks, Disney World and Planet Hollywood for example. Readers interested in the concept might consider Pine and Gilmore (1998).

Time out box II

1   The power of the Internet should not be underestimated. It is likely that consumers will increasingly make purchases in this way. However, as yet, e-fulfilment is far from satisfactory and the seamless shopping experience is still a long way off. We also believe the trend for 'customization' and 'personalization' will continue and this will have considerable implications for the design of our operating systems

2   A question that has troubled most firms at one time or another. Forecasting is clearly little help over longer time periods and with regard to events in the wider, macro environment. Possible answers lie in the education of management and the workforce to become 'boundary-spanning' and develop a collective awareness of change and future possible change scenarios.

Time out box III

There are many possible examples, including grocery goods that now carry much more information regarding their composition as well as web sites for recipes, food information, recycling information, etc. Smart tags on apparel also offer similar information and can track the life of the product, its use and even its geographical location: take care where you leave your jeans!

Time out box IV

A common misconception is that taxonomies are empirical while typologies are conceptual. Yet taxonomies do not have to be empirically tested, although there are strong reasons for doing so, and typologies can be tested quite rigorously. Another distinction often suggested is that taxonomies provide comprehensive classification systems (including 'good' and 'bad' phenomena) while typologies only describe ideal types. To a degree this is true: however, it is perhaps better to think of typology as a branch of knowledge that deals with *classes* with common characteristics, a study of types, while taxonomy is a systematic approach to classification of *individual* examples often relying upon empirical and quantified data.

Time out box V

Like many fast food restaurants, the Kentucky Fried Chicken operation relies upon standardization and the division of labour. Each product and process is standardized with little variety. The various tasks are analysed and well understood and consumer contact is relatively low (there is no personalized service). This standardized, high volume operation with dedicated technology can be highly efficient and fast. However, it is not well equipped to cope with variety, as flexibility levels are low. Just try asking for boiled potatoes instead of fries with your Kentucky Fried Chicken!

DISCUSSION QUESTIONS, WORK ASSIGNMENTS AND EXAM QUESTIONS

1   How would you define the role of operations management? Apply these definitions to a manufacturer, a bank and a health centre.
2   Why has the distinction between tangible products and services become increasingly blurred?
3   Discuss why flexibility is important in today's modern organizational environment.
4   How can flexibility be classified and what implications will each classification have for operations management?

Reader questions related to Clipper Navigation Inc. case study

1   How would you describe the product and service combination supplied by Clipper Navigation?
2   Describe the main subsystems of the Clipper operations. Can you group the vital activities under particular headings?

3   Their VP for Operations mentions the importance of horizontal and vertical partners. What products and services might these provide and what is the essential difference between the two categories?

4   Think about the need for flexibility necessary for Clipper Navigation. As we have seen, flexibility is a matter of both an internal and external response. What are the particular operational activities vital to ensure this flexibility? Can they be improved? Could the organization use demand data and information to better plan operations?

RECOMMENDED READING

Katz D. and Kahn R.L. (1978) *The Social Psychology of Organizations*, John Wiley & Sons Inc., New York.

Meredith J.R. and Amoaka-Gyampah K. (1990) 'The Genealogy of Operations Management', *Journal of Operations Management* 9, 2, 146–67.

Pine II B.J. and Gilmore J.H. (1998) 'Welcome to the Experience Economy', *Harvard Business Review* July–Aug 97–105.

Slack N., Chambers S. and Johnston R. (2001) *Operations Management*, Financial Times and Prentice Hall, Harlow (chapter 1 – for those still unclear about the nature of operations management).

Swamidass P.M. and Newell W.T. (1987) 'Manufacturing Strategy, Environmental Uncertainty and Performance: A Path Analytic Model', *Management Science* 33, 4, 509–24.

Vandermerwe S. and Rada J. (1988) 'Servitization of Business: Adding Value by Adding Services', *European Management Journal* 6, 4, 314–24.

Frameworks for the analysis of operations management

Chapter 2 examines three important conceptual approaches that are used as an aid to understanding operations management. Each of these frameworks provides a slightly different perspective that can be used to build a greater understanding and to aid analysis.

LEARNING OBJECTIVES

After considering this chapter, the reader will be able to:

- Appreciate the different perspectives from which operational management can be analysed
- Understand the nature of value adding
- Apply techniques and concepts of systems theory to operational situations
- Consider the complexity involved in operations

KEY TERMS

- Value adding
- General systems theory
- Complex adaptive systems

INTRODUCTION

Analysing any operational activity is not an easy task, and there are a number of important techniques to aid this process. We discuss three of the more influential approaches so that the reader will be aware of their utility as well as their drawbacks.

VALUE ADDING

Value added is essentially related to how well the organization matches its product and service combinations to the identified needs of its chosen customers. Sources of value added are many and varied. Michael Porter (1985) comments:

> In competitive terms, value is the amount buyers are willing to pay for what a firm provides them. Value is measured by total revenue, a reflection of the price a firms' product commands and the units it can sell. A firm is profitable if the value it commands exceed the costs involved in creating the product. Creating value for buyers that exceeds the cost of doing so is the goal of any generic strategy.

Value chain analysis can be used to describe the activities within and around the organization, and relate them to the competitive strength of the firm (its ability to provide value for money products and services). Thus the approach rests upon the need to identify separate organizational activities and assess their value added. The importance of organized activities and systems becomes clear. The various resources (people, machinery, information, etc.) must be deployed into activities, routines and systems that produce the necessary value. The ability to perform particular activities and manage the linkages between activities is the key source of competitive advantage.

In order to understand these value activities Porter developed the value chain. Here, we can divide activities into two categories: primary and support.

Primary activities

- Inbound logistics (receiving, storing and distributing the inputs to an organization).
- Operations (transforming inputs into outputs).
- Outbound logistics (storing and distribution and delivery of product and service combinations).

- Marketing and sales (means by which consumers are made aware of and can purchase products and services).
- Service (activities that enhance the value of a product or service).

Each of the primary activities is closely linked to each other and to the support activities.

Support activities

- Procurement (the process of acquiring the resource inputs to *all* the primary activities across the whole organization).
- Technology development (all activities have a technology – including know-how and knowledge, whether concerned directly with products and services or processes).
- Human resource management (those activities involved in recruitment, managing, training, developing and rewarding people).
- Infrastructure (systems of planning, finance, quality control, information management, etc.).

A single organization will not necessarily undertake all these primary and secondary activities. As we know, firms are increasingly reliant upon others in their supply network. Thus, we must also think of value as being at a system level. Value creation will take place at the level of the supply system and the wider process needs to be analysed and understood. Once more, the linkages are important as a source of competitive advantage.

The net result of this value added analysis is a better understanding of those activities that add value and those that do not, and the amount of added value that is created. In so doing, both commercial and non-commercial organizations are able to make the changes necessary to activities so as to contribute to competitive advantage (we will return to this subject in chapter 3).

TIME OUT BOX I

The 'value chain' and 'value system' are important strategic concepts. However, are there limitations to this approach?

SYSTEMS THEORY

Systems thinking and systems theory owes its roots to the ideas of organismic biologists during the first half of the last century. Its emergence was a profound revolution in Western scientific thought which threatened René Descartes' celebrated method of analytical thinking: in every complex system the behaviour of the whole can be understood entirely from the property of the parts. Twentieth-century science now had to accept that systems could not be fully explained by reductionist analysis. The properties of the parts could be understood only from the organization of the whole – the context was equally important.

This systemic context is the property of the whole and is destroyed when a system is dissected into isolated elements. Thus, we have a nesting of systems and subsystems at different levels of complexity. Each level will also exhibit an emergent property not visible at lower levels (the whole is worth more than the sum of the parts). Indeed, the various networks of relationships are of primary importance over and above the objects in the system. In every system structure is a manifestation of the underlying processes.

Of course, contextual and process thinking is not new. Its forerunners existed even in Greek antiquity. However, the English mathematician Alfred North Whitehead advanced the study when in the 1920s, he formulated a strong process-oriented philosophy. At the same time physiologist Walter Cannon refined the ideas of constancy in an organism's internal environment to arrive at homeostasis, the self-regulating dynamic balance. Similarly, at the beginning of the century, a Russian scientist, Alexander Bogdanov, developed a theory called 'tektology', which can be translated as the 'science of structures'. Bogdanov's work was subsequently published in the West in 1928.

These influences led directly to the 'theory of open systems' that was formulated in the 1940s by the Viennese biologist Ludwig von Bertalanffy. Bertalanffy's concepts of an open system and general systems theory established systems thinking as a major scientific movement with new methodologies and application – systems engineering, systems analysis, systems dynamics, etc. Most importantly, Bertalanffy pointed to an application for thermodynamics in this new field. Thermodynamics, the discipline that addresses the phenomenon of heat and its relation to mechanical and electrical work, had been formulated in the middle of the nineteenth century. The second law, the law of the dissipation of energy, described the trend in physical phenomena from order to disorder. Any isolated, or closed, physical system will proceed spontaneously in the direction of ever-increasing disorder, described and measured by the degree of entropy. Bertalanffy tentatively suggested that living organisms were open systems that could not be fully described by classical thermodynamics. They were open and fed on a continual flux of matter and energy from their environment to remain alive:

> The organism is not a static system closed to the outside and always containing the identical components; it is an open system in a (quasi-) steady state . . . in which material continually enters from, and leaves into, the outside environment.
>
> Bertalanffy (1968)

The open system was thus characterized by a state of dynamic or 'flowing' balance, a system capable of self-regulation.

The various system theory principles, derived primarily from the study of biological systems, are now widely used in the analysis of management and organization. We will now briefly highlight some of the main tenets of open system theory.

- The concept of an 'open' system. A continuous exchange with the environment in order to sustain the life of the system and self-maintenance in order to acquire negative entropy (see below).

- Importation of energy. As discussed above, open systems import energy from the external environment.
- Throughput. Open systems transform the energy available to them.
- Output. Open systems export some product to the environment.
- Cyclical. Open systems have a pattern of activity (importation, throughput and output) that is cyclical in character.
- Negative feedback. Inputs also consist of information that acts as a feedback upon the nature of the environment and the system's internal patterns of activity. This negative feedback allows the system to correct any deviations in its course to keep in balance or homestasis.
- Homeostasis. Self-regulation and maintaining a steady state, the control of subsystems and an exchange with the environment.
- Negative entropy. The second law of thermodynamics applies to all systems. No structure is fully self-sufficient or self-contained. Systems, and particularly closed systems, have a tendency to deteriorate and run down. Open systems attempt to sustain themselves by importing energy to delay the onset of entropic tendencies; they are characterized by negative entropy.
- Integration and structure. The structure, function and behaviour of all of the elements of a system are closely related. The behaviour of the system cannot be understood by a reductionist analysis that looks for simple cause and effect or stimulus and response. The system will have an emergent property (the whole being greater than the sum of the parts) that is a result of a balanced integration and differentiation of the parts.
- Requisite variety. The internal regulatory mechanisms of the system and its subsystems must be as diverse (and appropriately integrated) as the environment upon which it relies.
- Equifinality. A flexible pattern of organization that allows the achievement of specific results in a number of ways. In other words, a system can reach the same final state from differing initial conditions and by a variety of paths.
- Evolution. Systems will move to more complex forms of integration and differentiation, as the environment becomes more complex and dynamic. This differentiated growth and elaboration is similar to the cyclical process of variation, selection and retention witnessed in evolution and natural selection.

Those readers interested in exploring the application of open systems theory in more depth should consult the work of Katz and Kahn (1978).

Returning to operations management. Many of these concepts regarding open systems have been applied to the operational activities of an organization. In its most basic form, this can be demonstrated by the input–transformation–output process of an open organizational system that is embedded in a wider environment. The transformation can be tangible, transforming raw materials into goods, or intangible, when providing services and information, and the activities of nearly all firms can be described using this framework. This model describes how input resources, both transforming (needed to perform the transformation) and transformed (changed by the transformation) are altered into various output types.

CRITICAL REFLECTION

Value adding analysis and open systems theory are useful ways to attempt to conceptualize an operational system. However, they have been criticized and the reader should be aware of the main objections.

First, such models can be rather simplistic. They ignore the complexity that is our organizations and their operational systems. For example, the input–transformation–output process does assume linearity. In linear systems small changes produce small effects, and large effects are due either to large changes or to a sum of many small changes. In non-linear systems, by contrast, small changes may have dramatic effects because they may be amplified repeatedly by self-reinforcing feedback. Thus, amplifying, positive, 'runaway' feedback, which has traditionally been regarded as destructive, appears to be a possible source of new order and growth in complexity theory. This does not mean that operational systems are chaotic – merely complex. They are still deterministic; in other words, we can still make some predictions, as these systems are relatively stable and their behaviour patterns, although never repeated exactly, remain within certain overall constraints and boundaries. We can understand the qualitative features of the system's behaviour rather than the precise values of its variables at a particular time.

Second, systems theory in particular places substantial weight upon environmental determinism as a major influencing factor upon the system. However, critics believe that in fact there is a greater degree of strategic choice: more significance should be placed upon the internal environment and particularly the degree of discretion available to power-holders and decision-makers. Here we question the heavy one-to-one correspondence between organizational structure and the environment. Systems theory does assume causation is essentially one way, that the environment drives organizational structure, rather than the alternative, that organizations may affect environment and even control the environment by direct influence.

Third, classical organizational analysis was rightly criticized for the assumption that there is one best way of organizing that serves in multiple situations. The approaches used by value adding analysis, open systems theory *et al.* have translated this into an assumption that there are many equally good ways with the choice among them dependent on the nature of the environment. This is clearly an improvement on the classical model that ignored the embedded nature of an organization in its social context, but even so, it still ignores the fact that there may be a number of equally effective ways to deal with a given environment. Different organizations could approach a given environmental problem with any variety of strategies, and each of them could be successful. Further, what happens if an organization fails to adapt to its environment?

Fourth, given the importance that these approaches place on the environment, we may need to consider that the environment is in fact not an absolute, given entity. Two organizations may define the same market differently; thus approach it with different strategies, and both be successful. Is the environment an objective reality or is it simply what we make it to be?

continued

continued

Finally, these approaches to understanding an organization and its operations are, to a degree, prescriptive. The assumption is made that effective managers can control their organizations' fates by finding optimal adaptations to environmental contingency.

We end this critical reflection by playing devil's advocate and offering a devastating critique of systems thinking by Lilienfeld (1978):

> Systems thinkers exhibit a fascination for definitions, conceptualisations, and programmatic statements of a vaguely benevolent, vaguely moralising nature . . . They collect analogies between the phenomena of one field and those of another . . . the description of which seems to offer them an aesthetic delight that is its own justification . . . No evidence that systems theory has been used to achieve the solution of any substantive problem in any field whatsoever has appeared.

COMPLEX ADAPTIVE SYSTEMS – PART 1

At this point we briefly introduce some of the current perspectives regarding complex adaptive systems (CAS). In chapter 10 the reader is offered more detailed insights into these phenomena. At this stage, however, it is important to appreciate that organizations, their operations and their supply networks are highly complex and often far from easy to understand. Indeed, their behaviour is, as we have seen, non-linear. In other words, behaviour is never repeated exactly and cannot be extrapolated or forecast with high degrees of accuracy. Unfortunately, this factor makes analysis (using systems theory or value adding) all the more difficult.

The principles of complexity apply to many things: jelly fish to bees, swallows to steelworks and even whole economies. Complex systems consist of many agents acting in parallel, without hierarchical control, in multiple layers of structure. They are also, to a degree, self-developing or -making (the term used here is autopoiesis) in their ability to self-organize; to self-refer (an ability to recognize and learn in anticipation of environmental change) and to display emergent behaviour (the whole being more than just a sum of the parts). These systems are also subject to entropy (the second law of thermodynamics) and decay as they wind down unless replenished with energy. We should also note that some systems can be complex without being adaptive (the whirlpool or vortex in the bath). It is only living systems that can cope with their environment using predictive models to anticipate and proact. As Trosiglio (1995) suggests:

> Complexity deals with a world that is far from equilibrium [at the edge of chaos] and is evolving in ways that we cannot hope to predict. It points to fundamental limits to our ability to understand, control, and manage the world, and the need for us to accept unpredictability and change.

The following four principles apply to complex theory:

- Complex adaptive systems cannot exist in a state of equilibrium. Any CAS requires requisite variety to cope with external sources of change – bounded instability.
- Complex adaptive systems have a capacity for self-organization and emergent complexity.
- Complex adaptive systems tend to move towards the edge of chaos. It is in this region that new forms can emerge (something not possible in either a state of equilibrium or totally random instability).
- Complex adaptive systems are characterized by weak cause and effect linkages. Small and isolated changes in one variable can cause huge and unpredictable changes in another. Alternatively, large changes may have little effect. We see a disproportionate response to changes in the independent variable.

The important lesson of this subsection is the contention that organizations, their operations, supply networks, supply chains and material and information flows are dynamic systems. Cohen and Stewart (1994) use the terms 'simplexity' and 'complicity'. Simplexity is the tendency of a single, simple system to generate highly complex behaviour. This leads to the more subtle concept of complicity, which is when two or more systems interact with mutual feedback that changes them both, leading to behaviour that is not present in either system on its own. As Levy (1994) phrased it:

> By understanding industries as complex systems, managers can improve decision making and search for innovative solutions. . . . Chaos [complexity] theory is a promising framework that accounts for the dynamic evolution of industries and the complex interaction among industry actors. By conceptualizing industries as chaotic systems, a number of managerial implications can be developed. Long-term forecasting is almost impossible for chaotic systems, and dramatic change can occur unexpectedly; as a result, flexibility and adaptiveness are essential for organizations to survive. Nevertheless, chaotic systems exhibit a degree of order, enabling short-term forecasting to be undertaken and underlying patterns to be discerned. Chaos [complexity] theory also points to the importance of developing guidelines and decision rules to cope with complexity, and of searching for non-obvious and indirect means to achieving goals.

CONCLUSION

Three different perspectives have thus far been discussed to aid our understanding of the operational process. Value adding is an important approach in that it forces us to think about the value a customer or consumer seeks from the operational system. Systems theory or thinking emphasizes contextual thinking and networks or relationships embedded in larger networks – the relationships being primary. Complexity theory, however, introduces a new dimension. We become concerned not just with the substance or structure but also the form or pattern. The structure involves quantities while the form or pattern has to be mapped to capture its qualities, as it cannot be measured or weighed.

CASE STUDY – OPERATIONS STRATEGY IN ACTION

The Taiwan retail sports market – frameworks for the analysis of operations management

The Taiwanese retail sports market is subdivided into clothing, sports footwear and sports equipment. In Taiwan this sector is increasingly competitive, saturated and dominated downstream by independent SME retailers and upstream by large manufacturers such as Nike, Adidas, Elle, Converse, Mizuno, Kappa, *et al.* The market is heavily influenced by the following trends:

■ A growing interest in health and fitness by customers having more leisure time than ever before;

■ An increasing variety of international sports are now televised, stimulating greater participation;

■ Sportswear is now worn as leisurewear and has become an important element in street fashion;

■ Fashion trends from Japan and America have a large influence on this market;

■ Leading sports brands such as Nike, Adidas and Reebok are growing in popularity;

■ There is increasing competition from clothing discount stores, mail order companies, non-specialist outlets (street stalls, markets, and department stores), and imported clothing from China, Hong Kong, Korea and South-East Asia.

Market demand

The sports market has many similarities to other fashion sectors. Seasonality, short seasons, complexity, high inventories and volatility are all evident. Demand is very uncertain due to the following factors:

■ Many frequent sports activities in communities, universities, clubs, schools, etc.;

■ The rise and fall in fame of sports personalities can cause rapid changes in demand;

■ Sales tend to be linked to major professional sports events;

■ The weather is unpredictable and causes swings in demand.

Market distribution

Three main brands dominate the Taiwanese sports market: Nike, Adidas and Reebok. There are also local brand suppliers that are increasing market share by offering much lower cost. Specialist sports shops are the main outlets for sports purchases, although new chain stores are now gaining ground.

Manufacturing and sourcing

Taiwan has high labour and land acquisition costs. This has meant that a number of manufacturers have moved production to China and other parts of Asia offering lower costs due to lower wage economies. However, quality of fabric and material offshore can be uncertain, consequently many firms ship materials to contract manufacturers, who make the garments and then send them back. This has resulted in long lead times, low levels of flexibility, poor response and many hidden costs, including transportation.

Retailers in Taiwan will usually source goods by using one or more of the following purchasing strategies:

1   *Forward purchase offshore, low cost*. Chinese or other Asian suppliers are used. Orders are placed in advance of any season (6–12 months in advance). Fabric and trims are sent to the manufacturers who construct the garments/shoes etc., to specification. Normally the finished goods are then shipped back to Taiwan in the agreed quantity needed for the whole of the sale season prior to the start of that selling season. Purchasing decisions are made considerably in advance of the sale season and before any demand indication is known. Quality is reasonable, and the price of the finished goods is low (although there may be hidden costs). Reorders are not usually possible during the sales season as response is very slow. Relationships with these suppliers are at a distance and formal; there is no real flexibility for returns or exchanges at the end of the season.

2   *Domestic, responsive and flexible*. A Taiwanese manufacturer provides a proportion (for instance 40 per cent) of the goods needed prior to the start of the selling season. Thereafter, in season manufacturing is based upon a re-estimation of actual demand using PoS data provided by the retailer and reorder using Electronic Data Interchange (EDI). This provides for quick turnaround manufacturing and shipment of products that are in demand. The retailer can more accurately stock reflecting demand, increasing consumer service, and suppliers do not have a high inventory burden. Production and distribution costs are higher, however, and volumes are deliberately small. Such a strategy does rely upon a close, almost symbiotic, relationship between supplier and retailer.

3   *Combined*. An Asian offshore manufacturer ships a large proportion of the goods needed prior to the start of the season. During the season, the retailer then makes weekly replenishment orders using Taiwanese suppliers for small 'top-up' amounts. However, Point of Sale (PoS) data and derived information are not widely shared with this domestic supplier. Thus supply is often shipped from his stock holding built as a buffer against uncertainty. Here, quality can be controlled although prices will be higher. There is a faster response and some degree of flexibility due to smaller batch sizes, but there will be increased labour and transportation costs and suppliers bear the inventory burden.

ANSWERS TO TIME OUT BOX

Time out box I

First, the analysis that this encourages, albeit important, can be somewhat one-dimensional. It tends to compartmentalize our thinking and ignores the relationships and interactions between primary activities and support activities. It also assumes that the organization is part of a linear chain. In fact, although to a degree true, this is a little simplistic: in reality the term 'network' would be a better analogy. Finally, deciding upon what activities add value is not very easy to discern, from the customer's perspective. In truth this will rapidly change and often the end-customer is unaware themselves! These criticisms apart, it is still a valuable method of analysis.

DISCUSSION QUESTIONS, WORK ASSIGNMENTS AND EXAM QUESTIONS

1   What do you understand by the term 'adding value'? How does such a concept encourage an external orientation?
2   What are the advantages and disadvantages of systems theory? In what way does this approach force us to consider the relationship between an organization and its environment?
3   In what ways could complexity theory aid our understanding of operations management?

Reader questions related to the Taiwan retail sports market case study

1   Consider how the case above might be analysed in terms of value adding using the concepts of value chain and value system.
2   As we discussed in this chapter it is useful to think of an organization, or even an industry, using and input, output and transformation process model. Using the three different sourcing strategies above, construct a model for a Taiwanese retailer. What will be the main differences between the three?

RECOMMENDED READING

Katz D. and Kahn R.L. (1978) *The Social Psychology of Organizations*, John Wiley & Sons Inc., New York.

Chapter 3

An introduction to strategic management

Chapter 3 embarks upon a strategic theme in order to introduce the fundamentals of an operations strategy. We aim to provide the reader with a clear appreciation of an operations strategy, its role, and its setting in the context of other business or corporate strategies.

LEARNING OBJECTIVES

After considering this chapter, the reader will be able to:

- Appreciate the nature of strategy and its content
- Recognize the different strategic viewpoints or schools of thought
- Establish the basic grounds for competition and positioning in a competitive environment
- Appreciate the nature of an operations strategy, its links with other strategic approaches, and its deployment

> ## KEY TERMS
>
> - Corporate and business strategy
> - Adding value
> - Design versus process
> - Market-driven as opposed to the resource-based view
> - Strategic positioning
> - Operations strategy
> - Strategic hierarchy
> - Strategic genealogy

INTRODUCTION

Competitive strategy is about difference, the choice of certain activities to deliver a unique value-mix to a selected market. Strategy, then, is first about choices. Choices concerning markets, product and service combinations, resources in their widest sense and directions for the future.

This chapter has four main themes. First, to develop an understanding of the nature of strategy. Second, to discuss the various strategic viewpoints and different opinions that exist concerning the nature of strategy. Third, to assess what is meant by strategic positioning. Finally, to consider the character of an operations strategy: its nature and context, its genealogy, its links with the broader business strategy, how it is formulated, and how it is deployed to support the competitive aims of the organization.

WHAT IS STRATEGY?

We begin with the classical view of strategy. Corporate strategy can be described as an organization's *sense of purpose* – a guiding purpose or policy, a focus statement, even a philosophy, for the achievement of an objective. It is the mapping out of future directions that need to be adopted using the resources possessed.

CASE VIGNETTE **JACK WELCH**

Jack Welch was a legendary CEO of the General Electric Company (GEC). When asked, he described strategic management as:

- Understanding where the business is at the moment
- A clear view about where it wants to be in the future
- A wide-scale debate about how it will reach its future destination

The study of corporate strategy is a relatively recent phenomenon. Edith Penrose (1959) was one of the earliest academics to argue that what happened inside the firm was just as important as the marketplace outside the firm. Until this time, the main focus of economics had been upon the latter, with a detailed consideration of market demand and supply issues. Penrose argued that the growth of the firm was related to its use of resources, its past history and its evolution over time; previous history was a key influence on future development. The US strategist Alfred Chandler (1962) also published a substantial study concerning the growth of the firm. He argued, in support of Penrose, that the development of an organization over time is an essential element in understanding strategy.

At this point, a word about terminology. It is important to recognize that for many firms, there is a distinction between two levels of strategy: corporate and business (see the British Sugar plc example in Fig. 3.1).

At its highest level, we have a corporate, long-term plan. This seeks to determine the industries and markets in which British Sugar will compete. Investment, vertical integration, acquisitions and diversification, new ventures, divestment, allocation of resources to business units, will all be the type of decision made at this level.

The business strategy for British Sugar is concerned with how each factory or business unit competes in a particular industry or market to establish competitive advantage. This is the competitive strategy and describes the task of domain navigation as opposed to domain selection in the case of the corporate strategy (Bourgeois, 1980). The difference between the corporate and business strategies can be conceptualized by asking the following questions: 'What business or businesses should we be in (corporate)?' and 'How should we compete (business)?'

The next level of strategy concerns the functions and the so-called functional strategy to support the achievement of the corporate and business plans. Finally, the various strategies are deployed in the form of short-term tactics.

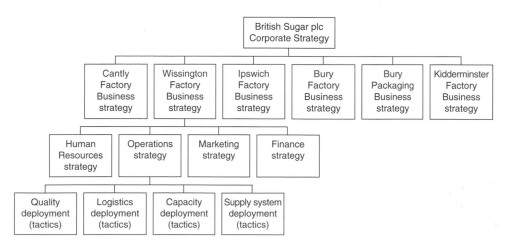

Figure 3.1 British Sugar's hierarchy of strategies

> ### CRITICAL REFLECTION
>
> There are two points of note concerning Fig. 3.1. First, we describe the logical, rational world of the classical strategist. As we will see later, not only is this often impractical, it is not always desirable. Second, as we have already discussed in chapter 1, many organizations will not have an identifiable operational function. For them the question of an operations strategy will be more complex — more of this later.

We can now define a strategy as:

Definition
The pattern of major objectives, goals and purposes and the fundamentals, plans, policies and philosophies for achieving those goals, that are declared in such a way as to define what business the firm is engaged in, or wishes to be engaged in, and the kind of organization it is or would like to be.

Strategy at the corporate or business level can be viewed from three vantage points:

1   Strategy formulation (developing a strategy);
2   Strategy implementation (putting a strategy into action);
3   Strategic control (modifying the strategy and/or its deployment to ensure desired outcomes are attained).

Thus, from the third perspective, every organization needs to manage strategies in three main areas:

1   The firm's internal resources;
2   The external environment within which the firm operates;
3   The firm's ability to add value to what it does.

We now deal briefly with each of these views.

Internal resources

Every firm needs to marshal and lever its key resources. A resource in this sense includes human resources, information and knowledge — as well as the traditional viewpoint of land, labour and capital. Strategies, in this classical view, attempt to optimize the use of these resources and to promote their combined distinctive capabilities in allowing the organization to survive and grow (we will return to the resource-based view of strategy later).

The business environment

Strategies cannot be developed in isolation. Regard must be had to the environment in which they operate and the effects of this environment. We can describe the environment as every aspect external to the firm; however, it is often very difficult to comprehensively analyse and assess all the various elements.

TIME OUT BOX I

The British Sugar operation in East Anglia is focused on refining sugar beet. The beet is a widespread crop in this area and grown over the winter for harvest in early February. Each processing plant runs a 24 hour, 7 day-a-week 'campaign' at this time to process the crops as they arrive. It is a massive logistical exercise to collect the sugar beet from rural and often inaccessible farms using third party hauliers.

Consider the business strategies for their processing units. What are likely to be the main environmental influences that will need to be considered and accounted for?

Organizations will attempt to develop strategies that are best suited for their strengths and weaknesses in the environment in which they operate – a match between internal capabilities and external environment. However, many commentators, such as Mintzberg (1987), suggest the environment is so uncertain that it may be impossible to plan on a long-term basis. Strategies may need to be *crafted*, built-up through learning and gradual experiment. In this viewpoint, the rapid changes in the environment may make it impossible to plan how value will be added.

For the modern organization, an awareness of the environment and ability to span the firm's boundaries is essential. The planning role here is one of attempting to monitor and analyse environmental conditions. The most commonly used framework is the separation of environmental factors into 'macro' and 'micro'.

- The wider, macro environment. Includes elements such as: economic (national or international), social, technological, demographic, governmental and natural environment factors.
- The closer, micro environment. This describes the industry or competitive environment that will include suppliers, competitors, consumers, etc.

In chapter 7 p. 136 we offer a framework for environmental factor analysis (EFA[12]) that can be used to guide this thinking.

It should be evident that these environmental forces can have dramatic consequences for a business (an unexpected major crisis such as the Foot and Mouth outbreak in the UK in 2001 or the collapse of Enron in the US, for example). In addition, we have already seen that an organization will often rely heavily on its external environment for key resource inputs. For the strategist, the environmental challenge is finding a 'fit' between the internal resources and core competencies of the organization and the opportunities and threats posed by the external situation.

Adding value

In chapter 2 we looked at three frameworks that can be used to analyse the operations of an organization: value added, systems theory and complexity theory. At a strategic level, these are closely connected. Using the systemic viewpoint, the organization, as an open system, seeks negative entropy. To stave off the effects of the second law of thermodynamics, and a move towards disorganization or death, any complex open system (whether natural, designed or a social system) must import and store more energy from its environment than it expends. For the organization, this energy is in the form of resources. From a strategic perspective, it is important to ensure that value is added to such resources for long-term survival. This means using operational activities to add value and then deliver the output to customers in the forms they require.

The purpose of the corporate and business strategies is to bring about the conditions under which the firm can create this vital additional value and pass it on to the customer – both now and in the future. The strategic task is to create a distinctive way ahead, using whatever core competencies and resources at its disposal, against the background and influence of the environment (both near and far). Through these distinctive capabilities the organization seeks sustainable competitive advantage.

STRATEGIC VIEWPOINTS

As with most academic disciplines, the study of strategy has divergent schools of thought. These can be traced alongside the development of the subject over time, as shown in Table 3.1.

We need to be aware that there are, for the moment, two major debates between strategic commentators:

- Process versus design;
- Market-driven view versus the resource-based view.

Design versus process

Design

The 'design or classical school' is based on the belief that senior managers can objectively appraise the enterprise, its resources and its environment, to formulate strategies that will maximize the chances of success in an uncertain future. In addition, they can then implement this strategy in order to achieve the desired consequences. Formulation and implementation work together (the former planning the latter) in a logical and rational progression taking into account all possible demands.

Table 3.1 The evolution of strategic management

	1950s	1960s	1970s	1970s–1980s	1980s–1990s	2000s
Dominant theme	Budgets used for planning and control	Corporate planning	Corporate strategy	Industry analysis	Competitive advantage	Innovation and creativity
Main issues	Financial control through budgeting	Planning for growth	Portfolio planning	Segments, choice, positioning	Sources of competitive advantage	Flexibility and responsiveness
Concepts and techniques	Budgets at all levels for directing and planning	Forecasting and modelling	Synergy, Strategic Business Units (SBUs), matrices and experience curves	Structure and competitor analysis	Resources, core competencies	Rapid diversification, knowledge and learning
Implications	Strength of financial management is crucial	Planning Departments and the five year plan	Diversification, multidivisional, globalization	Selectivity, restructuring, asset management	Business Process Re-engineering (BPR), outsourcing, restructuring and refocusing	Virtuality, knowledge bases, network management

Process

Opponents of the 'design school' will suggest this is largely fiction. The process is less structured and more diffused. The dichotomy between formulation and implementation is less apparent. Mintzberg (1978, 1985, 1988) is one of the leading protagonists of the process movement. For him, although senior management may have an *intended* strategy in mind, its development is far from rational as a process of negotiation, bargaining and compromise, involving individuals and groups, will decide its final shape. However, and here is the real difference, the realized strategy will only reflect between 10–30 per cent of that originally intended. In other words, a strategy will *emerge*, incrementally, with patterns of decisions adapting to evolving external circumstances.

The process school concentrates upon the realities of how a strategy might emerge and the processes involved. Meanwhile, the design school is more normative in trying to uncover factors that might provide sustainable competitive advantage.

One further debate is also pertinent here. Both design and process schools reflect the belief that strategic planning and thinking is the role of managers at the top echelons of the business. Yet we know that the organization must learn from daily experiences and make adjustments in that light. Henry Mintzberg (1987) uses the term *crafting* strategy to contrast this from the rational planning approach:

> Imagine someone planning strategy. What likely springs to mind is an image of orderly thinking: a senior manager, or group of them, sitting in an office formulating courses of action that everyone else will implement on schedule. The key note is reason – rational control, the systematic analysis of competitors and markets, or company strengths and weaknesses, the combination of these analyses producing clear, explicit, full-blown strategies.
>
> Now imagine someone crafting strategy. A wholly different image likely results, as different from planning as craft is from mechanization. Craft invokes traditional skill, dedication, perfection through the mastery of detail. What springs to mind is not so much thinking and reason as involvement, a feeling of intimacy and harmony with the materials at hand, developed through long experience and commitment. Formulation and implementation merge into a fluid process of learning through which creative strategies emerge.

Market-driven versus resource-based views

Market-driven

During the 1970s and 1980s the focus of strategic thinking shifted to environmental-based opportunities. The leading proponent of this approach is Michael Porter (1980, 1985). In his book *Competitive Strategy* (1980), which was written from the perspective of industrial economics, he introduced the five forces model and the concept of generic strategies. The argument is, that it is not the industry that an organization is in that counts, but where it wants to compete in terms of the nature of the competition. This competition is provided by the nature of the rivalry between existing firms, the threat of potential entrants and substitute products and the bargaining power of buyers and suppliers. The generic strategy adopted will offer an organization three ways of coping with these forces and achieving sustainable competitive advantage: overall cost leadership (traditionally based on economies of scale), differentiation (offering a product or service perceived in the industry as unique), and focus (using the low cost or differentiation in a niche or narrow segment). According to the theory, every business needs to adopt one of these strategies in order to compete in the marketplace. There are real dangers for a firm that engages in more than one and fails to achieve any of them – it is stuck in the middle. A firm in this position:

> Will compete at a disadvantage because the cost leader, differentiators, or focuser will be better positioned to compete in any segment. . . . Such a firm will be much less profitable than rivals achieving one of the generic strategies.

Current prevalent opinion, however, seems to be that companies can 'be all things to all people' – or most of them anyway. Good strategy, suggests Ghemawat (1999):

> Embraces the idea that competitive position must consider both relative cost and differentiation, and it recognizes the tension between the two. Positioning, in this view, is an effort to drive the largest possible wedge between cost and differentiation (or price).

Despite the fact that the market-driven views are still widely held, there are those that reject many of the aspects of this approach.

Resource-based

The resource-based view represents a substantial shift in emphasis towards the individual resources of the organization and away from the market-based view. Despite its recent popularity, the concept of resources and capabilities emerged from research into diversification. Wernerfelt (1984), for example, built on the economic theories of Penrose (1959) and viewed companies as a collection of resources, rather than holding market positions in the development of strategy. The notion of distinctive competencies, first discussed by Selznick (1957) and Ansoff (1965), was further reiterated by Prahalad and Hamel (1990). In their analysis, key resources, skills and technologies are called core competencies. Since the end of the 1980s, the resource-based view has been extended to the field of strategic analysis and strategic choice identifying the importance of resources in strategy development (see Rumelt, 1984).

A resource is a basic element that a firm controls in order to best organize its operational processes. A person, machine, raw material, knowledge, brand image and a patent can all be viewed as examples. Often the distinction is made between tangible and intangible resources (Godfrey and Hill, 1995). Kay (1993) identifies three of the most important resources as: the firm's ability to innovate; its reputation; and its network of relationships inside and outside.

A resource, or set of resources, can be used to create competitive advantage. The sustainability of this advantage depends upon the ease with which the resources can be imitated or substituted (Peteraf, 1993). When resources are combined they can lead to the formation of competencies and capabilities (Prahalad and Hamel, 1990).

Competencies refer to the fundamental knowledge owned by the firm (knowledge, know-how, experience, innovation and unique information). To be distinctive they are not confined to functional domains but cut across the firm and its organizational boundaries. Competitive advantage can come from a focus upon key competencies (those things the firm specializes in or does well). Capabilities, meanwhile, reflect an organization's ability to use its competencies. Capabilities refer to the dynamic routines acquired by the organization concerning the managerial capacity to improve continuously the effectiveness of the organization. According to Collis (1996), capabilities represent the firm's 'collective tacit knowledge of how to initiate or respond to change that is built into an organization's processes, procedures and systems, and that is embedded in models of behaviour, informal networks and personal relationships'. We should note, however, that resources, capabilities and competencies are dynamic and constantly changing (Teece, Pisano and Shuen, 1997).

The essence of the resource-based view is its focus on the individual resources, competencies and capabilities of the organization, rather than on the strategies that are common to all companies in the industry. Understanding the industry is important, but organizations should seek their own individual solutions in that context. Sustainable advantage comes from exploitation of the relevant resources of the individual organization.

The resource-based view draws attention to those internal resources created within a particular enterprise that cannot be purchased externally. Organizations are bundles and clusters of resources, capabilities and competencies and managers must develop these in unique ways. These can be managed and combined to create an organization's unique difference. They cannot be easily reshuffled to take account of market opportunities, but organizations must define opportunities in terms of existing internal capabilities and focus on the unique expertise (outsourcing anything that is not central to this).

TIME OUT BOX II

Fast food restaurants such as KFC, McDonald's and Pizza Hut are all relatively commonplace in most developed economies (with differing opinions as to their contribution to society!). Whatever views you hold as to their worth, they satisfy a demand and employ a large number of people. Pizza Hut, for example, is a US company that produces and markets pizzas nationally and in overseas markets. It consists of many outlets in the USA, UK and other countries worldwide. Its corporate strategy is set at HQ level with various business strategies for particular regions.

Spend a moment thinking about Pizza Hut's strengths, both externally and internally. What might be the main elements of its market-driven and resource-based strategies?

Before leaving the subject of business and corporate strategy, we must spend a little time looking at how a firm positions itself in terms of its market and industry. This positioning is vital as a way to align its core competencies with market opportunities. It also provides a key linkage mechanism to the various operations strategies the firm might adopt.

THE GROUNDS FOR COMPETITION

Whether the reader adheres to the resource-based or market-driven viewpoint, or a combination of the two, the comments made in the introduction still hold true: strategy is about choices. A competitive strategy is about difference, the choice of activities that will deliver a unique mix of value. As Michael Porter (1996) suggests, 'The essence of strategy is in the activities – choosing to perform activities differently or to perform different activities than rivals'. Choices have to be made concerning strategic positioning (conceptual and actual) and the use of particular competencies, capabilities and processes.

Conceptual strategic positioning

In making these choices firms will, according to Porter, adopt certain strategic positions that emerge from three distinct sources (although they are not mutually exclusive and can overlap):

- *Variety-based positioning*. Based on producing a subset of an industry's products or services using a distinctive set of *activities*. For example, specialist restaurants providing vegetarian and vegan organic foods or Asian foods such as Wok stir-fry cooking; automotive support services like Kwik-fit that specialize in tyre, exhaust and oil changes rather than a full garage service; specialist automotive insurance agents catering for niche driver groups; and third party logistics services that cater for chilled and frozen foods supplied to large grocery retailers. These are focused competitors with a value chain designed to serve a wide variety of customers but satisfying only a subset of their needs.
- *Needs-based positioning*. In this category the firm will try to serve all the needs of a particular group of customers. The customers will be grouped by differing needs and the firm's activities are tailored to serve all those needs – different price requirements, product features, information, support services, or even the same customer group having different needs on different occasions. The point is that an organization operating using this positioning has to configure different sets of activities to cater for the various needs, because the same value system cannot meet the needs of all groups (we will review the operations strategy implications later). Examples will include those retailers adopting a positioning to serve all the needs of their customers. In clothing, Marks and Spencer, Arcadia Group, J.C. Penney or Nordstrom; in groceries Tesco Stores, J. Sainsbury, Wal-mart Stores and in household furnishing, Ikea.
- *Access-based positioning*. The segmenting of customers who are accessible in different ways. Although their needs may be similar to other customer groups, the configuration of activities to reach them is different: different sets of activities may be

needed to reach customers in the best way. The rural post office or grocery store will, perhaps unwittingly, be using this positioning. Unable to compete on price, its use of local produce and its accessibility (open seven days a week and eighteen hours a day) enables a configuration of activities based upon accessibility for a local population (possibly without transport).

Core competencies, capabilities and processes

Before making decisions regarding strategic positioning, choices also have to be made concerning competencies, capabilities and processes. The important role of operational activities across the firm (and its supply network) can be developed by changing focus from function to process. In chapter 1 three definitions of operational management were offered. The third, a broad perspective, was as follows:

> *Definition*
> The design, operation and improvement of the internal and external systems and resources that create product and service combinations in any type of organization.

Involved in the management of these internal and external systems and resources will be the activities that Michael Porter refers to as being the essence of strategy. These activities cut across the firm and its supply system and some are also known as distinctive core competencies or processes (as we discussed in the resource-based view).

Sustainable competitive advantage can be built up over time based upon these unique competencies. They can be based upon knowledge, know-how, experience, innovation, and unique information use. The activities and processes utilizing these competencies are hard to replicate by competitors. Products and technologies provide only a short-term strategic advantage as they have a relatively limited life span and are easy to copy or improve upon. These core competencies or capabilities and processes cut across organizational boundaries: product development, order fulfilment and supply chain management, for example, all rely upon the co-ordinated contribution of all parts of the firm and other enterprises in its operating environment.

At a strategic level, the importance of these processes and core competencies must be recognized. This can be achieved in three ways:

- The value they provide to the customer must be continually augmented. In other words, determining the activities that the customer values most and working to improve the competencies related to them.
- Analysis of internal competencies and activities to convert them into goods and services with a market value. Capitalizing upon creativity and innovation to transpose internal expertise into value for consumers that can be sold. American Airlines first developed the legendary SABRE reservation system for internal use. However, it soon became clear that it had a spin-off value when it was converted into a product that could be sold to other airlines. The creative *conversion* of activities and competencies to goods and services will lead to the development of new and modified goods.

■ Development of new activities and competencies that can be used to enter new markets. The financial management expertise of many leading grocery retailers in the UK (Tesco Stores and J. Sainsbury, for example) has been developed into a new financial services for consumers. They now offer loans, mortgages and account handling facilities as products. This is a complete diversification from traditional business (retailing), but was accomplished successfully because it is built upon expertise in existing competencies and processes. Bearing in mind the importance of core competencies, we can now take to strategic positioning in practice.

Strategic positioning in practice

But the type of positioning described above has practical implications. Effective positioning defines how the firm will compete in the marketplace based upon the strengths and weakness of the organization (in particular its core competencies), the needs of its market and the position of the competition. In practice, choices have to be made between some of the following competitive options or grounds (many, however, are not mutually exclusive).

Cost

The relentless elimination of all waste in the entire cost structure. This is not a short-term strategy, it requires a long-term and thorough commitment to the search for operating cost reduction in order to achieve competitive advantage on the basis of being the lowest cost player. However, this does not mean cutting back on investment. Updated facilities, equipment, programs and systems to streamline operations, skills training and development are all essential capabilities.

Quality

Quality is not confined to eliminating defects and conforming to specifications. Quality should be viewed as an opportunity to seek out new ways to add value above and beyond the consumer's expectations. This of course relies heavily upon understanding the needs of the consumer and also appreciating the quality achievements of the competition.

Flexibility

As was discussed in chapter 1, there are a number of ways to classify flexibility. The ability to customize a wide range of products to individual tastes (mass customization), to introduce new products rapidly, to modify existing ones, and to react to individual value needs is increasingly being seen as a strategic weapon. Technology, the right skills and training and the blending together of operations strategies and operational activities in the necessary form is key to this approach.

Response

Closely related to flexibility, response, speed and time-based competition dominates many sectors. The flexibility to provide customized goods and services provides little or no competitive advantage if the consumer has to wait an inordinate time for delivery. As witnessed with many Internet shopping facilities, the problem of e-fulfilment currently exercises many organizations. Fast moves into new markets, adaptation and close linkages between operational activities are all essential. Decision-making must be encouraged at all levels, especially those dealing with consumers. Speed of response also involves whole supply systems in co-ordinated alliances and partnerships.

TIME OUT BOX III

In the previous exercise, we gave some thought to the market-driven and resource-based strategies of Pizza Hut. Building on this thinking, what strategic positioning does the firm seek to attain? First, is it based on variety, needs or access, or a combination? Second, what is the importance of cost, quality, flexibility and speed? Third, what are the core competencies and the activities or processes they support? Fourth, are they unique and a source of sustainable competitive advantages when compared to, say, technology or products?

Whatever the basis for positioning, the response of the firm requires a tailored or customized set of activities. To quote Porter (1996):

> Strategy is the creation of a unique and valuable position, involving a different set of activities. . . . The essence of strategic positioning is to choose activities that are different from rivals. If the same set of activities were best to produce all varieties, meet all needs, and access all consumers, companies could easily shift among them and operational effectiveness would determine performance.

We can now examine the role of an operations strategy in supporting the buiness strategy.

THE ROLE OF AN OPERATIONS STRATEGY

It has become clear that an operations strategy, like any strategy, revolves around a pattern of choices. The choices or decisions involved are concerned less with individual day-to-day, tactical activities and more with the whole transformation system that is part of the organization. As we shall see in a moment, the choices also reflect the changes in the wider competitive environment in which the firm is embedded. The pattern of decisions tends to be of a medium to long-term nature and supports both the core capabilities and competencies of the company, and how it uses resources and technologies to provide sustainable competitive advantage in the future. The types of judgements necessary for an operations strategy will vary from firm to firm and depend very much on the particular industry or sector. For example, they may cover:

- How to supply particular products and services;
- What capabilities or competencies will be needed in the future;

- What resources we will need to acquire;
- What work flows are necessary;
- What processes and technologies will be required;
- The capacity needed and the levels of flexibility involved;
- Human resource levels (skills, training, recruitment, selection and retention);
- Quality levels;
- What facilities are needed;
- Type of suppliers, relationships with them and sourcing and outsourcing (what do we make in-house what services do we buy in?);
- Decisions about the general operating systems and the resources needed long-term to maintain them.

To summarize the nature of such decisions. They are:

1   *Medium- and long-term.* In other words, we will be considering demand and how to satisfy its requirements over the next 1–5 years (shorter time spans are the remit of operational management).
2   *Analysis at operations level.* Thinking about the whole operations process, whether at a functional level or across the whole firm, but including its supply networks (the subsystems or processes within operations are the concern of operational management).
3   *Conceptualizing at operations level.* For example, what products and services and quality levels are required in the future? Operational management activities here would be actually providing the products and services on a day-to-day basis.
4   *Strategic rather than tactical.* Should we outsource any activities? Which key suppliers should be chosen for strategic inputs? Should certain suppliers become 'preferred' and close alliances developed with them? Tactical operations management will be concerned with improving purchasing systems or expediting supplies.

The following three case vignettes are provided to describe the nature of an operations strategy as opposed to operational management.

CASE VIGNETTE **SWISSÔTEL, ISTANBUL**

Voted one of the top ten hotels of the world, Swissôtel stands high above the sparkling Bosphorus river in the bustling and vibrant city of Istanbul. For many years the hotel was the playground and temporary home of the rich and famous. However, this clientele began to dwindle and senior management decided that they should enter a new market. A strategic business decision was made to offer completely new service – conference facilities – and given the grandeur of the setting, it was decided that these facilities would be of the highest quality and attract the patronage of leading international firms as well as serve as the stage for world conferences. Clearly the next step was to translate this vision into reality.

continued

53

continued

An operations strategy was needed to make decisions about the type of new facilities necessary; what services would be needed for the executive consumer; the suppliers and what elements of supply could be outsourced (catering was one possibility); technologies necessary for the hotel and its clients; human resource levels (including skills); quality levels; capacity and flexibility (demand profiles would change as many delegates would arrive all at once); and what processes and work flows would have to change as a result of this new strategic direction.

CASE VIGNETTE **FISHER FOODS**

Fisher Foods Ltd, part of the Albert Fisher Group plc, supply chilled and prepared salads, chilled and frozen seafood, vegetables and fruit. As became alarmingly clear to senior management, 40% of their business takes place in the six weeks prior to Christmas. At this point there is a huge surge in demand and the firm struggles to cope. It was decided, shortly after one such event, that an operations strategy should be developed to alleviate the problems at this time. As part of this strategy, it was planned to make major changes in the type of services provided, work flows, capacity and flexibility, human resource levels, supplier commitments, etc. Today, the structure of Fisher Foods differs enormously depending upon the season – it has now become two separate businesses in one, depending on the time of year. It also has two different types of operations strategy!

CASE VIGNETTE **UK ARMED FORCES**

In the early 1990s, the UK Government commissioned a strategic review of the Armed services. Following recommendations, a substantial reorganization was undertaken to adopt a new smaller, flexible, rapid response profile (as opposed to having a large potential army of occupation). It was intended that the new rapid response units would be able to move swiftly in and out of the trouble spots of the world without the huge build-up and lead times for response that were needed prior to the earlier Gulf War. However, to establish such a profile, major changes had to be considered as part of the operations strategy of the Army, Navy and Air Force. Equipment, facilities, capabilities, resources, technology, training, suppliers, capacity and flexibility decisions had to be made in the light of this new profile. An operations strategy had to be devised to plan the necessary changes well in advance of any new operational activity in the field. The strategy was, and still is, in need of constant change in the light of new engagements (the war and deployment of Special Forces in Afghanistan being a recent example).

The author is grateful to the MBA class of 2001 at UEA for their help with these examples.

To date, there has been a certain amount of confusion as to what does and does not constitute an operations strategy. Clarification is in order, and to do this we are going to propose a structure or genealogy as an overall guideline for the rest of the book. This can be done using a branch of study called *systematics*: the science of population difference and classification. The following genealogy (see Table 3.2) is proposed as a taxonomy.

We can begin at the bottom of the table with a distinct *species*. These are the generic building blocks of an operations strategy, but also can be part of a tactical, operational management approach (*genus*). The building blocks will, when deployed in practice, contain certain discernable elements (*subspecies*). Next, groups of building blocks (*species*) form a particular operational or tactical approach (*genus*). Medium- to long-term strategic decisions are then made about the building blocks (the *order*) as components of a distinct operations strategy. A particular identifiable type of operations strategy is then evident (the *class*) and constitutes the pattern of organization or form that is a qualitative set of relations. Thus, the *class* is an identifiable type of operations strategy for a type of operational situation.

Table 3.2 *Strategic genealogy*

Classification	Description
Kingdom (the highest category of taxonomic classification)	Organizational business strategies
Division or phylum (a generic group)	A generic model of an operations strategy that is not any particular identifiable type, but still containing interrelated building blocks.
Class (a grouping of organisms)	An identifiable type of operations strategy (supply network, quick response, efficient consumer response, etc.) demonstrated in a qualitative pattern of organization. This will then be physically embodied in an individual and quantifiable deployment (the structure) unique to each situation.
Subclass	A narrower operations strategy used in a linear supply chain, value chain or part of the chain (logistics strategy for example).
Order (taxonomic rank constituting a distinct group)	Strategic decisions made (medium- to long-term) about the various building blocks of an operations strategy.
Genus (taxonomic grouping containing several species)	Groups of building blocks (or *species*) form a particular operational or tactical approach, such as supply chain management and logistics.
Species (individuals with common characteristics — in practice the species will be made up from subspecies or elements)	Individual building blocks are the *species*: core competencies, capabilities and processes; resources; technologies; and certain key tactical activities that are vital to support a particular strategy or unique positioning. These building blocks are grouped into a *class* of operations strategy (a specific instance) or described in the generic form (the *phylum*). They can also be used at a more tactical level as a particular operational management approach (the *genus*).

This pattern of organization is then physically embodied in the structure, a unique, individual and quantifiable operations strategy evident, or actually deployed by an organisation (the physical embodiment of the class). These distinctions are discussed further in chapter 4. We can also see particular subclasses where the strategy is much narrower; as used, for example, in a linear chain (supply chain strategy) rather than a network or just part of a chain (logistics). The class then forms part of a higher, *division* or *phylum* that can be thought of as a generic model of an operations strategy; one that is not of any particular identifiable type, but still contains interrelated building blocks. Finally, the generic operations strategy belongs to a larger *kingdom* of business strategies.

Definitions from the literature

Much of the literature concerning the nature of an operations strategy is found wanting. It is hard to find commentators prepared to offer a definition. As we have seen in chapter 1, operations can provide support for the overall strategy of a firm and can also act as its distinctive competence. Slack and Lewis (2002) however, do offer an interesting viewpoint when they describe an operations strategy as: 'The total pattern of decisions which shape the long-term capabilities of an operation and their contribution to overall strategy'. They broaden this by offering a second perspective: 'The total pattern of decisions which shape the long-term capabilities of any type of operation and their contribution to overall strategy'.

They also draw a distinction between the *content* of the strategy (decisions and actions) and the strategy *process* (methods used to make the content decisions).

CRITICAL REFLECTION

This is an important point and one requiring care. Although it may seem obvious that strategy has a content and there is a strategy process, many contributors believe it is not that simple. Strategy for them involves many fine grained choices about how to configure particular activities and the overall supply network. Thus there may not be a clear-cut distinction between content, process and strategy implementation.

Slack and Lewis (2002) also reflect that there are four operations strategy perspectives:

- A top-down reflection of what the whole business wants to do;
- A bottom-up activity whereby operations strategy improvements build business strategy;
- A translation of market requirements into operational decisions;
- Exploitation of the capabilities of operational resources in chosen markets.

All of these points are certainly important and aid understanding – but are we any nearer a clearer appreciation of the nature of an operations strategy? As we shall see in chapter 4, there are in fact different types of operations strategy. To a degree, each operations strategy is unique and individual to the firm: nevertheless, we can in fact provide a fairly broad taxonomy of these strategies. Further, research tells us that many of these operations strategies utilize similar building blocks (see Table 3.2). That being the case, you quite rightly ask 'How can they also be unique?' We will be suggesting over the next few chapters that there is empirical evidence to show that it is the blending of these building blocks into an architecture that will make them unique.

A working definition of operations strategy

It is our opinion that the definition of an operations strategy is still somewhat haphazard, despite the excellent work of Nigel Slack *et al*. To this end, a further contribution is made. An operations strategy can be conceptualized at two levels:

> *Operations strategy definition 1 – the functional strategy*
> Major decisions about, and strategic management of: core competencies, capabilities and processes, technologies, resources and key tactical activities necessary in the function or chain of functions that create and deliver product and service combinations and the value demanded by a customer.

As with our definitions of operations management in chapter 1, the first is a narrow perspective. Here, we are thinking at functional level. For example, distinct operations or a manufacturing function that provides goods or services and the other supporting functions (purchasing, distribution, logistics) both internal and external (supply network or supply system functions).

A second definition evolves from the first. It is much broader and takes account of those firms, particularly in the service sector, which may not have a distinct functional approach. It covers all those activities; both within the organization and in the wider supply network, that add value to the final customer. However, we must be careful not to adopt an approach that attempts to cover the strategic management of all resources and activities used to produce goods and services. This would leave us open to criticism from other disciplines, such as marketing, which will have an equally important contribution to make.

> *Operations strategy definition 2 – the wider value delivery strategy*
> Major decisions about, and strategic management of: core competencies, capabilities and processes, technologies, resources and key tactical activities necessary in any supply network, in order to create and deliver product and service combinations and the value demanded by a customer. The strategic role also involves the blending of these various building blocks into one or more unique, organizational-specific, strategic architectures.[1]

---

1 As we have seen earlier, the strategic management role may not always be rational and planned. Some strategies will be logical and of a breakthrough nature, others will be adaptive, emergent and incremental.

In this definition we see that the strategic role is one of fusing certain operational building blocks (these may be internal or external) into a unique operations strategy. Each strategy will be different due to the manner and emphases of this blending activity. It should also be noted that a firm might in fact have more than one strategy (we return to this point later).

This second definition is a development of the first, as it also covers the narrower perspective. It has a number of important aspects:

1 It encompasses all three earlier definitions of operational management;
2 It embraces the situation whereby the operational activities are seen as the firm's distinctive competence;
3 It provides support for the implementation of the business strategy. The operations strategy links long- and short-term operations decisions to corporate strategy;
4 It is a definition that can easily apply to all organizations producing product and service combinations no matter what the mix (tangible or intangible); and
5 It places clear emphasis upon the strategic importance of *activities*.
6 It combines both the market-driven and resource-based views of strategy (p. 46).

Future discussions of operations strategy in the book will assume this second definition.

Ingredients of an operations strategy

From this second definition, an operations strategy is composed of a pattern of decisions. Medium- and long-term decisions are made regarding generic factors or ingredients. These include:

■ Core competencies, capabilities and processes;
■ Resources;
■ Technologies;
■ Certain key tactical activities that are vital to support a particular strategy or positioning.

These are the building blocks of the operations strategy and we will expand them further in chapter 5.

The role of the operations strategy

We now consider how the operations strategy can contribute to competitive advantage and its role vis-à-vis business strategies.

Porter (1996) describes activities as the basic units of competitive advantage. An organization, he suggests, will adopt a distinct strategic positioning; it will compete on the basis of flexibility, cost, quality, speed, diversity and variety, etc. Here, strategic positioning means 'performing *different* activities from rivals or performing similar activities in *different* ways'.

By contrast, Porter describes operational effectiveness as 'performing similar activities *better* than rivals'. Clearly, operational effectiveness depends upon the correct operations strategy, that unique architecture or blend that combines various generic building blocks, as described above. Our initial premise is that an operations strategy is aimed at performing key operational activities better than rivals, so as to provide support for the overall strategy of a firm as well as serving as a firm's distinctive competence. Companies can quickly imitate individual activities, but not the way they are combined in an architecture to form a unique operations strategy. One might also conclude that should operational effectiveness be achieved through the use of an operations strategy, then the latter would include both the performance of different activities to rivals as well as the performance of similar activities better than rivals.

In summary, then, we can combine the current dichotomy of strategic viewpoints (resource-based strategy as opposed to market-driven strategy) in a hierarchy as follows:

1   *Generic strategies* – based upon lower cost, premium price through differentiation, or combining the two either on a broad front or using a niche focus;
2   *Strategic positioning* – positioning the firm to compete on the grounds of flexibility, responsiveness, cost, quality, speed, variety, etc.;
3   *Operations strategies* – a unique resource-based fusion of core competencies, capabilities and processes; resources; technologies; and certain key tactical activities that are vital to support a particular strategy or positioning.

Finally, for completeness, we can see how operational management can then deploy the various strategies in order to achieve strategic objectives:

4   *Operational management* – the organization of operational management activities and management methods, both internally and externally, to provide a good or service in both profit and non-profit organizations.

The important role and contribution of an operations strategy as a vehicle for achieving competitive advantage seems apparent. What remains less clear are the types of operations strategy that might be employed and their exact composition. The next two chapters will attempt to shed some light on these issues.

TIME OUT BOX IV

This is the final strategic exercise concerning Pizza Hut. We have defined an operations strategy and suggested that it is a unique resource-based fusion of core competencies, capabilities or processes, resources, technologies and key tactical activities. Briefly, consider what competencies, processes, resources and technologies might be of most importance to Pizza Hut.

59

CONCLUSION

In chapter 3 we have extended the critical analysis from operational management to operations strategy. In order to do this, it has been necessary to gain an appreciation of the strategic setting. The nature of a business or corporate strategy has been examined from the viewpoint of internal resources, the influence of the environment and the need to add value. Strategy development, deployment and management involves some hotly debated schools of thought. The main debates were discussed, including whether strategy can be designed or whether it is a process, and the need for market-driven and/or resource-based strategies. The grounds for competition were also reviewed, in terms of conceptual positioning (by variety, needs and access) and the importance of certain activities, core competencies and processes, was stressed. The contribution of an operations strategy was examined and its genealogy suggested. Definitions were developed and the strategy outlined. Finally, strategic perspectives were summarized by describing a hierarchy of strategic thinking encountered in any business.

CASE STUDY – OPERATIONS STRATEGY IN ACTION

FlexLink Systems – an introduction to strategic management (www.flexlink.com)

FlexLink systems are an independent business partially owned by EQT Scandinavia and the Swedish SFK Group. FlexLink have been developing and supplying production process automation systems to a broad spectrum of industries for over two decades. Their birth was in 1978 as an internal project to develop a new conveyor system for the group's manufacturing lines. The brief was to build a system that would transport products horizontally and vertically to free up floor space and optimize manufacturing line layout. The solution they discovered was an innovative multiflex chain that was flexible, reusable, simple, and easy to use, design, build, change and operate on its own. This innovation had huge business strategy spin-off potential. In 1980 the trademark was registered and in 1981 FlexLink became an independent operating unit with SFK. Today, the culmination of this one-off project is an autonomous strategic business unit employing over 500 people, with a turnover of 1,000 million Swedish kroner, and an annual growth averaging 20 per cent. Now they are structured into three core business areas: automation, systems and components and are a leading international business, with sales, local support and expertise in over fifty countries.

FlexLink provide profitable automation to demanding industry consumers around the world. Based upon unique application experience and global networks, FlexLink offer innovative production solutions to the manufacturers of high volume, lightweight goods. They combine plastic chain conveyors, pallet-based systems, linear motion, structural and enclosure systems, drive units and integrated production lines into consumer-specific business solutions that embody one overarching strategy for all their business: flexibility. FlexLink believe that it should be possible to install, modify and change the systems on-site using standard hand tools. But this approach takes a great deal of industry knowledge, and in particular, knowledge of their customers' processes.

Having begun in the automotive mechanical parts industry, FlexLink now deliver complete lines for assembly, testing and packing to some of the world's largest sectors. These include general food processes, pharmaceutical personal products, automotive, tobacco, paper converting, electronics, electrical appliances and telecommunications; in fact, any production setting where processes are customized by high volume, advanced technology, short product life cycles and several product versions being produced in parallel. Knowing the customer's business and expectations in detail is essential when delivering a complete line. To create a unique solution, FlexLink has developed an expertise by being fully aware of the customer's production conditions and line output needs. Based upon this understanding, their business solutions (including the software and hardware) provide the efficiency necessary for high levels of production output.

FlexLink Systems grew out of a strongly held strategic conviction about providing unique customer solutions. They started with a clear intention to develop a company strategy based upon making their customers' lives easier. Their objective was to offer products and services that enable sometimes complex production problems to be automated using standard solutions provided quickly and easily, and available anywhere in the world. This includes everything from first analysis of customer requirements to after-sales support for the lifetime of the system.

FlexLink, as you would expect, are seriously committed to research and development. They continuously develop, test and evaluate new high quality solutions to future customer requirements, but they also insist that such solutions must be environmentally friendly and sustainable.

Quality is an integral part of all units and departments and firmly based upon, and measured by, a clear understanding of customer needs and expectations. In addition, any impact upon local and global environments is also carefully controlled. The consumption of natural resources is minimized where possible, and they will only use environmentally approved packaging materials and components designed for low energy consumption.

You might suspect that the foundation for success at FlexLink was an effective production system – but this is not the case. One of the reasons for their strong organic growth, rapid spread and penetration into all major markets has been their strict strategic outsourcing policy, which was adhered to from the very start of the company. They have no manufacturing facilities whatsoever, nor do they have any forwarding or logistics. They are in fact a virtual producer trading on their industry knowledge, their global application base, innovative products and processes and focusing on automation supplied to world leading customers. In practical terms, FlexLink consists of applications and systems engineering, research and development and marketing and sales. However, their competitive synergy is developed from less tangible, but equally important, strategic concepts such as vision, knowledge, creativity and innovation applied through the management of relationships. As they eloquently put it: 'Moving from components to concepts – from products to integrated solutions!'

FlexLink have built an extensive network of strategic outsourcing relationships. It is these relationships that make them flexible and allow the firm to focus upon developing and defining concepts then marketing and selling the final product after it has been outsourced to a supplier for manufacture. However, managing such a virtual business involves close attention to quality and supply chain processes and the ability to define and specify needs to suppliers, many of whom have grown with FlexLink over the last twenty years. Competitiveness and efficiency have been built as part of a supply network relationship strategy that allows each partner to focus upon its core business. Such an approach has also brought lower levels of cost and increased efficiency. Indeed, growth over the last twenty years has been almost entirely internally funded, based upon the cash and cash flow impacts of their strict adherence to an outsourcing strategy.

FlexLink Systems see their future as being a global, knowledge-based company within industrial automation. More effort will be put into software and hardware to add even more customer value: a people company, focused on customer processes and looking for new opportunities and supplier relationships in order to satisfy them.

FlexLink is growing fast in new market segments, especially auto electronics, pharmaceutical, electrical, personal products and confectionery sectors. They are consolidating existing markets as well as establishing new ventures for their dynamic assembly systems in the US, China, Poland, Hungary and Malaysia – these developments being built upon their ability to offer customers global support and competence.

However, the strategy of outsourcing remains a key cornerstone of sustainable competitive advantage for FlexLink. The management of a global people organization, through core values and core beliefs, is critical to their future success. Relationships, knowledge, vision and innovation continue to create the flexibility that is FlexLink.

ANSWERS TO TIME OUT BOXES

Time out box I

The environment can be classified into two 'domains': near and far. In the more distant, macro environment main influences will come from economic (national or international), social, technological, demographic, governmental and natural environment factors. For British Sugar examples might include a massive crop failure or disease reducing raw material availability (natural environment), a marked reduction in sugar consumption due to the establishment of strong links between sugar and terminal illness (social), a change in farming regulations concerning the methods of crop recovery and transport resulting in massive raw material price increases (technological and governmental) and inability to recruit sufficient staff to cover the long hours involved in a 'campaign' (demographic and social). Other influences will be at a competitive level and concern suppliers and competing firms.

Time out box II

As with many fast food outlets, one of the main strengths will be keeping costs low through standardization of products, processes and services. A weakness could be an inability to satisfy market demand for variety due to a lack of flexibility. In terms of market-driven versus resource-base strategies, this will have the following ramifications.

- *Market-driven.* Competition revolves around satisfying a need for fast food, at a reasonable quality, with speed and in a 'theme park' atmosphere. Positioning based upon low cost, needs and access. Providing, many would argue an illusion of value (the mark-up on each item is usually hundreds of per cent). In a market of intense rivalry, success is achieved by keeping costs low (with some variety) offering a fast and efficient service in a prime city centre site. The power of suppliers must be kept low (although an efficient supply system is extremely important) and they are usually locked-in in a relationship heavily determined by the restaurant chain.
- *Resource-based.* Here we see the importance of their business principles, which affect all outlets. Standardization, rationalization, efficiency, calculability (quantity rather than quality), predictability and control regulating the smallest detail. An atmosphere of diversion and amusement, for fun and drama, rather than just satisfying hunger. A culture that, it could be argued, ignores many of the health problems associated with fast foods and is dehumanizing for its workers. Although the workers are suggested as the most important resource, it may be the business system and the training schemes that are more valuable than the people (who can be replaced by other low-cost labour).

Time out box III

As we have seen above, the main conceptual positioning is a combination of needs and access. The actual positioning relies mainly upon low cost and speed. To support this the core competencies of the staff in delivering the business system and the structured, standardized and rational activities forming part of the business system, are key to its operation and more important than technology or even the products.

Time out box IV

The operations strategy for Pizza Hut exists at an individual store level. This means that each outlet at a micro level should plan effectively to deploy its resources efficiently in order for the organization at the macro level to achieve its corporate objectives, combining or blending various components or ingredients into an operations strategy to deliver the business system. For example, information, information communication technology, supply system coordination activities, shared planning and control with suppliers, logistical planning, etc., will all be important at an operations strategy level.

DISCUSSION QUESTIONS, WORK ASSIGNMENTS AND EXAM QUESTIONS

1   What is the overall purpose of a business strategy?

2   Discuss the differences between the two main strategic themes: the resource-based view and the market-driven view.

3   What do we mean by positioning? What are the different grounds for competition? Offer examples of firms or industries that might utilize different types of positioning.

4   What is the role of an operations strategy? What are its generic elements?

5   How does an operations strategy form a link with other elements of strategic management?

Reader questions related to FlexLink case study

1   Is it possible to describe the main features of the FlexLink Systems business strategy?

2   Is their business strategy market-driven, resource-based or both?

3   FlexLink adopt a fundamental strategic positioning. Can this be described?

4   In order to develop an operations strategy for FlexLink, what factors would be of most importance over the medium- and long-term?

RECOMMENDED READING

Grant R. (1991) 'The Resource-based Theory of Competitive Advantage: Implications for Strategy Formulation', *California Management Review* 33, 114–22.

Kay J. (1999) 'Strategy and the Delusion of Grand Designs', Mastering Strategy (Special feature), *Financial Times*, 27 September.

Porter M.E. (1996) 'What is Strategy?', *Harvard Business Review* November/December 61–81.

Prahalad C. and Hamel G. (1990) 'The core competence of the corporation', *Harvard Business Review* May/June 79–91.

Analysis and synthesis

The rules of the game:
Learn everything, inquire into everything ... when two texts, or two assertions, or perhaps two ideas, are in contradiction, be ready to reconcile them rather than cancel one by the other; regard them as two different facets, or two successive stages, of the same reality, a reality convincingly human just because it is complex.

Yourcenar (2000)

Part II explores the nature of operations strategies in more detail. The contribution of an operations strategy has also been outlined as part of a hierarchy of strategies that we might find in each firm. But what exactly *is* an operations strategy and what are its components? How easy is it to implement such a strategy and what can an organization expect from it? It is to these and other such questions that we now turn.

We start by detailing some of the classes of operations strategy currently witnessed. Chapter 4 offers an empirical taxonomy of strategy types and the general objectives or focus of each. These strategies have, we will also suggest, unique compositional elements (building blocks) that are blended or fused into distinct architectures. Chapter 5 examines these features and describes how such strategies evolve and develop in practice. In chapter 6 we consider strategic deployment, and the best methods that can be used to ensure these strategies are cascaded throughout the business. The broader tactical factors that are vital for a particular strategy, or strategic positioning, are then discussed in chapter 7. Chapter 8 returns to the strategic debate in order to ascertain the sources of competitive advantage possible from an operations strategy.

Finally, chapters 9 and 10 are somewhat of a digression. We suggest demand is the lifeblood of the organization and the *raison d'être* of an operations strategy (and management for that matter). Thus, we must understand demand for both services and goods. To this end, these two chapters assess the various methods available and the latest research being undertaken. We begin this task by examining, in chapter 9, the nature of demand. Despite its importance, many firms struggle to understand demand and all its implications; little solid research has been conducted into this subject. Finally, in chapter 10, we offer a review of some of the more promising attempts to better understand demand and deal with it in real time as opposed to over-reliance upon forecasting and other low value adding activities.

At this point, a cautionary note. Although all the above chapters are dedicated to different aspects of operations strategy, we are dealing with a complex web of relationships that is our organizations and their operational activities. As such, the various interconnections or correlations among these entities are equally important: an ability to see and appreciate the wider, whole picture will continually receive attention throughout the section.

CRITICAL REFLECTION

It is generally accepted that learning can take place over a number of progressive levels. We should be aware of the different perspectives and their implications:

- *Knowledge*. The ability to remember facts, terms, definitions (to identify, list, name, outline and state).
- *Comprehension or understanding*. The ability to translate ideas from one form into another (to explain, interpret, extend and generalize).
- *Application*. The ability to use general rules and principles in particular situations (to demonstrate, relate, use and apply).
- *Analysis*. The ability to break down and make clear the nature of component parts (to select, discriminate, separate and distinguish).
- *Synthesis*. The ability to arrange and assemble various parts so as to make a new statement, structure, plan or conclusion (to classify, compile, reconstruct, substitute and combine).
- *Evaluation*. The ability to judge the value of material or methods in terms of internal accuracy and consistency or by reference to external criteria (appraise, judge, evaluate, compare and contrast).

There are strong links between the chapters in Part II. As described above, we feel it is important to offer an *analysis* of operations strategies, their components, their deployment and the wider influences upon them, as well as a *synthesis* that places emphasis upon the interactive nature of all elements in dealing with demand. In reality, it is somewhat artificial to attempt the type of reductionism that deals with each in isolation and ignores the systemic nature of these subjects – a point we hope the reader will bear in mind throughout.

Chapter 4

Towards a taxonomy of operations strategies

In this chapter the reader will find that we adopt a unique research-based perspective that questions much current thinking on this subject. The main thrust of the chapter is to establish a taxonomy of strategies that is based upon a solid empirical and conceptual framework common to the social sciences.

LEARNING OBJECTIVES

After considering this chapter, the reader will be able to:

- Gain a firm understanding of the academic approach used in establishing taxonomies
- Appreciate how different operations strategies are evident in business communities and understand their main approaches
- Begin to appreciate the need for more than one operations strategy in an organization
- Develop a clear knowledge, through further research, of the various literature sources available for each particular strategy

> **KEY TERMS**
>
> - Taxonomy
> - Empirical operations strategy research
> - Form or pattern of organization (qualities)
> - Substance and structure (quantities)
> - Operations strategy

INTRODUCTION

A recent review of operations strategy research emphasized the need to promote a greater contribution from empirical, field-based research (Filippini, 1997). The writer also concluded that the discipline of operations strategy has concentrated upon two common themes: process and content. But according to Miller and Roth (1994) 'The development of strategic types is still lagging behind from both an empirical and theoretical standpoint'.

This chapter seeks to address this omission and to provide some clear guidelines as to the possible types of operations strategy available, as well as offering some practical implications for the development and implementation of such strategies. The chapter will first pose research questions that are particularly relevant for the study of operations strategy. Thereafter, a taxonomy is developed using a particular framework from the social sciences. Finally, in order to preserve the holistic nature of the subject, we introduce a model that stresses the various interconnections and guides the reader's understanding in this direction.

OPERATIONS STRATEGY RESEARCH

At this point, we offer five research questions that can be used to direct our thinking over the next few chapters. These questions are important and linked to an experiential learning cycle (Fig. 4.1).

In Fig. 4.1 we might start with the experience of an event or stimulus, which the individual then reflects upon in trying to make sense of it. This might lead to the generation of explanations of how or why something happened in the way it did. This is similar to an inductive process whereby we form theories from experience, observation and reflections. These theories can then be grounded by further observation. Alternatively, we can also start with guiding principles, abstract rules or theories that can be extrapolated or generalized to new events or stimuli. This is essentially a deductive approach whereby we infer from general laws to particular instances (i.e. we start with a theory that may well have been the result of another person's reflections). Whether the rule or theory is received from another or generated out of prior experience and reflection, its testing in new situations will create new experiences that enable consequent reflection, observation and ultimately new rules. There are two points of note: (a) particular individuals will place differing emphases on parts of the learning cycle due to the presence of particular predilections into which they

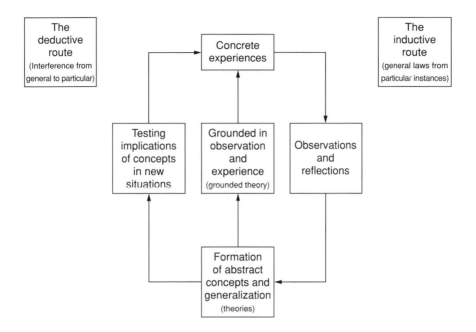

Figure 4.1 *The experiential learning cycle*
Source: adapted from Kolb et al. (1979)

have been socialized; and (b), in research quite often we will combine these approaches in a marriage between empirical conception and the certainties of deductive logic in something that has become known as the 'hypothetico–deductive model' of scientific explanation. For a further details the reader might consider Mintzberg (1979a).

We also have to remember that although operations management and operations research has quite a distinguished lineage, the contribution of an operations strategy, its composition and components is a relatively new phenomenon. Thus the need to develop guiding research questions to direct our thought processes.

Research questions

The important role of operations management and operations strategy has been touched upon in the preceding chapters. Other contributors (Hayes and Wheelwright, 1984; Anderson *et al.*, 1989; Hayes, Pisano and Upton, 1996; De Meyer, 1998; Loch, 1998; Slack *et al.*, 2001; Hill, 2000) also testify to the unique role of each. To date, however there is less clarity as to the exact nature of the latter.

A glance at the operational management literature will provide examples replete with descriptions of operational management methods, activities and technologies. However, all too often these are either glib eulogies without substance or advocation, or description without any attempt at order, quantification practical implementation. Worse, many such approaches have been offered with almost catholic applicability. It stretches credibility to accept, as many suggest, that such strategies can offer profound utopian benefits to every

69

firm and every industry: a universal panacea no matter what the ill! The complexity of our organizations and their contingent, embedded nature in their business and wider environments makes such claims naive and even misleading.

Over the next three chapters we will attempt to appreciate the true nature of an operations strategy, its composition and when, or if, certain operational management approaches can assume strategic status. The first research question reflects this:

■ *Research Question I.* Can a taxonomy of operations strategies be established?

We also suspect that many organizations may in fact use an operations strategy as a linking mechanism with their suppliers or customers. If this is the case, it seems logical that just as a firm may have more than one product, market, consumer or supplier, they might have more than one operations strategy (albeit each might use different nomenclature and occasionally have no actual title).

■ *Research Question II.* Do organizations have more than one operations strategy?

Until now we have spoken in generalities concerning an operations strategy. If, as we contend in the first research question, such strategies can be identified, is it not reasonable to assume we can also discover their composition? Chapter 3 offered our wider, working definition of the operations strategy:

> *Operations strategy definition 2 – the wider value delivery strategy*
> Major decisions about, and strategic management of: core competencies, capabilities and processes, technologies, resources and key tactical activities necessary in any supply network, in order to create and deliver product and service combinations and the value demanded by a customer. The strategic role involves blending these various building blocks into one or more unique, organizational-specific, strategic architectures.

We now need to discover exactly what core competencies, capabilities and processes, technologies, resources and key tactical activities might be involved in an operations strategy.

■ *Research Question III.* If an operations strategy is used or employed between an organization and its customers and/or suppliers, can the core competencies, capabilities and processes, technologies, resources and key tactical activities vital to support a particular strategy or positioning be identified?

This third research question forms the basis of chapter 5.

It seems evident from our discussions thus far that an organization will employ a number of core competencies, capabilities and processes, technologies, resources and key tactical activities. However, not all of these elements will assume strategic status, although, as we mentioned in chapter 3, some will be particularly important and 'fused' into unique operations strategy architectures. This provides research question four which will also be addressed in chapter 5:

■ *Research Question IV.* Are certain core competencies, capabilities and processes, technologies, resources, and key tactical activities vital to support a particular strategy or positioning blended or fused into particular and unique operations strategy architectures? Do these blends vary by particular operations strategy type or other influences, such as demand?

This chapter is concerned with the first two questions. We now examine the types of operations strategy currently being deployed by leading organizations.

A TAXONOMY OF OPERATIONS STRATEGIES

The close relationship between the next three chapters will emphasize the interrelationship between the types of operations strategy being employed, their composition and how they are implemented within the organization. Figure 4.2 demonstrates the interface in a graphic format.

To approach the task of developing a taxonomy of operations strategies, it is first necessary to address the theoretical perspectives involved. There are two distinct conceptual aspects in the process of classification: the *pattern of organization* and *structure*. We are following a procedure that has been adopted in a number of disciplines (see for example, Maturana and Varela, 1987; Maturana, 1988).

Pattern of organization (form and order – a qualitative perspective)

This is the study of form or pattern, in order to map a configuration of elements. Here, sets of relations between particular components are described. These relations characterize the system as belonging to a particular class. The pattern of organization of any system is the configuration of relationships among the system's components that determines the system's essential characteristics (certain relationships must be present to recognize, say, a chair, a bicycle or a tree). The description of that organization is an abstract description of relationships and does not identify the specific components (for example, retailers, bacteria, flowers or cats).

Structure (substance and matter – a quantitative perspective)

Actual relations among the physical components constitute the structure. In other words, the system's *structure* is the physical embodiment of its organization. The system's pattern

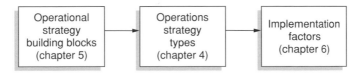

Figure 4.2 Operations strategy context model

of organization is independent of the properties of its components, so a given organization can be embodied in many different manners by many different kinds of components. The structure is constituted of actual relations among physical components: the physical embodiment of its organization (remember, organization is independent of the properties of its components). A given organization can be embodied in many different manners by different kinds of components (for example Top Shop or J.C. Penney, salmonella, a rose or a British Lilac cat). The structure can be measured, weighed and quantified.

The description of a pattern of organization involves an abstract mapping of relationships; the description of the structure involves describing the system's actual physical components – their shapes, chemical compositions, and so on. Let us use a bicycle as an example. In order for something to be called a bicycle there must be a number of functional relationships among components known as frame, handlebars, wheels, etc. The complete configuration of these functional relationships constitutes the bicycle's pattern of organization. All these relationships must be present to give the system the essential characteristics of a bicycle. The structure of the bicycle is the physical embodiment of its pattern of organization in terms of components of specific shapes made of specific materials. The same pattern 'bicycle' can be embodied in many different structures. The handlebars will be shaped differently for a touring bike, a racing bike, or a mountain bike. The frame heavy, solid or light; the tyres wide, smooth or heavy tread. All these combinations will be easily recognized as different embodiments or structures of the same pattern of relationships that defines a bicycle. Thus, we make a distinction between organization (the form or pattern) and structure (the substance).

We can now apply this conceptual thinking to operations strategies. Any strategy will have an abstract pattern of organization that describes the relationships between component parts. However, when such a strategy is adopted and deployed by a firm, we will then be able to see a particular physical embodiment of its organization: a unique combination of components. Thus, as we have noted, 'the system's organization being independent of the properties of its components' allows any generic type of operations strategy to be embodied in many different manners by many different combinations of components. Our hypothesis is that we may describe each organization as having an abstract type of operations strategy (the pattern of organization), and some may even have more than one, that will be evident in each instance from its physical embodiment (the structure). We summarize this conceptual approach in Fig. 4.3.

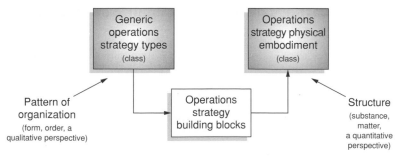

Figure 4.3 *Towards an operations strategy taxonomy I*

The figure introduces the link between generic operations strategy types having particular components and the physical embodiment of the operations strategy within a particular firm. We will build upon this figure in the next two chapters.

Operations strategies – pattern of organization (or form)

Returning to the taxonomy of operations strategies, it is now possible to think about the generic types available. To do this we can first remind readers of our earlier genealogy, as shown in Table 3.2, p. 55.

From the research conducted by the Strategic Operations Management Centre (SOMC) at the University of East Anglia, we have isolated both the generic operations strategy containing various building blocks

- Core competencies, capabilities and processes;
- Resources;
- Technologies;
- Certain key tactical activities that are vital to support a particular strategy or positioning;

and the particular classes possible. The reader should also be aware that here there are degrees of overlap. A firm may have more than one operations strategy (either the same or a different type). For example, it may be appropriate to require a quick response as well as time-based competition and strategic postponement. Lean production, just in time, strategic procurement and supply chain management are also frequently combined (Lowson 2001c). We will now detail the classifications identified, together with a short review and literature references for further research.

Quick response (QR) or planned product response

Developed in the textile/clothing industry for a large number of Stock Keeping Units (SKUs) with short product life cycles, high seasonality and high complexity, low inventory turnover and high gross margins to offset markdowns. The QR strategy links all activity to real time demand. It is customized by the individual retailer or manufacturer and is particularly suited to small- and medium-sized firms. It is designed to be context specific and to be contingent upon the setting. In the next section we provide a case study of QR in action. (Leading literature sources include: Gunston and Harding, 1986; Kurt Salmon Associates, 1988; Hunter, 1990; Suri, 1998; Lowson *et al.*, 1999; Lowson, 1999; Hadjiconstantinou, 1999; Hunter *et al.*, 2002).

Efficient consumer response (ECR)

Used in the grocery industry for fewer SKUs with lower unit value and seasonality, but which move at a much higher velocity with lower margins. ECR has four main elements: efficient store assortments, efficient replenishment, efficient promotion and efficient product introduction. The initiative is still current and some progress has been made in developing closer relationships with suppliers and various category management initiatives (see Kurt Salmon Associates, 1993, 1995; Sharp and Hill, 1998; Wood, 1993; Institute of Grocery Distribution, 1996).

CASE VIGNETTE **EFFICIENT CONSUMER RESPONSE**

Leading UK food producers such as Tesco Stores and J. Sainsbury have greatly refined their short shelf life ordering process using ECR. The system covers fresh produce, chilled foods and provisions, meat, poultry, and dairy products. Many of these goods have very short shelf lives and little or no stocks can be held. Lead times have been cut to nearly 24 hours in some cases. The store will generate orders on the morning of Day 1 and send them to suppliers electronically by midday. The suppliers will deliver to the retailer's depot the next day, as well as direct to store. Many suppliers now share close communication technology linkages with their retail customers. This allows orders to be placed electronically, open sharing of stock, manufacturing and distribution data by both parties, joint logistical planning, combined product development projects, and close working partnerships for merchandising and marketing. Many suppliers also have members of staff 'resident' at the retailers HQ in order to assist in the partnership planning and daily working.

Time-based competition (TBC)

Attributed to Japanese manufacturers such as Sony and Matsushita, the essence of TBC operations strategy is the ability to turn customers' desires rapidly into new product designs that will bring about faster obsolescence of existing offerings. It is an extension of just in time in manufacturing to the whole supply pipeline. The strategy involves more than just speed of response. It is concerned with reducing delays throughout all business cycles, reducing reliance on long lead times and, most importantly, the need to produce to forecast. In addition to rapid response, time-based competition requires expanded variety, flexible manufacturing, and increased innovation (see Ohmae, 1982; Abbeglen and Stalk, 1985; Stalk, 1988; Istvan, 1988; Stalk and Hout, 1990; Blackburn, 1991; Stalk and Webber, 1993; Hum and Sim, 1996).

Supply network strategy

This subsumes a number of operational initiatives including supply/demand management, supply management and value-stream management. These are intra-industry concepts that grew as an extension of supply chain management, logistics, materials management, systems dynamics and systems theory principles. Increasingly seen as a strategic issue, its aims are to co-ordinate the flow of materials and information in a network with the intention of satisfying end customers. Those organizations viewing the whole supply system as strategically important in providing sustainable competitive advantage will adopt this type of operations strategy. A supply chain strategy is a subclass that seeks close links between production and inventory throughout a chain of linear nodes. As such, it is a wider concept than logistics, although still a subclass of the supply network strategy. Increasingly these approaches have also been used as universal software solutions associated with distribution resource planning, manufacturing resource planning and enterprise resource planning packages. They are also disciplines rather susceptible to the latest fad and claims of profound utopian benefits and catholic applicability (see Forrester, 1961; Stevens, 1989; Johnson and Lawrence, 1988; Christopher, 1998; Hines, 1999).

Just in time (JIT), just in time II (JIT II) and vendor managed inventory (VMI)

An approach originating in Japan's shipbuilding and automotive industries. In the latter, it became widely known as the Toyota Production System. The JIT operations strategy covers a number of other manufacturing approaches. JIT can be considered as a philosophy for waste reduction and continuous improvement, a method by which to control and reduce inventory, a way of increasing throughput, and a production scheduling system. JIT is best applied to stable demand, higher volume products (due to the need for continual, high volumes to cover and buffer any constraints). JIT II is an extension of the close working partnership between supplier and customer in JIT. Here, personnel from the supplier organization work directly from the customer host and are authorized to purchase materials, etc. For VMI, responsibility for replenishment of a customer's inventory rests fully with the supplier who manages the whole process (Sugimori *et al.*, 1977; Hayes, 1981; Schonberger, 1986; Harrison, 1992; Pragman, 1996).

CASE VIGNETTE **PURE VENDOR MANAGED INVENTORY IN ACTION**

Montreal sleepwear manufacturer Claudel Lingerie Inc., after nearly two decades of steady growth, suddenly went into free fall. From sales of over $12 million (Can) in 1990, by 1995 this had fallen to $6.8 million (Can). The company blamed recession, a substantial increase in tax burden and a structural change in the whole lingerie industry. The latter had involved a change from primarily single owner stores to boutique chains such as La Senza. With the arrival of the chain stores many independents closed and with them the revenues that had accrued from a particular method of trading. 'The product was still the same' commented President Micheal Lapierre, 'it was still selling very much as a gift item with 40% of sales in December alone; it's the trading conditions that had changed, and we needed to get closer to our customers'.

Claudel looked to develop partnerships with their new customers, and one of their main weapons was a form of vendor managed inventory (VMI). Retailers carrying Claudel products could choose as much merchandise as they wanted, to be displayed separately in

continued

continued

their stores, and the supplier would not demand payment until they were sold. Retailers agreed to record sales daily and report them weekly, with Claudel guaranteed a payment electronically within a week. Items unsold after a certain period get marked down, with the retailers and Claudel sharing the proceeds.

Claudel found that their customers were keen to enter into this type of arrangement as their advance commitments involved only a space allocation (currently 90% of their customers use this method of operating). The advantages for Claudel included getting closer to the customer and having more data on demand preferences. Plus, with their knowledge of the product, they were better able to influence and manage the retailer's inventory in the most prominent position: the shop display. 'I have yet to sell one garment from the warehouse, there is no customer there' Lapierre comments. In addition, the stock remains the property of the vendor until sale, thus, if the retailer gets into financial difficulty, Claudel was not over exposed.

As an aside, we noted that Claudel employ approximately 150 people in its Montreal factory, including two whose only job is researching future trends. Another lesson for many firms!

Agility in the supply system, agile manufacturing, strategically flexible production or proximity manufacturing

Initially an apparel industry concept, but essential in any responsive operations system. Agile operations strategies grew out of the inability of Japanese manufacturing techniques to cope with a movement beyond variety to mass customization and personalization. The agile manufacturer aims to produce highly-customized products at a cost comparable with mass production and within short lead times. Combined with QR, the resultant tailoring of products to demand includes a higher element of service and thus greater added value. A flexible workforce, structure and production technologies (especially through the use of computer-integrated manufacturing) are all contained within a learning culture. Externally, the concepts of vertical integration and long-term partnerships are replaced with short-term, flexible contracts and horizontal outsourcing (see p. 77). These allow rapid response through an expansive system of communication networks (Hamel and Prahalad, 1990; Nagel and Dove, 1991a, b; Fralix and Off, 1994; Kidd, 1994; Goldman and Nagel, 1993; Upton, 1994, 1995; Duguay *et al.*, 1997).

CASE VIGNETTE **AGILE MANUFACTURING**

The Textile Clothing Technology Corporation (TC²) are an excellent example of agile manufacturing using 'real time' demand data. Based in Cary, North Carolina, USA, TC² is a 'teaching factory' with the aim of developing flexible and agile production using the latest technology. As well as its research role, it regularly produces batches of clothing for major US department stores. Readers are recommended to visit: http://www.tc2.com

Virtual operations strategy

As far as can be identified, the concept of the 'virtual' organization was first raised in 1992. INSEAD in France have carried out a survey of European manufacturing and practice every two years and reported that many manufacturers implementing various Japanese techniques had discovered that improvement on the factory floor had not been translated into increased profits and competitiveness. The firms taking part in the survey indicated an increased dependence upon their supply pipelines as relationships and dependencies were being formed externally. The compilers of the report suggested that this was a trend towards the 'virtual operations strategy': a situation where networks of outside resources are mobilized and configured for a particular task and then disbanded or reconfigured. Physical and information aspects of logistics operations are treated independently from each other. Ownership and control of resources is exercised at a distance using information and communication technology and through supply networks. This type of operations strategy does rely upon outsourcing and the fast formulation of organizational boundaries (De Meyer, 1992; Venkatraman and Henderson, 1998; Whicker and Walton, 1996; Clarke, 1998).

Strategic outsourcing

Closely connected to virtual strategy is the concept of an outsourcing operations strategy. Adherents believe that the organization should concentrate upon its core competencies or unique capabilities then aggressively seek ways to eliminate, limit, or outsource activities where the company cannot attain superiority to those firms specializing in that field; unless those activities are essential to its strategic focus. The key is to identify which activities are core and which can be sourced externally to the experts while at the same time retaining a degree of control. Today the most common examples include the devolution of responsibility to 'partners' for the provision of warehousing, transportation and information technology and administration services. However, loss of control of a vital function can be a long-term concern (Quinn *et al.*, 1990; Bowersox and Closs 1996; Vining and Globerman, 1999; Bryce and Useem, 1998; Baden-Fuller *et al.*, 2000).

CASE VIGNETTE **STRATEGIC OUTSOURCING**

Coats Viyella plc are an international group of companies operating in worldwide textile and precision engineering markets. With an annual turnover of £2.3 billion and a diverse product portfolio in sixty countries they are justly proud of their high levels of customer service.

In one particular market, their thread division, they offer a unique strategic outsourcing service to customers.

Coats supply numerous types of thread to clothing manufacturers. These are stored on site and only paid for when moved from the storage area to the production line. Thus, the manufacturer is only paying for what is used. Coats work closely with manufacturers in

continued

continued

order to keep them supplied in line with production schedules – full and frank information sharing is the bedrock of this agreement. They take full responsibility for the thread supplies, including ordering, delivery, storage and set-up of the manufacturer's machines with the right threads for a particular job. They also take responsibility for engineering work should any of the machines have thread-related problems – leaving the manufacturer to concentrate on other aspects. Coats even employ staff to work on the consumer's site advising line operators how best to use the raw materials. Consequently they form a unique partnership with manufacturers in managing their inventory from raw material to finished goods stage.

World-class manufacturing (WCM)

The capabilities that have to be developed to compete in export markets globally, or the level of performance that is exhibited by top manufacturers in the world. These rather unhelpful and tautological definitions have plagued this approach and by necessity link it to any operations strategy that is currently successful or in vogue (lean production for example). Hayes *et al.* (1988) describe key attributes of WCM as:

- Becoming the best competitor;
- Growing more rapidly and being more profitable than competitors;
- Hiring and retaining the best people;
- Developing top-notch engineering staff;
- Being able to respond quickly and decisively to changing market conditions;
- Adopting a product and process engineering approach which maximizes the performance of both;
- Continually improving – kaizen (see p. 83).

(See Hayes and Wheelwright, 1984; Schonberger, 1986; Hayes *et al.*, 1988; Giffi *et al.*, 1990.)

Lean production and lean thinking

Developed from the Toyota Production System with a clear focus upon removing waste from a system. The lean operations strategy

> uses less of everything – half the human effort in the factory, half the manufacturing space, half the investment in tools, half the engineering hours to develop a new product in half the time. Also, it requires keeping far less than half the inventory on site, and results in many fewer defects, and produces a greater and ever growing variety of products.
>
> (Womack *et al.*, 1990)

Its supporters suggest that it can be 'applied equally in every industry across the globe' (Womack *et al.* 1990) as a universal best practice. Unfortunately, such naivety has attracted many critics who point to its failure to recognize the contingency or context-specific factors of each organizational situation, its linear assumptions, and generalized, stereotypical, homogeneous ideas. Nevertheless, the approach does have its advantages in high volume, mass production markets. Its utility for more complex, flexible and fast moving markets populated by SMEs has to be doubted (Womack *et al.*, 1990; Williams *et al.*, 1992; Berggren, 1993; Womack and Jones, 1996; Ahlstrom, 1998).

Strategic postponement

Postponement is an operations strategy that aims at delaying activities until the exact attributes of demand can be identified. One of the leading practitioners of strategic postponement as an operations strategy is the clothing retailer and manufacturer Benetton. Postponement can take three forms: *time* (delaying activities until orders are received), *place* (delaying the movement of goods or services until orders are received), and *form* (delaying activities that determine final form of a good or service until demand is known). Benetton use the last approach by keeping greige – undyed products – waiting until last possible moment until colour preferences for a sale season are known. Postponement can apply to all operations activities as well as sourcing and purchasing. The use of a postponement operations strategy will assist the customization of goods. Dell computers and Hewlett-Packard provide examples from the electronics industry and National Bicycle and Honda in transportation. Postponement has also been described by the concept of the decoupling point. This is the point at which forecast driven and order driven activities meet in the goods flow: the point shows how deeply the consumer order penetrates the supply system (see chapter 13). Good literature source examples include: Bowersox and Closs (1996), Rovizzi and Thompson (1992), Feitzinger and Lee (1997) and Lee (1998).

CASE VIGNETTE **STRATEGIC POSTPONEMENT**

In the mid-1980s the National Bicycle Company of Japan faced immense competition from other manufacturers in a market that was steadily declining: the fight for market share was becoming more intense. Cost efficiency drives and new product introductions were having less and less impact and cheaper imports were flooding the market. A new approach was needed – a paradigm shift in the bicycle market. They decided to move into a market niche: customization through strategic postponement. But not customization on an individual scale – mass customization. But how could this be done without long lead times, huge component stock and high unit prices? Postponement was the answer. Traditionally bicycles had been built for stock and stored by retailer or manufacturer. National Bicycle decided to postpone frame welding, painting and assembly until individual tailored orders were known – these were faxed by retailers. Customers were individually measured by height and weight for each individual product (just like buying a tailored suit), and could choose from a wide variety of design elements (eighteen models, six handle stem extensions, 199 colour patterns, three toe clip configurations, six brake systems, frame

continued

continued

dimensions in 10 mm adjustments, three handle bar widths, two pedal types, two tyre types, two different name positions and five choices of script for the customer's name on the frame – a total of 11,231,862 variations). Lead times were kept to two weeks in Japan (three for export) and prices only 15% above the best mass produced cycle.

Similar postponement strategies are being seen in a wide range of sectors, perhaps the most prominent being Levi's 'personalized pair' system when buying jeans, the Benetton 'knit now dye later' system for fashion clothing, prescription glasses produced in one hour, custom-made pizzas in 15 minutes and full five course meals delivered to your door. Postponement is of course also widely used in the service sector, particularly in social/personal services (restaurants, health care, etc.) where the customer has to be present for the service to take place. Here, certain 'service modules' can be prepared in advance and then 'assembled' by individual order at time of delivery.

Logistics strategy

One school of thought views logistics as the umbrella strategy for many of the concepts we are discussing here (they are all relegated to implementation alternatives). Certainly the definition of logistics is: 'organising, moving and supplying' (*New Shorter Oxford Dictionary* 1993) and as such could encompass supply as well as demand. However, at a strategic level, the view is taken that logistics deals mostly with the micro activities (such as transportation) that take place after the production of a good or service (the demand side) in order to provide value in customer service. As such, it is a subclass of the supply network strategy, and sometimes even subsumed in supply chain strategy. However, if the demand side of a supply network assumes strategic importance for an organization (in e-commerce for example), a logistics operations strategy can be developed. It will concentrate upon distribution facility elements of supply rather than the whole (as in the wider supply chain strategy or supply network strategy).

Logistics has adopted a more strategic role with increasing globalization and the trend for geographic dispersal of firms (La Londe and Masters, 1994; Stock *et al.*, 1998; Kohn and McGinnis, 1999; Burnham and Natarajan, 1999).

Strategic purchasing or sourcing, strategic procurement, network sourcing, materials management

As the names suggest, these operations strategies deal with the supply side. All recognize the important contribution of purchasing and procurement and the handling of materials or service inputs before any transformation takes place. Once again, an organization seeking to achieve competitive advantage from this part of the supply network will develop an operations strategy to ensure operational effectiveness and a contribution to strategic positioning. Often, such an approach can utilize a tiered supply structure with heavy reliance upon SMEs. The particular strategy chosen may depend upon the particular corporate strategy direction (for example, low cost, differentiation through high quality, flexibility and responsiveness, etc.). Leading references include: Keough (1993), Lamming and Cox (1995), Anderson and Katz (1998), Thompson *et al.* (1998) and Narasimhan and Das (1999).

CASE VIGNETTE **STRATEGIC PURCHASING AND SOURCING**

This case study provides a pertinent example of strategic sourcing in action. We see how a firm initially sourced offshore for low cost reasons, then reversed the decision when it discovered that the other 'hidden' costs far outweighed the advantages. In fact, by returning to a more responsive and flexible domestic supplier it became more competitive in nearly all its markets.

LL Bean is a US catalogue retailer providing, among other products, a wide range of flannel and cotton garments. Prior to 1996, the fabric for these garments was sourced totally from Portugal – mainly because of the competitive price and high quality. This was shipped to the US and cut and sewn into shirts by a third party manufacturer. The offshore delivery process involved long lead times (10–14 weeks) and an order commitment well in advance of the sale season. The latter involved predicting the SKU mix quantities, and percentages of patterns and colours in advance of sale. The Northwoods line is a fashion item and has significant variances in colour and plaid pattern every year. This early ordering ensured that Northwood shirts were in hand in LL Bean's inventory in time to satisfy customer orders. Ordering additional fabric later in the season when demand was high was risky due to the long lead times. Yet the decision to source offshore did not seem unwarranted, since at this time both domestic and Portuguese manufacturers were typically requiring 10–14 weeks to produce and ship (70–98 days) products. Unlike domestic producers, the Portuguese production facilities did shut down for a month in August (this required even more advanced planning).

In 1995, LL Bean used their normal ordering procedures for the major sale period at Christmas. This was their 'cash cow' and confidence was high. That year, however, the flannel shirt market collapsed, leaving LL Bean with nearly a year's worth of inventory at the end of the season. They were forced to cancel all commitments to their Portuguese supplier who, faced with a year of spare production capacity, retaliated by refusing to supply LL Bean ever again if he was forced to offer the capacity to someone else. The search began for a new supplier.

In the past, cost had been the main criterion upon which to select a source of supply. Now they had to cast the net wider and considered all options. A detailed and extensive cost/benefit exercise was completed, and finally it was decided to source from Cone Mills – a domestic vendor! After lengthy negotiations a partnership between the two firms was embarked upon; one that was open and based upon full information disclosure. The result being that Cone has managed to drastically reduce the original (Portuguese) shipping time from 30 to 1–2 days. The yarn-dyed fabric production time is reduced to four weeks and costs are only marginally higher due to the influence of Quick Response and a proper understanding of the costs of imports. The replenishment schedule in Table 4.1 shows how the operation is more flexible and responsive. It encourages smaller shipments when demand is low, and reduced reliance upon forward commitments based upon forecast.

continued

81

continued

Table 4.1 LL Bean replenishment schedule

Order date	Cone Mills replenishment schedule		Portuguese replenishment schedule	
	Percentage of total order for season	Cumulative total	Percentage of total order for season	Cumulative total
February	30	30	100	100
April/May	30	60	0	100
Mid-June	10	70	0	100
Mid-July	10	80	0	100
Mid-August	10	90	0	100
Mid-September	10	100	0	100

LL Bean can now make decisions later in the season (in real time mode) when demand is known. For example, they now use early season sales data provided from catalogue sales as an indicator of later activity. Consequently their sales have increased and customer service levels on all measures are markedly better. With the knowledge gained and shorter lead times, LL Bean is now far more reactive and flexible to demand using its own QR approach.

For Cone Mills the arrangement to provide all the fabric for the Northwood line has doubled their business with LL Bean. It amounts to nearly two months full capacity for one of their mills. Plus the increased confidence that LL Bean now has in Cone to deliver has meant that they have increased their orders, in return Cone has been able to offer price concessions: all parties benefit from the relationship.

The partnership has been built upon freely available electronic data sharing. The timely flow of product, order and inventory information enables both firms to make faster more accurate decisions and reduce the pipeline delays. Interestingly, both parties are free to interrogate the others' major databases and pull files back and forth using the Internet and a secure software operation: surely this is the future for many firms in the textile and clothing industry.

Collaborative planning, forecasting and replenishment (CPFR)

An operations strategy developed specifically for the retail/supplier sector. Employs collaborative processes across a supply network, using a set of process and technology models that are:

■ Open, yet allow secure communications;
■ Flexible across the industry;

- Applicable to all supply system processes;
- Support a broad set of requirements (new data types, interoperability with different Database Management Systems (DBMS), etc.);
- Improving the partnerships between retailers and suppliers;
- Providing an environment for dynamic information sharing (DIS) that integrates both demand and supply side processes and effectively planning, forecasting and replenishing customer needs through the total supply system.

Generally, CPFR is aimed at the continual improvement of the flow of product and information throughout the entire supply network using a DIS model. For further information see: Voluntary Interindustry Commerce Standards (VICS) Association – http://www.cpfr.org and Sherman (1998).

CASE VIGNETTE **CPFR AT LEVI STRAUSS**

One of the most important elements in CPFR is the forging of proactive links between partners or allies at different stages of the supply pipeline. These need to be both strategic and tactical and require proper management as one of the resources of the organization.

An excellent example of this in action is to be found in the approach that Levi Strauss and Company take with its main suppliers and customers. Since the mid-1980s, the firm has constantly been trying to establish closer working links in the supply in a coordinated pipeline with the aid of its 'Levilink' communication services. One of the most successful initiatives was begun in the early 1990s by forging an alliance between Burlington Denim (a mill supplying denim and a division of Burlington Industries Inc.), Levi Strauss (the manufacturer and retailer of Levi jeans) and Mercantile Stores Co Inc. (a retailer with over 100 apparel oriented department stores in the US).

From Burlington's perspective, they focused upon three areas using the creation of three cross-functional teams: research and development, manufacturing, and facilitating. These were staffed by representatives of both Burlington and Levi Strauss. Burlington concentrated upon shortening its product development and manufacturing lead times. Levi's had realized that their aim of reducing the product introduction cycle to 'ninety days from concept to retail shelf' depended heavily upon CPFR as fifty days of this time was taken up with development and delivery of new fabric from Burlington.

Levi's had long been a pioneer of 'CPFR partnerships' with both customers and suppliers. Its three-prong strategy was based upon electronic commerce, internal process reengineering, fast reorder and re-estimation replenishment and strategic business planning relationships, in order to drive CPFR throughout its main supply pipelines increasing customer service and value added targets. The latter were ambitious and sponsored directly by senior management:

- A sharing of business plans and visions using common objectives and mutual profitability;
- Joint management of supply pipelines to share challenges and opportunities;

continued

continued

- Complete market differentiation and integration of marketing plans;
- Flexibility in all products and volumes;
- Rapid new product development and shared between pipeline members;
- A continual update process of existing products;
- Fast shipments;
- Immediate availability in store of all products through cross-docking and drop-shipping of logistics;
- Immediate re-estimation and reorder and replenishment to sale;
- Floor ready supply of all merchandise.

It was quickly realized that to achieve these aims a whole new style of business was needed under a CPFR umbrella. For example, first, a complete change in attitude and culture towards external collaboration and interdependence. Second, the removal of all barriers to information sharing in the supply system. Third, a performance measurement system that was mutually agreed and monitored by partnership members.

Mercantile Stores also saw communication and collaboration as the key to competitive success in improving customer service levels and controlling inventory. They identified the manufacturer (Levi's) as the conduit through which information could be exchanged in both directions along the pipeline and applied a 'partnership' approach at two levels: business strategy and technology. The former was based upon support and involvement throughout the whole organization for collaboration at numerous functional levels using open information flows, while the latter applied many of the operations strategy building blocks we cover in the next chapter.

This short case study is illuminating for three fundamental reasons:

1. The absolute necessity of such alliances and partnerships in a mutual CPFR network.
2. The proper development of such initiatives involves both a strategic and cultural change and should be 'driven' by senior management. Technology acts as a facilitator but it is insufficient on its own.
3. These partnerships are three-way and circular, not just between adjacent stages of the supply pipeline.

CONTINUOUS IMPROVEMENT OPERATIONS STRATEGY

As an effective operations strategy, continuous improvement must account for the needs of customers, the abilities of competitors, and it must build on the organization's core competencies and capabilities. As with all operations strategies, it must be woven into the fabric of daily activity and be meaningful as a mission (dealt with in chapter 7) to each and every employee.

Continuous improvement as an operations strategy originated in Japan where it was termed 'kaizen' – a strategy to continually, and incrementally, change and improve all operational components: equipment, procedures, skills, throughput time, quality, supplier relations, product and service designs and so on. One of the earliest examples of this operations strategy was to be found in the Toyota Production System (TPS), as such it has close connections to the lean production and lean thinking strategies.

The continual improvement strategy has three main objectives:

- Increasing and broadening managerial perspectives to encourage involvement;
- Changing values to encourage a culture of improvement and quality;
- Achieving effectiveness through leadership, motivation and goal-setting.

There are then ten guiding principles to further encourage development of an holistic CI operations strategy:

1 Process driven across all organizational functions;
2 Total employee involvement;
3 Good labour–management relations;
4 Effective leadership and cross communication;
5 Adaptability to a changing environment;
6 Visibility and control of all processes;
7 Reducing waste;
8 Customer orientation;
9 Standardization;
10 Quality awareness and quality control.

From a negative viewpoint, continual improvement is a focus mainly upon cost and waste. For enhanced flexibility and speed of response, it should be combined with other strategies. Further detail can be found in Huda (1992) and Imai (1996, 1997). This aspect is covered in more detail in chapter 14.

BUSINESS OPERATIONS STRATEGY
We deal with this subject in depth in chapter 14.

Operations strategies – the structure or substance

We now turn to an example of the structure of an operations strategy – the unique physical embodiment (see again Fig. 4.3). To do this we provide a case study taken from current research.

CASE STUDY – OPERATIONS STRATEGY IN ACTION

The Aztec Retail Group – towards a taxonomy of operations strategies

Using a quick response operations strategy as a platform for diversification

The Aztec Retail Group are a UK-based clothing retailer, known internationally for its 'social-occasion' clothing. With seventeen divisions and twenty-six labels it reaches into four segments of the clothing market: ladies' wear, menswear, children's wear and textiles. Aztec has also expanded globally and almost half of its business is done outside the UK. In addition to its London HQ and branches in Toronto and Vancouver, it has branches and showrooms in New York, Dallas, Los Angeles, Montreal, Mexico, Hong Kong, Osaka and Seoul. Aztec employs 240 people and in 1998 its sales were approximately £130 million. This success is, however, relatively new.

In the early 1990s Aztec went through many lean years until in 1995–96 it decided to restructure and deploy a QR operations strategy with its main suppliers. In order to first refocus it employed a '50–30–10' strategy. The plan was to reduce the design to sales cycle by 50 per cent, the inventory by 30 per cent and costs by 10 per cent in the hope of growing profit margins. Execution of the '50–30–10' strategy was largely accomplished by cutting back the size of the clothing lines offered as a method to prepare for future, sound diversification. 'With our infrastructure the way it is, we have the opportunity to increase business without increasing overhead . . . the real opportunity for us is in entering new markets', Elliot Lewis, MD. Focus was used to first narrow the product lines before diversifying into new markets using a QR strategy as a platform.

This initial focus also enabled a clearer understanding to be gained of the basic operational systems needed. As Lewis comments:

> We decided to map the various value streams and attempt to appreciate exactly what each product group demanded. It soon became clear that the different product and customer types were important. The same garment had completely different operational needs depending upon the type of customer, whether our own branches, other retailers, department stores or showrooms – all had unique requirements.

Aztec deployed a QR strategy and worked with its main suppliers to tailor the various QR elements to each product combination. As their MD comments:

> This may sound complex but it does in fact replicate the essential complexity in a supply situation. The type of product and/or customer combination will influence the demand patterns.

Aztec blended various operational management core competencies, technologies, resources and activities into what they called high level packages. For example, shared pipeline information systems, data interchange support, joint planning approaches, replenishment and re-estimation and reorder systems, and inventory management components, all of which contained a number of operational subsystems. These were then deployed by supply situation using different emphases dependent upon the unique product and/or customer behaviour needs: 'We now have three distinct operations strategies that use different packages (blends) of components parts'. It seems Aztec dealt with complexity, rather than artificially trying to smooth demand, and tailored their operations to real time demand patterns, rather than trying to rely upon long-term forecasts.

There are some very important points contained in this empirical case study:

- Aztec employed an identifiable operations strategy (Quick Response). As we speculated in the earlier research question (1), we have been able to identify operations strategy types both conceptually and empirically.
- As reflected in the second research question, organizations will often use more than one operations strategy, we will return to this point in chapter 6 (The deployment of the operations strategy). However, this is a key learning point from the research: just as firms will often have more than one product, customer or supplier, it seems only logical that they will have more than one operations strategy.
- Aztec also identified the main elements of their operations strategies. The next chapter will deal with the various building blocks discussed in chapter 1 that can compose an operations strategy: core competencies; capabilities and processes; resources; technologies; and key tactical factors that are *blended* in a *unique* strategy.
- The reader will note the italicized terms above. Again, an important research development. In chapter 6 we will demonstrate that not only do firms have more than one operations strategy, each is unique and customized as a result of certain forces and requirements. The customization is achieved by the blending or fusion of certain building blocks in a way that provides particular emphases.

TIME OUT BOX I

In the last decade there has been a substantial growth in the finance industry. New businesses are entering at a rapid rate, many of them from non-finance sectors (leading supermarkets for example). The more traditional institutions such as banks are increasingly under competitive pressure. In order to attract and maintain market share, attention has shifted to the competitive advantage an operations strategy can provide. As part of a group discussion, we suggest readers consider the following questions:

1 Under what circumstances might a major financial institution like a bank adopt more than one operations strategy?
2 From the generic operations strategies identified in this section, would there be particular types suited to this type of firm?
3 What are the key building blocks that a bank might employ as part of such an operations strategy?

CONCLUSION

There have been many historic changes in organizational theory over the twentieth century. Some can be directly assimilated as changes in operations strategy. It is clear that the provision of product and service combinations has witnessed substantial trends since the time of the Industrial Revolution of the late eighteenth and nineteenth centuries. We have certainly seen a move from craft production to the mass production of the Fordist era, this much is agreed. Less clear is our current status. Recent events have seen the rise, and decline, of lean production (Womack *et al.*, 1990) and a move towards flexible specialization (Piore and Sabel 1984) and mass customization (Pine *et al.*, 1993) with an emphasis upon satisfying an increasingly fragmented, volatile and ephemeral demand for customized and unique goods and services. Currently a debate rages between the need for agility (Kidd, 1994) emphasizing the ability to switch frequently from one market-driven objective to another, and the proponents of the neo-Fordist, lean production with a reduction of waste in all its forms. Others, possibly more correctly, stress that there is room for both strategies in the modern, globalized economies (see Brown *et al.*, 2000).

In this chapter, and indeed the book, we have taken a radically different route. As Harrison (1999) comments when contributing to the lean versus agile debate:

> The differences in emphasis do not imply that leanness is dead and that agility is the latest craze. What they do imply is that choices must be made in developing an [operations] strategy, and that you cannot have everything.

This is our very point. We are not witnessing what Brown *et al.* (2000) describe as a paradigm shift from one competing approach to another (Thomas Kuhn's vision of such changes was on a much larger and more profound scale – we are still tinkering at the edges of the current paradigm). We are now starting to understand that believing an organization must choose between competing operations strategies is in fact erroneous: life is more complex! As mentioned earlier, our research now suggests that there are in fact many operations strategies, constantly changing, some overlapping, and often a firm will have more than one – this is the picture of requisite complexity.

This chapter has demonstrated a taxonomy of operations strategies that has differentiated between the abstract pattern of organization and its physical embodiment, as seen in the Aztec Retail Group case. The next two chapters will examine the building blocks of any operations strategy, the unique blending and customization of such strategies to meet particular demand situations, and the competitive impact of these strategies.

ANSWERS TO TIME OUT BOX

Time out box I

As with many organizations, financial institutions are having to satisfy an increasingly diverse range of demands. Customers now seek unique product and service combinations tailored to their particular requirements. For example, loans, pensions, insurance policies, etc., are no longer standardized. They are customized to individual needs with repayments to suit income (even repayment holidays), returns and refinancing flexible to need, combined packages to suit type of employment, etc. If one adds to this the demand for many banks to offer other, more physical consumer facilities (such as ATMs, banking halls for deposit and withdrawal) and corporate facilities, we can see how such complexity necessitates a wide range of operational management activities and more than one operations strategy to suit the needs of a particular consumer group.

1   Clearly, financial institutions, such as banks, cannot hope to rely on one operations strategy to satisfy all consumer needs.
2   It is likely that competitive advantage for such organizations will come from being flexible and responsive as well customizing services to demand. Here, strategic postponement, time-based competition and QR are the operations strategies that might provide a competitive advantage.
3   As will be shown in the next two chapters, there are many possible building blocks of an operations strategy. It is the way that all these various elements or precepts are blended that will dictate when or if they assume strategic status. In the case of a bank, for example, information communication technology, multi-skilled personnel, high consumer and quality service levels, and to a degree some strategic alliances with technology providers, will provide the main elements of the operations strategy.

DISCUSSION QUESTIONS, WORK ASSIGNMENTS AND EXAM QUESTIONS

1   In what circumstances might a manufacturer, an insurance company, a theatre, and a hospital use an operations strategy? What types might be suitable for each and what benefits might accrue?
2   When might an organization employ more than one operations strategy?
3   What are the essential differences between the form or pattern of organization and the substance or structure?

Reader question related to the Aztec Retail Group case study

1   The Aztec Retail Group applied a quick response operations strategy. Discuss what other types of operations strategy might also be developed in these circumstances. What would be the advantages and disadvantages of using other approaches?

RECOMMENDED READING

Mintzberg H. (1979a) 'An Emerging Strategy of Direct Research', *Administrative Science Quarterly* 24, 582–9.

Lowson R.H. (2001) 'Customized Operational Strategies for Retailers in Fast-moving Consumer Goods Industries', *International Review of Retail, Distribution and Consumer Research* 11,2, 201–24.

Chapter 5

The essence of an operations strategy

In this chapter we attempt to ascertain some of the building blocks of an operations strategy. Until now, we have discussed these components in their generic form. We can now examine how these various components form particular types of operation strategy.

LEARNING OBJECTIVES

After considering this chapter, the reader will be able to:

■ Appreciate the building blocks or precepts used in an operations strategy

■ See the types of operations strategy which are used in a particular commercial sector

■ Describe how the various components are deployed

> ## KEY TERMS
>
> - Components or building blocks of an operations strategy
> - Types of strategy
> - Blending of key components
> - Operations strategy composition matrix
> - Empirical research

INTRODUCTION

In chapter 4, we introduced the concept that a number of operations strategy types exist. In Fig. 4.2 (p. 71), the link between operations strategy types (chapter 4), their building blocks (chapter 5) and implementation or deployment of the strategy (chapter 6) was suggested. Further, we can see how the taxonomy was formulated by identifying the interconnection between generic strategy types (the *phylum*) and their physical description and embodiment (the *class*) as in Fig. 5.1. The interface between these is provided by strategic decisions concerning the operations strategy building blocks (the *order*) and their unique fusion into a customized entity (the class or phylum).

In this relatively short chapter we discuss the research evidence to support the notion that there are certain building blocks of a strategy (core competencies, capabilities and processes, resources, technologies and certain key tactical activities that are vital to support a particular strategy or positioning.) In addition, the discussion of the finance industry in the last chapter highlighted the possibility that different organizations might employ various operations strategy building blocks in a particular blend or with particular emphases.

Returning to the earlier research questions:

- *Research Question I.* Can a taxonomy of operations strategies be established?
- *Research Question II.* Do organizations have more than one operations strategy?

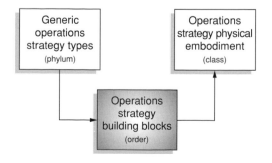

Figure 5.1 *Towards an operations strategy taxonomy II*

- *Research Question III.* If an operations strategy is used or employed between an organization and its customers and/or suppliers, can the core competencies, capabilities and processes, technologies, resources and key tactical activities vital to support a particular strategy or positioning be identified?
- *Research Question IV.* Are certain core competencies, capabilities and processes; technologies; resources; and key tactical activities vital to support a particular strategy or positioning blended or fused into particular and unique operations strategy architectures? Do these blends vary by particular operations strategy type or other influences, such as demand?

Chapter 5 is particularly concerned with the third research hypothesis.

THE BUILDING BLOCKS OF AN OPERATIONS STRATEGY

If an organization views particular building blocks as of strategic importance, then it will adopt an operations strategy reflecting this view. More likely, it will adopt an operations strategy that reflects the particular blend of these components; and one that is closely aligned to the organization's strategic priorities. In Fig. 5.2 we see a pictorial example of the matrix forming an operations strategy that is composed of certain generic building blocks:

- Core competencies, capabilities and processes;
- Technologies;
- Resources;
- Key tactical activities vital to support a particular strategy or positioning.

Each of the elements in the matrix will have a particular emphasis depending upon the firm and industry (hence the shading).

But does this mean that all the various types of operations strategy described in the last chapter are really synonyms?

Operations strategies employed

Chapter 4 outlined the various operations strategies that might be employed in business and commercial settings. In practice, particular types are to be found in certain sectors. In a recent survey, seventy-eight leading retailers in fast-moving consumer goods sectors (food, clothing, electronics, electrical, etc.) were questioned about whether they used an operations strategy, and if so, the type. The answers are contained in Table 5.1.

From the table we see that 66 per cent of the firms indicate that they use (either unilaterally or in conjunction with their suppliers) an operations strategy. Interestingly, a further three firms declared the use of a strategy, but could not give it a specific name. Clearly, as with wider business strategy, it is possible to possess a strategy without a given nomenclature. In addition, from this data it would seem that a number of retailers do in fact adopt more than one operations strategy (as speculated in our second research question). Further research is needed to ascertain the exact reasons that dictate the use of more than one.

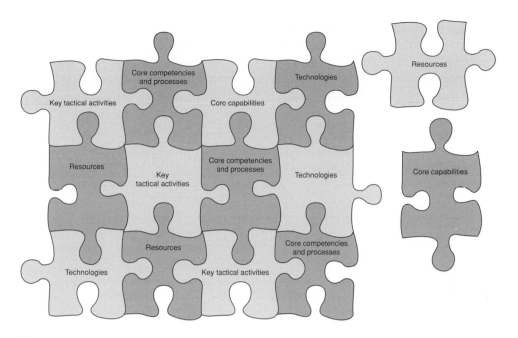

Figure 5.2 *Generic operations strategy composition matrix (OSCM)*

Table 5.1 *Types of identifiable operations strategy used (either unilaterally or with suppliers)*

Respondents	Sector	Operations strategy
17 firms	Grocery – Large multiple retailers	Efficient consumer response (7), Efficient consumer response and supply management (4), Supply management (2), Quick response and supply management (1), Efficient consumer response and time-based competition (1), Vendor managed inventory and collaborative planning, forecasting and replenishment (1), Logistics strategies (1)
7 firms	Grocery – smaller multiple retailers	Efficient consumer response and just in time (1), Supply management and vendor managed inventory (3), Supply management (1), Strategic procurement and lean production (1), Strategic outsourcing (1)
4 firms	Grocery – small independents	Supply management (1), Virtual organization (1), Supply management and time-based competition (2)
18 firms	Clothing – Multiple chains	Quick response (7), Quick response, supply management (2) Logistics strategy and strategic purchasing (2), Quick response and strategic postponement (2) Agile manufacturing and supply management (1), Just in time (2), Just in time and world class manufacturing (1), Virtual logistics and collaborative planning, forecasting and replenishment (1)
4 firms	Clothing – Speciality chains	Quick response (1), Quick response, agile manufacturing, time-based competition and Just in time (1), Postponement and world-class manufacturing (1), Supply management (1)

continued

Table 5.1 *continued*

Respondents	Sector	Operations strategy
3 firms	Clothing – Independents	Strategic purchasing and vendor managed inventory (2) Logistics strategy (1)
2 firms	Stationers – Retailers of books, periodicals, and general stationery material	Strategic purchasing and logistics strategy (1), Strategic outsourcing and Just in time (1)
2 firms	Electrical – Retailers of electronic car accessories to end-users	Supply management (1), Lean production/thinking and strategic purchasing (1)
2 firms	Electrical – Retail electronics for end consumer market (PCs, printers, and accessories)	Just in time and strategic outsourcing (1), Supply management and agile operations (1)
1 firm	Furniture – Furniture and household textiles retailer	Vendor managed inventory (1)
3 firms	General department stores – Clothing, electrical, furniture, accessories, etc.	Quick response and strategic purchasing (1), Logistics strategy (1), Time-based competition and supply management (1)
3 firms	Department Stores – Retailer of clothing and household goods	Supply management and virtual logistics (1), Quick response and agile supply/manufacturing (1), Just in time (1)
1 firm	Toys and games Retailer – Board games, plastic toys and models	Logistics strategy (1)

Source: from Lowson (2001a)

CRITICAL REFLECTION

At this point, readers should be aware that this text book is very much research led. Despite trying to take a balanced viewpoint and a comprehensive coverage of all views, we have deliberately based much of this work on the latest, leading-edge empirical research. Whilst having the advantage of being robust and fresh, it is also contentious. This is a new and unfolding discipline with many academics seeking answers to fundamental questions.

Indeed, as is typical of scientific discovery there will be much dispute and inevitable 'blind alleys'. There are two fundamental propositions we must consider:

- First, historically, many of the accepted scientific wisdoms we have today were at one stage shunned and ridiculed. The process of academic critique is normal and should be encouraged. There will be many that oppose the direction we take in this book.
- Second, as academics, a sense of proportion is needed. Always be aware that there are two sides to every debate.

TIME OUT BOX I

Why should the retailers in this study employ more than one operations strategy? Would you think it unusual for a number of operations strategies to contain similar components? After all, are business strategies unique to each firm?

Operations strategy building blocks

Having ascertained, (a) that there are a number of possible operations strategy types, and (b) that some firms may adopt more than one, our next consideration must be the composition of such strategies. Are the components generally similar? If so, are they then configured in different ways? What core competencies, technologies and resources might be blended to form a unique operations strategy?

The following paragraphs identify those building blocks most commonly used by retailers in this sector (it is important to bear in mind that the components will vary from industry to industry and even by individual firm). We are reporting only one particular study in consumer goods sectors.

CRITICAL REFLECTION

We make three very important points at this juncture:

1 The specific building blocks we are about to discuss will be common across a number of commercial sectors dealing with this type of product. However, there will be others essential to another type of industry and peculiar to that setting. Ergo, the list is not exhaustive.

2 Apart from these building blocks of an operations strategy, as we shall see in chapter 7, there will also be other influences upon the final shape of the strategy.

continued

continued

3   The elements are not in any particular order of importance. As the next chapter will confirm, the emphasis upon particular components is something that is unique to the organization in order to provide its sustainable competitive advantage.

Shared strategic operations planning with major customers/suppliers

Competition in many sectors is now quite rightly regarded as being between supply pipeline configurations. A number of firms in our research sample share quite a high degree of strategic and operational planning with their suppliers and/or customers. This involves regular collaboration over long-term direction of the particular partnership. The planning involved will naturally cover operational issues, but can also accommodate business issues concerning joint investment and even shared ownership in an organic partnership whereby each partner has a stake in the success of the other.

Joint product and merchandise planning between suppliers and customers

At a more practical level, retailers, customers and suppliers all combine in the concurrent processes of product development and modification and merchandise planning. Such cooperation allows the rapid development of samples or prototypes for in-store testing prior to sales season as well as a sharing of more detailed plans for the timing of product launches and new lines, etc.

Bar coded merchandise

Now an essential technology for supply systems no matter what the product and service combination. Bar coding enables the unique identification and tracking of all components and finished goods/services throughout a supply network. Many firms claim their operations strategies are only feasible with the use of bar codes, electronic data interchange (EDI) and point of sale (PoS) data sharing, thus firmly linking all activity in the supply system to the pull of real time, customer demand.

Small orders and batch sizes (both before and during a sales season)

Ensures that all activity matches the tempo of demand, paced to demand and customer behaviour. Consequently, many companies are reducing batch sizes of products in recognition that customers seek more individualized offerings and mass customization. Large stockpiles of homogeneous goods are becoming increasingly rare and an expensive method of operation.

Product data and information sharing with trading partners

This encompasses more than just information regarding inventory holding. New product/service development, promotions and other marketing initiatives, new developments in operational processes, goods availability, pricing strategies, costing, logistics programmes, etc. undertaken in an open book culture between enterprises where there is a high level of trust and openness.

Use of electronic data interchange (EDI)

A vital technological component enabling linkages between firms in a mutual operational network. EDI extends beyond the initial interconnection between retailer and supplier to an entire network. EDI is used as the medium to support electronic trading to facilitate global sourcing and acts as a low cost communication option.

Sales captured at item level

In conjunction with bar coding, it is necessary to be able to appreciate the flows of products and services at an individual level. If we are increasingly moving towards micro-marketing and segmentation at individual level, we need to understand how individual offerings perform. In other words, capturing activity at the level of individual item or Stock Keeping Unit (SKU) rather than in larger aggregates such as batches.

Continual and automatic replenishment systems

Despite the increasing individuality of product and service combinations, there will still also be room for more homogeneous offerings such as milk, socks, tins of beans and green Wellington boots (although the reader may well start to notice that even the purveyors of these items are seeking differentiation). These stable merchandise items ('basics' or value goods with little volatility and seasonality) can be replenished by a vendor or supplier to the exact rate of sale. Demand information can drive operational schedules and replenishment is direct from production output rather than stock holding.

Universal product codes (UPC) or article numbering in the supply system

For identification and tracking of goods using bar codes, these must be unique to individual SKUs and standardized throughout the supply system, as duplication causes inefficiencies. These UPCs are now beginning to be available via online catalogues that can be accessed by a number of firms in a supply network.

Electronic reordering

The ordering and reordering of services and goods (especially during a sale season) should be performed electronically to increase speed and accuracy and to reflect customer demand preferences for a particular, customized product and service. This element is closely linked to PoS data, bar coding and EDI.

Store or consumption ready deliveries

Time can be reduced in the delivery cycle by placing goods directly on shelf, or having goods and services ready for immediate consumption, once delivered. Price ticketing, specifications, packaging, etc., has to be completed to retailer or customer needs (each retailer/customer will have specific needs across a number of locations).

Shared and open inventory management systems

In many operational networks, information systems will often be shared and open to the members. Details of inventory (both raw material, work-in-process and finished goods as well as service provision) residing at all supply points (customer serving, retailer, manufacturer, assembly, etc.) will be open to access by any partner in the network.

Intelligent production and cellular manufacturing

For more tangible goods, intelligent production and modular or cellular manufacturing offers a far higher degree of response, speed and agility. Despite initial cost outlay, and time to fully implement, many supplier manufacturers are increasing the use of this form of production organization.

Fast re-estimation and reorder systems

For more volatile, short season or fashionable goods and services, many situations require fast re-estimation of sales and reorder during the season based upon real time demand. In this way, even fast-selling merchandise is restocked to match demand preferences. This reduces the likelihood of stockouts and unplanned markdowns of unwanted product.

Container shipping codes

Just as each SKU has a unique identification code, so does the container or batch of goods. These show the contents and destination and enable logistical tracking of merchandise deliveries so as to enhance speed of response and consumption-ready delivery.

Point of sale (PoS) data sharing with customers and suppliers

Point of sale data collection is vital, but it is of little use if retained in one organization. Essential for a flexible and responsive supply, without this data, large parts of a supply network will only be able to meet demand using forward inventory builds and forecasting rather than operating in-line with real time demand patterns. Unfortunately, the sharing of raw PoS data with other parts of the supply system still proves problematical in many cases.

Consumer demographic information systems

Consumer data 'mining' is now big business. Research indicates that many firms operating in mutual networks are prepared to share their demographic data and information about consumers for all to benefit in the targeting of micro-markets (micro segmentation and customization of segments) and overall category management.

Internet connectivity and e-business

Despite the rhetoric and hype, the Internet is an enabling technology – a powerful set of tools that provides a new way of conducting business: nothing more and nothing less (Porter, 2001). However, at an operational level, the Internet does have a profound impact upon the operational effectiveness and strategic positioning. For the former, the Internet allows a faster exchange of real-time data and information throughout the supply system; in the latter case it enables the value chain to be configured and tailored in a unique manner (we discuss this further in chapter 14).

The Internet also enables the concept of the electronic marketplace to be developed. A robust, secure and flexible data-sharing network enabling business-to-business connectivity. Some firms are also experimenting by using the Internet or Extranets (a supply pipeline application) to perform the various functions of more traditional EDI.

New logistics systems

Logistics, as discussed earlier, tends to occupy the demand side of any business (i.e. after the goods or services have been produced). With the prominence placed upon speed of response and the Internet, advantages that accrue in keeping pace with demand could be dissipated by delays in the logistics systems for finished goods. Many retailers were reported to be placing a much greater emphasis upon strategic logistics systems.

Compressing 'open-to-buy' periods

We mentioned in the last chapter those operations strategies that rely upon the manipulation of time: quick response, time-based competition, strategic postponement, etc. One of the essential components for such strategies is the manipulation of time prior to any selling point to ensure that the ordering of product and service combinations is achieved as close as possible to the start of the selling point. In other words, we try not to make bulk purchases of goods too far in advance of known demand preferences. In Fig. 5.3 we can see the dangers inherent in such a situation.

In this diagram the lead time represents the months ahead of a sale season (the point at which goods and services are available for consumption). The further we move away from this sale point the longer the lead time and the harder it becomes to forecast demand preferences accurately (hence the increase in forecast inaccuracy). The implication of this approach is further discussed in the case study 'Quick Response' at the end of the chapter.

Retailers are increasingly wary of placing orders for merchandise far in advance of a sale season (when demand is unknown). Research suggests that should such activities be

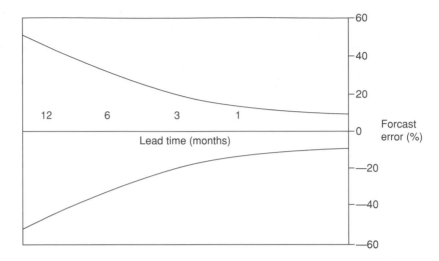

Figure 5.3 *Relationship between lead time and forecast error*

required, they be delayed to as close to the sale season as possible and be supported by a detailed analysis of the likely trends.

Pre-season delivery

In similar fashion to the above, many organizations have begun to question the practice of very early, pre-season delivery of merchandise (for those goods with distinct sales seasons). In the past, it has been common to deliver a high proportion of goods, if not all, prior to the start of the season. This entails a huge number of risks. Small pre-season shipments (sufficient for display and small inventory) followed by fast, flexible and responsive supplies during the season when demand preferences are known, is now the target for many.

Virtual product development

Fast new and modified products, developed using virtual teams from a number of networked organizations and virtual technology. It is now recognized that the new and modified products and services are required faster than ever. However, quality levels and customization issues are also vitally important. To satisfy all these, demands development processes are now undertaken in parallel using the input from a number of disparate, virtual groups in the supply network. Such groups remain responsible for the product and service combination for its whole lifetime, and also disband and reform with much flexibility.

Postponement of activities

The postponement of many supply system activities (usually the final form) until demand can be better identified is increasingly being used by organizations. Strategic postponement as an operations strategy has many benefits. However, it is complex and needs careful planning. Its main components include a precise understanding of demand preferences and how they take shape, that is communicated along various supply streams; good coordination between all the participants in the supply of goods; the flexibility in all operations to alter activities in-line with this changing demand profile and an extremely well-trained and skilled workforce.

Interface management and supply system visibility

Tracking all of the components, finished goods, and service offerings by individual SKU throughout the whole supply network. Modern operations rely heavily upon the ability to be able to track all these elements throughout their life cycle and throughout the entire supply system. This requires trust, openness and coordination from all stages of the system, as well as the ability to manage the various interfaces in the network for speed of response and to prevent stock/inventory duplication.

We have outlined some of the more important building blocks of an operations strategy used by retailers in this study. However, as we have seen in the Operations Strategy Composition Matrix (Fig. 5.2) there will also be less specific influences. In chapter 6 we will deal with these forces that tend to shape the resultant operations strategy in more detail.

The application of operations strategy building blocks

Returning to the empirical research, we can now consider an example of how these various building blocks are actually used. In Table 5.2 the respondents in our research identified the operations strategy ingredients used (either unilaterally or with suppliers). It is clear that certain elements are common within some sectors and, indeed, across a number of sectors.

From the table, the use of a number of building blocks across the various sectors involved is apparent. Quite a few elements are common. This leads us to ask: are the components of an operations strategy generally similar? If so, are terms used to describe such strategies really synonyms? Or, is each operations strategy configured in a different way? Despite the various building blocks being similar, are the various core competencies technologies and resources tailored and blended to form an operations strategy that is unique in each particular situation? It is our belief that the answers to the last two questions are in the affirmative and we will address these concerns in the next chapter.

CONCLUSION

Chapter 5 has described the use of empirical research in the fast-moving consumer goods sector. From the findings we can suggest that these participants used, either unilaterally or with others, certain types of operations strategy. Further, these strategies had common building blocks. However, despite the commonality of the ingredients each strategy was unique, as the ingredients had been given particular emphases. To demonstrate this feature we used a generic model – the operations strategy composition matrix (Fig. 5.2).

Table 5.2 *The application of operations strategy components*

Respondents	Sector	Operations strategy building blocks
17 firms	Grocery – Large multiple retailers	General product/data sharing with suppliers (94%) EDI and bar code use (91%) Shared strategic planning with suppliers (87%) Shared inventory management systems (85%) PoS data sharing (58%)
7 firms	Grocery – smaller multiple retailers	Shared inventory management (82%) Joint product and merchandise planning (77%) New logistics systems (66%)
4 firms	Grocery – Small independents	EDI and bar code use (62%)
18 firms	Clothing – Multiple chains	EDI and bar code use (94%) Fast re-estimation, reorder and replenishment systems (84%) Electronic reorder (78%) PoS data sharing (74%) Store ready deliveries (65%) Pre-season delivery (61%) Postponement activities (60%)
4 firms	Clothing – Speciality chains	EDI and bar code use (86%) Fast re-estimation, reorder and replenishment systems (78%) PoS data sharing (67%) Compressing 'open-to-buy' periods (64%) Pre-season delivery (60%)
3 firms	Clothing – Independents	Small orders and batch sizes (87%) EDI and bar code use (62%) Internet connectivity (55%)
2 firms	Stationers – Retailers of books, periodicals, and general stationery material	EDI and bar code use (78%) Electronic reorder (76%) New logistics systems (67%)
2 firms	Electrical – Retailers of car accessories to end-users.	Continual and automatic replenishment (67%) EDI and bar code use (67%)
2 firms	Electrical – Retail electronics for end consumer market (PCs, printers, and accessories)	EDI and bar code use (74%) Intelligent production (66%)
1 firm	Furniture – Furniture and household textiles retailer	Electronic reorder (100%) General product/data sharing with suppliers (100%) Continual and automatic replenishment (100%)
3 firms	General department stores – Clothing, electrical, furniture, accessories, etc.	Shared inventory management systems (78%) General product/data sharing with suppliers (68%) EDI and bar code use (58%)
3 firms	Department stores – Retailer of clothing and household goods	Shared inventory management systems (60%) PoS data sharing (55%)
1 firm	Toys and games retailer – Board games, plastic toys and models	Intelligent production (100%) Joint product and merchandise planning (100%) Electronic reorder (100%)

CASE STUDY – OPERATIONS STRATEGY IN ACTION

A quick response operations strategy – the essence of operations strategy

As we saw in the Aztec Retail Group case study in the last chapter, Quick Response (QR) as an operations strategy is designed to overcome the impact of seasonality in operations. The traditional practice is to manufacture as much as possible of the finished goods inventory before a season starts, then deliver a half or two-thirds of the estimated amount likely to sell in the season before the beginning of the season (point A in Fig. 5.4). The balance of the order is then delivered at a pre-agreed time during the season (for example, point B), or if selling above original estimates, reorders will be placed (point C).

The QR methodology takes a different route. As little as possible is made and delivered prior to the season. From day one, point of sale data are gathered, analysed, and used to get early indicators on style, colour, size and any other preferences. Manufacturing is then guided by continual (weekly/daily) PoS information. Accurate re-estimation/reorder then takes place (points A through B) during the early season allowing bar coded, shelf ready products to be delivered in line with demand requirement for the specific SKU mix.

The concepts behind Quick Response are elegantly simplistic, yet fundamental to competitive improvement:

- Forecasting, and particularly forecasting of short season goods with wide ranges of styles, colours, size, etc., is almost always wrong.
- The only time any certainty is introduced into a retailer or manufacturer operation is when a customer pays at the cash register and in QR terminology, registers a Stock Keeping Unit (SKU) 'preference' via a PoS entry.
- If a continual stream of PoS data can be reviewed at frequent intervals during a season, early indications can be obtained about likely volumes demanded and the mix of SKUs required by the customer. In QR terms this is demand estimation and re-estimation.

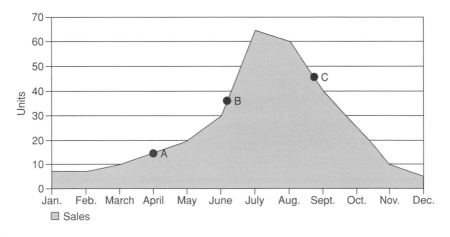

Figure 5.4 *Sales and order profile*

■ As opposed to the traditional practice of receiving most of the merchandise prior to the start of a season, the QR alternative of accepting only enough for store appearance or initial production run and then issuing frequent reorders based on the re-estimation of SKUs and volumes provided by PoS data now exists. In this way, the mix and volume of goods on shelf or at the manufacturing operation is continually adjusted to reflect true demand while keeping inventories small. Consequently, stock-outs are minimized and customer service levels raised, and at the end of a season, when unplanned price markdowns normally play havoc with financial performance, the volumes and SKU mixes are under control.

ANSWERS TO TIME OUT BOX

Time out box I

It is possible that strategies in a particular sector or industry might have similar compositional elements. The individuality comes from the blending of these building blocks.

DISCUSSION QUESTIONS, WORK ASSIGNMENTS AND EXAM QUESTIONS

1   In the operations strategy composition matrix certain generic building blocks were described. Give practical examples for each ingredient using: (a) a chain of restaurants, and (b) a department store.

2   How important are data and information to the role of an operations strategy? What data and information needs are strategically important for a chain of restaurants or a department store?

3   How might these data and information needs be met? What information systems and information technologies are suited to this purpose?

4   What might the role of e-operations be in these circumstances?

Reader question related to the quick response operations strategy case study

1   What are the main building blocks important for a QR operation's strategy? Why are they particularly vital in a retail industry (particularly clothing)?

RECOMMENDED READING

Porter M.E. (2001) 'Strategy and the Internet', *Harvard Business Review* March, 63–78.

Chapter 6

Deployment of an operations strategy

In this chapter we are concerned with how an operations strategy can be implemented and deployed. In chapter 5, various building blocks that are vital to support a particular strategy were described. As a reminder, these appertained to the particular sector under scrutiny and the components will vary by industry and even firm (this is the power of the concept). Here, we will show how these ingredients can be blended or 'fused' into particular and unique operations strategy architectures. Further, we hope to demonstrate how the various blends can vary by particular operations strategy type and other influences.

The chapter aims to review how each operations strategy has an individual composition matrix (something we introduced in chapter 5, Fig. 5.2) that allows for its customization contingent upon the circumstances. This process offers a unique strategic impact and sustainable competitive advantage. The chapter concludes with a review of the possible methods an organization might undertake in order to successfully implement its operations strategy.

LEARNING OBJECTIVES

After considering this chapter, the reader will be able to:

- Appreciate how the various components of an operations strategy are combined and fused in order to closely mirror the various demands placed upon an organization
- Develop an understanding of the ways in which various firms might customize their operations strategies for maximum strategic impact
- Consider the problems and approaches involved in implementation of a strategy

> ### KEY TERMS
>
> - Operations strategy composition matrix
> - Customization of an operations strategy
> - Demand and supply system behaviours
> - Mass customization
> - Strategic impact
> - Operations strategy implementation

INTRODUCTION

In chapter 3 we suggested that an organization may exhibit a hierarchy of strategies: generic strategies, strategic positioning, and operations strategy (followed by the operations management activities or components necessary to achieve strategic objectives). Thus, we can see that the operations strategy or strategies (and there may be more than one) in any firm, can provide a direct link to, and interpretation of, the wider business and corporate strategies.

Figure 6.1 demonstrates the perspective of this chapter and its relationship with the two previous. In chapter 4 we discussed the class of operations strategy and difference between generic types (an abstract pattern of organization – the *phylum*), the physical embodiment (the structure of the actual strategy when composed of a number of building blocks – class). Chapter 5 then reviewed research from one commercial sector that revealed some of the specific ingredients that might contribute to the latter physical embodiment.

Now we examine how the operations strategies are actually deployed (see Fig. 6.1) and the mechanism that provides their unique composition (as well as their competitive potential). We will examine how these strategies are formed and implemented using a composition matrix that customizes a strategy to the unique factors of its situation and environment.

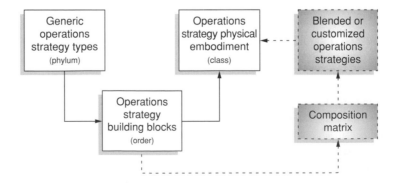

Figure 6.1 *Operations strategy deployment I*

This chapter considers the final research question:

- *Research Question I.* Can a taxonomy of operations strategies be established?
- *Research Question II.* Do organizations have more than one operations strategy?
- *Research Question III.* If an operations strategy is used or employed between an organization and its customers and/or suppliers can the core competencies, capabilities and processes, technologies, resources and key tactical activities vital to support a particular strategy or positioning be identified?
- *Research Question IV.* Are certain core competencies, capabilities and processes; technologies; resources; and key tactical activities vital to support a particular strategy or positioning blended or fused into particular and unique operations strategy architectures? Do these blends vary by particular operations strategy type or other influences, such as demand?

OPERATIONS STRATEGY COMPOSITION MATRIX

In the first chapter we suggested that there are a number of new demands affecting the modern organization. The cluster of value was suggested as a way to depict how multiple entities exert influences on an organization, and that these influences must therefore be taken into account when forming a suitable operations strategy. One of the strongest powers in this scenario will be that of the customer. With their diverse value needs and requirements, they will be the nucleus of activity. In the same way that customer groups and their demands are diverse, we posit that firms need to adopt unique operations strategies for each main type of demand. A majority of businesses will have more than one supplier, customer, product and/or service; it makes sense therefore that they employ multiple operations strategies, each tailored to address individual needs and circumstances.

TIME OUT BOX I

We have seen that the specific building blocks of an operations strategy may often be similar across the same commercial sectors. The various core competencies, capabilities and processes, resources, technologies and certain key tactical activities that are vital to support a particular strategy or positioning may be similar. Yet we know that in order to provide competitive advantage, a strategy should be unique. Two questions therefore arise:

1   How can these operations strategies be designed and implemented to become individual and unique?
2   What are the most important factors for an organization in achieving this customization?

We can speculate that the operations strategies employed by a firm in a particular sector are likely to contain certain components, but they are combined with particular emphases, and that the act of combination or blending will assume strategic importance. If, say, supply management and/or time-based competition and/or sourcing are of particular strategic importance to an organization, then it will accord operations strategy status to the combination of activities and elements that comprise them. Again, we make the point that:

- Some building blocks will be common across a number of commercial sectors dealing with particular product and service combinations. However, there will be others that may be essential to a specific industry that might be peculiar to that setting.
- Apart from these ingredients of an operations strategy, there will also be other generic influences upon its final shape (see chapter 7).
- The emphases upon particular building blocks are something that is unique to the organization strategy and does provide its sustainable competitive advantage.

These distinct operations strategy architectures reinforce Michael Porter's (1996) belief that strategy is mainly a matter of capability development and activities are the basic units of competitive advantage. To remind the reader, an organization, he suggests will adopt a distinct strategic positioning; it will compete on the basis of flexibility, cost, quality, speed, diversity and variety, etc. Here, strategic positioning means 'performing different activities from rivals' or performing similar activities in different ways'. In contrast, he describes operations effectiveness as 'performing similar activities better than rivals'. Clearly, operations effectiveness depends upon the correct operations strategy, that unique architecture or blend that combines various elements. Our premise is that an operations strategy is aimed at performing key operations activities better than rivals so as to provide support for the overall strategy of a firm, as well as serving as a firm's distinctive competence. Companies can quickly imitate individual activities, but not the way they are combined to form a unique operations strategy

However, in order to tailor an operations strategy in this way, we must first understand how the components of the strategic architecture can be put together. We define this as a composition matrix (Fig. 6.2). The matrix is composed of a unique blending of those components revealed from research reported in chapter 5. The reader should bear in mind that this figure is only an example. It is not exhaustive and it is conceivable that there will be others depending on the type of commercial sector. In addition, other external influences of a more general nature will also play a part (we deal with these in the next chapter).

For example, a particular operations strategy may rely heavily on shared strategic operations planning with major suppliers and less heavily on consumer demographic information systems. Although these are both possible building blocks of any operations strategy, one element might appear more prominently in a particular strategic composition matrix than another (hence the different shading). It is important, therefore, that an appropriate blend of building blocks is chosen for each situation, one that is individual to a known demand profile. After all, this is the principal aim of the operations strategy, as seen in the earlier definition:

Operations strategy definition 2 – the wider value delivery strategy
Major decisions about, and strategic management of: core competencies, capabilities and processes, technologies, resources and key tactical activities necessary in

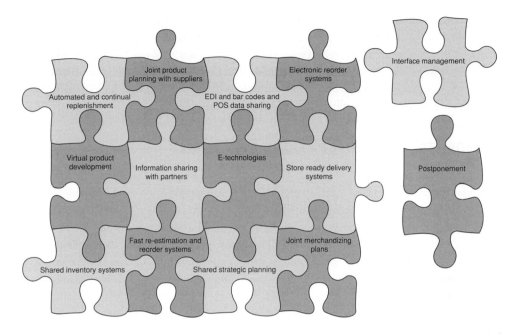

Figure 6.2 *An operations strategy composition matrix*

any supply network, in order to create and deliver product and service combinations and the value demanded by a customer. The strategic role involves blending these various building blocks into one or more unique, organizational-specific, strategic architectures.

It is the unique architecture of each operations strategy that provides an essential strategic contribution to achieve sustainable competitive advantage. From this we can speculate that organizations will have not one, but many operations strategies. Each may have common components, but each has a unique and individual emphasis that is dictated by a number of factors such as trading partners, supply system configuration and demand behaviours. In addition, these findings would seem to further expand and develop Fisher's (1997) conceptualization of supply chains. He argues that there may be a difference between physically efficient and market responsive supply chains that will be based upon their purpose in supplying functional or innovative products and their requisite demand patterns. Although Fisher confines his dichotomy to supply chains rather than the full range of operations strategies, he accepts the notion that different supply chains satisfy different demand types. This research allows us to advance two slightly different dimensions:

- It seems possible that a firm may use a number of building blocks that are blended into strategic architectures that match the exigencies of the competitive environment.
- We can also postulate that an operations strategy will have distinct building blocks that provide necessary and unique emphases to each situation.

109

The composition matrix shown in Fig. 6.2 details how individual operations components fit to deliver an operations strategy that is tailored and customized to the individual requirements of the business activity. The two shades are intended to show how an organization may place greater emphasis on some components rather than others. As demonstrated by the cluster of value in chapter 1, there are multiple activities taking place, therefore multiple strategies are needed, each tailored to individual circumstances.

CUSTOMIZATION OF OPERATIONS STRATEGIES

We now return to Research Question IV: what factors or situations might dictate that a particular blend of operations strategy ingredients be adopted. Do the particular blends vary by demand situation? Developing an optimal operations strategy is clearly a complex challenge. Detailed consideration has to be given to the blend of components and the emphases that each can provide in a particular consumer and/or product situation. Many firms operating in volatile markets are only now getting to grips with one operations strategy. Futuristically, they will have a number, each one holding a different significance; and perhaps more disturbingly, all being fluid and transitory.

We set out to identify which building blocks would blend well together and in which circumstances. In other words, what are the driving forces that dictate a particular fusion of core competencies, capabilities and processes, resources, technologies and certain key tactical activities. Research was conducted with two large multiple retailers of grocery products (see Table 6.1).

The two retailers supplied data concerning two classes of product. In order to develop an operations strategy it is important to understand the behaviours of supply and demand from two fundamental perspectives: (a) at the level of product/service combinations and (b) the supply system.

Product and service combination demand behaviour

This category includes:

- *Product attributes*. Such as durability of the product, price levels, shelf life (intrinsic – physical characteristics and extrinsic – customer taste changes), product complexity (number and variety of SKUs making up a product line), and product line dynamics (characteristics of slow-moving versus rapid turnover goods).
- *Demand patterns*. Demand periodicity (seasonality, aseasonality, cultural influences) demand uncertainty and the economics of products lines (unit margins), will all be in issue.
- *Customer behaviour*. The characteristics of the customer (in the case of another organization) or end-consumer (an individual purchaser) place different demands upon the supply pipeline and distort the pattern of demand. Different ordering processes, EDI usage, payment methods, logistical needs, promotional requirements, packing and shelving constraints, product characteristics (sell by dates, storage needs, transit

regulations, maintenance, information content, after sales support, repeat purchase patterns, etc.) will all vary by consumer, product group and individual product: all will change the demand pattern as well as the operations strategy necessary. Add to this the various seasonal effects, cyclical needs, fashion sways and partnership programme agreements, and the complexity and influence of individual customer behaviour begins to be seen.

Supply system behaviour

Analyses of:

- *Product Stream Value Flows*. Highly complex and dynamic. Such an approach requires the appreciation of supply system architecture and the intricacy of that architecture (length of pipeline, stages, firm sizes, product complexity and dynamism, information availability, customer demands, etc.); power of the participants (strengths/sizes/financial capabilities of the entities in the pipeline will have a marked impact on the way it operates) and integration of the supply system (data/information availability, technology, strategies used and culture).
- *Vertical Integration*. As suggested by Hayes and Wheelwright (1984), consideration of vertical integration strategies of pipeline members. This includes: direction of any expansion (upstream and downstream); extent of the process span required (number of supply system activities undertaken by firms) and the balance of the vertically integrated stages (capacity and operating behaviour) whether fully balanced or partially balanced.

Returning to Table 6.1, analysis of product and service combination demand behaviour has allowed the two retailers to rank the importance of all these factors affecting the two selected products (chilled ready meals for Acme Stores and tinned vegetables for Value Save) against the operations strategy components earlier revealed. The importance of each can then be scored using a maximum weighting of five. From the table, we can see that certain factors are more important than others for the two product categories (a score of > 4 or 5) and thus any operations strategy should incorporate these high scoring elements to give it a unique blend and emphases for the product group. Further, from the totals row we can see that the overall importance of an operations strategy clearly varies by product category (chilled ready meals scoring higher than tinned vegetables 75 > 48).

We now turn to supply system behaviour. Using the mapping analyses, the same approach can be used to rank importance of operations strategy ingredients by each retailer and/or supplier in a given pipeline situation. Again, some components are clearly more important than others and score more highly, as does the overall importance of the oper-ations strategy (Acme Stores versus Value Save 71 > 40). We begin to see how the operations strategy can be customized by each retailer and supply situation. Before going further, we will briefly discuss the importance of customization.

Table 6.1 Customizing an operations strategy for Acme Stores and Value Save

Operations strategy building blocks	Product behaviour (Chilled Ready Meals – Acme Stores)	Product behaviour (Tinned vegetables – Value Save)	Supply system behaviour (Acme Stores)	Supply system behaviour (Value Save)	Individual component weighting (Max. 20)
Shared strategic operations planning with major customers and suppliers	3	2	4	2	11
Joint product and merchandise planning with coustomers and suppliers	3	0	4	2	9
Bar coded merchandise	5	2	5	3	15
Small orders and batch sizes (both pre- and during a sales season)	5	2	4	3	14
Product data and information sharing with trading partners.	3	2	4	2	11
Use of Electronic Data Interchange (EDI)	4	2	5	3	14
Sales captured at item level	4	2	4	3	13
Continual and automatic replenishment systems	3	5	4	2	14
Universal Product Codes (UPC) in the supply system	4	4	3	2	13
Electronic reorder	4	4	4	3	15
Store ready deliveries	5	3	5	2	15
Shared and open inventory management systems	4	3	4	1	12
Intelligent production and cellular manufacturing	0	0	0	0	0
Fast re-estimation and reorder systems	5	0	4	1	10
Container shipping codes	5	2	2	2	11

	Product behaviour (Chilled Ready Meals). Weighting Max. 115	Product behaviour (Tinned vegetables). Weighting Max. 115	Supply system behaviour (Acme Stores). Weighting Max. 115	Supply system behaviour (Value Save). Max. 115	Customized operations strategy architecture. Max. 460
Point of Sale (PoS) data sharing with customers and suppliers	5	5	4	1	15
Consumer demographic information systems	0	1	1	0	2
Internet connectivity	3	4	2	1	10
New logistics systems	3	4	3	1	11
Compressing 'Open-to-buy' dates	5	0	2	1	8
Pre-season delivery	1	1	2	3	7
Virtual product development	1	0	1	2	4
Postponement of activities	78	50	74	41	243
Totals	**75**	**48**	**71**	**40**	**228**

Mass customization

Over the last decade, management literature has been replete with calls for mass customization, for example, Westbrook and Williamson (1993), Pine *et al.* (1993), Fincke and Goffard (1993), Kotha (1996), Fisher (1997), Gilmore and Pine (1997), Fung (1998) and Zipkin (2001). This movement recognizes the increasing need for individual, customized and personalized goods and services with the need for volume. To put the debate into context, the modern operations era can be described using the following evolutionary milestones:

- *Mass production.* High volume, standardized goods and services. Low variable cost and economies of scale with little or no variety (Skinner, 1985).
- *Lean production.* Focused on the Toyota Production System, the removal of all waste from the operations environment (Womack *et al.*, 1990).
- *Mass customization.* Similar to mass production, but with variety. Instead of selecting one variety of a product, each customer provides unique information so that the product can be tailored to her or his requirements. Requires flexible production processes and delivery capacity. Sometimes also referred to as 'superficial customization'.
- *Agility and flexible operations.* The agile manufacturer aims to produce highly-customized products at a cost comparable with mass production and within short lead times. The tailoring of products to demand includes a higher element of service and thus greater added value. A flexible workforce, structure and production technologies (especially through the use of computer-integrated manufacturing) are all contained within a learning culture. Externally the concepts of vertical integration and long-term partnerships are replaced with short-term, flexible contracts and horizontal outsourcing that allow rapid response through an expansive system of communication networks (Kidd, 1994).
- *Flexible specialization.* In order to satisfy a new demand pattern moving towards individualization, a rejection of Fordism and mass production. A return to a craft form of production, based upon the use of information technology and customized, short-run manufacture, in a network of small firms operating in niche, segmented, markets, (Piore and Sabel, 1984).
- *Operations strategies.* As this book has been suggesting, we are now beginning to witness a new trend. Recent empirical research (Lowson, 2001c) suggests that many organizations are reacting to the demand for variety by adopting an operations strategy. Research has also confirmed three major implications. First, just as a firm may have more than one product or customer group or operate in more than one market, it will often also use more than one operations strategy. Second, these strategies can often be customized to meet the individual needs of each situation, for example, a particular customer or product group – an operations strategy for each individual demand situation. This simple, yet powerful approach provides organizations with the ability to match and respond to the demand complexity of the value stream using unique operations strategies. Third, the operations strategies deployed are intended as integrative relationship devices in a supply network and, as such, they are broader in scope than a functional strategy such as manufacturing or production.

Looking again at Table 6.1, this approach answers the calls for greater mass customization of products and services, by offering a customized operations strategy (by both product/service combination and/or organization of the supply system). Using the operations strategy component weighting in the last column of the table, the importance of each operations strategy element can be ranked across a range of products or services and manufacturers and retailers in a supply system. It is likely that groups of organizations and products can be addressed by particular operations strategy configurations: an operations strategy for each individual demand situation. This approach provides organizations with the ability to match and respond to the complexity of the value stream by 'blending' unique operations strategies to match demand (as suggested in Research Question IV at the start of the chapter).

The strategic impact of customized operations strategies

The customization of an operations strategy will have profound competitive implications. The subject of an operations strategy as a source of competitive advantage is dealt with in more depth in chapter 8. At this juncture we propose to offer a short example of the possible impacts.

CASE STUDY – OPERATIONS STRATEGY IN ACTION

Omicron Foods Part 1 – deployment of an operations strategy

Customization of an operations strategy

The Strategic Operations Management Centre (SOMC) at UEA undertook a detailed research project with Omicron Foods, a small UK food manufacturer with two plants in Norfolk, over an eight month period. The Company employs nearly 200 staff and was a management buy-out from a US international parent company in 1995. Omicron manufactures and supplies snack foods to four leading grocery retailers as well as a number of trade wholesalers. We conducted value and demand analyses of both product and supply system behaviour in respect of three of the four retail consumers in order to achieve a clearer understanding of the basic operational systems employed. This involved an examination of the following demand behaviours:

- Product behaviour (see p. 110); and,
- Supply system behaviour (see p. 111).

Despite acknowledging that they had an operations strategy, the only one openly referred to by Omicron was supply network management. As observed by Omicron's Operations Director:

Once we decided to map the various value streams and attempt to appreciate the exact behaviour of each supply system and customer grouping, it soon became clear that the different product and customer types were important. The various 'behaviours' meant that groups of SKUs [Stock Keeping Units] had completely different operational needs depending upon the type of retail customer, etc., – they all had unique requirements.

Omicron Foods did in fact use three distinct types of operations strategy,

- Efficient consumer response (ECR),
- Supply network management (SNM), and
- Just in time (JIT).

Each strategy had a slightly different emphasis that depended upon the retail customer involved, the supply system structure and the demand behaviours. Thus, although many elements were common across all three operations strategies, a particular emphasis upon certain precepts was in evident in each strategy (see Table 6.2).

Here, we see a similar approach to the customization of operations strategies for the retailers Acme and Value Save in Table 6.1. In Table 6.2, the product and supply system behaviour for each of Omicron's retail customers has been analysed in terms of the categories listed above. The demand behaviours were then ranked by Omicron against the main components common across such operations strategies. Three fundamental points should be noted here:

1   The various components were suggested by Omicron and they will of course vary by each organization (this encapsulates this contingency of each situation);
2   The type of analysis seen in Table 6.2 can also be conducted at both product and product group level; and
3   We are attempting to deal with Omicron's operations strategies at supply system level and not just the interface between them and their retail customers.

Returning to the table, the demand behaviours for each retailer were ranked in order of importance against the various operations strategy building blocks used in the supply system. We can see immediately that for each retailer supply system, and of course their suppliers, those components scoring highly (in comparison with others in the same column) are particularly important and should receive attention. In this way the resultant operations strategy is blended and customized by retailer and demand behaviours. The fourth column gives Omicron Foods an indication of the importance of the component across its customer base. Finally, the total row for each retailer supply system indicates the overall importance of an operations strategy for that organization. Here, for example, ECR is particularly prominent and Omicron can assess the level of resource to be devoted to this operations strategy, (taking into consideration the importance, or otherwise, of the particular customer account).

In conclusion, the customizing approach was summarized by Omicron's Director:

Table 6.2 *Omicron Foods operations strategy building blocks weighted by product demand and supply system behaviour for major customers*

Operations strategy building blocks	Product demand and supply system behaviour weighting (max 20)			Component weighting bands (max 60)
	Retailer I* (ECR)	Retailer II (SNM)	Retailer III (JIT)	
Shared strategic operations planning with major customers and suppliers	17	17	12	46
Joint product and merchandise planning with customers and suppliers	19	10	0	29
Bar coded merchandise	20	18	10	48
Small orders and batch sizes (both pre- and during a sales season)	11	14	5	30
Product data and information sharing with trading partners	17	9	14	40
Use of Electronic Data Interchange (EDI)	19	19	12	50
Sales captured at item level	19	14	10	43
Continual and automatic replenishment systems	18	8	12	38
Universal Product Codes (UPC) in the supply system	15	12	1	28
Electronic reorder	19	12	15	46
Store ready deliveries	10	7	13	30
Shared and open inventory management systems	9	7	12	28
Intelligent production and cellular manufacturing	11	5	7	23
Fast re-estimation and reorder systems	18	7	16	41
Container shipping codes	10	5	3	18
Point of Sale (PoS) data sharing with customers and suppliers	17	17	12	46

continued

Table 6.2 continued

Operations strategy building blocks	Product demand and supply system behaviour weighting (max 20)			Component weighting bands (max 60)
	Retailer I* (ECR)	Retailer II (SNM)	Retailer III (JIT)	
Consumer demographic information systems	7	1	0	8
Internet connectivity	8	17	4	29
New logistics systems	9	8	3	20
Compressing 'Open-to-buy' dates	5	0	1	6
Reducing pre-season delivery	4	15	6	25
Virtual product development	7	1	1	9
Postponement of activities	14	14	16	44
Interface management and supply system visibility	18	13	17	48
Totals	**321** Retailer I demand behaviour. Max. score 480	**250** Retailer 2 demand behaviour. Max. score 480	**202** Retailer 3 demand behaviour. Max. score 480	**773** Customised operations strategy architecture. Max. score 1440
	These three columns demonstrate the importance of the operations strategy fusion by demand behaviour associated with a particular retailer and its individual supply system			This column demonstrates a unique operations strategy architecture linked to the identified demand behaviour pattern across a group of consumers

* This analysis can also be conducted at the level of individual products or product groups rather than customers.

This may sound complex but we can now see that it does in fact replicate the essential complexity in a supply situation. The type of product and/or customer combination will influence the demand patterns and require discrete competencies, resources and technologies for each customer, supply system and even product type.

For Omicron Foods, each of the three operations strategies were important and played an essential role, although a slightly different one, in managing the demand and supply system. The result, as can be seen in Fig. 6.3, is a distinct and individual portfolio of operations strategies as used by Omicron – an architecture of components blended and influenced by product and supply system behaviour for a particular retailer (as suggested in Research Question IV).

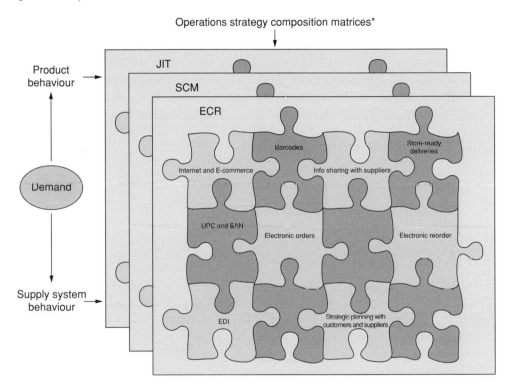

Figure 6.3 *Customizing operations strategies to demand: Omicrom Foods – operations strategy portfolio*

* Unique 'blends' or architectures reflecting core competencies, capabilities and processes, resources, technologies and certain tactical activities that are vital to support a particular strategy or positioning.

IMPLEMENTATION FACTORS

We have seen how demand can be used to provided a customizing influence upon the operations strategy. This is perhaps one of the key drivers involved: satisfaction of customer needs and values being the *raison d'être* of the operations strategy. Nevertheless, there will be other influences upon the shaping of such a strategy and these fall into three main categories. Thus we now have:

- Product and supply system behaviours (covered in this chapter);
- Performance factors. The factors that are primarily concerned with the impact of the operations strategy, in other words its quantitative performance and its ability to offer sustainable competitive advantage; and
- Tactical factors. Broader considerations that in their specificity will be peculiar to each individual firm, its circumstances and its environment (for example, quality requirements supply chain relationships, human resources *et al.*)

These factors are summarized in Fig. 6.4.

We can put the operations strategy of any organization into a context using this model.

- *Box 1* shows the operations strategy component profiles. These are the unique blends of building blocks, whether referred to as supply network management, quick response, JIT, time-based competition, lean manufacturing, etc.

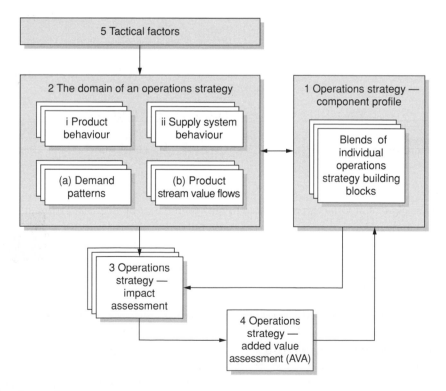

Figure 6.4 *Operations strategy context model*

- *Box 2* shows how these strategies are influenced by the domain in which they are cultivated by (i) product behaviour and (ii) supply system behaviours in turn composed of (a) demand patterns and (b) value flows.
- *Box 3* demonstrates the influence of the various performance factors. It will be inevitable than any operations strategy will reflect the ability of its various components to increase the overall performance of the firm and hopefully lead to competitive advantage.
- *Box 4* added value assessment. From this perspective, the financial performance of the organization and its operations strategy can be reflected in a more qualitative assessment of those activities that add value and those that do not.
- *Box 5* The tactical factors individual to the situation (dealt with in chapter 7) that shape each operations strategy in order to be unique and closely aligned to the individual organization and industry circumstances – strategy is about the difference that creates value!

We now turn to Boxes 3 and 4. First, the performance factors, and the possible link between these and the various components of the operations strategy, second, the assessment of added value.

Performance factors

In order to assess the likely impact of an operations strategy, we return to the Omicron Foods case study.

CASE STUDY – OPERATIONS STRATEGY IN ACTION

Omicron Foods Part 2 – impact of an operations strategy

Operations strategy impact

Senior management at Omicron were asked to rank both the competitive advantage (current and likely) and the impact upon performance (profit, sales/turnover, quality and customer service) of each of the operations strategy components or building blocks – see Table 6.3.

Component competitive advantage

First, we will look at component competitive advantage. Here, we see that the Omicron management team examined each component and ranked them in terms of the current and likely amount of competitive advantage that might accrue from its use (negative, low, medium and high). For example, Internet connectivity was ranked as a future component likely to offer a relatively high degree of competitive advantage. In the medium strength column, EDI, PoS data and bar coded merchandise ranked highly as current contributors.

121

Table 6.3 *Omicron Foods impact analysis. Operations strategy components (or building blocks) degree of competitive advantage (current and likely) and impact upon performance (% of respondents)*

	Component competitive advantage (current and likely)				Component impact upon performance*			
	Neg	Low	Med	High	Pr	Tu	TQM	CS
Shared strategic operations planning with major customers and suppliers	6	12	82	0	12	0	68	20
Joint product and merchandise planning with customers and suppliers	0	19	80	1	2	11	10	77
Bar coded merchandise	0	0	89	11	14	10	0	76
Small orders and batch sizes (both pre- and during a sales season)	0	0	58	42	28	22	8	42
Product data and information sharing with trading partners.	0	17	72	11	2	8	32	58
Use of Electronic Data Interchange (EDI)	0	2	92	6	27	12	11	50
Sales captured at item level	4	37	59	0	47	32	21	0
Continual and automatic replenishment systems	21	9	70	0	48	32	0	20
Universal Product Codes (UPC) in the supply system	3	73	20	4	17	39	37	7
Electronic reorder	3	43	52	2	47	40	7	6
Store ready deliveries	6	23	70	1	4	28	10	58
Shared and open inventory management systems	0	48	52	0	11	17	37	35
Intelligent production and cellular manufacturing	0	22	48	10	10	10	58	22
Fast re-estimation and reorder systems	2	14	76	8	15	11	47	27
Container shipping codes	0	10	88	2	9	11	32	48
Point of Sale (PoS) data sharing with customers and suppliers	0	7	93	0	62	0	0	38
Consumer demographic information systems	0	98	2	0	4	10	36	50
Internet connectivity and E-commerce	0	12	22	76	13	25	22	40
New logistics systems	5	11	26	58	3	7	9	81
Compressing 'Open-to-buy' dates	15	25	55	5	27	26	24	13
Pre-season delivery	1	46	42	11	22	19	47	12
Virtual product development	3	32	61	4	12	31	17	40
Postponement of activities	15	15	10	60	7	45	10	38

* Pr = Profit, Tu = Turnover, TQM = Total Quality Management initiatives, CS = Customer service levels

At the other extreme, the sharing of consumer demographic information systems with their retail customers was not expected to provide very much advantage and the automatic replenishment might, in some instances, prove a cost to Omicron.

Component impact upon performance

In these columns the management team attempted to quantify some of the likely benefits of the various operations elements. To do this they agreed upon four potential categories where any change was likely to be significant:

- Profit;
- Turnover/sales;
- Total quality management initiatives;
- Customer service levels.

In this type of analysis we can see both the impact of some building blocks (new logistics systems for example), as well as the relationship (customer service in this example). The following then can be identified as correlated impact factors:

- *Profit* The use of shared PoS data;
- *Total quality management* Shared strategic operations planning with major customers and suppliers;
- *Turnover* Postponement activities;
- *Customer service levels* Joint product/merchandise planning with customers and suppliers, use of bar codes and new logistics systems.

CRITICAL REFLECTION

Clearly, some caution is advisable here. Statistically there may be a degree of correlation for some of these relationships; however, it is not possible, without further research into the mechanisms that link the variables, to suggest any form of causation. Nevertheless, for the first time, we are able to identify not only ingredients used but also how they influence key organizational performance indicators. This, together with a better understanding of product and supply system behaviour (see case study Part 1), enables a customized operations strategy to be developed, if necessary by each product and/or customer; something previously unavailable at a management level. Although we have moved a little closer to a qualitative understanding of the impact of the building blocks an operations strategy (Research Question IV), further research is needed to quantify these strategic advantages and provide more detail.

Table 6.3 also allows an organization to consider each operations strategy component and examine the likely impact across a range of factors (of course the factors that are important will vary from one organization to another – making this strategic approach unique).

Added value assessment

The assessment of performance conducted by the Omicron Foods management team in Table 6.3 was based mainly upon an internal perspective. In other words, the management team asked themselves 'How will these operations building blocks, admittedly operating in a wider supply system, impact upon our internal performance?' While this thinking is important, it does not fully reflect the notion that performance measurement is also an external activity. In the earlier parts of this book we placed a strong emphasis upon the idea that competition is now at supply pipeline level – this is nothing new. However, the idea that we should measure performance at this level is a development towards new, *external*, pipeline scoring methods.

Suppliers and retailers in a supply system will often evaluate each other's operations performance and the total business they are both involved in. Retailer systems to measure their suppliers and vice versa are nothing new. What is particularly innovative is the new form of 'Added Value Assessment' (AVA) now beginning to emerge in many vendor–retailer relationships. This concept brings together the participants in a supply channel as equal partners. A methodology is then applied to identify activities that:

■ Add value;
■ Do not add value;
■ Are necessary at the moment, but not adding value longer term.

An agreed financial scoring system or collective reward system is then evoked to provide the motivation for continual improvement in the supply channel. Consequently, actions adding value throughout an integrated supply system are rewarded, while those continuing to subtract value are penalized. In this way there is an increased motivation on the part of all enterprises in the supply pipeline to consider activities beyond their boundaries and their impact throughout the network. An independent adjudicator can also be used to administer the scheme and ensure equitable decisions as well as to enforce confidentiality agreements.

TIME OUT BOX II

At this point, the readers might like to contemplate what supply system performance measurements a clothing retailer such as Spain's Zara or Mango and their vendors might agree upon as part of a meaningful contribution to what might add value and what might not?

The AVA approach encourages far better supply performance from all members, as well a more open sharing of information. Clearly, the continuing feedback from both the internal and external performance assessments seen in Fig. 6.4 can also guide the blending, deployment and control of the various operations strategy components.

CONCLUSION

A brief resumé may be in order. This chapter has attempted to provide a long overdue synthesis in the strategic operations management and mass customization debate. We have seen that the building blocks of an operations strategy can be viewed as forming a composition matrix that fuses them together as a reaction to the demand and supply system circumstances. The unique architecture that is formed is in some degree individual to each strategy, business and sector and provides strategic impact and competitive advantage due to its emphasis upon particular performance factors. The operations strategy is then contingent upon its particular circumstances: a factor that has considerable benefits to its subsequent implementation.

The rationale for this chapter was summarized in Fig. 6.4. Here, we described how different types of operations strategy were evident and these were cultivated in a particular domain of influence that included various performance factors. It was also pointed out that each situation would also involve various tactical factors that would have a wider impact and shape the resultant operations strategy. It is these perspectives to which we now turn in the next chapter.

ANSWERS TO TIME OUT BOXES

Time out box I

1   One approach will be to fuse these various building blocks into a unique architecture. It is the way they are blended, with a greater emphasis being placed upon some components rather than others, that will provide unique combinations that are difficult for rivals to copy. This will give the firm an individual strategic positioning rather than just operational effectiveness.

2   There will be many tactical factors that must be considered (these are dealt with in the next chapter), however, given the importance we have placed upon demand as a driving force, this will be a major deciding factor.

Time out box II

There are a number of issues (not all of them operational) that will be important in this fast-moving and complex fashion supply system. As pointed out earlier, often the exact nature of performance measurement will be unique to the circumstances. As such, it is not easy to be prescriptive, however, our suggestions are as follows:

1   Decision making
- Decision cycle time
- Time lost in decision making.

2   Processing and production
- Product creation and manufacture
- Inventory turnover and work in progress levels
- Quality and conformance to specs
- Asset utilization and plant efficiency
- Cycle times
- Quality levels
- Workforce turnover
- Product and process flexibility.

3   Product category management
- Category strategy
- Category measures
- Category processes
- Data/information requirements
- Category capabilities
- Activity based costs
- Category relationships.

4   New product introduction
- Market/segment research
- Development and execution
- Number of new introductions
- Time from idea to market
- Design for manufacture rating
- Rate of introduction
- Percent first into the market
- New vs. existing sales levels
- Assessment of effectiveness.

5   Product merchandising
- Managing product categories
- Managing store operations
- Developing brand propositions
- Managing channel strategies
- Managing trade sales
- Retailer and supplier levels of gross margin return on inventory (GMROI).

6   Product promotion
- Programme planning
- Forecasting and deployment
- Execution
- Assessment.

7   Replenishment
- Management of store inventory and orders

- Logistics performance
- Material procurement
- Order fulfilment cycle times
- Product records
- On time shipment.

8   Distribution

- Flow-through distribution
- Shipping accuracy
- Shipping cycle time
- Cost of shipping
- Floor ready units
- Inventory accuracy
- % auto replenishment
- Cross-docking capabilities
- Direct to store delivery.

9   EDI and bar coding technology

- Degree of electronic data interchange adoption in supply channel
- Depth of EDI implementation
- Percentage of products bar coded
- EDI integration
- Per cent of Universal Product Code (UPC) or European Article Number (EAN) compliance
- SKUs on electronic catalogue
- % shipping cartons with Universal Product Code (UPC) container code.

10   Customer service

- Response time
- Order lead time
- Deliveries on time
- Line fill and order fill.

11   Quality and reliability

- Adherence to quality procedures
- Quality performance
- Quality failure level (internal and external)
- Accuracy of interpretation of customer needs and requirements
- Level of customer input through initiatives such as quality function deployment (QFD)
- Customer satisfaction with product life cycle and new product introduction.

DISCUSSION QUESTIONS, WORK ASSIGNMENTS AND EXAM QUESTIONS

1   In what ways might a customized operations strategy lead to competitive advantages? What are the advantages and disadvantages?

2   To what degree will mass customization and the provision of individualized goods and services be a factor in future commerce (for both goods and services)?

3   Can such goods and services ever be totally individualized? What are the main hurdles in achieving this status?

Reader questions related to the Omicron Foods case study, Part 1

1   The various building blocks comprising an operations strategy for Omicron are clearly specific to their sector (grocery production and retail). Can similar components be identified for other commercial ventures, such as the financial services or a restaurant?

2   In teams or groups, consider other instances when a firm might want to adopt different operations strategies. It may be constructive to consider this question in relation not only to the grocery retailing and manufacturing industries, but also the service sector. Might this strategic approach also be relevant to non-profit making firms?

3   Part 1 of the Omicron Foods case demonstrated that an organization might customize an operations strategy for each major customer. Consider if this could be done for product types or groups in the financial services sector or healthcare sector.

4   What advantages and disadvantages might operations strategy customization have for a firm?

Reader question related to the Omicron Foods case study, Part 2

5   The impact assessment conducted by senior managers at Omicron was ostensibly an internal exercise. Could a similar analysis be undertaken across a wider supply network gaining the input from other firms? Could you suggest what performance measurements might be agreed upon between firms in such a setting? How could they be reinforced in a meaningful way that would add value to the supply network?

RECOMMENDED READING

Fisher M.L. (1997) 'What is the Right Supply Chain for Your Product', *Harvard Business Review* March/April, 105–16.

Zipkin P. (2001) 'The Limits of Mass Customization', *Sloan Management Review* Spring, 81–7.

Chapter 7

Tactical factors that shape an operations strategy

This chapter deals with the tactical factors and contingency issues that shape an operations strategy. We can think of these at three levels:

1   At the level of building blocks. The individual core competencies, capabilities and processes, resources, technologies and certain key tactical activities that are vital to support a particular operations strategy;
2   The influence that these elements will have in making each operations setting, and to a degree, strategy, unique; and
3   The way these tactical factors can be used internally, as management levers, to enhance the competitive potential of an operations strategy.

LEARNING OBJECTIVES

After considering this chapter, the reader will be able to:

■   Appreciate the mission of an operations strategy
■   Explain the strategic positioning an operations strategy can support
■   Understand how certain key tactical factors can be used as management levers to shape an operations strategy
■   Appreciate how contingency issues in an external competitive environment will shape such a strategy

KEY TERMS

- ■ Tactical factors
- ■ Contingency issues
- ■ Mission
- ■ Positioning
- ■ Products and processes
- ■ Operational system
- ■ Data and information
- ■ Human resource management
- ■ Quality
- ■ Sourcing and purchasing
- ■ Structure
- ■ Supply network

INTRODUCTION

This chapter continues to examine the context of an operations strategy by reviewing the wider perspectives that will shape both its development and performance. All organizations are embedded in an individual context. Although, for example, there will be certain common factors across an industry, and firms may even share common operations strategy building blocks, the particular blend of these elements will be unique to both the commercial enterprise and its sector. Chapter 6 demonstrated how operations strategies could be customized to reflect various demand and supply situations. There will also be other, more general, tactical factors and contingency influences upon the unique composition and deployment of such a strategy – it is these that are the subject of this chapter.

At the outset, we post a warning to the reader. The various tactical factors and contingency issues covered in this section can only be described in general terms. They will be individual to each situation (and to a degree each strategy) dependent upon the organization circumstances – hence the earlier comment that strategy is all about the differences that create customer value and the competitive advantage these may secure.

The various tactical factors we will describe exist both internally and externally (in the organizational domain) and will often be connected to the various 'bundles' of resources or core competencies of the firm.

TIME OUT BOX I

At this juncture, the reader might speculate on the type of tactical factors that are likely to shape the operations strategy of an organization.

CRITICAL REFLECTION

The reader might reflect upon the individuality and contingency of each organization and its particular setting. We should be aware that this uniqueness is a fundamental factor in the study of organizational theory and that far too often it is overlooked.

Much management literature (and indeed, a great deal of management consultancy) is devoted to the provision of solutions that will address common problems across a number of firms and sectors. There is considerable criticism of such 'best practice' models. In particular, the fact that they assume implicit simplicity in transferring stereotypical ideas of homogeneous, static systems from one organization or industry to another (Thompson and McHugh, 1995).

This catholic applicability stretches credibility, in asking us to accept, as many supporters suggest, that such broad solutions can offer benefits to every firm and every industry: a universal panacea no matter what the ill! This situation has been brought about as much by the peddlers of software reputed to provide an all-embracing management solution, as it has by the misinformed supporters. The complexity of our organizations and their embedded nature in their business and wider environments makes such claims naive and even misleading. In truth, any improvement approaches have to be contingent upon all the circumstances, including the socio-economic environment and spatio-temporal setting; a fact conveniently overlooked in the face of such intricacies. For example, complexity and dynamism are often conveniently side-stepped as the supporters of these all-embracing solutions apply their techniques in established industries exhibiting relatively stable demand patterns. In practice, it is suspected that very few industries will display these characteristics in the future; the majority will be attempting to cope with multiple differentiation through rapidly changing value chain configurations.

In Fig. 7.1 we can see how the tactical factors will shape each operations strategy and its composition.

TACTICAL FACTORS AND CONTINGENCY ISSUES

This main section is divided into four interrelated parts:

1   The mission of the operations strategy;
2   The operations strategy positioning;
3   The external competitive environment.
    These three subsections are short and set the scene by way of describing the overall directions that could shape the strategy (mainly through external influence).
4   Tactical factors and contingency issues as management levers.

In the fourth section, we discuss the tactical factors and issues that are likely to have a bearing on the operations strategy. Thus, these tactical factors will need to be measurable

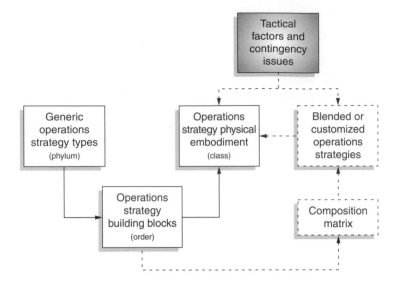

 Figure 7.1 *Operations strategy deployment II*

and contribute to the performance, impact, and added value assessment we described in the operations strategy context model in chapter 6 (see Fig. 6.4, boxes 3 and 4). In this figure the reader can also see the link to the factors we are about to describe. Fig. 7.2 sets the scene by showing the influence of these factors and their contribution to the operations strategy areas covered thus far.

TIME OUT BOX II

In Fig. 7.2 the term 'operations strategies' is used in the plural. Why is this the case?

These tactical factors and contingency issues are inevitably interrelated and in some cases will cross functional boundaries within and beyond the organization. Harrison (1993) describes them as being 'Directly concerned with the transformational processes' as follows:

- *How are the transformational processes defined?* The scope of the individual system models. How can we define the transformation systems and processes?
- *How are the transformational systems linked?* The material or client or product and service combination flows.
- *What are the basic operations principles of each transformation system?* The process choice and infrastructure needs. Is the process based upon leanness, flexibility, batches, projects, continuous flow, a line, a modular cell, etc.?

132

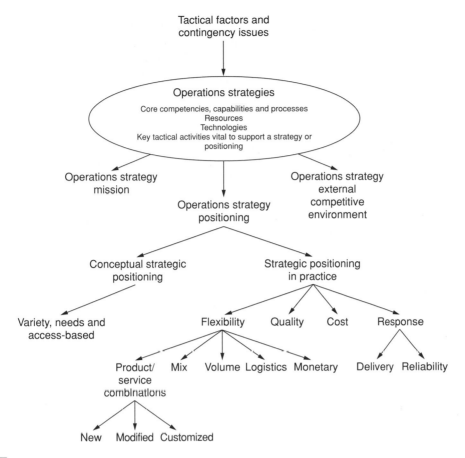

Figure 7.2 *An example of how tactical factors and contingency issues influence the operations strategy*

- *How is the transformation actually carried out?* The mixture of human labour and technology. The socio-technical mix that involves job design and the human–machine interface design.
- *What are the quantitative limits of the transformational process?* The capacity of the transformation system. How many burgers, haircuts or clients can be coped with at any given time?
- *Where is the process located?* These decisions will dictate customer convenience for a service as well as warehousing and supply issues for a tangible product.
- *How is the process physically organized?* The layout and arrangement for the movement of material, people and goods.
- *Who owns each transformation system?* Are the processes conducted in-house (if so do they map to functional boundaries or do they cut across), are they provided by a supplier, outsourced to a third party, subcontracted, etc.
- *How are product and service attributes arrived at?* What are the steps in the design process? How does the introduction of new or modified designs impact upon the transformation system and the customer or client?

133

- *How is quality controlled and improved?* What are the levels and tolerances? What improvements should be made? How will any changes influence the product and service combination and the customer/client?
- *How is the flow of materials, (services) and people planned and controlled?* Material, service component or people flow through the transformation process.
- *How are the informational needs of operations met?* This relates to the information systems and information technology requirements: the data demands and the information outputs of the transformation system.
- *How are human resource needs met?* Issues such as recruitment, training, motivation, working practices, health and safety and employee well-being.

At a strategic level, all of these factors will have to fit with the mission, positioning and competitive environment of the operations strategy. Before looking at the tactical factors in more depth, we will first consider the mission, positioning and environment in more depth.

The operations strategy mission

We remind readers that operations strategy has two roles:

- It can provide support for the overall strategy of the firm;
- It can serve as the firm's distinctive competence.

The mission of an operations strategy will outline and define its overall direction. However, the mission needs to be meaningful and one that is not vague and lacks quantification. Employees should be able to associate with, and buy into the mission, as a meaningful purpose in their everyday tasks. Hence, care must be taken to ensure that such a statement is capable of relevant interpretation at each level throughout the firm and that it fits consistently with the ethos and values espoused. Needless to say, the mission must also proclaim those areas of excellence and core competencies that are capable of securing competitive advantage; as such, there will be a strong link between the mission and the business strategy.

CASE VIGNETTE **KLM ROYAL DUTCH AIRLINES**

The '24-hour industry'
We hear much of the '24-hour economy'. For KLM Royal Dutch Airlines the 24-hour industry is nothing new. Every second of the day one of their aircraft is flying to somewhere around the world. Founded in Amsterdam in 1919, KLM have synchronized schedules and code-share operations over a worldwide network of more than 350 cities in more than 80 countries. To achieve this coverage on their own would require a huge operation at vast cost with all the problems of control found in many diversified international corporations. With safety and consumer service such prominent and critical factors in this type of service industry, how do they achieve this vast coverage yet maintain localized

integration? They think globally, but act locally through a number of strategic alliances and network agreements.

The current KLM fleet consists of 120 aircraft, but through their partnership agreements this is increased by 981 to 1101 that covers nearly every part of the globe. Some of the partners include: North America (Northwest Airlines and Alaska Airlines); South America (Surinam Airways); Europe and Africa (Air A!ps, Air Lingus, Braathens, Czech Airlines, Cyprus Airways, Kenya Airways, KLM Cityhopper, KLM Exel, KLM UK, Lithuanian Airlines, Hungarian Airlines, Martinair, Meridiana, Swisswings, Transavia Airlines and Ukraine International); Middle East and Asia (Garuda Indonesia, Japan Air System, Jet Airways and Malaysia Airways).

These are however, more than just partnerships in name. KLM have deliberately sought close operating links that will allow the sharing of major resources such as facilities, staff and aircraft across the normal organizational boundaries, so offering consumers a seamless service providing extra destinations, more frequent flights and smoother, quicker transfers. As Leo van Wijk, President and Chief Executive Officer of KLM, declared: 'We have worked hard with a number of prominent partners, who were once competitors, to build a long-term vision of an enduring, world-embracing airline alliance'.

Their operations mission is simple yet enduring for consumers and employees alike: 'Strategic cooperation to make air travel easy, fast and safe. *Welcome on board!*'

The operations strategy positioning

At the next level, positioning, measurable goals are necessary (another important reason why the mission can at least be perceived in quantitative terms) so that we can tell if objectives are being achieved. The definition of these goals must be clear and precise.

In chapter 3, the grounds for competition were discussed. Here, we outlined:

- Conceptual strategic positioning (variety-based, needs-based and access-based);
- Strategic positioning in practice (cost, quality, flexibility and response/speed).

Positioning relates directly to how the firm will compete. Returning to Fig. 7.2, we can see how the operations strategy can be positioned, both conceptually and in practice, by making choices between a number of options – flexibility, quality, cost and speed – some of which will not be mutually exclusive. For example, if we take the flexibility option, we can see from the diagram that this involves a number of other choices that will have a wider impact. Flexibility in logistics will have an effect upon cost, quality and speed. Changes to delivery times will alter speed of response, reliability, cost quality and flexibility.

TIME OUT BOX III

How can this interrelationship be described in systemic terms?

The objectives of strategic positioning should be complementary, (because they are inter-connected) ranked and measurable in a meaningful sense (for example, quality measurement at a hospital is very different from that of KFC). However, there will inevitably be trade-offs, as improvements in some areas may well be at the expense of others, for example, a decrease in delivery speed might improve reliability but will also affect consumer service and stock-holding (this reinforces the need for quantification). Finally, these objectives are dynamic and will change constantly. It is therefore important that the operations strategy can be reviewed to effect continual improvement in a rapidly changing environment. For an interesting account of the role of operations strategy positioning and its part in strategy formulation, read-ers are recommended to read: Strategy formulation, chapter 2 in Russell and Taylor (2001).

The external competitive environment

Finally, the external competitive environment. A source of contingent influence that will impact both upon the wider operations strategy as well as various tactical factors. We can consider this environment using the following broad, factor analysis.

Twelve point environmental factor analysis (EFA[12])

1 *Political factors* – Government policy and legislation;
2 *Economic factors* – financial markets, interest rates, inflation, recession, exchange rates, the Euro, etc.;
3 *Sociological factors* – demography and lifestyles;
4 *Technological factors* – obvious advances in product and process technology, etc.;
5 *Environmental or 'green' factors* – the pressure for environmentally safe goods, reductions in pollution and resource depletion;
6 *Ethical factors* – concerning products, working practices, resources, impact upon local population and investment issues;
7 *Market factors* – demand for niche products, short product life cycles, increasingly global competition, resource availability;
8 *Competitor factors* – competitor's objectives, resources, performance, products and services and strategies;
9 *Customer factors* – immediate customer base, wider customer base, market segmentation, customer values, customer service and quality.

We can then add to the power of this analysis by considering the impact of all of the above using the final three factors:

10 *Complexity factors* – the degree to which the environmental factors are likely to witness *changeability* (the environment affected by internationalization, technological, social and political issues) and *novelty* (the degree to which the environment presents the organization with new situations);
11 *Predictability factors* – the degree to which such changes can be predicted (the visibility and predictability of such changes);

12 *Dynamic factors* – the speed or rate that any of the above factors are likely to change and the possible appropriate responses that the organization may be able to muster prior to, or after, such change.

The operations strategy will be cognizant of the EFA[12] factors, as well has having to ensure a fit with their demands. It is vital that the operations strategy finds a balance with the demands and influences of the mission, positioning and external competitive environment. One way to ensure this, is to view the tactical factors and contingency issues not merely as forces to which one must react, but also as proactive levers that the organization can adjust to fit the exigencies of its competitive setting.

Tactical factors as management levers

We now turn to the question of how the various tactical factors and contingency issues will provide a unique shape to each operations strategy (depending upon its particular sector and environment). It should be remembered that in addition to the impact that these various areas will have upon the operations strategy, they are also management influences to pursue the measurable operations objectives of the organization. There are eight general management levers we will briefly cover (although the list is by no means exhaustive – the peculiarities of the industry may dictate there are others):

- Products and processes
    Order winning and qualifying
    New products
    New services
    New processes, core competencies and technologies
- The operations system
    Flow strategy
    Process choice
    Production planning and control
    Location, capacity and facilities
- The role of data and information
- Human resource management
- Quality
- Sourcing and purchasing
- Structure and infrastructure
- Supply networks

Products and processes

The structures and procedures behind the introduction of new and modified product and service combinations are a key part of the operations strategy. These core processes cut across both organization and supply system boundaries and can involve a broad spectrum of individuals and firms. Growth and success are based to a large extent upon the

137

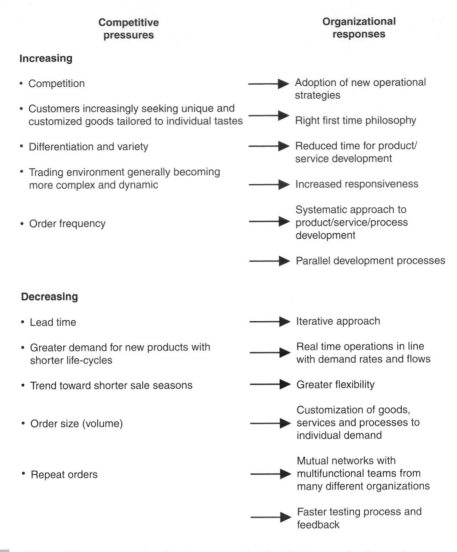

Figure 7.3 *Major trends affecting new product/service/process development*
Source: adapted from Hunter et al. *(2002)*

organizational capacity to introduce new and develop existing products and services at the right point in a product life cycle. Indeed, as research shows (Hunter *et al.*, 2001; Barclay *et al.*, 2000), increasing external competitive pressures are being placed upon the product/ service/process development process (see Fig. 7.3).

The products and services that the firm offers will be as a response to its market, but these will in turn define which markets the firm will operate in. They will also dictate the new processes and core competencies the firm will require. There is a strong link between these three elements. An effective New Product Development process (NPD) will aim to:

1   Match product and service combination characteristics with consumer requirements;
2   Ensure that customer requirements are met in the simplest and least costly manner;
3   Reduce the time required to design a new service or product;
4   Minimize the revisions necessary to make design workable.

ORDER-WINNING AND QUALIFYING

An interesting way to think about the likely success of a new or modified product and service combination is to conceptualize the order-qualifying and order-winning criteria (Hill, 2000).

- Order-qualifiers are those criteria that a company must meet for another firm to even consider it as a possible supplier or for a customer to consider a purchase;
- Order-winners will actually secure the selection of the product or service.

TIME OUT BOX IV

What order-qualifying and order-winning criteria would you use when selecting a medical or dental practitioner?

NEW PRODUCTS

The development and modification of products involves four closely coupled sets of activities: customers, marketing, design and operations. These activities will take place in a feedback loop:

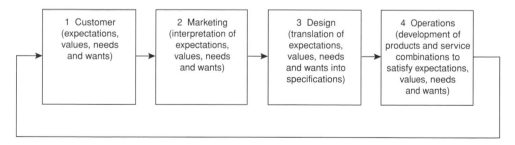

New and modified product/service/process development is an organized, procedural activity. Traditionally, development and modification of new products would generally run through a lateral sequence of activities:

- *New/modified product strategy*. The direction and focus that integrates the activity.
- *Idea generation*. Systematic generation of ideas, not only by NPD teams, but from sources both internal (all employees), and external (customers, competitors, distributors and suppliers).

- *Idea screening.* To reduce the number of ideas.
- *Concept developing and testing.* Developing ideas into product concepts and product images. The concept is a more detailed version of the idea. Image is the way consumers perceive the potential product. Here, the firm may use target consumer groups, both symbolic and physical.
- *Marketing strategy.* The marketing strategy outlines the intended target market (the segment), the planned product positioning (how we will market it) and the sales, market share and profit goals. For example, the target market for our new sports model is younger, well-educated and high income. The positioning will be on economical, fun to drive and green.
- *Business analysis.* A review of sales, costs and profit projections to evaluate whether these factors satisfy company objectives.
- *Product development.* So far the new product may have only existed as a concept or a crude mock-up. Now it is developed into physical, workable product. This calls for investment. Prototypes are then tested (for safety and working, etc.) and there may also be a degree of customer testing.
- *Test marketing.* Product and marketing programmes are introduced in more realistic market settings, for example, in-store style testing. Standard market tests are used (test cities) and controlled test markets (research firms might be used to keep controlled panels of customers in a simulated test market).
- *Commercialization.* The launch or introduction.

We can immediately see that this is time consuming, and does not fit easily with the major new commercial trends depicted in Fig. 7.3. Nor will it help speed of response or flexibility (if that is the positioning of the operations strategy – note the systemic influences and possible conflict). Consequently, many firms attempt to improve the design process. This can be done by:

- Using concurrent or parallel design processes that integrate the various activities involved in the customer, marketing, design and operations cycle;

CASE VIGNETTE **HEWLETT-PACKARD**

The design and development of the HP Deskjet printer was an early attempt by Hewlett-Packard to integrate manufacturing, marketing, quality assurance and finance with the needs of the customer. Multifunctional groups worked in constant communication to identify what activities could be performed concurrently to reduce both the development and manufacturing time and cost. This resulted in a Deskjet printer offering a competitive advantage from both cost and speed.

Interestingly, HP were also one of the first firms to introduce the use of NPD project teams that stay in touch throughout the whole life cycle of the product. Thus, the same team will meet to discuss progress, problems, modification and even phasing-out of the product.

- Using multifunctional design teams;
- Designing for manufacture, assembly and service provision (taking into account the problems that are concerned with the actual delivery of the product);
- Designing with environmental factors and their implications in mind;
- Measuring the various influences and trade-offs that changes to the product or service might make (so that costs and benefits are visible).

NEW SERVICES

Designing or modifying a service is, like new product development, a creative process. It begins with a concept to provide a service with features that will differentiate it from the competition. Issues such as location, facility design, layout, workflow, procedures and job definitions, quality measures, customer involvement, equipment and capacity are all important. In fact the design process never finishes as services are continually improved and modified.

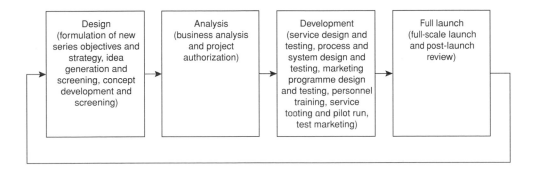

This process utilizes various 'enablers' comprised of people, products, technologies and systems (see Fitzsimmons and Fitzsimmons, 2001, p. 111).

NEW PROCESSES, CORE COMPETENCIES AND TECHNOLOGIES

New and modified processes include the introduction of new technology and the automation necessary to produce and deliver product and service combinations. Technology need not be confined to hardware, however, as it also includes innovative systems such as electronic funds transfer or automated multiphased testing in healthcare. In manufacturing many processes and technologies are often an integral part of the product. For services, however, the process is the product because customers participate directly in the service delivery. The success of a new technology, automation or process is therefore dependent upon customer acceptance (and often the learning of new skills) and their willingness to be active participants in the service process (a point to be borne in mind when designing the service).

The operations system

For any organization, the operations system, whether a single function or encompassing the whole firm and its supply system, (see definitions p. 57, chapter 3), is the key to providing the value consumers seek in product and service combinations. At a tactical level, this operations system will have a number of practical considerations.

FLOW STRATEGY

Earlier we saw how different operations strategies can be developed and how they can be positioned to align with the firms competitive priorities (positioning on cost, quality time, flexibility, etc.). Clearly, the operating system at a tactical level must reflect this positioning and translate the corporate strategy into key operations decisions. As Krajewski and Ritzman (1999) comment:

> Based on the firm's competitive priorities for its products and services, the operations manager must select a flow strategy, which determines how the operations system is organized to handle the volume and variety of products and services for a specific market segment. A firm may employ more than one flow strategy for its operations, depending upon the competitive priorities for each set of products or services it wants to produce. With a flexible flow strategy the system is organized around the processes used to produce the product or service [for example, a health clinic where patients may flow between different processes, in different sequences dependent upon the type of illness]. With a line flow strategy the system is organized around the product or service itself [line flows are typically seen in many mass production plants, the product flows along a line of processes]. Flexible flow and line flow strategies are extremes; many other strategies fall between the two [intermediate flows].

PROCESS CHOICE

Processes must also be designed and chosen to support the flow strategy. There are five basic types, which form a continuum (although these will often overlap:

- *Project* – building an office block or a luxury cruise liner;
- *Job* – customized machining, special mail deliveries, emergency care;
- *Batch* – scheduling air travel, a bakery, processing mortgage loans;
- *Line* – producing automobiles, fast-food restaurants;
- *Continuous* – petrol refining, chemical plants, electricity generation.

We can see that some of these processes are designed to handle smaller volumes and are consequently far more flexible. Others, meanwhile, have low customization levels but produce a high volume. Similarly with services, the degree of labour intensity and customization is high in a low volume professional service (e.g. a medical practitioner) compared with low level, high volume, customer involvement in a service factory such as a clothing catalogue.

PRODUCT PLANNING AND CONTROL

Production planning and scheduling focuses upon controlling and planning the transformation system. This must also form a close fit with the operations strategy and its various elements. The production plan (also known as the aggregate plan) needs inputs from functions and involves decisions regarding production rates, inventory holding, staffing and labour related factors, machine capacity and utilization, costs and budgets, material requirements, etc.

LOCATION, CAPACITY AND FACILITIES

Location can be important for a number of organizations. For retailers and service providers, for example, it can become a strategic factor that makes the difference between success and failure. For manufacturers, location also has a role to play when considering supply, raw materials and logistical issues.

Decisions regarding capacity interact with location decisions. They involve not only the volume of goods/services produced but also limits as to raw materials and component usage, storage, distribution, employee levels, etc.

Facilities decisions concern the location and focus of operations units and distribution centres. Are several needed? Does each facility perform the same function, or do they focus on a particular market, process or product and service combination?

The role of data and information

The processing of data, information and the use of Information communication technology (ICT) has revolutionized business, commerce, and of course, operations. Information systems, as opposed to information technology, now drive the activity in many organizations (indeed, in the service sector, information is often the product).

At an operations level, flows of information both internally and externally (in the supply system) are vital for the proper development and deployment of an operations strategy. Information provides the ability to set objectives and also to give feedback upon performance. At this level, the operations strategy relies heavily upon the contribution of information systems (internally and externally) and the technology that enhances them.

Retailers, distributors, transport, hospitals, banks etcetera all use information systems and information technology as a vital integrated feature of the competitive strategies. Today, many firms will deliberately develop information and information technology strategies that underline the importance of this role. Knowledge is power. In supply systems, information is power. It provides the decision-maker with the ability to compete, to operate a business smoothly and efficiently and it helps us to understand increasing complexity (although in some cases it can also cause it).

We should also note the role of technology in enhancing the supply of data and information. In recent times, the impact of bar coding, provision of point of sale data, electronic data interchange, computer-aided design and manufacture and the Internet has provided the tools enabling business to be conducted in a completely new way. A word of warning though: these are enabling tools and technologies and as such are only components of an operations strategy – new ways of conducting business, perhaps, but they are not strategies in themselves (for an excellent coverage of this debate see Porter, 2001).

143

Human resource management (HRM)

The selection, training and continued development of the organization's most important resource is crucial to strategy at any level, whether corporate, business, operations and functional.

The concept of HRM can be traced to the early 1970s. Prior to this, employees were regarded as a cost (although this was by no means universal, some wealthy Victorian benefactors such as Jeremiah Coleman went to great lengths to organize trade union representation and supply extensive employee benefits). With the development of theories concerning human capital, employees came to be seen as assets and resources. By the 1980s it was clear that the management of human resources was a professional task and one that should be addressed by the wider business strategy.

There is much literature regarding HRM and time precludes a full review. However, according to Van Looy *et al.* (1998), its essence and applicability to operations strategy can be encapsulated in three integrated models:

- *The Michigan model* – the ideas of strategic matching and the basic components of HRM;
- *The Harvard model* – the diversity of stakeholders and the four Cs of HRM;
- *The Warwick models* – the processes involved in HRM.

THE MICHIGAN MODEL

The function of the model is to link HR practices and business requirements by emphasizing the importance of human resources (Tichy *et al.*, 1982; Fombrun *et al.*, 1984). People are resources and should be managed in a way that is consistent with organizational requirements. The fit or congruence between organizational strategy and effectiveness is underpinned by human resources. Thus, human resource management and human resource systems (selection, performance appraisal, rewards and development) should support business goals.

The model prompts us to consider the importance of developing human resource practices that are aligned to the type of strategy being pursued. This does have shortcomings, however. HRM is depicted rather negatively, in a reactionary manner that reduces the importance of such resources and may lessen motivation. In addition, it is assumed that strategy is always planned and rational. As we have seen earlier, despite the existence of generic strategies, there is still much overlap in terms of positioning and approaches such as differentiation and cost leadership are often not mutually exclusive. Strategy can be incremental and has much to do with process rather than content alone; similarly HRM practices are not always as narrow and clear cut as merely selection, performance appraisal, rewards and development.

THE HARVARD MODEL

Developed by the Harvard Business School and less prescriptive, (Beer *et al.*, 1984, 1995). This work covers a broader range of practices than the Michigan model, and includes:

- *Human resource flows.* Activities related to managing the flow of people in, through and out of the organization: recruitment and selection, placement, development, performance appraisal, promotion and termination.

144

- *Reward systems.* Implies everything that is related to attracting and retaining employees: pay systems, motivation and benefits.
- *Employee influence.* Levels of employee power and authority and the way these systems are designed.
- *Work systems.* The way work is designed and the arrangement of tasks and technology to achieve optimal performance and results.

The model recognizes different stakeholders as each having their own objectives: shareholders, management, employees and unions, government and the community. Outcomes that need to be achieved within these different policy domains and among the different stakeholders involved are called the four Cs:

- *Commitment.* By employees to their work and organization.
- *Congruence.* Between the objectives of the various stakeholders – employees and their families, the organization and its objectives, shareholders, community and society at large.
- *Competence.* Both now and in the future. To what extent can one attract, keep and develop the skills and knowledge of the people involved.
- *Cost effectiveness.* The consequences of certain policies in terms of wages, benefits, turnover, motivation, employment and so on. Costs can be considered at individual, group, and organizational and societal levels.

The model focuses upon the management role and integrates stakeholders as well as the content and process of HRM and the strategy. Management develops a vision of how employees are treated and involved in the organization. This is translated from strategy formulation into HRM practices and employee behaviours, with management as the driving force.

THE WARWICK MODELS

The Warwick models provide a more balanced viewpoint in which processes and context are at the forefront (Hendry and Pettigrew, 1986; Hendry, 1991). In reviewing the transition of HRM, Sparrow and Hilltrop (1996) suggest the following starting point:

- Strategy should not be seen as a ready-formed output to which HRM can be easily moulded. Changes in HRM areas (culture, structure, etc.) can precede and even shape strategy in a bottom-up fashion;
- Changes in strategy and HRM often have long timescales. As such, the process of change is as important as the output. In addition, this process is often anything but rational.

The Warwick models emphasize a number of different HRM context-specific pathways that can achieve the same end result. However, they are less prescriptive and not seen as a best practice example that can easily be transferred from one company to another. Some formulas may be transferable but they must be contingent upon individual settings and circumstances (a debate we encountered at the beginning of this chapter).

145

CASE VIGNETTE **HRM AT SUN MOUNTAIN LODGE**

The Sun Mountain Lodge sits astride the stunning Cascade Mountain range in Washington State, USA. We will be looking at their operation in far more depth at the end of the chapter. Acknowledged as one of the world's top hotels, HRM practices are especially important for this service organization. Their HRM strategy places considerable importance upon continuous employee development, establishing collaborative relationships and empowering service employees. They see a clear strategic relationship and a mirroring effect between customer satisfaction (a key business strategy aim) and employee satisfaction (an HRM strategy aim). The latter is mainly achieved through enhancing the processes of competence and empowerment.

Quality

The techniques and tools used to achieve quality objectives comprise the total quality management lever. We can think about quality using two perspectives: the quality objectives – definitions and measurable targets – and the means to achieve these targets. Once again, the writings of quality gurus (much of which is mere common sense), quality approaches and concepts and total quality management, occupy a wealth of business and management literature (see Dale and Plunkett [1990] for a review of the quality movement evolution). Here, we can only suggest some broad perspectives:

- Quality management approaches will vary dependent upon the industry;
- Quality is linked to value and the value adding process that emphasizes both internal and external customers. Every operations activity should add value to an individual customer (internal or external);
- Quality relates to the whole package that we term product and service combinations.

Garvin (1988) offers the following definitions of quality:

- *Transcendent quality* – an indefinable condition of excellence;
- *Product-based quality* – related to difference in product attributes;
- *User-based quality* – the capacity to satisfy user needs and preferences – fitness for use;
- *Manufacturing-based quality* – conformance to requirements design or specification; and
- *Value-based quality* – excellence for use in a given situation for a given price.

Clearly, quality covers a huge number of dimensions in the delivery of products and services: performance features, reliability, conformance, durability, serviceability, aesthetics and perceived quality, to name but a few. In service provision, issues such as personal attention, dependability, empathy, knowledge, security, kindness, etc. head a huge list of required virtues (see Stewart *et al.*, 1996).

For the service sector, quality begins with identifying customer requirements. Parasuraman *et al.* (1985) identify ten dimensions of service quality:

- *Tangibles* – physical appearance of the facilities, staff, buildings, etc.
- *Reliability* – ability to reproduce the same service level (presumably high?) again and again.
- *Responsiveness* – the speed at which inquiries and queries are dealt with.
- *Communication* – the clarity and understandability of the information given to the client.
- *Credibility* – the trustworthiness of the service provider.
- *Security* – the physical safety of the consumer or security of client information.
- *Competence* – the actual technical expertise of the service provider.
- *Courtesy* – the attitude of the service provider and manner adopted by the server (the reader may well refer back to the section on HRM and wonder if the term 'server' really does engender a true mirroring of customer satisfaction with employee satisfaction?).
- *Understanding* – how well the provider of the service understands the client's needs.
- *Access* – how easy is it to reach the service provider (physically, temporally or spatially).

Finally, we mention the Total Quality Management (TQM) movement. This takes quality to a more strategic level and is well explained by Kanji (1990) in the following terms:

> Quality – is to satisfy customers' requirements continually.
> Total quality – is to achieve quality at low cost.
> Total Quality Management – is to obtain total quality by involving everyone's daily commitment'

Oakland (1989, p. 40) provides a TQM model that links the quality process between a customer and supplier (both internal and external) using teams, systems and tools in an environment of quality communication, culture and commitment. He also provides a useable definition of TQM:

> Total quality management (TQM) is an approach to improving the effectiveness and flexibility of businesses as a whole. It is essentially a way of organizing and involving the whole organization; every department, every activity, every single person at every level.

Sourcing and purchasing

Purchasing may be defined as:

> The function responsible for obtaining by purchase, lease or other legal means, equipment, materials, components, suppliers and services required by an undertaking for use in the added value process of providing product and service combinations.

147

Sourcing, purchasing and procurement often assume strategic status within organizations – hence becoming operations strategies in their own right. Given the importance of resource inputs to nearly every type of organization, this is a key management lever and influence upon the operations strategy. The activity encompasses purchasing, distribution and logistics. Decisions involve from whom to order, from where to order, when and how much. There is obviously a close interface between purchasing and operations. Sourcing and purchasing activity includes:

- Selecting, evaluating and developing sources of materials, supplies and services;
- Maintaining and developing close relationships with suppliers;
- Negotiating and control quality, delivery, payments and returns;
- Seeking new material and products and new sources of better materials, products and services;
- Negotiating and acquiring raw materials, capital equipment, consumer goods and services at competitive prices consistent with quality levels;
- Cooperation in cost reduction activities and long-term sourcing planning;
- Maintaining effective communication systems both internally and externally.

We can see that the sourcing activity involves decisions regarding value, make or buy, outsourcing and third party logistics, prices, quantity, quality and delivery.

Structure and infrastructure choices

A brief mention of the operations system or network is in order. Every transformation activity is part of a wider and larger interconnected network that has design considerations in terms of the layout and flows, processes and jobs. The flows of goods and services, as well as data and information, must be co-ordinated both internally and in the wider supply and demand echelons of the network. The design of the network revolved around issues such as:

- *Vertical integration*. How much does one operation shape the entire network? How much of the network should an operation own? These make or buy decisions are the locus of vertical integration. Some firms will supply raw material, make all the components, perform final assembly and distribute goods. Others will rely on suppliers for some of these tasks. In between are the quasi-ownership agreements involved in outsourcing, third party arrangements, vendor managed inventory, and even partially owned suppliers in preferred supply networks.
- *Operation location*. Where should each part of the network be located? These are vitally important decisions (see the operations system p. 143).
- *Capacity*. What is the physical capacity of each part of the network? What longer term capacity decisions are needed?
- *Expansion*. What is the direction of any *vertical* integration or capacity expansion planned (backward or upstream towards suppliers or forwards, downstream towards customers)? Are there plans for *horizontal* integration (other firms at a similar network

point or node)? What is the extent of the process span required (one or more operations in a supply system)? What is the balance among the remaining vertical activities (the operating behaviour and balance – not necessarily ownership)?

All these decisions can affect the quality, speed, dependability, flexibility and cost of the entire supply system or network.

Supply network

Network supply is a distinct operations strategy (see chapter 4) that is used by a wide number of firms. A subclass of this is the supply chain strategy that covers a linear chain of supply. Unfortunately, the term 'chain' fails to sum up the complexity involved in these activities; thus we prefer to refer to network or system. Further the strategy, as we will see, has more to do with demand than supply. Supply chain management is mentioned here not because of its ubiquitous business application, but due to the fact that the various relationships, activities and linkages in a supply system will have a profound effect upon any operations strategy. Hence there are various tactical issues to do with the supply system that will influence any operations strategy adopted.

The supply network adopts a focus upon the dealings with suppliers and customers. The management of the supply system in fact involves both the supply and demand sides of the organization and its value chain. We also saw in chapter 1 the concept of the value chain:

> Competitive advantage cannot be understood by looking at a firm as a whole. It stems from the many discrete activities a firm performs in designing, producing, marketing, delivering, and supporting its product. Each of these activities can contribute to a firm's relative cost position and create the basis for differentiation . . . The value chain disaggregates a firm into its strategically relevant activities in order to understand the behaviour of costs and the existing and potential sources of differentiation. A firm gains competitive advantage by performing these important activities more cheaply or better than its competitors.
>
> Porter (1985, p. 33)

Michael Porter emphasizes the importance of primary activities such as inbound logistics, operations and outbound logistics. He also confirms that these activities take place in a wider value system, comprising a number of firms' value or supply networks and chains.

We can define supply chain management as: 'The management of upstream and downstream relationships with suppliers and customers to deliver superior customer value at less cost to the supply chain as a whole' (Christopher, 1998).

There are many terms and phrases (and inevitably acronyms) covering this area in the current business literature. We will now attempt to distinguish between some of the various concepts, although the reader is again referred back to our original operations strategy genealogy (chapter 3, p. 55).

- *Purchasing and supply management (genus).* A focus upon organization of the supply-side, upstream business activities.

149

- *Physical distribution management (genus)*. Similar to the above, but on the downstream or demand side.
- *Materials management (genus)*. Involves both supply and demand but limited in scope to tangible items before, during and after the operations transformation.
- *Inventory management (genus)*. Encompasses decisions on supply and demand sides (internal and external) regarding purchasing, distribution, materials management and logistics and addresses when and how much to order as well as storage and movement.
- *Logistics (genus)*. A broader activity than just physical distribution. Covering mainly the demand side of the organization and it involves planning of product and information flows through a business to the customer. Ostensibly a tactical approach (although the logistical strategy is one type of operations strategy adopted by firms that focus heavily on these activities). (See genealogy in chapter 3.)
- *Supply system management or supply chain management (genus)*. An operational management activity concerned with the linkages in the whole supply and demand system, from origin of material to consumption and disposal and covering a number of entity relationships in the pipeline.
- *Value chain management (genus)*. We suggest that value chain management is perhaps a more conceptual approach that places an emphasis upon the underlying value creating activities in either a value chain or value system. Value can simply be defined as the gap between cost of producing a good or service and the price one can charge (profitability, in other words).
- *Operations strategies (class)*. The types of strategy developed by firms to encompass the primary value adding activities of inbound logistics, operations and outbound logistics (strategies such as supply network, quick response, supply chain, just in time, time-based competition, lean production, strategic alliances, procurement, etc.) These strategies also rely upon some of the tactical factors touched upon above that are vital to support a strategy or particular positioning.

CONCLUSION

To conclude, we remind readers that this chapter has examined the tactical factors and contingency issues that form an influence upon the operations strategy. To do this we have placed the operations strategy in a wider, competitive, business environment and considered its mission and positioning vis-à-vis that environment. The operations strategy is also influenced by a number of tactical or support activities that can be thought of at three levels:

- At the level of building blocks. The core competencies, capabilities and processes, resources, technologies and certain key tactical activities that are vital to support a particular strategy or positioning;
- The influence that these elements will have in making each operations setting, and to a degree, each strategy unique; and
- The way these building blocks can be used internally, as management levers, to enhance the competitive potential of an operations strategy.

All the above factors should be consistent with the operations strategy as they form the distinctive competencies that inform the objectives, mission, operations and business strategies. The alignment of all these elements will offer the firm grounds for a sustainable competitive advantage through the deployment of its operations strategy – the subject of chapter 8.

CASE STUDY – OPERATIONS STRATEGY IN ACTION

Sun Mountain Lodge – tactical factors that shape an operations strategy (www.sunmountainlodge.com)

As if hewn from the very landscape itself, the Sun Mountain Lodge stands on a 3000 feet high mountain top with a 360 degree view of mountains wilderness and valleys. Situated near Winthrop in the Cascade range in north-central Washington State, USA, this is the home of Sasquatch and grizzly bear and the gold, silver and copper mining boom of the 1890s which created Methow Valley millionaires overnight. Sun Mountain Lodge has achieved international acclaim with awards for the hotel, guest rooms, cuisine and an unmatched experience in excellent service.

Constructed entirely of local boulders, fossil-embedded stones and mammoth timbers, every aspect mirrors the view and its history. From huge chandeliers to willow chairs, hand-made quilts, and local art in all 112 rooms and cabins, the Lodge oozes luxury. Guests can soak in the scenery from whirlpool baths, hot-tubs, jetted tubs, and wet bars, heated swimming pools inside and out, fitness rooms, spas and beauty centres, private balconies, conference and meeting facilities. For the more active, the award-winning hospitality also includes 3,000 acres of hiking, mountain biking, walking and horseback riding on more than 100 miles of trails. Every season reveals new outdoor options – white water raft trips, helicopter skiing, snowmobiling, sleigh rides, snow shoeing, ice skating, cross-country skiing, fly-fishing, river rafting, lake boating, tennis and golf to name but a few. The Lodge combines the highest-quality creature comforts and nature: a peak experience of service and amenities, rivalled only by the one outdoors.

Sun Mountain has become the Northwest's premier four season resort with a unique combination of privacy, tranquillity and serenity balanced by the highest standard of excellence in service and guest amenities. Sun Mountain has pursued a deliberate business strategy to position itself both as a high quality and premium service provider combined with catering for the guest wanting to experience nature and the wilderness first-hand. This positioning has to be reflected in the operations strategy positioning as well as certain tactical factors that are vital to support it. These tactical factors or management levers include decisions about:

■ Services or products and processes – including order qualifying and winning criteria, new services, new processes and technologies.
■ The operations system – the flow strategy, process choice, planning and control systems, capacity and facilities.

- Data and information – what is required, how it is processed, to whom it is provided, what is strategic and what is tactical information.
- Human resource management – selection and recruitment, but more importantly perhaps, the necessary training and development of staff and management.
- Quality – what value is sought and what are the value adding processes using the ten dimensions of service quality discussed earlier.
- Sourcing and purchasing – analysing core strategic inputs, supplier selection and relationship development, setting quality standards, communication systems, etc.
- Structure and infrastructure – degree of vertical integration, location, capacity and expansion.
- Network supply – the various operations strategies necessary.

ANSWERS TO TIME OUT BOXES

Time out box I

Tactical decisions in operations can involve:

- Product and service provision decisions (e.g. make to order, make to stock, assemble to order, etc.);
- Processes (project, batch, mass, continuous);
- Technologies, capacity and facilities (how much capacity required – demand and what facilities needed);
- Human resources (skills, autonomy, training, recruitment and selection, performance, compensation, tasks and teams, levels of management);
- Quality (target level, how will it be measured, training, responsibilities, evaluation);
- Sourcing (vertical integration and make or buy decisions); and
- Operations system decisions (how the operating systems will execute day-to-day decisions to support the firm in uncertain conditions).

Time out box II

The reader should remember that research conducted in this discipline indicates that organizations may in fact adopt and use more than one operations strategy. Consequently, each strategy will have its own mission, positioning, competitive environment and components or elements. Each will also be influenced by tactical factors and contingency issues.

Time out box III

Chapter 1 discussed frameworks for the analysis of operations, one of which was systems theory. We can see an example of 'nesting' of systems and their subsystems in Fig. 7.2. There is interdependence and changes to one part of the system will have ramifications for the rest. This is also an example of emergent property; that is, the interconnected system as a whole is capable of achieving certain objectives that various parts alone would not – the whole is greater than the sum of the parts!

Time out box IV

We would assume that any medical practitioner would need to achieve certain standards to enter the marketplace in order to be considered as a possibility (order qualifying). For example, she/he is qualified to practice, possesses the latest technology, has reasonable premises, has not had too many accidents or litigious encounters for malpractice or negligence, etc. To win your selection (order-winning), you might look for the practitioner to specialize in a particular area and be an expert in that field with a proven success rate. She or he might provide unusual approaches: hypnotism, acupuncture, sedation therapy for nervous patients, cosmetic treatment, virtual treatment (joke!); their premises might be particularly convenient or accessible, or they might be pioneers of the very latest technology.

DISCUSSION QUESTIONS, WORK ASSIGNMENTS AND EXAM QUESTIONS

1   What do we mean by the term tactical factors? How will they influence the transformation process of operations?
2   If a firm chooses to adopt a particular positioning, how can the operations strategy be of unique support?
3   The business environment is an important source of influence upon an organization. What factors can we use to analyse and classify the forces involved?
4   We have described a number of tactical factors that may need to be considered as part of an operations strategy. Choose four of these and discuss the extent to which they will influence the strategic decisions of a retailer, a manufacturer and a service provider.

Reader questions related to Sun Mountain Lodge case study

1   What are the main assumptions behind the operations strategy of Sun Mountain Lodge?
2   Can the core capabilities or competencies and processes necessary to support this strategy be identified?
3   What technologies and resources are also vital for the operations strategy to be effective?
4   Finally, we have seen that certain tactical factors are also fundamental as part of an operations strategy to support both the wider business strategy and the unique strategic positioning the organization seeks. Discuss which of these tactical factors or management levers are of particular importance for Sun Mountain.

RECOMMENDED READING

Dale B.G. and Plunkett J.J. (eds) (1990) *Managing Quality*, Philip Allan, New York.

Fitzsimmons J.A. and Fitzsimmons M.J. (2001) *Service Management*, 3rd edn, Chapter 5, 'Service Development and Process Design', McGraw-Hill, New York.

Porter M.E. (2001) 'Strategy and the Internet', *Harvard Business Review*, March/April 63–78.

Russell R.S. and Taylor B.W. (2001) *Operations Management*, Chapter 2, 'Strategy Formulation', Prentice Hall, New Jersey.

Sparrow P. and Hiltrop J.M. (1996) *European Human Resources Management in Transition*, Prentice Hall, Harlow, England.

Chapter 8

Operations strategy as a source of sustainable competitive advantage

At this point, a brief summary may be in order. Part I dealt with understanding – an introduction to operations management and to organizational strategy. Part II (analysis and synthesis) has so far demonstrated that:

1 We can classify types of operations strategy;
2 They have a particular essence, a blend or fusion of building blocks that give each a unique composition, customized to the embeddedness of the situation; and
3 These various operations strategies have a number of tactical factors or contingency issues that influence the deployment of the strategy and also act as management levers to enhance its competitive ability.

In this chapter we examine the support that an operations strategy can provide to an organization's competitive strength. Fig. 8.1 demonstrates the contribution to the wider debate thus far.

In the figure, we can see the contribution of the tactical factors discussed in chapter 7 that contribute to operations strategy positioning – flexibility, quality, cost and response – and act as management levers. This positioning will lead to competitive advantage by (a) providing a lower cost product or service; (b) differentiation offering a better quality or more variety; (c) a faster, responsive service; or (d) a combination of these in either a broad focus or particular niche market.

LEARNING OBJECTIVES

After considering this chapter, the reader will be able to:

- Appreciate the strategic role of an operations strategy
- Analyse its competitive dimensions
- Plot the life cycle of such a strategy

KEY TERMS

- Competitive dimensions
- Operational implications
- Product and service attributes
- Competitive priorities
- Strategic fit
- Strategic development
- Strategic life cycle
- Competitive advantage
- Evolution

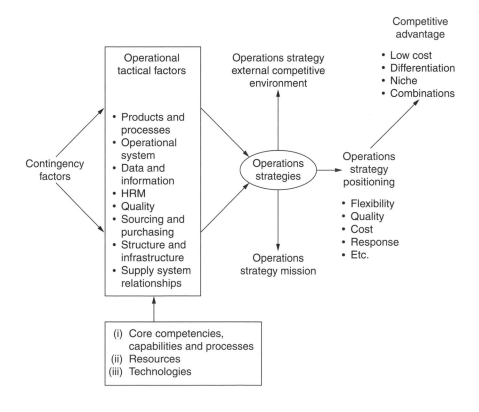

Figure 8.1 *The source of competitive advantage*

INTRODUCTION

The aim of this chapter is to firmly locate the competitive contribution of an operations strategy. To do so, we examine the competitive dimensions involved. The latter involves a close fit between:

1   Corporate objectives
2   Marketing strategies
3   Product and service attributes
4   Operations strategy competitive priorities; and
5   The development and deployment of the operations strategy.

THE ROLE OF OPERATIONS STRATEGY

The operations strategy has two main functions:

- It must make decisions addressing the strategic and long-term functional aspects of operations. The direct responsibility for creating and delivering product and service combinations to external customers (other firms) and consumers (individuals). Here, we are concerned with the basic input – transformation – output activities.
- To guide the operational activities performed by all personnel throughout the organization. Here, we recognize the important notion that operational activities take place across the whole of the organization as part of a value chain that resides in a wider value system. As such, there will be many value adding customer–supplier relationships, both internal and external.

Clearly, not all organizations will have a distinct and separate operations function. The operations strategies used by a firm (remembering that there may be more than one) will need to be closely aligned to the general business strategy. It may be timely to remind readers of our earlier definitions of an operations strategy. The first was a narrow, functional description:

> *Operations strategy definition 1 – the functional strategy*
> Major decisions about, and strategic management of: core competencies, capabilities and processes, technologies, resources and key tactical activities necessary in the function or chain of functions that create and deliver product and service combinations and the value demanded by a customer.

The second is a much broader perceptive covering the value adding activities across a whole supply network:

> *Operations strategy definition 2 – the wider value delivery strategy*
> Major decisions about, and strategic management of: core competencies, capabilities and processes, technologies, resources and key tactical activities necessary in

157

any supply network, in order to create and deliver product and service combinations and the value demanded by a customer/consumer. The strategic role involves blending these various building blocks into one or more unique, organizational-specific, strategic architectures.

The operations strategy cannot be designed in a vacuum. It must be linked both to the customer and to other parts of the enterprise and the supply network. We now examine these wider competitive dimensions.

COMPETITIVE DIMENSIONS

The operations strategy has an important role in coordinating the operational goals to those of the organization. However, the objectives of the organization will change over time; hence the need for the operations strategy to anticipate future needs. In this way it acts as a portfolio that can adapt to the changing product and service combination needs of the final customer – a clear point of reference to our discussion in chapter 5 regarding the essence of the operations strategy (the blending of certain building blocks into a unique and a customized architecture).

The keys to competitive success for the operations strategy lie in:

- Understanding target markets;
- Identifying the priority choices;
- Understanding the consequences of each choice;
- Appreciating the various trade-offs.

Thus the starting point of any competitive analysis must be a basic understanding of the organization's markets and then the choices that customers face when deciding which product or service to buy.

We can use this understanding of markets and choices to develop an operations strategy competitive framework that will emphasize the procedure involved as well as the strong links between operations and marketing (see Fig. 8.2).

From Fig. 8.2, we can see the main steps necessary to perform both a competitive analysis and the development of the operations strategy.

Stage 1 – developing properly defined corporate objectives;

Stage 2 – determining marketing strategies to meet those objectives;

Stage 3 – appreciating the operational implications for the markets in which the firm operates;

Stage 4 – understanding the essential attributes of product and service combinations;

Stage 5 – establishing operations strategy competitive priorities using the main building blocks of the operations strategy (tactical and support activities, core competencies and processes, resources and technologies);

Stage 6 – determining the strategic fit between these building blocks, the operational implications of the market and the choices customers make, in particular product or

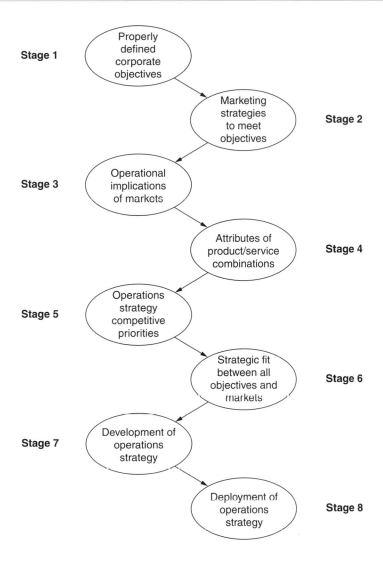

Figure 8.2 *Operations strategy competitive analysis*

service attributes. We can use the operations strategy composition matrix introduced in chapter 5 as a 'blending' and linkage mechanism in order to establish the correct infrastructure;

Stage 7 – practical development of the operations strategy;

Stage 8 – deployment of the operations strategy.

Stages 1 and 2 – corporate objectives and marketing strategies

We will assume that stages 1 and 2 have been completed as they are beyond the remit of our debate. We can move directly to the third stage – understanding the operational implications of the marketplace.

Stage 3 – operational implications of the marketplace

Markets and marketing are not the same thing. Marketing is a business function whereas markets constitute the essence of business. There will be several markets and submarkets for each firm. Some of these will be new, some established and others in decline. It is vitally important that the business fully understands its markets and their current and future fluctuations – the role of data and information is key here. Unfortunately, as Terry Hill (2000) points out, 'Current approaches to corporate strategy development fail to provide adequate insights on which to build functional strategies'. In other words, the descriptions developed of organizational markets and their similarities are inaccurate and without proper meaning. Consequently, they cannot easily be translated into operations strategies. According to Hill (2000), this is due to a number of factors.

- Markets often being viewed and described only from a marketing point of view with the description of segments typically being based on very broad perspectives; for example, Europe and North America or financial services. Although these may be sensible from a marketing perspective (for sales promotions and activities), they lack coherence at the level of operations management and operations strategy. As we have already seen in chapter 6, the demands from different sets of consumers within any of these segments may be completely different. In other words, the operations strategy will have to be customized at a much more focused level. The Omicron Foods case study (chapter 6) demonstrated that although the marketing function may have described the firm's main consumer group as large grocery retailers, from an operational perspective, many of these retailers required individual, customized operations strategies.
- If the view of a market is positioned too high in the strategy process, the essential differences are overlooked through lack of data and analysis. Rather than broad-brush generalities, market descriptions require more insight and consideration as to the operational elements involved. The market segment description of customers as 'large grocery retailers' will take on a new meaning when analysed at the operational perspective of Wal-Mart, J.C. Penney, Nordstrom, Tesco Stores, J. Sainsbury, et al.
- The two factors above are further compounded by the use of general phrases to provide market descriptions and values. Phrases such as 'customer service' and 'delivery' do little to capture the insights and complexity of the markets and their value needs. They also provide little guidance for the development of the operations strategy.

Stage 4 – the attributes of product and service combinations

In chapter 3 we discussed the importance of strategic positioning. This positioning has two dimensions: conceptual (variety, needs and access) and practical (flexibility, quality, cost, response). We now examine what this positioning seeks to achieve in terms of the practical product attributes. Chase et al. (2001) defines the major competitive dimensions that form the position of the company in terms of its product attributes. These are the grounds of competition translated into the types of products and services on offer – the elements that form the bases of choice for the customer and consumer. Once these are established, the operational system and its strategy can be shaped as a delivery mechanism.

Cost – make it cheap

Within every industry, there is usually a segment of the market that buys solely upon cost. To be successful in this sector a firm must compete as a low-cost producer with an operations strategy that is positioned to compete upon saving cost and reducing waste (lean production or lean thinking, for example). A low-cost strategy does not imply low value or low quality. It is a long-term, relentless approach to achieve maximum value, as defined by your customer, but at the same time, driving down all costs and waste by utilizing resources effectively and spreading overhead cost.

CASE VIGNETTE **COMPETING ON COST**

Flying Southwest Airlines on the US West Coast is a novel experience. Their short-hop fights between San Francisco and Seattle, for example, are more like travelling on a bus or coach. The operations strategy is designed to drive down cost by flying only Boeing 737s (no variety necessitating different training and skills), using smaller airports and terminals, no allocated seating, fewer fare options, no meals only snacks, smaller crew numbers with more flying hours, no ticket offices, reusable boarding passes, faster turn around of flights (often only 20 minutes), and maximum utilization of routes to suit the planes being used.

Wal-Mart (now the owner of Asda Stores) has been a low-cost market leader for nearly twenty years. The firm seeks to drive down overhead, shrinkage and distribution costs. Rapid transportation, reduced warehousing, direct delivery, vendor managed inventory, etc., have sustained the achievement of maximum value at the lowest possible cost.

TIME OUT BOX I

Why is it often very difficult for the low-cost producer to succeed and be profitable?

Differentiation of product quality and reliability – make it good

Differentiation is concerned with providing uniqueness. This is not something that is associated with a particular department or function, but is a core competence across the whole organization. It can apply equally to both the product and the service in the value provided as part of a product and service combination. To achieve competitive advantage here, the operations strategy must ensure close attention to the value customers seek. These can be quality, reliability, variety, features, services, location, delivery, after sales support and so on.

161

For example, quality can be divided into two categories: product quality and process quality. The level of quality will vary depending upon the market segment (higher levels might be expected in medical services compared with, say, refuse services (prices will also vary). It seems evident that close attention to the values sought by the customer are key to competing in this sector. A number of different operations strategies can be used to achieve differentiation; much depends upon the circumstances.

TIME OUT BOX II

We need to consider what priorities and dangers there are for those competing in a high product quality and reliability segment.

Response – make it and deliver it fast

Response refers to flexible response as well as speed and reliability in both the development and delivery of a product and/or service.

A flexible response is the ability to match changes in the marketplace with new/modified product and service combinations, a change in volume, mix, logistics, monetary contribution and or consumer contact (see chapter 1).

Reliability can also be an issue here. If the end-consumer values reliability in delivery or scheduling, for example, then the operations strategy can be designed to compete in this area (clearly, there are also quality implications).

Speed of response, whether in production or delivery, will also be a ground for competition. Quick Response has been used in the complex textile and clothing industry for many years. It is particularly adept at matching a volatile demand, using a huge number of possible stock-keeping units, while at the same time ensuring that product assortment and availability remain high in the styles, colours and sizes that are important. The following case vignette explains some of the problems.

CASE VIGNETTE **COMPETING ON RESPONSE**

In 1999 more than 17.6 billion units of apparel were purchased in the US (an increase of 0.6 billion since the previous year). However, of those garments purchased, only 47 per cent were sold at regular prices and 51 per cent at discounted prices. This difference of 4 per cent may at first sight seem rather inconsequential – but it represents an estimated $64 billion in lost revenue for retailers!

In previous years the loss in revenue has been even higher (see Table 8.1). Here, we see the percentages of clothing units purchased at regular and discounted prices for the last eight years. Clearly the units bought at a discount have declined, yet overall, the majority of apparel items purchased are done so at markdown prices. This has ramifications for the whole industry.

Table 8.1 *Percentage of clothing units purchased: normal vs. markdown price*

Year	Normal price	Markdown price
1992	44	54
1993	43	55
1994	42	55
1995	43	55
1996	45	49
1997	45	51
1998	47	51
1999	47	51

Source: NPD Group

Clothing purchases tend to peak in August and December (back-to-school promotions and holidays) and markdown buying follows a similar trend. In fact, the proportion of garments bought from month to month at a discount price follows a similar trend for normal purchases. Fig. 8.3 shows the monthly pattern.

Research from the Cotton Inc. Research Group Lifestyle Monitor for 1998 suggests that 58 per cent of customers would rather wait and buy a garment in the sale at the end of a season, than pay full price at the beginning. This is partly to do with style preference (waiting for a new style introduction) and lower price opportunity. However, two-thirds of customers name price as the most important attribute when considering a purchase.

Women buy approximately 80 per cent of all clothing purchased and 52 per cent is at markdown prices (47 per cent for men). In 1997 the average price paid for branded goods

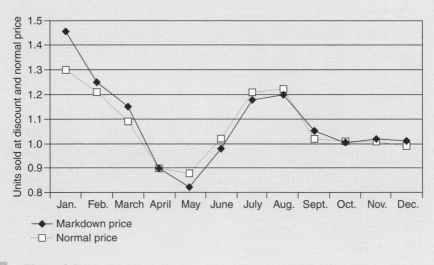

Figure 8.3 *Monthly clothing purchases – normal vs. markdown price*

continued

continued was 20 per cent less than private or own label, and 60 per cent less than the price paid for designer goods. It seems, logically, that there is a positive correlation between the price and the time consumers will wait to purchase during a markdown. In 1997, women waited for discounts to purchase 55 per cent of designer garments, 52 per cent of private garments and 51 per cent of branded garments. The average discount was 36 per cent for designer labels, 29 per cent for brands and 27 per cent for own label garments (see Table 8.2).

Table 8.2 *Average discount on purchases (%)*

Year	Designer labels	Brands	Own labels
1995	35	29	28
1996	33	29	27
1997	36	29	27

Source: NPD Group

The percentage of clothing bought at markdown prices also varies by outlet type, as shown in Fig. 8.4.

In 1999, purchases at markdown prices accounted for 75 per cent of clothing unit sales to women at department stores, 69 per cent at chain stores, 60 per cent at speciality stores, 41 per cent at mass merchants, and 29 per cent via direct mail. The average discounts were 30 per cent at speciality stores, 29 per cent at chain stores, 22 per cent at mass merchants and 12 per cent using direct mail. Interestingly, jeans tend to be sold for smaller discounts than any other type of garment.

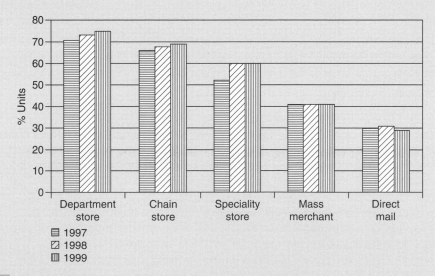

Figure 8.4 *Discount purchases by women by outlet type (% of units)*

From this case study, we can see some of the problems for the clothing sector. Add to these the facts that for sale seasons are becoming short, diversity and variety greater and the fact that the industry has a unique pipeline structure relying on many SMEs, the complexity and volatility is evident. Clearly, the trend for customer purchasing of markdown clothing will not decrease unless a Quick Response operations strategy, for example, is used to ensure far higher customer service levels than at present. Unfortunately, in many cases the rails of clothing on display represent more often what is not selling rather than what is. In addition, customer perceptions of what adds value need to be changed; influencing buying behaviour. Both of these approaches will help to minimize forced markdowns and discounts and ensure more sales take place at a normal retail price.

The niche – a combination

Finally, some product attributes may require a combination of the three competitive dimensions (cost, differentiation and response). Often, this is described as a focused, niche market, where one or more elements can be combined (however, some firms can achieve all competitive dimensions in a broader market). Here, a number of operations strategies will become important in order to achieve flexibility, low price, delivery and quality.

CASE VIGNETTE **COMPETING WITH A FOCUS**

Tesco Stores is currently the leading UK food retailer. Its competitive advantage is built around a focus upon high quality as well as low cost. Using an Efficient Consumer Response operations strategy, they offer a high quality service and product availability, but at the same time keeping waste and costs low (elements of a supply network and lean production strategies). They also recognize that different operations strategies should be used for different product groups and characteristics. In addition, they increasingly seek competitive advantage from niche operations by tailoring the goods supplied to the needs of the geographic region (even down to a micro-segment representing a suburb of a town).

Another focused operation is that of the fashion chain Yves St Laurent. Recognizing the unique demands of a fashion niche, their operations strategy employs a focus upon providing high quality, latest styles and fast response – all more important than cost!

The concept of trade-offs

We have described three basic categories of product and service attribute (cost, differentiation and response), as well as the combined focus or niche. For each one of these, certain operational elements will be important for the appropriate operations strategy. However, there will be cost/benefit trade-offs to consider.

An organization cannot excel simultaneously in all competitive dimensions. Consequently, in practice, decisions have to be made regarding which parameters are critical to the firm's success, then concentrating upon the operations strategy that will address these particular characteristics.

For example, speed of response will often preclude a huge variety of goods. Low cost may not allow a large degree of variety or flexibility. Low cost may also prevent exceptionally high quality. It is at this point that we can see the importance of using different operations strategies for different product groups – this will allow the organization more than one product and service focus.

Unfortunately, many firms will attempt to straddle two or more competitive positions using one operations strategy. The result is that they fail to satisfy the values sought by any particular group of customers. Trying to compete at an operational level in two incompatible ways at once will incur enormous penalties.

CASE VIGNETTE **BRITISH RAILWAYS**

Since privatization, the various independent companies that now comprise the British railway system have been dogged with problems. All but a very few have been able to position their product using an operations strategy to achieve any level of competitive success. For this industry, safety is paramount, whether competing on cost, differentiation or response, and a series of accidents have dented public confidence. The train operating companies have struggled in vain to achieve a safe, reliable and high quality operational service at reasonable price. The question has to be posed: are they attempting to straddle two competitive positions and failing to provide an operations strategy that provides the full value sought by any one group of customers? The reader may like to examine the 'flight experience' on VIA Rail Canada (www.viarail.ca) and compare the product attributes, strategic positioning and operations strategies of the two railway sectors.

Finally, we should remember that the positioning of a firm to offer a particular choice in product and service combinations requires a close interface between operations and marketing. To appreciate both of these perspectives we revisit the order winning and order qualifying concepts introduced in chapter 7 (p. 139):

- *Order-winning*. The criterion that differentiates the products or services of one firm form another. For the British Rail operating companies, for example, the order winning criteria may be price and reliability, convenience and quality of experience (although in practice there is little alternative choice).
- *Order-qualifying*. The screening criteria that permit a firm's products to even be considered as possible candidates for purchase. For the train operating companies, this will include the safety record, qualified staff, adequate rolling stock and a reasonable timetable.

Stage 5 – operations strategy competitive priorities

Once we have gained a clear understanding of the operational requirements and challenges of the market and attributes of our products and services, we need to translate this knowledge into the operations activity and strategy (the competitive priorities). A firm will gain competitive advantage with its operating system by outperforming competitors in terms of one or more of these capabilities. The reader will immediately see that these capabilities match many of the product attributes just covered. This is an important point. We are attempting to demonstrate how the product attributes are, in effect, two sides of the same coin. On the one hand, they consist of the choices a customer will make, on the other, they drive the operations strategy in terms of the fundamental requirements necessary. They shape the core competencies and processes, the resources, technologies and key tactical issues that comprise an operations strategy. Thus, they translate product attributes into operational capabilities and implications.

There are eight possible competitive priorities for operations that fall into four groups:

Cost	Low cost operations
Differentiation	High performance design
	Consistent quality
Response	Fast delivery time
	On-time delivery
	Customization
	Flexibility
Combined	Combination in a focused, target market

A firm may employ, as we have already said, one or more operations strategies dependent upon the requirements of various customers. However, there will be trade-offs involved, and attempting to compete using incompatible operations strategies will be fraught with the danger of trying to straddle too far a divide, and failing to properly satisfy any particular customer group.

Cost

Lowering prices for goods and services also lowers margins, if the product or service cannot be delivered at a lower cost. To compete on cost, any operational system and its strategy must examine labour, materials, waste, overheads and other costs to design a system that lowers the cost per unit of a service or product. Often, lowering cost also requires additional investment in automated facilities and equipment.

Differentiation

Differentiation can be based upon a number of factors, in particular, high performance product and service package design and consistent quality. High performance design determines the level of operations performance required in making a product or service. Consistent quality measures the frequency with which the product and service meets design specifications. Operations strategies in this environment need to be designed to control and monitor errors. A lack of differentiation consistency in a global competitive market will quickly lead to failure.

Response

Response involves a number of factors. Flexibility (customized goods and services and flexibility in volume, mix, logistics, monetary contribution and/or customer contact) and time (fast delivery time, short lead time, on time delivery, fast development, and general time-based competition). Response dictates that the operational system and strategy must be flexible enough to handle variety and specific customer values and rapid changes in that value. This necessitates an understanding of both the volatility and complexity of the market.

Combined

It is, we suggest, possible for an organization to have more than one strategy. In certain situations firms can compete using a number of diametrically opposed operations strategies. However, this is a far more risky strategy. In certain situations a firm can compete on a number of competitive positions. For example, a manufacturer will wish to reduce defects in order to improve quality, reduce costs and cut delivery time.

There will come a trade-off point when improvements in one area will start to detrimentally affect others. For example, research shows that raising the degree of customization or producing high-performance design products may lead to both higher costs and higher prices (Safizadeh *et al.*, 1996). Thus there needs to be a careful selection of competitive priorities. We must also bear in mind that there are also certain competitive priorities that are mandatory – these are the order qualifiers discussed above.

We can now examine the strategic fit between product attributes, markets and the major components of the operations strategy.

Stage 6 – strategic fit

We have analysed: (1) the operational implications of the various markets; (2) the various choices that customers make when considering product or service attributes; and (3) the operations strategy competitive priorities. We now turn to the essential fit between the three. As we know, an operations strategy is composed of building blocks:

- Core competencies, capabilities and processes;
- Resources;
- Technologies;
- Certain important tactical activities vital to support strategic positioning.

In chapter 6 we demonstrated that an operations strategy is composed of a number of these building blocks that are fused together in a unique and customized strategic architecture. Thus, all of these components are related to one another in a holistic or systemic fashion to support the firm's business strategy. Earlier we saw how Southwest Airlines compete on cost. They achieve this through an operations strategy composition that is blended in a manner that allows it to focus upon certain components and avoid others. Figure 8.5 demonstrates this fit using the operations strategy composition matrix (OSCM) developed in chapter 5 and extended in chapter 6.

The composition matrix in Fig. 8.5 is an example of some of the possible components; there will be many others. However, this shows how the operations strategy translates the business strategy and deploys it through various activities and components. For more information on the contribution of activities to a business strategy see Porter (1996). We can also see that the resultant operations strategy for Southwest has an emphasis upon a number of key themes (in white) which are linked and integrated through other clusters of tightly linked activities (black). As we demonstrated in chapter 5, to be properly deployed and customized to the situation, the operations strategy requires a fusion between all the building blocks. It is this blending and reinforcement of the operations strategic architecture that translates the business strategy into operational activity and then offers a unique and sustainable competitive advantage through having the correct infrastructure.

Using the case study in chapter 6, we began to examine how the operations strategy can be blended and customized to product and supply system behaviours. The resultant operations strategies for Omicron Foods allowed the firm to tailor their approaches for each of their main retail customers and enhance their competitive position. The development of operations strategy in practice is now covered in a little more detail.

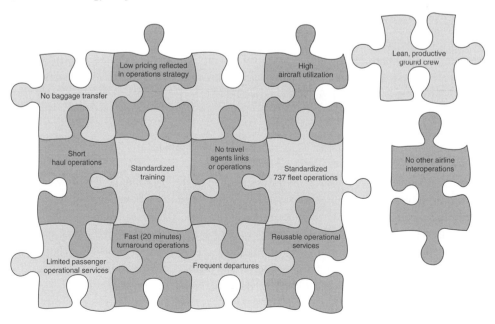

Figure 8.5 *Operations strategy composition matrix (OSCM) for Southwest Airlines*

CASE VIGNETTE **THE DYNAMICS OF AN OPERATIONS STRATEGY**

At the time of writing (11 September 2001) the devastating and horrific events surrounding the terrorist attacks on the Twin Towers in Manhattan and the Pentagon are unfolding. Anyone who has used domestic flights in the US will know the operations strategies of many such airlines translate a business strategy that is based upon convenience, speed of turnaround and low cost 'as easy as hopping on and off a bus'. Unfortunately, such operations do not entail elaborate security checks prior to booking-in. Looking again at the OSCM for Southwest we see it is not a key component of their operations strategy. Nevertheless, as environmental circumstances change, commercial organizations must adapt – this necessitates continual change to both business and operations strategies. In future, we are likely to see much tighter airline security across the world. Firms cannot, in a dynamic and complex business world, afford to stand still!

Stage 7 – developing an operations strategy in practice

Developing an operations strategy, or strategies, will be, to a degree, a unique activity for each organization. Despite some similarities between their components, these strategies are often comprised of a singular configuration and architecture that is customized to the exigencies of the organization and its environment. As such, we are forced to offer only general guidelines as to development and deployment.

As we saw earlier, operations strategies are composed of a pattern of decisions regarding:

■ Core competencies, capabilities and processes, these can be process-based (derived from transformation activities), system or subsystem-based (across the entire operation system), organization-based (across the entire organization), and network-based (covering the whole supply network);
■ Resources;
■ Technologies;
■ Key tactical activities vital to support strategic positioning.

The development of an operations strategy involves the blending of the above components using tools such as the operations strategy composition matrix. This will ensure that the resultant strategy is shaped to wider requirements (such as demand, the supply system, performance needs, etc.) The strategy must also be related to the identified values and needs of various products and markets (see p. 160 above). However, each of these choices will reflect a trade-off that will have implications for the final operations strategy, its operational system and the various product and service combinations.

CRITICAL REFLECTION

In modernist organizational theories, the organizational environment is viewed as an entity that lies outside the boundaries of the organization. The organization, for its part, faces uncertainty about what this environment demands, while at the same time it depends upon many of the environmental elements.

Symbolic-interpretivists or social constructionists view this environment as a social or theoretical construct formed by beliefs about their own existence and constituted by expectations set in motion by these beliefs.

Postmodern theory offers many approaches to the study of organization and the environment. In fact, increasingly followers suggest that there is little distinction between the two concepts. Hence, we see the boundaryless, virtual and networked organization.

The study of organization–environment relations tends to focus upon mainstream, modernist theories. These have arisen from two influential movements: systems theory and contingency theory. The former stressed that the organization is open to the environment and interacts with it to secure its very existence (as opposed to the Classical, closed viewpoint). This places an emphasis upon an assumed influence of, and relations with, this environment.

Contingency theory has developed in a number of directions: defining types of environment (stable or rapidly changing) and organizations best suited (mechanistic or organic) to the requisite variety of that environment using a process of matching or isomorphism; resource dependency theory, the environment is a powerful constraint on organizational action through which managers have to navigate using various power/dependence relationships; population ecology, populations of organization evolve using Darwinian concepts of variation, selection and retention; and institutional theory, organizations adapt and then become institutionalized to the values, both social and cultural, of the external society which exerts certain pressures (coercive institutional pressures, normative institutional pressures, and mimetic institutional pressures).

Stage 8 – implementing an operations strategy

In chapter 6 the practical deployment of a customized operations strategy was explored. Implementing the strategy involves translating the various components or elements into relevant actions; this is far from easy as management involves the application of knowledge.

TIME OUT BOX III

When we describe management as an 'applied' rather than 'knowledge-based' field we are referring to different levels of learning. What do we mean by this?

Knowing which approach to follow for best results and making the developments happen is an underlying management capability. What to do and how to do it will vary from one situation to another. As we shall see in Part III (Applications), the deployment of the operations strategy will depend upon a number of factors (including environmental constraints, type of sector and even type of organization).

To conclude the review, we will spend a moment considering the dynamic nature of operations strategy.

THE LIFE CYCLE OF AN OPERATIONS STRATEGY

In order to examine the temporal dimensions of an operations strategy it is necessary to understand the relationships between the components involved and how these are shaped and changed. An operations strategy will evolve over time as certain elements receive more or less emphasis (the Internet and electronic commerce being a current case in point).

We have seen how the strategy develops a particular composition (for example, the operations strategy composition matrix in Fig. 8.5). Any operations strategy will in fact contain a number of similar building blocks. However, they are assembled in such a fashion as to give a unique or customized strategy that matches particular circumstances (for example, demand and performance requirements, etc.). Although all possible components of the strategy might be present, in practice, some will appear more prominent for any given demand or supply system situation. It is important, therefore, that an appropriate blend of components is chosen – one that is individual to a known demand and performance profile. It is this unique architecture that provides the essential strategic contribution.

The organization's composition matrix will evolve over time through dealings with suppliers and consumers – many of the components may in fact be introduced at their behest. Further, the model changes constantly as new technologies, resources and core competencies and processes are introduced. It is not linear, and its history will determine which of many (rather than one) final states it will adopt. At any particular point in time, the matrix as a system may encounter a bifurcation point, when it will branch off into an entirely new state.

This inherent complexity, however, provides the strength of the operations strategy. The complementarity or cohesion between the various elements (those having both a strong and weak emphasis) will determine the difference between:

- world-class operations;
- efficient operations;
- sub-optimal or dysfunctional operations.

Contribution to competitive advantage

As the Southwest Airlines Composition Matrix (Fig. 8.5) demonstrated, certain building blocks have been combined with a particular low-cost emphasis. This act of combination or 'blending' provides the Airline with an operations strategy fusion that assumes strategic status. If, say, supply network and/or time-based competition and/or sourcing are of particular strategic importance to an organization, then by blending certain key elements, it will accord operations strategy status to that combination. These distinct architectures reinforce Michael Porter's belief (1996) that strategy is mainly a matter of capability development and that activities are the basic units of competitive advantage.

We now seek to discover the exact nature of the various forces that shape that evolution and direction.

Shaping operations strategy evolutionary paths

As part of our research, a number of retailers and manufacturers in consumer goods sectors were asked to rank the most important influences upon their operations strategies and operational activities. In other words, what where the main factors that shaped the development of such a strategy. The following influences consistently scored most highly:

1   Those associated with the demands of the product or product group (78 per cent);
2   Those associated with the structure of the supply system (74 per cent); and
3   Those associated with the performance of certain metrics within that supply system (66 per cent).

In chapter 6 we demonstrated how the operations strategy is deployed through a customization of the composition matrix using an analysis of product and service demand behaviour and supply system demand behaviour. As a reminder, these covered the following:

INFLUENCES ASSOCIATED WITH THE DEMANDS OF THE PRODUCT OR PRODUCT GROUP
■   Product attributes
■   Demand patterns
■   Customer behaviour.

INFLUENCES ASSOCIATED WITH THE STRUCTURE OF THE SUPPLY SYSTEM
■   Product stream value flows
■   Vertical integration
■   Individual firms sizes and power.

We can now build on these by describing the third influence upon the composition of an operations strategy:

INFLUENCES ASSOCIATED WITH PERFORMANCE METRICS WITHIN THE SUPPLY SYSTEM
In addition to the influences associated with the demands of the product or *product group* and structural demands of the *supply system*, a third factor is important in the evolution of an operations strategy: *supply system performance metrics*. Here, we are concerned

to understand how factors such as lead time, inventory, supplier service performance and customer service level might be used to place an emphasis upon certain elements of the operations strategy. To appreciate the underlying impact of these performance measures, Fig. 8.7 displays the relationships involved in what we have termed the LISP interactions.

There are four fundamental quantities in any supply system:

■ Lead time for supply;
■ Inventory at a particular supply pipeline stage;
■ Customer Service level; and
■ Supplier Performance, this involves two factors: supplier service level and supplier process time (to convert raw materials or components into finished goods and services).

These components interact and the implied value for one is derived from the other three. The result of this interaction is also another important determinant of the composition of an operations strategy. Figure 8.7 sketches these connections between supply system tiers.

Fisher (1997) points out that speed and flexibility of the supply system can help overcome the impact of uncertainty, but typically at a cost. For any operation there are a number of relationships that can be used to assess these performance trade-offs. Thus, we need to quantify these LISP relationships in order to examine in detail the performance of a supply system. In the next chapter we will examine the LISP relationships to show how different types of demand behaviour and performance in any supply system can be used to tailor an organization's operations strategy.

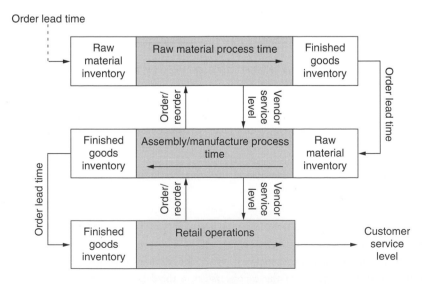

Figure 8.6 LISP interactions in a supply system

Evolution of operations strategies

The adoption of an operations strategy can, it seems, be by design or almost accidental. When asked, 80 per cent of our research respondents declared that they had deliberately adopted and designed an operations strategy as part of a clear, planned, evolutionary path. A further 6 per cent, however, stated that such a strategy was almost accidental and had just grown in a piecemeal and fragmentary way as a result of various external influences. We then asked *all* the respondents declaring the use of a strategy (planned or emergent), to classify the most important influences upon its development and evolution. To do this the retail population were asked to describe climatic forces in their domain (what Webster's dictionary calls the prevailing temper of environmental conditions characterising a group or period) that might have had, or is likely to have, an influence on the evolution and development. Table 8.3 details the outcomes.

To briefly deal with the findings. The influences of technology and economic imperatives (Hall, 1977), are reinforced by international considerations and the physical needs for goods to be available when and where required (Sethi, 1970). Khandwalla (1977) shows the effects of environmental turbulence together with diversity and technical complexity. The rate of environmental diversity, instability and turbulence is further supported in the Aldrich (1979), Miles (1980) and Emery and Trist (1965) classifications (although in the latter case many respondents also declared the environment to be relatively simple and stable). The adaptation from Porter (1979) shows industry rivalry to be most important (interestingly, power of suppliers and consumers is lower – perhaps due to many of the respondents being retailers). Finally, as discussed above, product demand and supply system demand behaviour, together with supply system performance metrics (as part of the LISP interconnections), also seem equally important influences for these retailers.

In addition to the above, for those with a designed and planned strategy, there will also be strong internal pressures, possibly, we would suggest, as a result of these external powers.

Operations strategies are fluid and transitory. They will evolve over time, despite their initial origins (planned or accidental). Whatever the type of operations strategy, it is now clear that their performance might be ranked (world class, efficient or suboptimal, etc.); and that this performance might be a function of the unique blending of their building blocks. However, additional research is needed to ascertain if there is any correlation between ultimate performance of the operations strategy, its origins and its evolution.

CONCLUSION

In this chapter we have set out to expand upon, and confirm, the contribution of an operations strategy to competitive advantage. In so doing, a phased approach has been used. This both guided development and deployment, but also to make it abundantly clear that the operations strategy, like any other, does not exist in a vacuum: the power lies in its close interface with other strategies and parts of the business.

Table 8.3 *Operations strategies – evolutionary influence*

Descriptions of substantive climatic or domain environmental conditions (categorization source)	Degree influence for each classification (%)
1 Hall (1977)	
Technological	21
Legal	6
Political	11
Economic	25
Demographic	14
Ecological	6
Cultural	7
2 Sethi (1970)	
Physical	32
Social	14
Psychological	11
International	43
3 Khandwalla (1977)	
Turbulence (dynamic, unpredictable, fluctuating)	41
Hostility (risky, stressful, dominating)	11
Diversity (heterogeneity)	21
Technical complexity (high technical sophistication)	20
Restrictiveness (many constraints)	7
4 Aldrich (1979)	
Resource capacity (rich–lean)	4
Homogeneity – heterogeneity (diversity)	27
Stability – instability	26
Resource concentration – dispersion	6
Domain consensus (territorial legitimacy)	7
Turbulence (disturbance via increasing rate of interconnection)	30
5 Miles (1980)	
Statics (complexity, routineness, interconnectedness, remoteness)	12
Dynamics (change rate, unpredictability of change)	56
Receptivity (resource scarcity, output receptiveness, domain choice, flexibility)	32
6 Emery and Trist (1965)	
Placid-randomized (simplicity and certainty, no interdependency of behaviour – trial and error to survive)	4
Placid-clustered (relatively simple and stable, clusters of components, conditions of risk)	54
Disturbed-reactive (more complex, dynamic and uncertain)	40
Turbulent field (highly dynamic and uncertain)	2
7 Porter (1979 – adaptation)	
Level of industry rivalry (existing competition)	42
Threat of new entrants (new competition)	21
Power of suppliers (power of the supply system)	17
Power of customers (consumers)	3
Threat of substitute products (new operational management methods, etc.)	17
8 Lowson (2001b)	
Product demand behaviour	42
Supply system demand behaviour	33
Supply system performance metrics	25

The next two chapters take a slight digression. Hopefully, it is clear that an operations strategy can provide substantial benefits to the firm. However, before going further it is now necessary to consider its primary role in this respect; the satisfaction of the demand and value needs of the customer.

CASE STUDY – OPERATIONS STRATEGY IN ACTION

Norwich International Airport[1] – operations strategy as a source of sustainable competitive advantage (www.norwichairport.co.uk)

> Every airport is unique and to that end Norwich International Airport is no different.

Norwich International Airport (NIA) prides itself on being a passenger friendly airport, offering a full range of services the traveller would normally expect, such as its airport shops, catering facilities, car hire, parking and so on. There is, however, quite a subtle difference: flights are rarely delayed, car parking is cheap, and most of the airport functions are provided in-house. This means that the airport provides a service that is reliable, comfortable and standardized. In fact, one of the first things you notice as you enter NIA is the calm. None of the visible chaos and disorderly hustle and bustle you normally encounter upon entering a busy airport. This is what differentiates NIA from its larger counterparts and it is a positive product of the airport's operation.

Based just outside Norwich, in the heart of East Anglia, NIA has at present 380,000 passengers using the airport a year, but this is anticipated to rise to 1 million in the next five years. This is partly due to the UK Government's recent announcement that the cost of flying from Heathrow airport near London is to be substantially increased in a bid to encourage travellers to take advantage of smaller regional airports.

The NIA operation

The main consumers of NIA can be divided into 3 categories:

- *Aviation operators* – certain services have to be offered to aviation operators. These include the use of the runway, hangars, maintenance, apron services, air traffic control and fire and rescue services.
- *Service Operators* (e.g. car hire firms, caterers, newsagents and other retail outlets) – these organizations are able to rent retail space to run their enterprises from an airport location.
- *Passengers* (these can be subdivided into business and leisure) – airline passengers expect safety, security and being able to relax in a well maintained and furbished

---

1 The author is indebted to Nicola Burgess of the Strategic Operations Management Centre at UEA for contributing this case study.

terminal lounge with easy access to all their travelling requirements including refreshments, duty free, and up-to-the minute information on flight schedules and the like.

The airport's dominant carrier is KLM UK, who offer a service that allows passengers to fly anywhere in the world via its Amsterdam, Schiphol hub. The popularity of this service is, however, marred by the fact that it charges its passengers more to fly from Norwich due to limited capacity relative to the larger London airports. In addition, the size of the KLM operation discourages competition from other airlines at NIA and this has created a high price monopoly situation.

Norwich International Airport also operates its own in-house charter service. This is run using its own travel shops that are strategically placed in five locations throughout East Anglia. Using the charter service NIA is able to offer seats to major tour operators such as First Choice, Thomas Cook and Thomson Holidays. This is an attractive option to these tour operators as the airport takes all the risks when adding new destinations. The introduction of new destinations helps stimulate the marketplace and attracts new operators and airlines to use the airport. Over the last six years this has been a successful strategy, increasing the throughput of passengers by 120,000.

Despite these efforts, and recently attaining International status, NIA could still be regarded as a small airport, with most of its passengers being local businessmen and oil rig workers travelling up and down the UK's north sea coast via small regional carriers such as Eastern Airways.

Norwich International Airport is aware that it has a number of exceptional opportunities for expansion and growth. Future demand projections suggest a massive increase in passengers. This means that NIA must increase the current passenger capacity ceiling to provide operational facilities for this increased business. To date, they have not taken advantage of the available land at the airport that provides opportunities to extending runways and increase the volume of carriers using NIA. They are also in a position to diversify their services to provide training facilities and a helicopter service for the East Coast offshore energy industry.

An analysis of NIA's strengths, weaknesses, opportunities and threats reveals some favourable conditions for the development and growth of the airport (see Fig. 8.7).

Future operations

In order for NIA to embrace these opportunities and maintain their image as a reliable and friendly airport, it will need to consider the deployment of a new operations strategy. However, to do this NIA will need to reconcile the interests and activities of many stakeholders, including:

■ Aviation operators;
■ Service operators;
■ Passengers;
■ Airlines;

Strengths	Weaknesses
• Nearest competitor is 90 miles away • Services delivered are mainly in-house (standardized to lower cost) • NIA provides its own in-house charters which are sold through its own travel shops • Clear management structure • NIA owns five travel shops throughout East Anglia promoting the airport and its in-house charters • Cheap car parking in comparison with other airports • Amsterdam hub offers 230 destinations to NIAs passengers (one third of all passengers use this service)	• Communication links are under developed • Limited schedule service operation • Very few flight destinations direct from NIA • Over-priced fare structures imposed by carriers • Dominant airline KLM can be restrictive when trying to encourage new operators to use the airport in terms of competition • Poor public transport system, including poor road access • No direct rail link
Threats	**Opportunities**
• Low cost airlines running from larger London airports • Dualling of A11 – main road to Norwich from London (ease of access to London airports from East Anglia) • Local residents complaining of pollution and noise	• NIA has a largely untapped catchment area (approx. 1.6 million people in East Anglia) • Very little competition • Large acreage (airfield is underutilized and large future developments are possible by means of capital investment) • Introducing new 'hub' similar to Schiphol, e.g. Paris, Birmingham or Brussels • Dualling of A11 – main road to Norwich from London

Figure 8.7 *Norwich International Airport – strengths, weaknesses, opportunities and threats*

■ The tour operators;
■ Maintenance and security staff, baggage handling employees and so on.

It also remains vital that the airport's operations remain fully integrated and seamless to maintain the current relaxed atmosphere unique to NIA.

As we read in chapter 3, an operations strategy is composed of a pattern of decisions. These are medium and long-term decisions are made regarding certain generic factors or ingredients. The building blocks include:

■ Core competencies, capabilities and processes;
■ Resources;
■ Technologies;
■ Key tactical activities that are vital to support a particular strategy or positioning.

Further, if NIA wishes to customize its operations strategy for each major customer or service provided, it will also need to decide which of the factors or components should receive more emphasis as higher order strategic themes.

ANSWERS TO TIME OUT BOXES

Time out box 1

Products and services sold on the basis of cost are typically commodities. They will be similar to many others in the marketplace with very little variety. This type of market segment is usually very large as many firms are lured by the appeal of high profits associated with high volumes, the learning curve and economies of scale. However, competition and industry rivalry is fierce as the barriers to entry are relatively low, substitute products freely available and powerful customers and suppliers. Failure rate in this environment is also high as all the players scramble to be the one and only low cost producer who will establish the selling price for the market.

Time out box II

First, the firm must establish the value sought by the customer (this is not always easy). For example, over-designed products with too high a quality may be prohibitively expensive.

Second, process quality is equally important in providing the correct specifications and the right quality levels.

In the marketplace, this type of organization is seeking to compete on differentiation. That is, providing a product that stands out from the rest. To do so can be expensive and involve high quality components or raw materials. The cost of entry and operation in this market is therefore high and attention to the changing values that customers seek crucial (no matter how high the quality levels, manual calculators will not sell!). Competition is not likely to come from new players (due to the high cost of entry), but from existing firms making breakthrough improvements in products or processes or introducing new substitute goods and services.

Time out box III

Bloom and Krathwohl (1956) described increasing levels of learning:

- Evaluation – appraise, compare, conclude, contrast, interpret and explain.
- Synthesis – classify, compile, design, modify, reorganize, formulate, reconstruct and substitute.
- Analysis – select, discriminate, illustrate, separate, and distinguish.
- Application – demonstrate, relate, use, compete and prepare.
- Understanding – explain, extend, generalize, infer, summarize and estimate.
- Knowledge – know, identify, list, outline and state.

Knowledge and understanding are the lower level, easier elements of learning. Higher levels are concerned with application, analysis, synthesis and evaluation. For the manager, the most difficult task is to perform effectively. This requires application of knowledge, the analysis of the results of that application, the building of the results into an improved form (synthesis) and then evaluation of what else needs to be done. Effective managers are continually developing these capabilities through their own responsibilities.

DISCUSSION QUESTIONS, WORK ASSIGNMENTS AND EXAM QUESTIONS

1   What do we mean by the term 'operational implications'? In what ways does the under-standing of the market have important implications for operations strategies?
2   What are the main product and service attributes of:
    - The emergency services?
    - A high quality hotel?
    - An automotive manufacturer?
    - An electricity supply company?
3   What are the main competitive priorities for each of the above sectors?
4   Discuss examples of firms with different operations strategy life cycles. They can be viewed as being at different stages as well as performing at different levels (world-class, efficient or suboptimal).

Reader questions related to the Norwich International Airport case study

1   Discuss the possible components of NIA operations strategy given the changes that are likely in the next five years.
2   In Fig. 8.5 an example operations strategy was developed for Southwest Airlines. This showed how certain factors could receive a particular emphasis depending upon the type of consumer or product. Analyse the change in emphasis necessary to customize an operations strategy for each of the NIA main customers:
    - Aviation operators;
    - Service operators (e.g. car hire firms, caterers, newsagents and other retail outlets);
    - Passengers (these can be subdivided into business and leisure).

RECOMMENDED READING

Porter M.E. (1996) 'What is Strategy', *Harvard Business Review* November/December, 61–79.

Lowson R.H. (2001c) 'Retail Operational Strategies in Complex Supply Chains: Analysis and Application', *International Journal of Logistics Management* 8, 1, 97–111.

Chapter 9

Understanding demand complexity

Demand is important to all organizations whether large or small, commercial or non-profit, providing goods or services, or both. Demand, and its understanding, plays a large part. In fact, for operational management and operations strategies, the proper satisfaction of demand is fundamental. There seems little point in undertaking either activity if demand is ignored; yet that is precisely what happens in many organizations. Demand understanding and planning is only considered in a tactical sense; it is a reactive afterthought. Admittedly, the ramifications of demand are felt most strongly at this short-term level; however, it makes more sense to plan longer-term. In fact, it may be sensible for organizations to have demand strategies. Very few will have and this omission can be rectified by an operations strategy. First, we need to understand demand.

LEARNING OBJECTIVES

After considering this chapter, the reader will be able to:
- Appreciate the need for demand management
- Consider the types of demand
- Understand the factors affecting demand and the strategies for managing demand

INTRODUCTION

Demand links the operations strategy to the marketplace. It is the lifeblood of any enterprise and affects activities throughout the organization. Yet most firms know relatively little about demand and the strength of its influence.

In chapter 8 we were reminded of the two definitions that can be used to describe the role of the operations strategy. It is worth looking at one of these again in a little more detail.

> *Operations strategy definition 2 – the wider value delivery strategy*
> Major decisions about, and strategic management of: core competencies, capabilities and processes, technologies, resources and key tactical activities necessary in any supply network, in order to *create and deliver product and service combinations and the value demanded by a customer*. The strategic role involves blending these various building blocks into one or more unique, organizational-specific, strategic architectures.

The italic type emphasizes the importance of demand: 'To create and deliver product and service combinations and the value demanded by a customer'.

Demand tells us exactly what product or service combinations and value customers and consumers seek. In other words, as Lauterborn (1990) suggests, identifying and delivering the four Cs:

■ Customer needs and wants;
■ Cost to the customer;
■ Convenience;
■ Communication.

Clearly, we do not suggest that all of the above activities are the exclusive domain of the operations strategy. However, demand permeates the whole enterprise and is a key concern of all employees. Indeed, we could go as far as saying that all activities should closely mirror and reflect demand information. Not only what we do, but when, where and how. This is the importance of demand as the nucleus and driving force behind all activity in the cluster of value (see Fig. 1.3, p. 18), and the reason why demand needs to be managed.

183

DEMAND MANAGEMENT

The management of demand encompasses a number of activities, depending upon the type of industry concerned.

TIME OUT BOX I

What are the major demand considerations for:

1   The public services in the UK?
2   Clothing retailer The Gap?
3   KLM Royal Dutch Airlines?
4   Robinsons Britvic, manufacturer of soft drinks?

To a degree, demand behaviour is individual and unique to not only the industry, but also to the firm. There will of course be certain well known trends and cycles (turkeys are always in demand around Thanksgiving and Christmas) and some general considerations apply to most producers of goods and services. Before looking at these, it may be interesting to examine another case study to see how demand drives operations.

CASE VIGNETTE HOW LEVI STRAUSS ALIGNS ITS OPERATIONS STRATEGY TO DEMAND

San Francisco based Levi Strauss and Co. are one of the largest producers and retailers of denim jeans. They use a particularly innovative operations strategy to support a flexible response to demand and high levels of product diversity. There are six core operational competencies that are seen as critical for future success:

1   *The alignment of organizational activity to demand.* This is a fundamental principle and a core business process. All activities within the enterprise are paced to demand and customer behaviour. Products are designed, produced and delivered in the variety and volume that matches demand. Activity moves to the 'beat of this drum'. Swings in demand are closely monitored; too little or too much leads to waste and inefficiency. For example, if in a particular week customers will on average buy 55,000 pairs of original, shrink-to-fit 501 jeans, that's all the company will make.

2   *Linkages between demand and supply.* Given the importance of the alignment activity described, a strategic understanding of demand and its synchronized connection with supply is imperative. Improvements in supply are important, but not to the detriment of real time demand understanding. Demand is the target; no matter how sophisticated the supply weaponry, it will be ineffectual if the target is not understood.

3   *Demand relationships.* A recognition that both customers/consumers and products have demand behaviours that are dynamic and place unique claims on the organization. Identical products, 501 jeans for example, will have unique product flows depending upon the customer (department store, speciality store, supermarket, wholesaler, independent, corner store) or consumer (you and me) buying behaviour. Similarly, product attributes will vary by garment, for example volume and flow characteristics, demand patterns, seasonality, promotional strategy, cyclical needs, information content, credit terms, customer incentives, repeat purchase patterns, etc. These different behaviours will customize and tailor supply channels.

4   *Resource configuration.* Operations strategy thinking is at a network level that will encompass many external interconnections in the supply system.

5   *Time.* As a strategic weapon, time is vital to Levi Strauss. Careful assessment of how time can be reduced in the business cycle allows a quicker response to demand. The adroitness and dexterity to move fast to satisfy unplanned demand or a previously unrecognized market niche requires the correct operations strategy.

6   *Information.* Data and information are the foundation of the operations strategy. As an information business, Levi's recognize that timely and accurate flows enable fast and accurate response.

Concepts and terminology

Different approaches to demand will reflect the varying emphases or objectives that the firm has. For example, the type or nature of demand and whether we are planning to satisfy that demand over the long, medium or short term.

Objectives

Planning for demand and developing responsiveness and flexibility. Capacity, resource planning, staffing, scheduling, training, investment in technology, and so on, are all important elements. This also includes an understanding of:

- *Sources of demand* – understanding internal and external customers and the value they seek as well as potential changes in these sources.
- *Operational processes* – how the operations strategy can be shaped and customized to the sources of demand and their individual behaviours.
- *Nature of demand* – the type, timing, quantity of demand and how these can be better understood and manipulated.

Types of demand

There are a number of ways to classify demand. Here, we will cover the four main approaches used in operations:

- *Dependent versus independent demand.* Dependent demand is demand that is relatively predictable because it is dependent upon some factor that is known, Slack (1999). Items forming part of a larger good or parent product are dependent upon demand for that finished product. For example, demand for bread buns, meat patties, lettuce, mayonnaise, relish and cheese slices will all depend upon the demand for McDonald's cheeseburgers. The process for understanding dependent demand is thus relatively straightforward and can be calculated. Independent demand is far less predictable and more random, as its causes are less well understood. Decisions may have to be made without any firm visibility of customers' orders. This involves risk and guesswork.
- *Inputs and outputs.* Demand for outputs covers the product and service combinations provided by the firm. We also need to consider dependent demands for inputs, the raw materials, components, labour, machine time, etc., which will also be involved.
- *Push and pull operational systems.* In the push system we are producing product and service combinations in advance of demand and awaiting order. This will have adverse inventory implications but will allow a faster response. In the pull system, the customer triggers activity with an inquiry or order. Here we make to that order rather than stock. The system involves less finished goods inventory and is more flexible, although response to peaks of demand may be poor.
- *Aggregate and item demand.* Aggregate demand is total demand, not broken down into component, item or category. Item demand, as the name suggests, will involve the parts or operations or activities. Aggregate or item demand can be dependent or independent and can also be an input or output.

Planning time frame

Demand management aims to meet short-, medium- and long-term needs. There is a direct link between the length of the planning horizon and the difficulty or complexity involved in understanding the implications. In Fig. 5.3 (chapter 5) this lesson was demonstrated. The planning horizon also involves understanding lead times (the time taken to get things done) and cycle or throughput times. Unfortunately, the more distant the time horizon, the less we know about demand. This problem is then compounded by the use of long-term forecasts, which are, no matter how sophisticated, often guesswork.

Factors affecting demand

The total demand that faces any enterprise is a result of a number of market forces. The size of the total market, the market share an organization has, various trends, seasons and cycles, and even random fluctuations will all affect the demand patterns. We now examine a few of these in a little more detail.

The business cycle

Sales are influenced by demand and demand can in turn be affected by a large number of features. One particular macro factor is the status of the economy as the business cycle moves through various phases of recovery, inflation, recession and depression. These cycles, plus the intervention, to greater and lesser degrees, of different governments, will all influence the demand a business may face.

The product life cycle

As we know from our marketing colleagues, product and service combinations all pass through a life cycle (some longer than others). During this life cycle, there can be numerous interventions that will alter the profile of the cycle and reflect changes in market share.

There are a large number of factors that can influence demand. Their interrelated, systemic nature demonstrate (a) the complexity involved in understanding demand, and (b) the difficulties of trying to forecast its variation. Figure 9.1 summarizes the situation (although this is somewhat simplified).

Product and service demand behaviour and supply network demand behaviour

In chapter 6 we saw how the operations strategy was customized to reflect the influences of the particular product or service and its supply system. The act of customization was deliberately designed to match or blend the composition of an operations strategy to these behaviours. Thus when discussing demand influences we must be clear that both goods and services as well as supply structures are considered. In the case of the former, we can demonstrate this by comparing the differences, for example, in product behaviour for

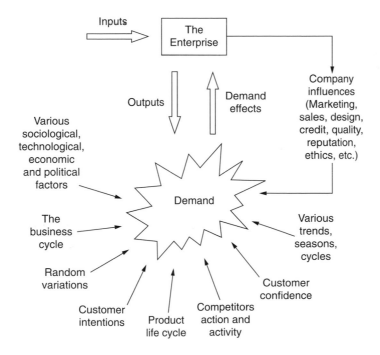

Figure 9.1 *A picture of demand*

clothing and grocery items in Table 9.1. We can see that in a number of dimensions, the products exhibit different behaviour patterns. In addition, within these groups there will also be subgroups that may also have differences – basic, seasonal and fashion or short season, for example.

The structure of any supply system also influences demand behaviour. As mentioned in chapter 6, the various stages, types of firms involved, flow of information and products, etc. will all have a bearing. Some of these points can be graphically demonstrated in the next case study.

CASE VIGNETTE **BRITVIC SOFT DRINKS**

Britvic Soft Drinks are the largest soft drink producers in the UK. Main brands include Robinsons, Tango and Pepsi. These products suffer from extremes of seasonality usually caused by the vagaries of the British climate. Sales rocket one week only to plummet the next. In addition, these swings are exaggerated by what is known as the Forrester effect. Also known as the 'bullwhip' or 'whipsaw', this describes a picture of demand distortion that grows in amplification. Perceived demand rather than real demand will cause a variation that increases with each activity in the supply system (Forrester, 1961; Burbidge, 1961).

At Britvic in the early 1990s, senior management were becoming increasingly alarmed at the high cost and waste associated with these patterns. Was all this activity really due to the consumer purchasing patterns? Or were other factors at work that were not as yet understood?

A large research programme was launched in order to try to analyse the demand patterns. Leading retailers became involved and product flows were scrutinized over a period. As the graph below shows, individual products were tracked and the consumer purchase data from retailers was used to demonstrate the seasonality of the product. As we can see, the orders placed by retailers upon Britvic were even more extreme than consumer purchasing and the manufacturing production activity worse still. This is a classic example of the Forrester Effect where volatility increases in oscillation the further away

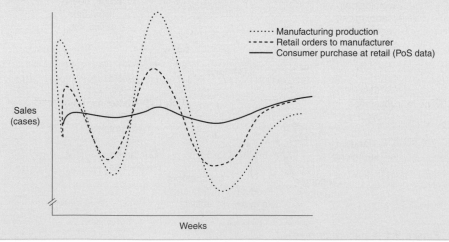

from its source. But other strange influences also became apparent. For example, the retailers would often indulge in a forward purchase or investment buy. If a product was being promoted by a cut in price over, say, a week, the retailers would often place a spot purchase – they would order 2–3 months of their usual requirement in one week then nothing more for the next three months. To the manufacturer this was consumer demand gone mad. Overall, the exercise enabled Britvic to better understand demand and to obtain advance information of investment buys. It opened the channel of communication between them and their retailing customers. In addition, they began to link their internal activity to external demands of unique product flows and consumer behaviour by producing and delivering every product every week, or day, in line with actual sales to consumers.

Strategies for managing demand

Ideally, a firm seeks to match supply and demand. We have much more control over the former than the latter. Managing supply involves issues such as changing capacity, employment levels, training, scheduling, etc.

Changing capacity to manage supply

In many operations, changing capacity is an important aid to flexibility. For tangible goods, this can be achieved by changing output using increased labour, machinery, material, etc. For services, even more flexibility is possible using the following:

- Customer participation – customers participate in the operational process providing capacity exactly when need (for example, self-service petrol stations).

Table 9.1 *Differences in product behaviour*

Product behaviour	Clothing	Grocery
Average stock keeping units (SKUs) per average retail store	High (500k–2m)*	Low (25k–30k)
Inventory turns	Low (2–5 times per annum)	High (10–25 times per annum)
Unit value (value to weight or cube ratio)	High	Low
Markdown frequency	High	Low
Gross margin	High (35–50%)	Low (20–25%)
Product life cycle	Short	Long
Seasonality	High	Low
Incidence of product substitution	Low	High
Cost of being out of stock (estimated to be approx. 3 times purchase prices of each lost sale)	High	Low
Purchase frequency	Low	High

* k = 1,000 and m = 1,000,000 SKUs

- *Core and secondary capacity* – providing stable, core capacity to meet basic demand (i.e. permanent staff) and adjustable, secondary capacity to meet extra demand (temporary staff at Christmas, for example).
- *Flexible capacity* – meeting unexpected fluctuations in demand using multi-skilled staff who can perform more than one task when required.
- *Short-term capacity* – adjusting to meet demand peaks by using employees to work overtime.
- *Absorbing and releasing capacity* – subcontracting, deferring work or even bringing it forward.

In Fig. 9.1 the impression was given that a firm will be reactive to demand. This is not always the case. As demonstrated in the figure, an enterprise will influence demand in a number of ways. Further, excessive fluctuations in demand need not always be accepted as inevitable. There are certain active and passive measures that can be taken to smooth demand; this is especially the case in the service sector. We now review some of the approaches used to manage demand.

Partitioning to manage demand

There will always be certain patterns in demand. For example, some groups of people will use bank facilities at certain times of day or on particular days of the week. Some customers will fly only at weekends or on weekdays. Walk-in demand for a surgery or health clinic may be higher on Mondays than any other day of the week (Rising *et al.*, 1973). Once these patterns are identified and have been analysed, smoothing strategies can be used. For example, the demand may be partitioned so that in the case of the health centre, Mondays are reserved for emergencies and walk-in patients and less urgent cases are given appointments for other days in the week.

Price incentives to manage demand

Creating differences in price can also be used too manipulate demand. Here, we can use examples of off-peak or weekend telephone rates, 'happy hours' in bars and birthday parties in fast-food restaurants as ways to utilize spare capacity through complementary services and pricing changes. The strategy also enables full utilization of scarce resources.

Promoting off-peak demand

Creative use of off-peak capacity provides different demand sources. Apart from the telephone example above, many mountain ski resorts will use off-season to promote business conferences or different types of activity (walking and hiking – see the Sun Mountain case study in chapter 7).

Complementary services

Bars, restaurants and shops at major airports not only generate revenue; they also serve to keep waiting passengers entertained and calm frayed nerves. Complementary services are also a natural way to diversify and keep capacity balanced throughout the trading period.

Reservation systems

Making a reservation sells the potential service. As reservations are made, demand can be scheduled. For customers, they reduce waiting and guarantee service. However, reservation systems have to cope with customers failing to honour appointments. Often, a charge is made or a deposit lost. Many airlines in fact overbook to cover the percentage of no-shows and avoid empty seats. This does on occasion lead to overbooking problems when the airline has to compensate passengers or tempt passengers into taking a later flight.

Demand forecasting

The final section of this chapter examines some of the basic forecasting methods traditionally used to attempt to appreciate future demand.

Many firms attempt to plan future activity based upon demand forecasting. Unfortunately, as we know, forecasting is really guessing (no matter how sophisticated the equipment used). Trying to predict the future, especially long-term, is a risky business (if you want to make God laugh, tell him your plans!). Forecast errors increase with lead time (see Fig. 5.3, p. 100). These errors can be negative – the firm runs out of finished goods, components or raw materials, leading to lost sales, or positive – we are left with high levels of costly inventory. Forecasting requires an understanding of the business cycles, the time involved, lead time composition, sources of business forecasting data and the implications of forecast error. Forecasting approaches can be broadly categorized as (a) subjective and (b) objective.

Subjective forecasting methods

These are mainly qualitative, opinion-based and judgmental – they are none the less just as valid, and can often be combined with mathematical models.

FIELD SALES FORCE
One of the most effective methods of forecasting is asking the people responsible for sales to estimate likely demand. Often, people such as sales staff, retail shop floor staff, service providers and the like are the first line of contact with the customer. They will have an excellent understanding of short-term demand (volumes, mix, type, etc.) and the likely future trends. Aggregated, such data is extremely valuable and is often overlooked in many organizations.

CUSTOMERS AND CONSUMERS
Research concerning the needs and purchasing plans of both customers and potential customers is also a valuable source of information. Information as to product and service advantages and disadvantages as well as possible modifications should be constantly monitored. In addition, this approach can also be used to compare the firm's offerings with that of their competitors.

DELPHI METHODS

These are a group of methods that seek the contribution of a panel of experts. They have the advantage of utilizing expertise and knowledge as to future trends and changes. For example, they are frequently used by organizations attempting to construct futuristic scenarios that extrapolate the implications of major changes in society.

Objective forecasting methods

These are quantitative forecasting methods that attempt to model the relationship between demand and other independent variable(s). There are two main types:

TIME SERIES MODELS

Here, time is the independent variable and demand patterns are projected against this variable in an attempt to predict future trends. Time series involves the collection of historical data such as sales patterns. This data can be broken down into its main constituent components:

- *Trends* – the general upward or downward movement of the average level of demand over time.
- *Seasonal* – the reoccurring fluctuation of demand above and below the trend value that has a fairly consistent repetition. This could be weather related, as we saw with Robinsons Britvic soft drinks, or attached to a particular season such as holidays or Christmas. Seasonal patterns can also repeat weekly or monthly.
- *Cyclical* – reoccurring upward or downward movements that repeat with a frequency longer than one year. This is usually related to business cycles (inflation, recession, etc.).
- *Random* – a series of short, erratic movements without evident pattern.

For forecasting purposes, trend and seasonal demand data is the most frequently modelled and projected in order to predict demand (although there is always a large element of uncertainty when trying to accurately understand the future).

CAUSAL MODELS

These are also known as explanatory or associative models. The forecaster attempts to use another independent variable (apart from, or in addition to time) with which demand, the dependent variable, has shown a strong past relationship. This model offers us leading indicators of future trends. For example, over time (independent variable) the levels of childbirth (independent variable) may be correlated or related to the demand for baby food (dependent variable).

For those readers interested in further information regarding forecasting methods and techniques, reference should be made to Makridakis *et al*. (1998).

CONCLUSION

The nature of demand has been explained and its management suggested. The chapter has shown that there are many factors affecting demand as well as possible strategies for longer-term planning for demand influences. We have also described, briefly, the nature of forecasting, although in practice firms find longer-term forecasting increasingly problematic and inaccurate. It is in this light that chapter 10 continues the debate by examining some of the more recent research into demand management.

CASE STUDY – OPERATIONS STRATEGY IN ACTION

Weathering an industry's 'perfect storm' – understanding demand complexity[1]

If the hit movie *The Perfect Storm* was recast into an apparel industry drama, it would tell the story of two market forces that collide simultaneously: markdowns and stock outs. The first wave leaves in its wake massive amounts of inventory that will not sell, while the latter washes away hot-selling garments that cannot be replenished.

In today's retail world, perfect storms are increasing in frequency, wreaking havoc with operations and bottom-line profits. Faced with this constant pummelling, clothing companies and retailers must focus upon trying to accommodate the uncertainty and variance associated with fast-changing customer demand, while leveraging the network's supply ability to deliver the right product at the right time.

Time delays wash profits away

A key element affecting the amount of damage inflicted by the apparel industry's perfect storm is network supply time delays. Yet many retailers and manufacturers have shifted a tremendous amount of consumer goods manufacturing to low-wage countries throughout the world, without careful consideration of the hidden costs of both logistics and inflexibility that reliance on forecasts that accompany importing will bring. When companies calculate gross margin (revenue minus the cost of goods), they assume that the revenue side of the equation is unaffected by the production source. In this calculation, choosing the cheapest production source is sure to maximize gross margin.

However, there is an error in this logic. The longer and more inflexible the network of supply, the more a company must rely on long-range forecasts that push the merchandise towards the retail stage; and this scenario spawns the conditions necessary for the perfect storm. In the aftermath, companies are stuck with excess inventory and are forced to sell more merchandise at discounted prices. Moreover, there is greater consumer dissatisfaction, lost sales and ultimately, reduced profits. Consider the facts: industry estimates have revealed that more than 33 per cent of all merchandise is sold at markdown prices, while about one in three customers with specific purchases in mind is not able to find what they want in stock when they reach the retail store.

....

1 The author is indebted to Professor Russell King of North Carolina State University for his help with this case study. A full transcript can be found in the January 2001 issue of *Bobbin* magazine.

Now contrast this scenario with a fast, flexible, responsive and efficient network supply that is able to operate using a pull or just in time system. Since production decisions can be delayed and based more on actual consumer demand, the right inventory can be pulled through the supply chain. Reduced time in the supply system will of course (as we saw in chapter 5, Fig. 5.3) substantially reduce forecast error.

In an integrated network supply system the tight coupling of entities, freely shared information and consumer demand pulling inventory through the network progressively removes time from the rest of the chain. However, as the chain lengthens, uncertainty increases both risk and exposure, until the cost advantage of a cheaper supplier is offset by increased logistics and flexibility costs as well as reduced and lost sales and markdowns. Where this break-even point falls is dependent upon the product and supply system structure.

There are almost always hidden network supply costs associated with production, most are typically lost within the umbrella category of 'overheads'. Fundamentally, the cost of a product has five major components: materials, labour, gross profit, network supply and overhead. In more detail, there are eight major cost categories associated with network supply, each of which offers a significant opportunity for cost reduction:

1 *Forecasting, planning, scheduling and purchasing.* This area includes systems (equipment/software), staffing, information systems and internal, outbound and inbound communications.
2 *Inbound cost.* Freight, tax, tariffs, duties, losses and gains associated with variance, penalties and rebates, returns and inbound planning are included in this category.
3 *Receiving.* The main components here are equipment and labour.
4 *Inspection.* This area includes equipment and labour for incoming, in-process and final inspections.
5 *Warehousing.* Space, equipment and staffing for raw materials, work-in-process and finished goods are the primary costs in this area.
6 *Inventory.* Losses and damages as well as carrying and obsolescence costs are factored into inventory.
7 *Internal material movement.* This includes in-process losses and damages, equipment and staffing.
8 *Outbound cost.* Freight, tax, tariffs, duties, losses and gains associated with variance, penalties and rebates, returns and shipment planning are included in this category.

Analysing cost components

The hidden costs of network supply can amount to as much as 20 per cent of any supply situation. This can double when the hidden inflexibility costs of sourcing offshore are also taken into account (Lowson, 2001d; King and Hunter, 1997). The apparent advantages of cheaper offshore labour are belied by increased network supply and inflexibility costs that are often hidden and not easy to compute.

ANSWERS TO TIME OUT BOX

Time out box I

1   Many of the public services in the UK are free at the point of use. In other words, services such as education, water, roads and health care are, although some controversial exceptions exist, free when consumed. These services are all perceived as vitally important for society in general and their consumption is rising rapidly. Demand planning is difficult and has to ensure that significant inequalities and inefficiencies are avoided. The quality levels must be constant as must access to all groups of society, no matter the race, gender, age or income − often a difficult balancing act.

2   For The Gap, demand is also a big problem. The apparel business is hugely complex. It is, perhaps, the most demanding of sectors in which to satisfy demand − hundreds of colours, thousands of styles and sizes, and millions of SKUs on the retail shelves at any one time. In addition, the average shelf life of these merchandise items shorten with each passing year until we reach continuous fashion (seasons as short as 6–8 weeks). Further, customers increasingly seek an individual look.

   A couple of examples may help the reader to understand the complexity of the apparel business. Suppose sardines were to be offered in cans of a dozen or so sizes, in at least as many shapes, and 30–40 colours. Worse, every three to four months, the cans not sold would have to go into the sale because they are now out of style. That is not even close to the diversity and complexity of the clothing business.

   Forecasting in such a sector, especially long-term, is particularly inefficient. Retailers like The Gap have to rely upon operations strategies that ensure speed of response and flexibility. To do this, acute awareness of real time demand trends are vital.

3   KLM Airlines, like many other international carriers, try to maximize the capacity of aircraft. They charge multiple fares on single flights. This represents decisions made to hold seats until the last minute to attract full-fare business travellers, but at the same time allowing many seats to be purchased earlier by a cost conscious tourist traveller. Any empty seating before scheduled departure can also be sold at a bargain price to those passengers in a position to drop everything and fly. A degree of passenger demand forecasting is used, but often the complexity of multiple fare structures relies upon experienced and well-trained sales staff and controllers who will know the flight profiles and the types of demand likely to be placed.

4   For a producer of soft drinks like Robinsons Britvic, demand is highly seasonal in two ways. First, at certain times of year, such as Christmas, summer and Easter, demand will tend to increase. Second, demand in this industry is very much weather related. For example, normal weekly sales in April or May could quadruple due to an unusually hot spell. In countries like the UK, where weather patterns are unpredictable, forecasting such events is nearly impossible. Producers of such goods have to use other techniques and approaches to cope with demand.

DISCUSSION QUESTIONS, WORK ASSIGNMENTS AND EXAM QUESTIONS

1   Identify the four Cs for a bar of chocolate and a railway journey from Reykjavik to Oslo.
2   What is meant by dependent and independent demand and push and pull systems?
3   Are business cycles important for all organizations? Can examples be found where they are not?
4   Will strategies for managing demand become more important in the future for, say, an enterprise such as Amazon.com?
5   What are the main problems associated with long-term forecasting? In what industries might such activities be easier or harder?

Reader questions related to the 'perfect storm' case study

1   How would a better understanding of demand alleviate the perfect storm of markdowns (too much inventory) and stock-outs (too little inventory) and the need to operate using long-term forecasts? What are the factors of demand that are important in the manufacture and retail of clothing goods for sale in most high streets?
2   The case study describes the situation where retailers increasingly use foreign, offshore manufacturing suppliers for garments due to cheaper labour costs. These costs are, however, offset by the hidden costs of the supply network and inflexibility. Consider how these hidden costs might be quantified and what categories might be used to classify them.

RECOMMENDED READING

Makridakis S., Wheelwright S.C. and Hyndman R.J. (1998) *Forecasting: Methods and Applications*, John Wiley & Sons Inc., New York.

Lowson R.H. (2001d) 'Retail Sourcing Strategies: Are they Cost-effective', *International Journal of Logistics* 4, 3, 271–96.

Chapter 10

New research in understanding demand

The final chapter in this section concludes our examination of demand. Here we consider some of the latest research being conducted into the subject in order to assess its utility for organizations and their operations.

LEARNING OBJECTIVES

After considering this chapter, the reader will be able to:

■ Debate some new approaches to demand management

■ Offer comment on their worth for organizations and possibly suggest other fruitful avenues of exploration

> **KEY TERMS**
>
> - Shadow demand
> - Real time demand
> - LISP performance interactions
> - Complex adaptive systems
> - Typology

INTRODUCTION

As we saw in chapter 9, demand is neither easy to quantify or predict in today's organizational climate. This being so, perhaps new frameworks are needed that concentrate less on prediction and smoothing and more on detailed understanding of the complexities involved. This chapter discusses a few possible avenues of research that may bear fruit. There are of course others currently under examination, and the reader should remember that many are exploratory in nature. Nevertheless, it is wise to be aware of new advances.

DIRECTIONS OF DEMAND RESEARCH

Much of this research is highly exploratory and leading-edge. As such, it gives the reader an indication of the latest work in progress.

Shadow demand

Shadow demand describes the situation when demand is lost for a number of reasons – in other words, what happens when customers learn that the products or services requested are not available. Often known as 'stock-outs', these situations are surprisingly common. Most firms will measure their order fill rate, that is the percentage of orders that are properly met (85–90 per cent is deemed to be good). However, many of these systems fail to recognize earlier customer decisions. These include the various choices made once informed an item is out of stock. Once this shadow demand is included, these order fill rates look far less satisfactory.

Upon being told a product is unavailable, a customer will typically make one of three choices:

1 Accept a later delivery date when in stock (a *backorder*);
2 Substitute another item; or
3 Leave the purchase situation.

What happens next to this demand is little understood. In Fig. 10.1 we highlight the possibilities.

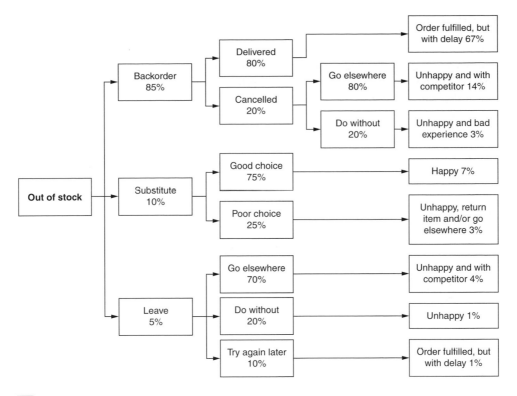

Figure 10.1 *Shadow demand*

We can see that upon encountering a product or service that is out of stock customers exercise three options: backorder (85 per cent), substitute (10 per cent) leave (5 per cent). We can now examine the outcome in terms of customer satisfaction:

1 *Backorder.* Of those choosing to wait, 20 per cent will eventually cancel and either go elsewhere or do without – in either case, this results in lost sales and unhappy consumers with a bad experience of trading with the firm. The remaining consumers are reasonably happy but encountered delays (67 per cent).

2 *Substitute.* Some of those accepting a substitute service or product will be happy (7 per cent). However, 25 per cent will not, and will be unhappy with the firm, themselves and the whole experience. They are also highly likely to go to a competitor.

3 *Leave.* Consumers leaving the purchasing experience will go elsewhere and use another supplier, do without and be totally disaffected, or try again later. The latter may lead to an order finally being fulfilled, but at a cost in terms of customer experience. In the right-hand side boxes we see the overall percentage for the final outcome. It is clear that there are very few possibilities that leave the customer happy with the overall encounter. Add to this the loss of customer loyalty and the damage to reputation from word of mouth communication, and we can see that shadow demand is very important.

199

Real time and surrogate demand

Many organizations now adopt operations strategies that can respond to known, real time demand. Strategies such as QR, time-based competition, agile operations, just in time and strategic postponement will all endeavour to promote a fast, flexible and agile response to known demand. Working to known demand has the advantage of avoiding the guesswork involved in forecasting. This allows accurate delivery of the product and service combinations that are known to be required. In so doing, the enterprise avoids unnecessary duplication of activity and waste.

TIME OUT BOX I

What are the disadvantages involved in trying to operate to real time demand?

Customer demand can also be viewed not as a monolithic concept but rather as consisting of two parts – namely, direct and indirect, or surrogate, demand. A surrogate can be thought of as 'one appointed to act for another'. Total demand would therefore be equal to direct plus surrogate demand. When a customer buys a kilo of potatoes in the supermarket, that is direct demand as there is no surrogate or third party involved in the transaction. On the other hand, when the customer employs an architect for an addition to the home, it is the architect that then determines the amount and direction of spending.

With the advent of technology and the Internet, the individual customer is relying increasingly upon surrogates of one kind or another. In a similar way to direct and indirect demand (chapter 9), the organization must take into account surrogate demand and its complexity – a result of the demand source being further removed from the organization finally satisfying its implications.

LISP performance interactions

In chapter 8 (p. 172) we examined the life cycle of the operations strategy. We noted that research had shown three main influences involved in shaping the strategy:

1　Those associated with the demands of the product or product group (78 per cent);
2　Those associated with the structural demands of the supply system (74 per cent); and
3　Those associated with the performance of certain metrics within that supply system (66 per cent).

Categories (1) and (2) were dealt with in chapter 8 under deployment and customization of the operations strategy. We will now expand upon supply system performance as a demand influence.

Linking all operations to real-time demand is a major strategic objective for many organizations. However, as explained above, it is far from easy to achieve and requires a fully synchronized supply network in which information is shared openly and all firms act in unison. To achieve this, the performance of the supply system must be examined as a whole; in other words, a network focus upon the interactions and relationships rather than just the objects or enterprises. We can now explore how different types of demand behaviour and performance in the supply system can all be used to tailor an organization's operations strategy to real time demand understanding. To do this we will use an extended case study.

CASE STUDY – OPERATIONS STRATEGY IN ACTION

Rosebud – new research in understanding demand

Rosebud is a medium-sized, niche, high street operation trading under two brand names. It supplies high quality, fashionable apparel, with both men's and women's ranges, aimed at the 20–30-year-old consumer. It has outlets in most North American and European cities. The various garments it supplies can be classed as:

- Basic (generally sold all year round with infrequent changes);
- Seasonal (shelf life of, say, 12 to 25 weeks);
- Short-season (shelf life of 6 to 10 weeks or less).

Rosebud were attempting to introduce three operations strategies (for each of the garment classifications above) that could be tailored to the demands of its main produce classifications. As we saw from Omicron Foods in chapter 5, more than one operations strategy may be needed for main product groups. To do this, senior managers knew that they had to carefully analyse three interconnected elements:

1 The customer demands placed upon the organization (product demand behaviour);
2 The structure of the responding supply system (supply system behaviour);
3 The performance of the supply system (supply system performance metrics).

It chose three products that were representative of this generic garment classification: a short-season product (women's styled summer shirts), a seasonal garment (women's denim jeans) and a basic item (women's underwear). We now follow the work of Rosebud's management team.

As we know from chapter 5, there are a number of building blocks that might comprise an operations strategy in the retail sector. Table 10.1 shows the full range of components for Rosebud's retail supply system.

Rosebud ranked the various building blocks of its operations strategy against the product groups. This is done by analysing the product group demand behaviour (discussed in chapter 6) to provide a score reflecting their importance. The results were:

- In the totals row, an individual score for each product group reflects the overall importance of an operations strategy to that group (333, 174 and 69) and the

Table 10.1 *Rosebud's operations strategy building blocks by product group demand behaviour*

Operations strategy building blocks	Product group demand behaviour			Component weighting bands (Max. 60)
	Women's styled summer shirts (Max. 20) (SS)*	Women's denim jeans (Max. 20) (S)*	Women's underwear (Max. 20) (B)*	
1 Shared strategic operations planning with major customers and suppliers	17	12	6	35
2 Joint product and merchandise planning with customers and suppliers	19	10	0	29
3 Bar coded merchandise	20	11	7	38
4 Small orders and batch sizes (both pre- and during a sales season)	20	14	5	39
5 Product data and information sharing with trading partners	17	9	3	29
6 Use of Electronic Data Interchange (EDI)	19	10	4	33
7 Sales captured at item level	19	9	3	31
8 Continual and automatic replenishment systems	16	8	2	26
9 Universal Product Codes (UPC) in the supply system	19	7	1	27
10 Electronic reorder	19	8	4	31
11 Store ready deliveries	10	7	2	19
12 Shared and open inventory management systems	9	7	2	18
13 Intelligent production and cellular manufacturing	11	5	0	15
14 Fast re-estimation and reorder systems	14	7	2	23
15 Container shipping codes	10	5	3	18
16 Point of Sale (PoS) data sharing with customers and suppliers	17	7	4	28
17 Consumer demographic information systems	7	1	0	8
18 Internet connectivity	8	5	4	16
19 New logistics systems	14	8	3	25

No.	Activity	Product group demand behaviour. Max. score 480	Product group demand behaviour. Max. score 480	Product group demand behaviour. Max. score 480	Customised operations strategy architecture. Max. score 1440
20	Compressing 'Open-to-buy' dates	5	0	1	6
21	Reducing pre-season delivery	4	3	2	9
22	Virtual product development	7	1	1	9
23	Postponement of activities	14	7	2	22
24	Interface management and supply system visibility	18	13	7	38
	Totals	**333**	**174**	**68**	**575**

These three columns demonstrate the importance of the operations strategy fusion by product class behaviour

This column demonstrates a unique operations strategy architecture linked to the identified demand behaviour pattern for the group

* SS = Short season, S = Seasonal, B = Basic

necessary component emphasis. For example, high scoring elements (numbers 2, 3, 4, 6, 7, 10 and 24) should receive greatest emphasis and will become higher order strategic themes which are linked and integrated through other clusters of tightly linked activities. In a similar fashion, Rosebud can then continue to categorize the components of its strategy according to their weighting.

- The final column gives an overall component weighting across a number of product groups that reflects the strategic elements of most importance to the firm.
- With this knowledge, any subsequent operations strategy adopted by Rosebud will reflect different emphases for each product and supplier either by individual product group or across a range of goods.

This approach can also be used at subgroup or even individual product level. For example, the analysis completed by Rosebud for various styles of women's top could equally well be applied to size and colour characteristics (i.e. at SKU level).

Rosebud also conducted a similar analysis of their supply system behaviour (again covered in chapter 6) that also led to a second set of scores.

In addition to the influences of product demand behaviour and supply system behaviour Rosebud were convinced that a third factor was important in developing an operations strategy customized to demand: supply system performance metrics. They were concerned to understand how factors such as lead time, inventory, consumer service level and vendor performance might influence the use of certain building blocks in an operations strategy. To appreciate the underlying impact of these performance measures the LISP interactions were used (introduced in chapter 8, Fig. 8.7). To reiterate, these involve:

- **L**ead time for supply;
- **I**nventory at a particular supply pipeline stage;
- Customer **S**ervice level;
- Supplier **P**erformance, this involves two factors: supplier service level and supplier process time (in this retail case, to provide finished goods in the form of clothing for retail sale).

The LISP interactions allowed Rosebud to undertake a three-dimensional analysis of various supply system variables. It is important to remember that they were looking at a method to quantify the performance of each of the variables:

- Lead time;
- Supplier service level;
- Supplier process time.

Each in a relationship with:

- Customer service level;
- Inventory for retail finished goods levels.

We are not just dealing with individual and isolated measures of performance (for lead time, for example). Fig. 10.2 portrays this more graphically.[2]

These interactions, chosen by Rosebud, were considered in the following format for the three product groups:

- *Case 1*. An interaction between lead time (dependent variable a) and customer service level and inventory (independent variables);
- *Case 2*. An interaction between vendor supplier level (dependent variable b) and customer service level and inventory (independent variables);
- *Case 3*. An interaction between supplier process time (dependent variable c) and customer service level and Inventory (independent variables).

These supply system performance metrics were important because when combined with product and supply system behaviours, they would allow the retailer to better understand demand and cope with uncertainty.

For Rosebud, uncertainty comes from many sources. In particular they identified the following main causes:

- Inability to forecast customer demand;
- Complexity in the manufacturing supply process;
- Primary and secondary tier manufacturer reliability/quality (especially offshore);
- Logistical system reliability;
- Inaccuracies in PoS data or bar codes.

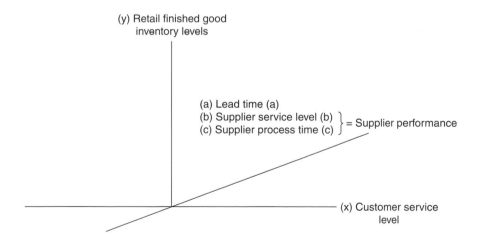

Figure 10.2 *LISP variables in three-dimensional format*

---

2 This approach can also be portrayed in a topological, finite 'phase space' portrait, (Jules-Henri Poincaré is generally credited with this mathematical concept and there are many applications, including Holmström and Hameri, 1999).

Fisher (1997) points out that speed and flexibility of the supply system can help overcome the impact of uncertainty, but typically at a cost. For the retailer there are a number of relationships that can be used to assess performance. In the next three figures we will demonstrate how Rosebud quantified these LISP relationships.

First, Fig. 10.3 examines how customer service level is related to retail store inventory for short, medium and long order and reorder lead time performance.

Rosebud adopt a quantitative measure for lead time performance, whether long (1–50 per cent) medium (51–80 per cent) or short (81–100 per cent). They were then able to plot the LISP relationships for each of the lead time performance profiles. For example, at 25 per cent along the lead time contour, Rosebud's finished goods inventory levels are likely to be relatively high (the aim being to decrease them to a holding level matching real time customer demand), and customer service levels low (line $a - a$). In the medium range, at performance point 75 per cent, the reduction in lead times would have a proportionate effect upon customer service levels and inventory (line $b - b$). With much shorter lead time (say, performance point 90 per cent) we can see that again customer service level and retail finished goods inventory levels for Rosebud improves (line $c - c$). However, in real life things are not always this simple. These relationships will not always be linear, that is, continual improvement in lead time will not continue to provide similar sized improvements in customer service and inventory statistics (Hunter *et al.*, 2001). As shown in Fig. 10.4, an optimum point for improvement will often be reached. After that, further reductions in lead time for Rosebud between the performance points 90 per cent and 100 per cent, although bringing commensurate increases in customer service, will be at the expense of slightly increasing finished goods inventory needed to support an improvement in the other variables. Thus, for Rosebud, the first lesson learnt was that operational improvement is to some degree a matter of moving between curves, rather than along them.

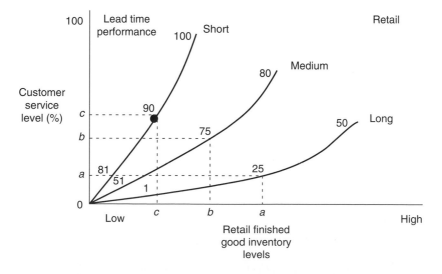

Figure 10.3 *The relationship between customer service level and inventory for lead time performance*

Rosebud now undertook a similar analysis for the relationship between customer service levels and retail finished goods inventory for high, medium and low supplier service performance (see Fig. 10.4).

The interactions in Fig. 10.4 are the first element (supplier service level) in an examination of supplier performance. These demonstrate the effect of Rosebud increasing supplier service level from low or medium to high. There are subsequent improvements upon both finished goods inventory at store level (a reduction) and customer service level. However, there will again be a critical point after which further improvement in supplier service level will be at the expense of increasing Rosebud's inventory levels over and above what is needed to satisfy customer demand.

The final LISP example is shown in Fig. 10.5. This is the relationship between customer service level and inventory of finished goods for low, medium and high vendor process time.

This is the second element of supplier performance (process time). In this scenario, as the process times improve we see a related reduction in Rosebud inventory levels and an increase in customer service until the watershed point. Thereafter, a continued reduction in process time will eventually start to drive up finished goods inventory in order to ensure satisfaction of forecast customer demand requirements. We then have a situation whereby the supply system is using buffer inventory, as the process time is so short that Rosebud is over-stocked. The above analysis could be performed equally well for a supplier rather than a retailer, and could be focused up or downstream. However, further research is required for all the LISP interactions to better understand and quantify this break-even or watershed point.

Rosebud could now use the results of the analysis into supply system performance metrics in a similar fashion to those for the product demand behaviour and supply system behaviour. Table 10.2 shows the ranking given by Rosebud for supply system performance metrics

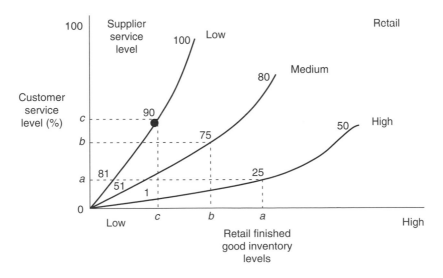

Figure 10.4 *The relationship between customer service level and inventory for supplier service level*

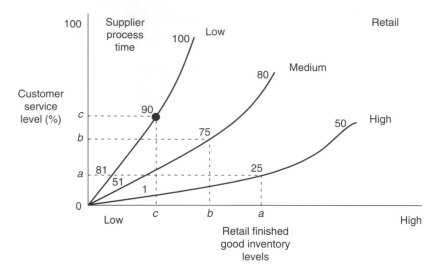

Figure 10.5 *The relationship between customer service level and inventory for supplier process time*

(lead time, supplier service level and supplier process time) against a sample of the various operations strategy building blocks.

A moment's explanation is in order. Table 10.2 uses only four operations strategy components as an example. As before, each is ranked against a product group (although the analysis could again be at individual product level as well). For each product group, a weighting (out of thirty) was applied by Rosebud to reflect the influence of the three dimensional supply system performance variables (lead time performance, supplier service level and supplier process time).

We can now see how Rosebud used all these various factors:

- The customer demands placed upon the organization (product demand behaviour),
- The structure of the responding supply system (supply system behaviour),
- The performance of the supply system (supply system performance metrics)

in order to shape and customize their operations strategies to demand.

Table 10.3 demonstrates how this process was undertaken using just four elements of any possible operations strategy as an example. We should remember that in practice there will be many more, and that Rosebud was hoping to devise three operations strategies.

The retailer scored out of a maximum of thirty each of the operations strategy components against the product demand behaviour (P) and supply system behaviour (S). The supply system performance metrics (M – the LISP interactions) were also scored from a maximum of ninety. This gave a subtotal for each component in each product group (**T**) that indicates the importance of that element for any operations strategy. In the right hand column (component weighting bands), the importance of the component across a number of product groups (that may be provided by the same supplier, for example) can also be assessed and

Table 10.2 Rosebud's operations strategy components by supply system performance metrics

Operations strategy components	Supply system performance metrics									Component weighting bands (Max. 270)
	Styled summer blouses (SS)*			Women's denim jeans (S)*			Women's underwear (B)*			
	LT**	SSL**	SPT**	LT	SSL	SPT	LT	SSL	SPT	
Store ready deliveries	24	25	20	17	22	19	10	9	8	154
Compressing 'Open-to-buy' dates	20	17	15	14	12	12	9	7	4	110
Internet connectivity	12	17	10	11	9	6	4	6	2	77
Intelligent production and cellular manufacturing	9	7	19	5	6	14	2	5	7	74
Totals	**65**	**66**	**64**	**47**	**49**	**51**	**25**	**27**	**21**	**415**

* SS = Short season, S = Seasonal, B = Basic

** LT = Lead time performance, SSL = Supplier service level, SPT = Supplier process time

Table 10.3 Rosebud's operations strategy composition

Example operations strategy components	Operations strategy composition summary												Component weighting bands (Max. 450)
	Styled summer blouses (SS)*				Women's denim jeans (S)*				Women's underwear (B)*				
	P**	S**	M**	T**	P	S	M	T	P	S	M	T	
Fast re-estimation and reorder systems	27	24	78	129	19	14	39	72	16	12	33	61	262
Shared and open inventory management systems	24	20	45	89	7	12	36	55	10	9	25	44	188
Container shipping codes	20	17	32	69	13	10	34	57	7	5	12	24	150
Consumer demographic information systems	14	10	24	48	9	7	21	37	5	3	10	18	103
Totals	85	71	179	335	48	43	130	221	38	29	80	147	703

* SS = Short season, S = Seasonal, B = Basic

** P = Product group demand behaviour (= Max. 30), S = Supply system behaviour (= Max. 30), M = LISP supply system performance metrics (Lead time, supplier service level and supplier process time = Max. 90), T = Subtotal for product group (= Max. 150) scored from a maximum possible of 450. Finally, in the total row at the bottom of the table we can see the individual influences of demand behaviour etc., upon all the possible components in an operations strategy.

For Rosebud, the outcome of this work has brought two fundamental benefits. First, they have been able to develop three operations strategies, one for each major product group. Second, their understanding of product demand behaviour, supply system behaviour and supply system performance (through the LISP interactions) has ensured that these strategies are composed of the most important elements or components for that product group. Further, the resultant operations strategy takes full account of demand and is customized to the performance of each supply system.

Complex adaptive systems – Part 2

The research directions described above hint at the complexity of supply systems. As mentioned in chapter 2, the systemic organizational model of inputs, transformation and outputs may be rather simplistic. In its place, many academics are now exploring the concept of organizations being complex adaptive systems as we introduced in chapter 2 (see for example Lowson *et al.*, 1999; Marion, 1999; Stacey *et al.*, 2000; and Homstrom and Hameri, 1999). This has fundamental implications for demand knowledge and management.

Complexity when applied to organizations is a recognition of non-linearity. The behaviour of an organizational system is to a degree deterministic (if we set out to produce cans of beans we will not get cars) and falls within certain wide boundaries. However, such behaviour is non-linear, it never repeats itself exactly (we cannot predict with any accuracy that each can will have exactly the same number of beans week after week). Traditionally, enterprises were analysed as though they were linear systems (plotted on a graph using a straight line). We thought of a factory as a linear system with certain inputs, transformations and predicted outputs: the system is deterministic (and one in which forecasting is both possible and accurate). In actuality, a factory is non-linear, as with most systems in nature, and outputs are not easy to predict using straight lines on graphs. This is the reason why the use of performance indicators and benchmarking is much more haphazard than many textbooks would have us believe.

Science has for centuries been divided between those who believe that the universe is a coherent whole, having a large number of subsystems all cooperating to achieve some greater result in accordance with a predetermined plan. At the other extreme, there are the atomists who place their faith in a world that is nothing more than atoms in a void with no overall long-term plan. These ideologies fall within the opposing camps of holism and reductionism respectively.

Complexity theory, in fact, demonstrates that both viewpoints are valid, dependent upon the level of analysis. All systems have different properties and varying degrees of unpredictability and determinism that alter in line with the viewpoint: classical or quantum. Once the dynamics of complex systems are examined, it becomes clear that awareness of their initial condition will not help prediction of the final outcomes: determinism. For example, the input of raw materials, energy and people into the factory system will not always guarantee the output of goods in the right quantity or quality.

Orderly determinism with perfect knowledge of outcomes was the foundation of traditional or classical science as propounded by such people as Isaac Newton. Unfortunately, at a certain level, systems fail to comply with the Newtonian viewpoint because they are:

- *Non-linear*. There is synergy; the whole is worth more than the sum of the parts.
- *Large in numbers of components*. Complex systems are more than just complicated versions of simple systems. They have identities of their own and their many elements have high degrees of freedom.
- *Open*. Complex systems are open to environmental influence and the driving forces contained therein and produce a 'rich' behaviour.
- *Unpredictable*. Complexity appears abruptly with little warning and does not slowly evolve. It is aperiodic.

All systems, whether they are work systems or weather systems, have complex or chaotic elements, and even the simplest displays a mixture of chaos and order to varying degrees. In the past, scientists have ignored the elements of complexity as merely background noise, a random element that had no part of the system under study; not appreciating that it did, in fact, constitute *the* system and without it, the system would cease to exist. In fact, we need to think about these systems as complex and chaotic but not actually random – there is a pattern.

Closely associated with complexity is the butterfly effect or more technically *sensitive dependence on initial conditions*. The concept means that with a complex, non-linear system, infinitely small changes in the starting conditions of the system will result in dramatically different outputs for that system in the future. If we cannot take into account the action of a butterfly flapping its wings in Montreal in our weather predictions, then we will fail to predict a thunderstorm in Norwich two weeks from now because of this dynamic. Small errors in the quality of inputs to a complex system can lead to dramatic and unforeseen consequences.

CASE VIGNETTE **THE CHALLENGER**

Perhaps one of the most regrettable examples of this was the loss of the space shuttle Challenger on 28 January 1986. A relatively small quality defect involving rubber seals, coupled with a series of poor management decisions driven by a need for NASA publicity, led to an enormous consequential loss of lives and dollars.

Changes and uncertainties multiply, cascading upward through a chain of turbulent features, from dust devils and squalls to eddies the size of continents. Even if computerized sensors were to be placed a foot apart over the whole earth, and then rising at foot high intervals into the atmosphere, it would still not be possible to predict with any certainty the weather in Seattle in six hours time. The spaces between the sensors would still hide minute fluctuations; these small errors would continuously grow and magnify across the globe.

Complex systems contain order and disorder, form and chaos, complexity in apparent simplicity, simplicity in apparent complexity, and regular irregularity. What then of management and business?

Organizations are complex systems; they are unpredictable and indeterministic to varying degrees and contain many 'soft' elements. Strategies are often emergent. Controls need to be simultaneously loose–tight. Performance measurement and evaluation is notoriously difficult. Forecasting is fraught with error. Functions require a degree of differentiation in order to interact properly with a corresponding subset of the environment. Complexity and difference between departments thus needs integrative devices.

Uncertainty in markets and demand leads to increased transaction cost. Excessive hierarchy in the business structure brings confusion. Highly diversified companies have control predicaments. Organizational visions and mission statements rarely convert perfectly into practice.

Organizations are open systems with little consensus as to the meaning and significance of their own constituents. Complexity and unpredictability are unavoidable and in fact, like noise, should not be ignored or removed as they are probably the very essence of the system wherein the potential lies for competitive advantage. Order and chaos are reciprocal, with both elements present in any management situation.

A fascinating application of the principles of chaos and the use of information is to be found in Levy (1992). The search for artificial life provides a pertinent example, one highly applicable to organizations and their supply pipelines. Living systems are typified by the degree to which information can move freely or be retained. If the value (dynamical state) is low, this represents a regime in which information is frozen. It can easily be retained through time, but cannot move. If the value is very high, then information moves very freely and chaotically and is difficult to retain. On the other hand, there is a certain area where information changes but not so rapidly that it loses all connection to where it had just been previously: it is this regime that supports the kind of complexity that is the mark of living systems.

The reader will no doubt be struck by the immediate comparison between the above and supply networks. Complexity is essential, but a proper degree of complexity that allows it to:

> Spit in the face of entropy – hung on a cliff side. On a precipice to its left is a barren regime where not enough information could move; to its right was a swirling maelstrom where information moved so wildly that chaos ruled.
>
> (Levy, 1992)

For optimal operation, supply networks, and the companies that compose them, there is a need to operate 'On the edge of chaos . . . at the edge of a phase transition between desert and cyclone' (Levy 1992).

We can think of our enterprises as self-organizing systems. In other words, they are capable of self-organization and the spontaneous emergence of new structures. The

Russian-born chemist and physicist Ilya Prigogine described such systems as 'dissipative structures'. Being complex, non-linear, and unstable in a state far from equilibrium, the system reaches a critical point of instability when a new pattern emerges. In other words, the dissipation of energy (the second law of thermodynamics) is not necessarily associated with waste, but a source of new order. The structure not only maintains itself in a stable state, but is also capable of evolution. Prigogine (1997) showed that while dissipative structures received their energy from outside, the instabilities and jumps to new forms of organization were the result of fluctuations amplified by positive feedback or reinforcing loops. This amplifying, 'runaway' feedback, previously regarded as destructive in cybernetics, was a source of new order. He described these structures as:

> The state of a system far from equilibrium, that develops amplification processes through positive feedback loops giving it the appearance of instabilities which actually lead to the creation of new forms.

> (Prigogine, 1997)

This circular type of system is self-organizing as well as self-referring in the continual creation of new networks – something later to be called *autopoiesis*[3] (Maturana and Varela, 1980).

This new thinking regarding complex adaptive systems is now being applied to the study of organization. In the past, we assumed linearity and an input–transformation–output operation that was kept in balance using negative feedback loops. This is to a degree still valid; however, we now know that it is vastly oversimplistic. Our firms, as complex adaptive systems, have a capacity to self generate and are not totally dependent upon the environment – they demand as much from the environment as it demands of them. We also suspect that they are also much more dependent upon positive and self-amplifying feedback than was previously realized. This type of feedback is necessary for the system to adapt and evolve. In linear systems small changes produce small effects, and large effects are due to either large changes or to a sum of many small changes. In non-linear systems, by contrast, small changes may have dramatic effects because they are amplified repeatedly by this self-reinforcing, positive feedback (similar to the Forrester effect described in the Robinsons Britvic case vignette in chapter 9).

We can think of our commercial enterprises as being dynamically stable, (possessing both complex and chaotic as well as stable characteristics and existing at a point far from equilibrium – the edge of chaos), but able to drift over a fairly wide range of structures and behaviours without threatening relative stability. However, they are also capable of changing dramatically when needed. Some disturbances, whether internal or external in origin, and the continual build-up of amplifying, positive, runaway feedback, will push the system into a bifurcation point. Here, it will dramatically branch off in a different and unpredictable direction before settling down again into a new region and new source of order that maintains its dynamically stable structure – the system has evolved through dissipation into a new form of organization.

....

3 *Auto* meaning 'self' and *poiesis* which derives from the Greek for 'poetry' and means 'making' – self-making.

We can plot the trajectories that a complex system (a commercial organization for example) might go through using a visual mathematical technique called topology. The mathematician Jules Henri Poincaré first developed this approach at the turn of the twentieth century. The patterns of a complex system can be displayed in an abstract mathematical space called 'phase space'. Every variable of the system is associated with a different coordinate in this abstract space. For example, to describe a pendulum motion correctly we would need variables: angle of swing (positive and negative) and velocity (again, positive or negative). With these two variables we can depict the motion of the pendulum completely at any moment in time. Using horizontal and vertical axis in a cross-hair graph we can mark points of angle and velocity – this will generally form an ellipse as the pendulums trajectory in phase space (see Fig. 10.6).

In this picture a single point describes the entire system in terms of angle and velocity. In this example, there are only two variables. Some systems can be described by many more – we could, say, have sixteen variables and a sixteen-dimensional phase space.

In this ideal example, the pendulum continues swinging without change; there is no friction to slow it down. Without intervention, however, the pendulum would eventually come to a halt. We can plot this in the same way as Fig. 10.6, but instead of an ellipse the picture would be one of a line spiralling towards the centre as eventually velocity and angle reach zero. This trajectory is called a point attractor, as the system's trajectory is drawn towards a final resting point. By contrast, the closed loop, frictionless trajectory is a period attractor. Point attractors correspond to systems reaching a stable equilibrium; period attractors correspond to periodic oscillations. We also have strange attractors. In this instance the trajectory we plot for these systems never repeats itself exactly, each cycle covers a new region of phase space. However, they are not entirely random, there is a complex, highly organized pattern that almost repeats itself, but not quite. The system is always within certain boundaries (it is deterministic, in the UK we probably will not get six feet of snow in summer) but we can never forecast weather accurately (a non-linear system – we cannot be sure exactly what weather we will get next summer).

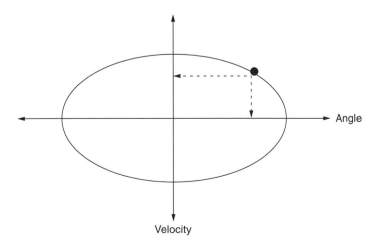

Figure 10.6 *Trajectory of a pendulum in phase space*

Many now believe these systems describe the complexity of our modern organizations. Because of dynamic instability, the system being far from equilibrium and *sensitive dependence on initial conditions*, minute changes in the initial state will lead over time to large-scale consequences. Add to this the continual amplification of positive feedback loops and we can see that organizations are in fact, over time, structurally unstable and have critical points of instability (bifurcation points) when the system is capable of branching off in a new direction (evolution). Accurate predications are only possible regarding the qualitative features of the systems behaviour, rather than seeking to quantify the precise values of its many variables at any given time.

It is instructive to think of organizations as existing in a complex environment as described above. The demands they face for their product and service combinations will also increasingly fall into these categories.

Other areas of research potential

Finally, we provide a brief literature review of some other new areas of research in connection with demand understanding.

The value stream

The value stream is a wider concept than the supply chain and closely related to the value chains (see Porter, 1985, ch. 1). In essence, it describes the combination of actions that are required to add and deliver value to the consumer. In Hines *et al*. (2000) some interesting research reported a two and three-dimensional view of supply or value chain dynamics. Using geographic analogies, the authors demonstrate the complexity of parallel value streams. Using a systems dynamics framework, they show the flow of information and physical return of products with beach and wave comparisons. The descriptions of supply chain dynamics and the influences of push and pull demand add new conceptual understanding. However, their findings in support of generalization and validity in a wider population are less persuasive.

The whole area of value stream mapping is further considered and seven value stream mapping tools introduced in Hines and Rich (1998). These incorporate an analysis of process activities, response, variety, mapping for quality, demand amplification, decision points and physical structure. The research offers an improved methodology for the application of lean thinking (see chapter 4) and some fundamental lessons for the management of a value stream.

CONCLUSION

The chapter concludes Part II of the book. The reader is now armed with the necessary knowledge concerning operational management, operations strategy and the nature of demand, to apply these lessons to the many firms that comprise the business and commercial sectors. In Part III we will examine how particular organizations develop and deploy operations strategies in these domains.

ANSWERS TO TIME OUT BOX

Time out box I

Identifying what is being demanded and then reacting to it is not as easy as it might at first sound. In providing a service, a firm can, to a degree, often produce that service when it is demanded. For example, a haircut or a meal. However, even here we need to ensure raw materials and capacity are available. When it comes to more tangible goods there are a number of problems. Obviously, some firms can make to order, especially highly customized one-off products such as providing a new airplane or office block. When it comes to goods that are more homogeneous, such as clothes or groceries, then there are problems. Waiting until demand is known before producing some of these items involves a very fast and flexible response. To achieve this, there must be a high level of information flow and cooperation in the supply pipeline. This will allow some goods to be replenished as sold (linking manufacturing activity to the sale of products) and a more accurate re-estimation and reorder as sales trends become clear. Some stocks will always be needed, however, but operating to real-time demand drastically reduces these and allows the enterprise to mirror demand in the activities it performs.

DISCUSSION QUESTIONS, WORK ASSIGNMENTS AND EXAM QUESTIONS

1   Why is demand understanding becoming more problematic for many organizations?
2   How will an understanding of complexity help firms in the future?
3   In what ways can we measure value?

Reader questions related to Rosebud case study

1   Use the basic LISP interactions to compare the supply system of an automotive manufacturer with a grocery retailer.

RECOMMENDED READING

Priesmeyer H.R. (1992) *Organizations and Chaos: Defining the Methods of Nonlinear Management*, Quorum Books, Westport, CT.

Applications

There are no such things as applied sciences, only applications of science.

Louis Pasteur

Part III examines the application of an operations strategy. The first ten chapters have prepared the reader for this point. Having discussed the nature of an operations strategy, and its role, advantages, customization possibilities and deployment, the next task is to consider how the strategy can be applied in an organizational setting. At the very beginning we spoke of the need for strategies to recognize the contingency of the situation. Research has led us to the belief that every operations strategy is, to a degree, unique and customized to its situation. Thus, unlike many management books we must recognize this axiom and not be tempted to discuss the strategy as if it applied, equally well, to each and every organizational domain. Although, for the purposes of this text, we cannot afford the luxury of working totally at an individual firm level, we can use specific firm examples within certain segments of the organizational population.

Bearing the above in mind, Part III will discuss operations strategy applications in four distinct sectors: retail and manufacturing applications (chapter 11); small and medium-sized enterprises (SMEs) and the service sector (chapter 12); global and supply network applications (chapter 13); and finally, e-business and strategic coordination settings (chapter 14). We consider what essential differences an operations strategy might exhibit in each of these environments, as well as the unique benefits that such a strategy might bring.

Operations strategy
Retail and manufacturing applications

Chapter 11 is set in the world of consumer goods retailing and manufacturing. A turbulent and complex domain, with much waste due to stock-outs (too little inventory of the right type) and markdowns (too much inventory that no-one wants). In this chapter we will examine the unique operations strategies necessary for the demands witnessed. To do so, we again use the notion of core building blocks as a framework for analysis.

LEARNING OBJECTIVES

After considering this chapter, the reader will be able to:

- Have an appreciation of the problems associated with these particular sectors
- Understand the key building blocks of retail and manufacturing operations strategies
- Discuss the formulation of manufacturing and retailing strategies
- Appreciate the competitive advantage accruing from a manufacturing and retailing operations strategy

> **KEY TERMS**
>
> ■ Strategic triangle
> ■ Filtration process
> ■ Building blocks of operations strategy
> ■ Formulating a strategy
> ■ Strategic frameworks for manufacturing
> ■ Competitive advantage

INTRODUCTION

Market leaderships can be achieved in one of three ways: through product leadership, customer intimacy, or through operational excellence (Treacy and Wiersema, 1997). It is the latter element that forms the key focus of this chapter.

The essence of any strategy was described by Kenichi Ohmae (1982) as a focus upon customers, competitors and the company itself – the three components he called a strategic triangle. In other words, the strategy must:

■ Fit the existing and potential environment. Addressing the needs of customers, the capabilities of customers and the anticipated change in response likely to be needed;

■ Provide a linkage mechanism for key organizational partners in a supply or wider mutual network;

■ Incorporate the activities of all major line functions of the firm;

■ Extend into staff activities, so that individuals can clearly visualize how their activities contribute to wider aims;

■ Specify the performance required to achieve strategic aims;

■ Promote a culture of continual improvement and development of both activities and strategic aims.

This rather rational view of strategy aims to keep the firm, its customers and its competitors in clear focus, while at the same time incorporating the need for resources, including supply partners, that are continually undergoing change. All of these elements form part of the strategy and each are subject to certain current and future performance objectives. Chapter 11 now examines the more practical applications of an operations strategy for consumer goods retailing and manufacturing.

The unique and individual nature of an operations strategy can be seen in Fig. 11.1.

As we have seen, organizations will utilize one or more operations strategies. These strategies are composed of a long-term pattern or cluster of strategic decisions made regarding the generic building blocks:

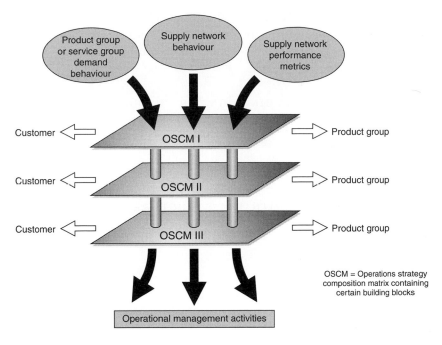

Figure 11.1 *Operations strategy filtration process*

■ *Core competencies, capabilities and processes.* These are (a) process based (derived from transformation activities), (b) system or coordination-based (across the entire operation system), (c) organization-based (across the entire organization), and (d) network-based (covering the whole supply network);

■ *Resources.* These depend upon the industry and the firm, but can be thought of at two levels: individual resources of the firm (capital equipment, skills, brands and so on); and the way they work together to create competitive advantage. Given the individuality of a resource-based strategy, for our purposes we will have to think of resources as being: (a) tangible (physical, technologies and financial, etc.); (b) intangible (communication and information systems, reputation, culture, brands, and so on); and (c) human (specialized skills and knowledge, communication and interaction, motivation and so on).

■ *Technologies.* In addition to being a resource used in the general sense (equipment, etc.), technology will have an increasingly important role to play as it also includes core technological know-how in product and process innovation across the whole organization and its supply network); and,

■ *Tactical activities.* Key activities that are vital in order to support a particular strategy or positioning. The continuation of certain core tactical activities will be vital to sustain a particular operations strategy or business positioning.

These various components may be similar across a number of operational situations. At this level we have only a collection of components, however their strategic nature, and inherent competitive advantage, comes from the unique way in which they are customized. As can be seen in the diagram, there are a number of distinct flows or driving influences that filter through the operations strategies composition matrices I, II and III that contain the building blocks. These flows include:

PRODUCT AND SERVICE COMBINATION (OR PRODUCT AND SERVICE GROUP) DEMAND BEHAVIOUR

- Product attributes;
- Demand patterns;
- Customer behaviour.

INFLUENCES ASSOCIATED WITH THE STRUCTURE OF THE SUPPLY NETWORK

- Product stream value flows;
- Vertical integration;
- Individual firm's sizes and power.

INFLUENCES ASSOCIATED WITH PERFORMANCE METRICS WITHIN THE SUPPLY SYSTEM

These are the three-dimensional LISP interactions we encountered in chapters 8 and 10:

- **L**ead time for supply;
- **I**nventory at a particular supply pipeline stage;
- Customer **S**ervice level;
- Supplier **P**erformance, this involves two factors: supplier service level and supplier process time (to convert raw materials or components into finished goods and services).

The three streams in Fig. 11.1 act as a shaping mechanism for each operations strategy composition matrix and will determine not only the elements in the matrix but their unique fusion, that is, which of the various components are higher order strategic themes and which are less important. The influential streams will also dictate they way in which all the elements in the OSCM are interconnected in various relationships.

Finally, we reach the situation whereby the organization has developed an operations strategy composition matrix that is customized by individual consumer group and/or product and service combination. From this, we can also develop the operational management activities necessary to support that particular strategic focus.

RETAIL OPERATIONS STRATEGIES

As we have seen from the filtration diagram, the essential architecture of an operations strategy will vary, to some degree, from industry to industry and even firm to firm. For retail operation there is an undoubted emphasis upon communication due to the complexity and volatility of the products being offered.

CASE VIGNETTE **WAL-MART**

Wal-Mart Stores are the dominant discount retailer in the US, and now making inroads in Europe through ownership of Asda Stores. They began life in 1972 as a small rural chain operating thirty stores in Arkansas, Missouri and Oklahoma. Steady expansion and an unwavering operations strategy has been based upon two key components: the use of technology and information to track sales and coordinate replenishment along the entire supply pipeline.

However, technology alone was not sufficient, as Wal-Mart's competitors soon discovered. Of equal importance was the establishment of proper information system procedures to ensure that the data used was accurate, relevant and timely (the technology was only a facilitator). This involved careful data and information system analysis as well as a considerable amount of skills training for staff. These were the difficult areas for competitors to replicate and the subsequent scanning, product procurement and inventory control systems provided substantial competitive advantage through a unique and customized operations strategy.

In addition, Wal-Mart also successfully employed a location advantage. In the early stages of development they deliberately chose rural locations so as not to compete head-to-head with larger competitors. Only when they had perfected their operations strategy could they move to more urban areas.

Finally, in developing this operational system, they placed much emphasis upon other important building blocks: a culture of supporting values, skills, technologies, supplier–consumer relationships, human resources, and approaches to motivation that were all difficult to replicate by the competition.

Most large multiple retailers will tend to construct operations strategies that differentiate them from the competition. These can include, for example, sophisticated information communication systems to manage the flow of products from manufacturing suppliers via distribution centres and warehouses to stores.

From the Wal-Mart case study we can see how a retailer can develop an operations strategy from particular 'buildings blocks' (in the composition matrix previously described in chapters 5 and 6).

Retail operations strategy building blocks

Using the Wal-Mart case we can now analyse and identify some of the components of their operations strategy composition. As seen above, these include a number of decisions on certain strategic building blocks as follows.

Core competencies, capabilities and processes

There are four kinds.

1   *Process-based capabilities* (the transformation activities). In Wal-Mart's case, these are the activities that transform information received to provide advantages such as low cost, responsiveness, speed, flexibility and high quality produce.
2   *System or coordination-based capabilities* (that is, found across the entire operations system). Here, Wal-Mart ensures its operations strategy underpins sources of competitive advantage such as, fast replenishment of goods, short lead times from suppliers, vendor-managed inventory, broad variety of products and services, the ability to customize individual stores and product ranges to demand and the ability to modify and develop new products quickly.
3   *Organization-based* (across the entire enterprise). Operating capabilities to adopt and quickly utilize new technologies, fast design of new products and a short life cycle to bring them on-stream, ability to open new stores and source goods faster than competitors, etc.
4   *Network-based* (covering a whole supply network). Wal-mart would have been unable to achieve its levels of success in isolation. Its competitive advantage has stemmed directly from its unique competence to create a network of supportive trading relationships (particularly with its suppliers). Without the cooperation of these other firms many of its operations strategies would have been ineffective. However, this capability is not easy to attain and will take time to incubate. It involved all employees, and particularly managers, being able to recognize that Wal-Mart did not exist alone. There were no real boundaries around the firm and all activities and functions were in fact boundary spanning, to a greater or lesser degree. In addition, the ability to negotiate, openly share information and plan activities jointly with other enterprises is a culture that many firms still struggle with.

Resources

As part of their operations strategy, Wal-Mart was able to dedicate particular key resources. These included the skills of their workforce, technological priority in investment, use of dedicated and key suppliers, alliances and partnerships with other service providers and the selection and development of key geographic sites for stores.

Technologies

As we have discussed, the possession of technology alone was not a key to competitive advantage. It is the use to which it is put and the information that it provides that is difficult to replicate. Nevertheless, Wal-Mart invest heavily in technology and information systems design with an annual technology budget of US$500 million.

Key tactical activities to support a strategic positioning

The necessary shorter term, tactical activities that support fast and effective procurement of goods, transportation, warehousing, logistics, etc., to ensure accurate replenishment of goods to real time demand levels. In other words, the ability to co-ordinate supply system activity to be driven, or more accurately pulled, to the pace of customer demands.

Finally, we should note that these building blocks of an operations strategy are not achieved over night; in Wal-Mart's case, for example, they took nearly twenty years to perfect. This is not to say that once it is perfected that is the end of the matter. In chapters 9 and 10 we looked at strategies for managing demand and complex adaptive systems. The operations strategy can be thought of as a complex adaptive system enabling the organization to react to the various demands placed upon it. As such, it is dynamic and changes over time. Competitors will constantly be trying to catch up. Thus, a retailer like Wal-Mart must ensure that invention and creativity is constantly applied to its strategies. It must be aware of new technologies, new processes and methods. Learning, change and adaptation are vital for all employees as well as the organization itself, as the operations strategy will evolve using both continual improvement (small incremental changes) as well as other larger step changes (the introduction of a major new technology for example).

MANUFACTURING AND PRODUCTION OPERATIONS STRATEGIES

In manufacturing or production, the operations strategy or strategies direct the translation of competitive and market aspirations into tangible goods. In other words, having ascertained the value sought and the various order qualifiers and winners, it is necessary to arrive at an operations strategy that will make decisions about how these products and product groups will be made and delivered.

Formulating a manufacturing operations strategy

The operations strategy cannot be designed in a vacuum. It requires the input of customer needs and requirements as well as resource and capability considerations. The subsequent strategic vision will have to be aligned to the wider business strategy in making decisions about the target market, product groups and core enterprise and operational competencies. We must also remember that these decisions are strategic, however, and often will involve radical step changes. To create a distinctive or core competence Skinner (1996) suggests that 'tinkering with the current system' and just adding new technologies is not enough. In a complex and dynamic commercial environment, new techniques must be replaced by 'a whole new product realization system that is different and better than any competitors' (Skinner, 1996).

An operations strategy for manufacture of goods is directly concerned with the transformation of raw materials and components into goods. Often these physical transformations will take place as part of a function (operations or manufacturing) and the operations strategy is this case is at a functional level. Chapter 7 (p. 132) summarized the type of strategic decisions to be made under the following categories (Harrison, 1993):

■ How are the various product transformation processes defined?
■ How are these transformational systems linked?
■ What are the basic operational principles (processes and infrastructure) for each transformation system?

- How is the actual transformation carried out?
- What are the quantitative limits of the transformational process?
- Where is the process located?
- How is the process physically organized?
- Who owns the transformation system?
- How are the design attributes arrived at?
- How is quality controlled and improved?
- How are the informational needs of operations met?
- How are human resource needs met?

Hill (2000) provides an important and explicit framework for a manufacturing operations strategy reflecting the close link between both manufacturing and corporate decisions. His approach to developing a strategy places a strong emphasis upon strategic integration – in particular the link between manufacturing and marketing. We have adapted this framework to include the following steps (although in reality the process will be iterative and much more complex).

Step 1 – corporate objectives

The objectives for the business: the basis for establishing clear, strategic, directions with an awareness and willingness to succeed. The directions also define the boundaries and parameters against which the various inputs can be measured and established – a coherent corporate plan. Of course, the various objectives will vary from one enterprise to another and will mirror the economy, markets, opportunities and preferences of the situation. These broad objectives may include growth aims, survival, profit expected, return on investment and other financial measures. But they can also reflect other concerns such as environmental resource issues, employee policies, etc.

Step 2 – strategic positioning

As discussed in chapter 3, the firm needs to adopt a particular strategic positioning that will underpin both its corporate objectives (Step 1) and marketing strategy (Step 3). We can immediately see the difficulty in a linear approach to this. Positioning can be conceptual (variety-based, need-based and access-based – or a combination of all three), or practical (based upon cost, quality, flexibility, response, etc.). This positioning involves a set of decisions that will take into account strategic priorities but will also dictate the operational activities that will be necessary to achieve these priorities.

Step 3 – marketing strategy

The marketing strategy is just one of the many functional strategies the organization may choose to adopt. These include, for example, an operations strategy, financial strategy, human resource management strategy, an information systems and information technology strategy, etc. In Fig. 11.2 (adapted from Harrison, 1993) we can see how these various elements form a strategic framework that links together strategic thinking and choice.

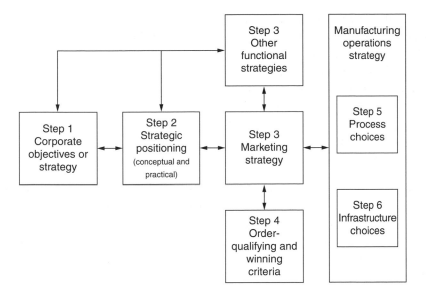

Figure 11.2 *Manufacturing strategy framework*

The marketing strategy will include:

- Marketing planning and control. Establishing the target markets for various product groups;
- Analysis of product markets to estimate value sought, trends, buying behaviour and competitive activity;
- Identifying target markets and agreeing objectives for each, both short- and long-term, and the action plans necessary.

In addition, the marketing plan will need to establish levels of support and the various resources necessary to meet objectives. The output of the marketing strategy will determine and identify product markets and segments; the range, mix and volumes of products involved; the various product attributes necessary to satisfy value demands and the overall marketing strategy for the various target markets (for example, a leader, aggressive competitor, new player, follower, etc.).

Step 3 – other functional strategies

In parallel to the marketing strategy, other functional strategies will need to be developed. These will cover a number of areas, but for our purposes, the main functional strategy will be that of operations. Here, it will be important that the operations strategy supports both the corporate and marketing strategies as well as being compatible with other functional strategies. Thus the decisions about, and strategic management of, operational activities, core competencies and processes, technologies, resources and key tactical activities used in the organization and its supply network must reflect the value demanded by a customer as well as the strategic priorities of marketing and the business as a whole. The resultant operations strategy blends the various components into a strategic architecture with various levels of emphasis. As we have seen in Fig. 11.1, the approach allows each strategy to be customized and to fit the requirements of not only the marketing strategy, but also the target markets for each product or customer group.

Step 4 – how products qualify and win orders in the market

The task of the manufacturing strategy is twofold. First, to meet the criteria necessary to qualify for the market through operational effectiveness (performing similar activities better than rivals). Second, to win orders and sustainable competitive advantage through differentiation from competitors (performing different activities from rivals or performing similar activities in different ways). The qualifying criteria are the essential features of a product, while order-winning criteria provide the basis for customer choice between alternative qualifying offerings. The following list shows some of the possible customer choice criteria which, in differing circumstances or product life cycle stages, may be either qualifying or order-winning:

- Total price;
- Specified product or service attributes;
- Quality of the product;
- Design and design flexibility;
- Delivery arrangements;
- Delivery performance;
- Volume and mix flexibility;
- Speed of quotation service;
- Product features;
- After-sales support;
- Stability of continuing customer support.

The decisions in step 4 are strategic and need to be taken at a cross-functional level. They are not the prerogative of one function, as there will be many perspectives of a firm's products and markets. This underlines the strong link necessary between corporate marketing proposals and commitments and the operations processes and infrastructure necessary to support them.

Step 5 – manufacturing strategy (process choice)

There will be number of alternative processes available to make particular products. In making such choices, the key considerations will include: volume, degree of customization, mix, complexity in the production process and the necessary order winning criteria. However, each type of choice involves both current and future trade-offs, often involving issues such as cost and variety levels.

Process choice relates to the basic mode of operation of a system. For example, producing one-off projects designed for a specific consumer at one extreme and continuous production, of say petroleum or chemicals, at the other. The process choice will involve decisions regarding:

- The use of alternative processes;
- The trade-offs embodied in the process choice;
- The role of inventory in the process configuration;
- Decisions whether to make internally or buy parts or components externally;
- Capacity decisions (size, timing location).

Step 6 – manufacturing strategy (infrastructure choice)

This concerns the non-process features within the production strategy. It can include the procedures, systems controls, compensation systems, work-structuring systems, and organizational issues within manufacturing. Infrastructure choice includes:

- The necessary support needed for the operations function;
- Planning and control systems;
- Quality assurance, management and control systems;
- Manufacturing systems engineering;
- Data and information requirements;
- Clerical and informational procedures;
- Compensation agreements;
- Work structures;
- Organizational structures.

Competitive advantage from production operations strategies

Nigel Slack (1991) addresses the notion of a 'doctrine of competitiveness'. Competitiveness, in his view, can be achieved through the manufacturing contribution to creating strategic advantage. In this context, the author refers only to a narrow range of operations strategies (those concerned with physical production), and as we know, there are many types of operations strategy that apply in non-production settings. Nevertheless, his contention is that manufacturing advantage can be achieved by 'Making things better' and this has clear resonance for operations strategies in general, and is a good point of departure for considering their competitive priorities.

Making things better than the competition, according to Slack, involves five essential propositions:

1   *Making things right* – the quality advantage;
2   *Making things fast* – the speed advantage;
3   *Making things on time* – the dependability advantage;
4   *Changing what is made* – the flexibility advantage;
5   *Making things cheap* – the cost advantage.

These performance objectives are the basic elements of competitiveness for manufacturing. Yet they also provide an indication of the wider contribution that any operations strategy might offer as an implementer, supporter and driver of the overall business strategy: to translate competitive market requirements into performance objectives (Slack *et al.*, 2001). Clearly the role of the operations strategy is to ensure, no matter what the particular competitive advantage sought, that these objectives are translated into operational activities.

Manufacturing operations strategy building blocks

As we described in the first retail section, we can now examine manufacturing or production operations strategies from the perspective of each having unique building blocks. Once more, we will do this by using a small case study.

CASE VIGNETTE **DESIGNER ISSEY MIYAKE**

Production and manufacturing does not always imply heavy industrial engineering with large processing machines, automated assembly lines, hard mindless labour, noise, sweat, the smell of oil and clouds of steam. The production task can also be artistic, intricate, passionate and an opportunity for flair, creativity and innovation to satisfy the most ephemeral and mercurial of demand. This case study highlights some of these more unusual production attributes.

Issey Miyake regards himself as both fashion designer and fashion producer. His creations are unrivalled in the haute couture industry and he is regarded by the Sunday Times as one of the top 1000 personalities of the world. A specialist in fabulous pleats – garments as light as leaves – in fabrics crumpled, crimped, embossed or pleated like tree bark or in zigzags, lending scintillating, vibrant three-dimensional flows to the purest geometric lines. Yet Miyake's 'visual creations' have never lost their primary vocation as functional tools. The seemingly fragile, fan-like gowns, undulating capes and candle-blouses can nevertheless be machine-washed, drip-dried as easily as bathing suits and rolled up in the travellers baggage. 'When I design, or better still, produce new fabrics and styles, my main objective is to make them wearable'. All manner of materials are also used: bamboo, string, rubber, paper, plastic, silk, cotton and gauze. The most extraordinary textures and refined nuances are achieved with each one. Whether twisted, lacquered, tied, bleached, quilted, crumpled, recycled or metallicized, all the materials reveal astonishing modernism and audacity, ever more beautiful, supple, brilliant and simple to care for. They are quite simply manufactured masterpieces.

Miyake in fact considers himself more a clothing manufacturer than a fashion designer, and spends huge amounts of time innovating new techniques of sewing and producing garments, which catapult his creations into the future. The 'Just Before Technique' is a classic example. A forty-metre long tube of black jersey is produced by a computer-controlled hosiery-knitting machine. A silhouette of the pattern to be cut appears in the fabric itself, with cutting lines at the armholes, neck and hem. A myriad variations can be produced from this unique prototype – long or short, symmetrical or unconstructed, wide or narrow – with just a few snips of the scissors.

The 'Colombo Process' is another innovation. It involves neither scissors nor needle and thread, and produces a seamless dress. It consists of a square piece of fabric thermally cut, to which a few snaps are added in strategic spots to give exquisite shape to a draped gown in the ancient style of the Far East.

In the 'Tubed Veil' technique, a long tube of extremely light material is folded and rolled so as to make a double thickness. The inner layer of the garment is subjected to crumpling by means of a chemical treatment, which gives the fabric a delightfully airy feel against the skin. The outer part is left as it is, to be draped around the body. Two dresses become one with the wearer not only looking good but being as Miyake describes: 'carefully and beautifully massaged and stroked by the material during even the slightest of movements'.

In his 'Star Burst Collection', Miyake systematically uses recycled clothes to which thin membranes of metallic leaves are thermally pressed on the garments using supple fabrics, sweeping the body's shape with silver, gold and copper splashes of light. Prism collage combines superimposed and inlaid materials – at the same time, coloured, matte and translucent – creating the effect of a peeling, yet masked and superimposed fresco.

Issey Miyake's success has given him strength, as he explains: 'In other words, more humility. I'm here to show what can be produced with joy, pleasure and discovery.' Miyake's story is a lesson in operations. Creativity, learning and innovation are still a fundamental part of the process – and in the future, they will prove to be even more important for an operations strategy!

We can now look at the strategic decisions necessary for a production or manufacturing operations strategy in more detail using the Miyake case. In this way, it is hoped that the reader can appreciate the wider implications for the strategy.

Core competencies, capabilities and processes

In manufacturing, as with other operational settings, distinctive competencies and processes are those special attributes or abilities possessed by an organization that give it competitive edge – they relate to the way the firm competes. As we noted previously, these can include:

- Price (Travel Lodge hotels);
- Quality (Sony, Lexus, Kodak and Disneyland);
- Time (McDonald's, Express mail and UPS);
- Flexibility (a hospital emergency and casualty facilities and Tesco Stores);
- Customer service (Nordstrom, Disneyland, five-star restaurants and hotels);
- Location (shopping centres or malls, service stations and ATMs).

Using an historical example, we can also see that since the Second World War, Japanese manufacturing companies have employed a number of distinctive competencies:

- *Low labour cost strategy* – using an inexpensive labour pool that existed shortly after the war;
- *Scale-based strategy* – in the 1960s capital intensive methods to achieve high productivity and low unit cost;
- *Focused factory strategy* – smaller factories were used in the 1970s to focus on narrow product lines and specialization for higher quality;
- *Flexible factory strategy* – time-based reduction in new product and process delivery and design times. High quality with increased variety;
- *Lean production* – reducing all waste while maintaining product variety and quality.

The approach to distinctive competencies is built upon customer needs and values and a close attention to competitor activities. It also involves a liaison between operations and marketing functions to appreciate both customer and product demands.

We can now examine the core competencies and processes that are important for Issey Miyake's organization and its operations strategy. The various core competencies can be divided into four classifications as in the Wal-Mart case:

1   *Process-based capabilities* (the transformation activities). Undoubtedly, these will be first and foremost the design creativity of Miyake himself. But we can also think of these skills a little more broadly, as they will have to be continually developed and honed and are dynamic. In order to stay at the forefront of design, Miyake will also rely upon information about the trends and fashions, other fashion developments, new technology and new materials. Although hard to quantify, this knowledge is a vital part of the design process and the capabilities of the organization in supplying these data will be important.

2   System of coordination-based capabilities (found across the entire operations system). We can now add to the design capability of Miyake himself, the other key skills of those around him that will also help transform product designs into extremely high quality clothing. The skills of the support staff in such an operation are paramount and some of the leading exponents of pattern making, cutting, fusing, sewing, trim design and pressing will be employed to support the design team. Design ideas have to be translated into garments that can be worn!

3   *Organization-based* (across the entire enterprise). At this level we can expect to see the importance of sourcing, the latest technologies, and the highest quality inputs. In addition, close liaison with both customers and suppliers will also be crucial.

4   *Network-based* (covering the whole supply network). The reliance upon high quality materials supplied by responsive organizations willing to innovate and experiment with new specifications is one of the keys to Miyake's success. Plus, the ability to understand, communicate and translate customer demands will also be important.

Resources

As mentioned above, access to the latest fabrics, materials and trims or components are vital in supplying haute couture fashion. At the same time the suppliers of such resources must be at the forefront of innovation and willing to create and develop new and unusual fabric products (both in terms of colour, weight and texture).

Technology

Perhaps less important as a core capability, but nevertheless necessary to ensure the latest technology is available and used to create high fashion clothing.

Key tactical activities to support a strategic positioning

For a successful strategy, the Miyake organization must ensure an efficient and effective operation at two levels: upstream and downstream. The former involves all those activities necessary to secure excellent quality materials and process machinery. The latter involves very close communication and a working partnership with individual clients, as well as fashion show organizers and leading retailers in major cities throughout the world.

CONCLUSION

In chapter 11 operations strategies for retail and manufacturing were discussed. To do this, we used the concept that certain forces can influence the shape of the core building blocks. A practical demonstration is now provided using two case studies. In the next chapter we will examine how SMEs and the service sector can develop and deploy operations strategies.

CASE STUDY 1 – OPERATIONS STRATEGY IN ACTION

Zara and Mango – operations strategy: retail and manufacturing applications (www.zara.com, www.mango.es/e/)

The first Zara clothing store opened in 1975 in Spain as a small retailer selling men's and women's clothing. Since then the Zara chains have grown into retailing giants with nearly 500 stores worldwide and an impressive sales record. Mango's store in London, part of the same Spanish retail group, has a turnover of £420,000 a month and is expected to gross more than £4 million a year. Both of these retailers are expanding rapidly and are very good examples of the success of cross-border European strategies.

The success of these firms is partly to do with the appeal of their men's, women's and children's fashions and accessories that display a unique style but at real world prices. But it is also partly as a result of their collaborative, digital networks that link them with their suppliers and customers. These advances have enabled both firms to deliver tailored products quickly and reliably, creating what they term a 'value net' for all the firms in the supply network. This value net is a key part of their operations strategy, allowing customer choices to be simultaneously transmitted to all supply partners who then deliver components as needed by other partners. The company at the centre of the operations strategy co-ordinates all activity, provides continual updates to all players, and captures significant value for its efforts.

The particular operations strategy used by both Zara and Mango helps them respond quickly to shifts in customer demand and build powerful new brands. They estimate that it takes only two weeks to convert design ideas into products on the shelf to satisfy its young, hip, clientele with fashion for the masses. Store employees regularly tour urban hot spots looking for new trends and reporting back to designers. Knowing what's in today and may be out next month is the secret of the success of these Spanish retailers, as is the ability to apply an operations strategy that puts new fashion concepts on the shelf in twelve to fifteen days. As part of this strategy, capital-intensive steps are executed in factories owned by Zara and Mango's parent company, while labour intensive operations are outsourced to small shops and manufacturers with whom Zara and Mango have collaborative partnerships that include providing them with the necessary technology and logistics capabilities. Customers seem to relish the results of this high velocity operation and are often seen queuing outside stores on designated delivery days – a phenomenon recently dubbed 'Zaramania'.

CASE STUDY 2 – OPERATIONS STRATEGY IN ACTION

National Starch and Chemical – operations strategy: retail and manufacturing applications (www.nationalstarch.com)

National Starch and Chemical are a leading member of the ICI Group of Companies. In their company brochure they boast an immense product portfolio that 'enhances the lives of people from tiny babies to senior citizens' across markets as diverse as food to health-care to construction. The enterprise is structured around four divisions: adhesives, speciality starches, speciality synthetic polymers and electronic and engineering materials.

With a turnover of just under $1.9 billion, 10,570 employees, thirty-one manufacturing companies, an international network of 160 manufacturing and consumer service centres over thirty-seven countries and six continents, National Starch embody the ICI vision of 'competitive advantage from devolved decision making at local levels'. In so doing, they have also had to become extremely adept at managing complex global trading relationships.

With such product and process diversity, coordination and control is vital if National are to achieve their strategic goals: 'Delivering market-driven innovation in products and services to win in quality growth markets worldwide using inspired and talented people and an operational performance that is constantly improving'. But how is this strategic vision translated into operational reality? This was the big question for National Starch and a key foundation of their current success.

With its global resources, advanced technologies and unparalleled customer service, National Starch and Chemical is in a unique position to supply products that answer the major challenges of its customers and the service needs of its suppliers around the world. Its mantra, 'People, Products and Customers', underlines its business philosophy and operations are a second foundation necessary to deliver competitive advantage.

National has been manufacturing adhesives, for example, for over seventy years and has seven advanced production facilities and twelve technical centres in locations across Europe. Senior management recognize that the time, expense and effort involved in the research, development and innovation cycle, must be matched by growth and evolution of its manufacturing processes. Nowhere is this more evident than the recently constructed, state-of-the-art, waterborne adhesive formulating plant at Warrington in the UK that can service a large part of the European market. This facility is one of the most progressive in the world, and is a clear example of how National can support its diverse range of technically advanced products yet at the same time retain high levels of customer service and product quality.

National Starch invested US $10 million in building new facilities at Warrington and they were, remarkably, brought on-stream in less than twelve months from the planning stage to the first production run. As part of their European production strategy, the decision to develop this greenfield site was driven by a recognition that sustainable competitive edge could only be established by a wide range of products with high quality, but at a lower cost than competitors. According to Ron Lane, European Manufacturing Director:

> Competitors could easily copy our product ranges; industrial espionage and reverse engineering are relatively easy in this industry. But they could not match our combination of quality together with a very low cost of supply – something the Warrington operation gave us.

The Warrington development brought synergy. It allowed National to position a raw material supplier of polymers (a key ingredient of adhesives) on the same site as their new adhesive manufacturing capability. This unique, integrated partnership now offered flexibility as well as minimizing unit cost through a reduction in the complexity of network supply. The advantages, according to Ron Lane, were immediately evident:

> We work in a very fragmented market with high competition. We had the diversity of products and a high quality reputation, Warrington meant we could also now position ourselves as the lowest cost supplier. But it was important for us to operate in profitable, healthy and growing markets rather than just at the low cost end.

The National supply network is now closely integrated and transparent. Demand information from the customer can be fed upstream to the adhesives manufacturer and polymer producer and then further back to raw materials. This means a greater flexibility and higher level of customer service. In addition, the operations strategy is now so slick that in many cases they produce to real time demand and make to order. As Allan Kerry, the site Production Manager points out:

237

Warrington brought us tremendous benefits. We now have very close coordination across the two divisions (the supplier of polymer and the manufacturer of adhesives); and, with our sources of supply on-site, we no longer have to transport materials all over Europe. Interestingly as well, the speed of response and flexibility has not meant a higher cost – quite the opposite.

The benefits from this investment are not only commercial. Environmental impacts have also been substantially minimized. The shorter supply system has allowed mix sizes to be reduced, thus optimizing production and lowering scrap and waste costs. Energy consumption per ton is also less, in line with the newer mixing technologies and smaller batches. The environmental impact of transportation has been cut as there is no longer a need to ship raw materials to a number of disparate sites.

The new plant, then, has brought considerable benefits to the company; not only in terms of technology and cost, but also by providing, for example, one of the most advanced, fully automated, packaging facilities in the industry (traditionally a very complex and labour-intensive activity). The collaboration between the two divisions extends into joint research and development teams and to a number of other projects undertaken by combined initiatives from both firms.

Warrington is also an investment for the future. The venture was deliberately designed with new markets and future capacity in mind. The base loads can be increased as part of National's drive to improve both polymers and adhesives. In fact, Warrington is a key long-term part of their policy for aggressive growth and profitable volume. European production strategies are built upon continuous improvement as standard, but they also recognize three other vital ingredients for future success:

1   Operational excellence by smoothing the supply chain and increasingly making to order using real time demand information;
2   Introducing lean production and manufacturing operations strategies to cut capital cost and waste;
3   Minimizing capital outlay by developing autonomy and empowerment in human resources through skills-based training and intensive continuous improvement.

As Ron Lane contends: 'Our strategies of diversification and growth rely upon collaboration with our partners – and this includes our workforce.'

Anticipating the needs of markets and customers is vital to every activity at National. Another bedrock of competitive success is National Starch's commitment to being responsive to their customers and developing close working relationships with them through the use of solid industry knowledge. As Jim Owens intriguingly suggests: 'Our goal is to help them make their products successful, but we can also offer much more!'

National work hard throughout all their adhesive business to develop individual customer solutions. By understanding their industry they aim to establish close working bonds with their customers to help them seize competitive edge. The secret for the company is a firmly held conviction and belief that to remain competitive it is not enough to simply supply high quality products. It also takes a creative approach to business – for manufacturers, suppliers and customers alike.

This innovative approach is the secret of success. National's key partnerships with customers and suppliers do more than just provide goods and services – they are an investment and commitment in the competitive success of a joint alliance. Jim Owens expands on this:

> Relations with customers, getting close to customers, and developing service relationships is crucial. In Europe, where there are so many diverse cultures, we have pan-European customers and very local customers. Customer relations are a complex yet essential part of our business. It is a key management objective for National to be proactive and help our partners achieve success and grow – we recognize that our own success is symbiotic and depends very much upon these relationships.

The development of strategic alliances with the right suppliers and customers has become a policy imperative for National Starch and Chemical. They understand, as an international competitor offering vital product differentiation in a crowded marketplace, that there is a core need to build synergistic businesses with external firms. All employees are encouraged to look outward as part of their continual development programme. Internal improvements must be matched by external linkages across a number of networks formed with partners. These mutual alliances provide National with a core strength that confirms the old adage that 'the whole is worth more than just the sum of the parts'. This strategy offers an extra competitive dimension from the emergent power of such alliances.

The philosophy of partnership can be seen across the whole organization. For their customers, National provides a unique business benefit – they have recognized the importance of customization. Operations strategies and operational activities are now firmly tailored to the needs of each customer. An understanding that in a complex and dynamic business world, high levels of product variety can only be supported by operational systems and strategies that are developed with, and for, each individual customer.

Long gone are the times when an organization such as National could provide just one general operations strategy for all. Each purchaser now requires a service that is different and matches their unique value needs. For example: product development utilizing the valuable input of suppliers and customers; support services that keep the customer constantly in touch with expert advice; assistance from industry experts to offer help with technical problems and optimize production processes; operational audits to select the correct applications and manufacturing process; advice on how to avoid wastage and improve product efficiencies and innovative delivery, handling and storage systems – can all be adapted to suit each individual customer. These fast, flexible and responsive unique solutions are designed for the requirements of each customer. In so doing, National Starch helps build its own and its partners' competitive strength through a belief that customer satisfaction is all part of the service.

For customers and suppliers alike, individual and customized relationships and operational support is now part of National's culture – it has become a way of doing business!

National's customers are in dynamic markets that always require new methods of processing and new products. In addition, these customers encounter problems related to the environment, production, safety, economics and competition. It is these marketplace dynamics that spawn the future opportunities for National to develop new and improved products and services. The company has met the needs of its customers for over a century, it is determined to continue to meet those needs with diversified, exciting new products and customized operations and service solutions that support its trading relationships in a mutually beneficial way. As the company proudly states: 'Our strength lies in the strength of our partners and our relationships with them!'

DISCUSSION QUESTIONS, WORK ASSIGNMENTS AND EXAM QUESTIONS

1   Why are data and information flows of particular importance to a retailer like Wal-Mart?
2   What do the terms 'order qualifiers' and 'order winners' mean? Why are these concepts necessary for an operations strategy?
3   What is the 'doctrine of competitiveness'? How does the concept ensure a manufacturing contribution to strategic advantage?
4   What are core competencies, capabilities and processes? In discussing these frameworks, provide examples from both manufacturing and retailing.

Reader question related to the Zara and Mango case study

1   The operations strategy described in the Zara and Mango case study relies heavily upon fast information flows. Discuss the necessary capabilities or competencies that these firms must posses to (a) capture particular types of data (what types are necessary), (b) transform data into information and (c) facilitate these information flows. As a reminder, these capabilities can be categorized as:
   ■   Process-based (the transformation activities);
   ■   Coordination or system-based (across the entire operation system);
   ■   Organization-based (across the entire enterprise);
   ■   Network-based (covering the whole supply network).

Reader question related to the National Starch case study

1   At the beginning of this chapter we introduced the 'filtration model' (Fig. 11.1). This allowed an organization to customize its operations strategy using the influences associated with:
   ■   The demand behaviour of products;
   ■   The structure of the supply network; and
   ■   The performance metrics of the supply network.
In groups, discuss these examples and how they might be particularly important for a manufacturer such as National Starch.

Chapter 12

Operations strategy
SMEs and service sector applications

We now turn our attention to small and medium-sized enterprises (SMEs) and the service sector. Both of these communities, and of course the two overlap, are of immense importance for economic wealth. Unfortunately, however, their needs in terms of operations and operations strategies have been greatly overlooked in many academic publications: especially in the case of the former. Clearly, many SMEs are manufacturers and/or service providers, nevertheless, we will suggest that size and structure in their case does present many unique opportunities and, indeed, hurdles.

LEARNING OBJECTIVES

After considering this chapter, the reader will be able to:

- ■ Formulate a strategy for SME operations
- ■ Appreciate an SME operational structure
- ■ Apply the operations strategy building blocks to SME organizations
- ■ Appreciate the nature of services and the service sector
- ■ Develop an operations strategy for service sector communities
- ■ Understand the business choices and integrative elements of a service strategy
- ■ Discuss the building blocks of a service strategy

> **KEY TERMS**
>
> - SME operations environment
> - SME operations structure
> - SME operations strategy building blocks
> - The nature of services
> - Business choices
> - Integrative elements
> - Service operations strategy building blocks

INTRODUCTION

As with the previous chapter, there are two distinct sections, covering services and SMEs. First we will discuss the various organizational aspects that make such communities unique and second, formulate operations strategies using the concept of building blocks.

THE SMALL AND MEDIUM-SIZED ENTERPRISE

SMEs form a vital part of many economies. The definition of an SME varies, but for our purposes we suggest the following:

1 A firm employing no more than 250 people;
2 An annual turnover of not more than 50 million euro or an annual balance sheet of less than 43 million euro;
3 Where not more than 25 per cent of the capital or voting rights are owned by another single enterprise, or jointly by several other enterprises, falling outside the definition of an SME as given under (1) and (2) above. Exceptions include public investment corporations, venture capital companies and, provided no control is exercised, institutional investors.

We can classify SME organizations as:

- Micro (employing 1–9);
- Small (10–49);
- Medium (50–249).

The importance of SMEs to an economy is undoubted. In the UK, organizations employing less than 250 people account for 57 per cent of all employment. The UK Small Business Service estimates (2000) that there are in the region of 1.1 million private sector SMEs in the UK. These firms employ over 9 million people and have a combined annual turnover of nearly £950 million. The picture is similar in the rest of the European Union and North America. In fact, SMEs are extremely important for Western economies.

SMEs are also fundamental for the operation and success of many supply pipelines. For example, the clothing industry, both in Europe and North America, relies heavily upon SMEs to provide the bulk of manufacturing. In the UK service sector, it is estimated that 42 per cent of firms are SMEs. In FMCG industries, SMEs form the bulk of the manufacturing stage either as first, second or third tier suppliers.

FORMULATING AN SME OPERATIONS STRATEGY

In developing an SME operations strategy, particular attention must be paid to the commercial environment.

The SME operations environment

The scale of SME operations means they have a relatively low impact on their surroundings and have a limited power to influence environmental forces in their favour – this will include both their suppliers and customers. However, their weakness in these areas can be countered by their ability to react quickly to environmental change. Fundamental shifts in social values, consumer tastes, technological developments, managerial techniques, financial markets and so on, have brought about more complex and dynamic commercial environments. For the SME, their less bureaucratic structural arrangements, together with concentration in the power of the owner, allows growth-orientated small ventures to capitalize on opportunities that emerge from such environmental changes.

Small organizations usually thrive in a changing environment, although it must not be unduly complex in terms of the number of variables involved or the speed of their change (Mintzberg, 1979b). It is further suggested by Mintzberg (1982) that the SME nimbleness in response to change is due in part to the fact that senior managers or owners formulate strategies that are closely connected with the work of the organization and with other workers and managers. Control and tactical decision making is not separated and distanced from ownership or senior management. In other words, such firms tend to be task continuous; there is a close link between management, planning and the work activity. Larger firms on the other hand are task discontinuous; there tends to be a separate and discrete planning and management structure (Off, 1976).

Given the limits imposed by small scale operations, evidence suggests that growth-orientated managers and owners pursue opportunities vigorously, flexibly and with innovation. They will pursue a number of opportunities and often refuse to be constrained by the assets currently under their control. They make tentative investigations of promising projects and frequently assume that the techniques and technologies not currently available can be developed in the near future. In this way riskier opportunities are explored, despite not immediately having sufficient resources to underwrite their opportunities. Managers and owners are prepared to pursue, evaluate and resource new opportunities in the full confidence of their ability to make things happen (Stevenson and Gumpert, 1991).

SMEs do encounter difficulties in acquiring resources. Their scale of operation and lack of specialist expertise result in a lack of purchasing power. In addition, in turbulent conditions the variation in demand for final products and services will be reflected in intermittent demands by the SME for resources – the alternative being to hold high levels of inventory. Thus, difficulties in procuring resources will result from (a) changeable demand and (b) lack of power or leverage.

Changeable demand

SMEs tend to avoid permanent or binding linkages with suppliers and other network contacts. Their flexibility relies upon the transient nature of their relationships with other organizations using short-term, entrepreneurial contracts – an ability to utilize resources carried by others (Stevenson and Gumpert, 1991). Colllins and Moore (1970) suggest:

> Entrepreneurs develop a transactional mode of personal relationships, which are useful to the entrepreneur . . . the entrepreneur quickly learns to end abruptly all relationships which hamper his present action and restrict his future . . . permanent associations greatly inhibit their desire to pursue, evaluate and reject immediately projects that do not look promising.

Increasing leverage

Here, SMEs face a dilemma. In seeking new opportunities and being nimble and fast they need instrumental relationships; in managing their current business they need strong, more permanent relationships. The two are to a degree exclusive. One solution seems to be the development of new ventures alongside existing ones. The flexibility of the SME often allows this type of project management operation, with resources being switched between current and new activities (Lowson, 1998). Small and medium-sized firms also suffer a power imbalance when dealing with larger suppliers and customers, with both sides regarding the relationship as somewhat temporary. This arrangement certainly offers greater degrees of flexibility, but is also highly speculative and makes operations planning very problematical. The following SME case study demonstrates some of the problems.

CASE VIGNETTE **DENNERGATE LTD**

Dennergate are a small to medium-sized Welsh clothing manufacturer employing just over fifty people. They produce fashion garments and their largest regular customer is a UK high street retailer called Next. Approximately 80 per cent of the finished goods produced by Dennergate are sold to Next for use in Next Retail, Next Catalogue (Next Directory), Next Franchise and Next Export sales. The remaining production capacity is supplies of one-off orders from retailers such as Monsoon, Mango and Top Shop. Dennergate have a turnover of just under £1 million per annum and produce nearly 5,000 garments a week.

Next often use their clothing catalogue as a method to trial new designs. For example, a new garment is introduced in the catalogue and its sales levels (by colour, style and size) will guide the decisions over how much and what particular style, colour and size is likely to sell well in-store. The seasons for most of these clothing lines is very short, as little as eight to twelve weeks; as such Next relies upon speed of response and flexibility from its vendor manufacturers.

Next source the bulk of their garments from suppliers in the Far East. These manufacturers can provide large orders and can offer very low purchase prices due their low cost and low wage operations. However, they are not very flexible and cannot adjust their production schedules easily to counter any change in demand: domestic SMEs such as Dennergate are used for this purpose. So, if a particular garment size, colour or style is selling well, Next will approach Dennergate and other SMEs to provide small top-up production.

Dennergate are what is known in the clothing industry as a CMT (Cut, Make and Trim) operation. The retailers will supply an order with fabric in rolls, patterns, labels, hangers and packaging. Dennergate do not provide any design input to the process and only have to provide labour, equipment and cotton.

Once fabric and style design is agreed by Next an order is placed with Dennergate for a sample batch. If this sample is approved by Next, the fabric is ordered and Dennergate is told the amount of garments that are needed. On average, there is a gap of two months between agreeing the sample and the amount needed and final delivery date. One week after delivery to Next, the clothes go on sale. During a sale season reorders will be placed depending on sales levels, and usually giving Dennergate four to six weeks to produce the reorder amount. Dennergate get very little advance notice of an order (it can be as little as two weeks) and will have to produce set amounts every week that are then collected until the full order is satisfied. In addition, Dennergate cannot plan on a longer-term basis as there is no agreement over pre-booked capacity – they are very much reacting to demand. In fact they are 'blind' as far as future orders are concerned. On the one hand, they cannot rely upon Next placing orders with them in any particular sale season (much depends upon the popularity of the garment). On the other, if they risk committing their capacity to another retailer, and have then to refuse a Next order, it is highly likely that Next will not use them again in the future – truly, a no win situation!

The SME operations structure

Larger firms have the capability to break tasks down into their component parts and assign specialist staff. Specialization is only economically feasible if the output of the firm is sufficiently large so the time and work of specialists or experts can be fully utilized. Therefore, the advantages of specialization will often be lost to the small firm.

Specialism also requires a degree of stability so that the same task can be performed repeatedly and skills can be perfected. However, the strength of the SME is in seeking new opportunities, as such specialist skills can quickly become redundant and the more flexible and adaptive generalist becomes more valuable. The SME resides in a changeable environment, has a small output and is a flexible and responsive generalist organization. These firms are ideally suited to providing a variety of customized product and service combinations in response to constantly changing customer needs (Lowson, 1998).

Small firms have less sophisticated, flexible and organic structures. They tend to adopt what Piore and Sabel (1984) describe as 'flexible specialization'. This is a rejection of the mass-production techniques of Fordism and a return to a craft form of production, based upon fewer rules and procedures, flexible working practices, the use of information technology and customized, short-run manufacture, in a network of small firms operating in niche, segmented, markets.

In addition to size, Woodward (1958) also demonstrated that operations methods can have an impact upon organizational structure. She showed that firms with different operational technologies tended to have different structural arrangements and managerial practices. She compared these variables in firms producing small batches of goods, mass operation and continuous operations. In general, the volume of the products or services produced tended to dictate the size of operational scale. Small-scale operations tended to be less specialized, had fewer levels of management authority and a small span of control for supervisors and managers. This type of firm tended to utilize flexible teams with a range of roles, and there was no large gap in status and authority between those doing the work and those managing or supervising. The SMEs functioned around the skills and expertise of the employees, with harmonious relations and high levels of verbal communication being used to coordinate activity – far less of the 'brainwork' of operations had been separated out and delegated to staff experts. Workers were given more autonomy and responsibility for organizing work procedures, processes and systems.

SME operations strategy building blocks

We can now examine the decisions that combine to form the potential building blocks of an SME operations strategy.

Core competencies, capabilities and processes

Any SME, no matter whether it offers tangible goods or services, will have certain key competencies, capabilities and processes. In making longer-term decisions regarding its operations strategies, these firms will be particularly concerned to enhance and build their flexibility, responsiveness and diversification platforms. Table 12.1 suggests possible areas where organizations might seek particular core competencies, capabilities and processes. A contrast is then drawn between small and medium-size firms and their larger counterparts (although it should be borne in mind that as we are looking at the body of SMEs as a whole, these are by necessity generalizations).

As is evident from Table 12.1, the SMEs can seek core capabilities from a number of sources in order to bring about greater degrees of organizational flexibility. The key to such flexibility is the aptitude and capacity to customize both products and processes by SKU, logistics flow and stocking policy, market segment, geographical area, customer (for example a particular retailer), and even individual store.

Another fundamental element in realizing the requisite levels of flexibility lies in the reduction of uncertainty. Traditional methods of operation rely heavily upon sales forecasting systems which drive all activity. This leads to large amounts of uncertainty and

Table 12.1 SME core capability sources

Sources of core competencies, capabilities and processes	Small and Medium-sized firms	Larger firms
Operations strategy, philosophy and culture	Mass customisation and individual customisation ■ Variety and diversity in product and service combinations and processes ■ Demand driven 'pull' systems ■ Understanding and operating in real time demand mode ■ Flexibility in product and service combinations, mix, volume, logistics, monetary and customer contact ■ Mutual and supportive networks ■ Virtual operations and collaboration in external relationships ■ Proactive in seeking new niche opportunities and the necessary resources to support them	Mass production ■ Homogeneity and superficial differentiation ■ Resource driven 'push' system ■ Rigidity in operations with long batch runs and a production to stock ■ Difficulty in changing direction to take advantage of new opportunities ■ Stable relationships with suppliers and customers ■ Strong bargaining power in resource and supply relationships ■ Ability to attract and efficiently employ specialist labour ■ Heavy reliance upon forecasting
Branding	■ Unique brands as symbols and images	■ Little real difference behind a promotional facade of choice
Operational processes	■ Economies of scope ■ Small batch flexible operations of a variety of product and service types ■ Built-in quality with little stock ■ Functional, numerical, financial, technological and temporal flexibility	■ Economies of scale ■ Mass production of homogeneous products ■ Uniformity and standardization ■ Quality issues due to scale and buffer inventories against demand ■ Extensive research and development and new product introduction capabilities ■ Ability to satisfy high levels of demand
Technology	■ Primacy of individual consumer data/information flows along supply network and electronic platforms ■ Flexible operations technology and multi-purpose systems CAD/CAM ■ Importance of Information Communication Technology (ICT) ■ Extensive use of EDI, UPC, PoS, etc.	■ Data/information capture and interrogation does not differentiate between elements of customer base ■ Islands of technology with little integration either internally or externally

continued

Table 12.1 continued

Sources of core competencies, capabilities and processes	Small and Medium-sized firms	Larger firms
Supply network management and logistics strategy	■ Networks. Large numbers of external negotiations and transaction with partners ■ Logistically distinct businesses ■ 'Customization' of supply channels ■ Outsourcing non-core activities. Strategic alliances ■ Time as a critical source of competitive advantage that is closely linked to customer requirements ■ Product velocity, diversity and flexibility as a prime measure of success ■ Flow-through 'tailored' logistics and consolidation centres	■ Endogenous organization focus and little external integration ■ Universal logistics approach ■ Uniform stable and reliable supply streams ■ Internal transactions in hierarchy ■ Gains in operations time often dissipated by slow sales, marketing, and distribution functions ■ Measures based upon lowest cost and gross margin ■ Stocking points and little value added from lengthy storage and handling of products
Structure	■ Flat, and organic with matrix and cross-functional teams ■ Emphasis upon processes ■ Integration of departments and a market network ■ Cross-functional strategic planning ■ Close link between management and workforce ■ Multi-skilled, flexible workforce. Continual improvement and training ■ Job rotation	■ Hierarchical with little integration and stress upon functional 'silos' ■ Mechanistic structure ■ Strategic planning within specialist department or at pinnacle of organization ■ 'Taylorisation' of work routines, task specialization, rigid division of labour, and task fragmentation
Product and process development	■ Fast-cycle product development linked to customer needs ■ Individual customers integrated into design process ■ Importance of innovation and R&D ■ In-store style testing and feedback before launch of new products	■ Little innovation with only superficial change when absolutely necessary ■ Any product development applies to whole customer base ■ Extensive R&D resources

consequent holdings of buffer stocks in order to combat unknown demand. Fast and flexible response, however, reduces forecast reliance and removes uncertainty by applying different operational practices to individual product groups, distribution channels, retailers, etc. Hence, true demand patterns become evident and easier to satisfy. We can now discuss the four core competency or capability categories.

1   *Process-based* (derived from transformation activities). The transformation activities for SMEs can be many and varied, depending on the type of industry or product being provided. However, it seems clear that an SME cannot always rely upon the stability of long-term relationships (either customer or supplier). Consequently, transformation activities constantly undergo a degree of variation and change. Often these fluctuations can be small and incremental; occasionally they will involve large changes in direction, or step changes. A core capability for the SME at a transformation system level is to manage change and adapt without major disruption being caused to operational structures and processes.

2   *System or coordination-based* (across the entire operation system). Here, SMEs will seek to ensure they maximize the opportunities for flexibility and responsiveness, using human resources, having multiple skills and utilizing multi-purpose technology that can be devoted to a wide variety of product and service combinations.

3   *Organization-based* (across the entire organization). The majority of SMEs reside in a complex and dynamic environment. In addition, their size makes them vulnerable to external forces, reducing their ability to dictate terms in relationships. Core competencies and processes at this level will involve an ability to anticipate as well as react to these various forces. Research has shown (Lowson, 1998) that successful SMEs have an extended ability and awareness of their close or micro environment. They have developed processes and procedures to scan this environment for potential changes and to proactively make adjustments before any particular damage may be caused. This entrepreneurial competence and risk taking comes partly from the fact that ownership and management are closely connected to the work of the organization. There is, as we saw above, task continuity. Planning and management are closely linked to operations – the brainwork of operations resides at all levels across the organization. Understanding the close environment and having the ability to be proactive and responsive to change also requires excellent coordination skills. Here the SME, due partly to its size and flat structure, is in an excellent position to utilize strong communication linkages between processes, systems and people.

4   *Network-based* (covering the whole supply network). As the Dennergate case study revealed, SMEs suffer from frequent changes in supplier and customer configurations. They cannot rely on stability in these areas. Consequently an innovative and creative ability to secure new markets and new sources of supply is vital for these firms. This necessitates the development of supportive networks, both horizontal and vertical. The former allows the SME to share work and to subcontract and outsource some tasks in a mutual network of small firms. The latter offers opportunities to switch between different suppliers and sources of necessary inputs (raw materials, components, etc.) as well as being able to find new markets and purchasers of outputs.

249

Resources

The SME has little bargaining power when it comes to resources. Suppliers will often be larger and more powerful and can raise prices, reduce quality and restrict supplies as a means to squeeze SME profitability. The SME has to be careful to avoid the high switching costs involved in changing supplier. The fixed costs buyers face in changing suppliers can include:

- Being tied to a particular source of supply due to product specification;
- Investment in ancillary equipment or learning how to operate suppliers equipment;
- Production lines being closely connected to a suppliers';
- The use of a core input that is only available from a limited source with no alternatives possible.

If switching costs are kept low, the SME can utilize its flexibility and constantly seek new and innovative sources of inputs.

Technologies

Most firms will rely upon some form of technology, either for products or processes. Often SMEs will lack the financial resources for high levels of investment in these areas. As a consequence, flexibility is again the byword for the SME in ensuring that technologies can be adapted for multiple purposes.

TIME OUT BOX I

How can an SME such as Dennergate ensure that any technological investment is flexible and suitable for multiple purposes?

Key tactical activities to support a strategic positioning

As with other organization types, certain short-term tactical activities will be vital to support a particular strategy or positioning; for example, particular linkages across the firm or externally with suppliers and customers. As the Dennergate case study revealed, despite having an inherently flexible structure, it is important that the SME develops this attribute operationally. Many of these organizations are particularly vulnerable to the decisions of powerful suppliers and customers. Flexibility in both looking for new sources of raw materials (or other inputs) and new markets must be matched by internal operational flexibility that supports rapid changes and diversification in product and service combinations. Thus, flexible operations strategies are built upon a foundation of flexible tactical and support activities.

SERVICE SECTOR OPERATIONS STRATEGIES

The provision of services now plays a vital part in most Western economies. In the US, for example, services account for 80 per cent of employment (US Bureau of the Census, 1990: 395). In the UK it is estimated that 75 per cent of the workforce are engaged in the service industries.

The nature of service provision

In previous chapters we have emphasized the importance of thinking in terms of a product and service combination. In fact, we can consider all commercial offerings to have an element of both product and service. The degree of tangibility varies from one instance to another depending upon whether we are supplying pure goods or pure services (see chapter 1). The intangibility factor also causes some problems, particularly with pure services. What is included as part of the service and what is not? For example, a customer's opinion of a visit to the bank will depend upon the 'moments of truth' that vary from the cleanliness of the floor, the length of the queue or even the cheerfulness and attractiveness of the teller.

There are three vitally important aspects of service provision: paying attention to competencies and their continuous development, establishing collaborative relationships and empowering service employees. A service capability is further defined by Heskett *et al.* (1997) as being composed of several elements:

- A latitude in delivering results to customers;
- A clear expression of boundaries within which front-line employees are permitted to act;
- Excellent job training;
- Well-engineered support systems, such as service facilities and information systems;
- Recognition and rewards for doing jobs well, determined at least partially by the levels of customer satisfaction achieved;
- Rigorous recruitment and selection practices.

The value of a service can be modelled to give a focus on what the customer seeks in each service delivery. The model of service value can be viewed as having six essential parts (Zeithaml, 1998, as adapted by Haksever *et al.*, 2000):

- *Perceived quality*. This can be thought of as 'fitness for use', customer satisfaction or internal and external customer satisfaction (Juran and Gryna, 1993). These definitions of quality capture the essence of value by emphasizing the importance of customer perception. Expectations are formed through word of mouth, communication, personal needs, past experience and external communications from the service organization. If the perception of what is received matches or exceeds customers' expectations, they will be satisfied and value will have been created. The higher the perceived quality the higher the value of the service.

- *Intrinsic attributes*. The benefits provided to the customer; these can be both core services and supplementary services. The former are the basic, or minimum, benefits the customer expects. The latter are the additional 'comfort' factors that enhance the experience. For example, a flight from Helsinki to Oslo 'transports passengers on an airplane from one airport to another safely and comfortably'. That is the core service. The supplementary services include food and beverages, newspapers, pillows and blankets and airline information. The core service is clearly essential and some supplementary services are always needed for its successful delivery. Indeed, to be competitive, creating more value by increasing supplementary services is often the main weapon a firm will use to increase market share (although these are transitory gains that can often be copied by a competitor).

- *Extrinsic attributes*. These are related to the service but exist outside the service package and are not directly related to the service itself. For example, the reputation of a hospital, the location of a restaurant in a fashionable waterfront neighbourhood on Lake Washington in Seattle. These are psychological benefits that the service provider may not always control directly, but they can greatly enhance value to the customer.

- *Monetary price*. The sum of the expenses incurred by the customer to obtain a service – the price charged as well as other expenses (including travel to an airport or hospital for example). Often a low monetary price will create customer value, providing that the lowering of prices will not affect other necessary attributes of the service.

- *Non-monetary price*. A perceived sacrifice over and above financial expense will be a non-monetary price. Time, anxiety, inconvenience, perception of risk, and other psychological costs can greatly influence the perception of value.

- *Time*. The time element of value creation can be construed in three ways. First, the time needed to use the service. In general, the less time that is required to use a service the greater the value. There is an important connection between time and service quality and the perceived non-monetary price. Second, service as a time-saving alternative to another service. Here, value is created through saving time for the customer and replacing, albeit sometimes only briefly, another competing service. Third, the time horizon required for the service to provide benefits. Value for the customer can be created over different time periods. For example value now and for a short period of time (a haircut and meal in a restaurant); value now and for an indefinite period of time (mail delivery, television broadcasts, inoculations); value in the future for a limited period of time (building a new school or restaurant); and value in the future for an indefinite period of time (university education, health checkups, cosmetic dentistry).

A service can be considered as being a package of features. Fitzsimmons and Fitzsimmons (2000) consider this bundle to consist of four elements:

- *Supporting facility* – the physical resources that must be in place before the service can be offered (for example, a hospital).

■ *Facilitating goods* – the material elements of the product service combination (equipment in the hospital, patient records, medical supplies, etc.).

■ *Explicit services* – the benefits that are readily observable to the senses and consist of the essential, *intrinsic* features of the service (the absence of pain after breaking a leg or the cure of an illness).

■ *Implicit services* – the psychological benefits that a customer may only sense vaguely or the *extrinsic* features of the service (the status of the hospital as a teaching facility, for example).

All these features are experienced by the customer and form the basis of her or his perception of the overall or total service – the various 'moments of truth' throughout experience (the total service can be ruined by one bad moment!).

When designing the product and service combination, decisions must be made regarding a number of strategic objectives. These objectives include both structural and managerial elements.

Structural

■ *Delivery system* – front and back office arrangements, degree of customer participation and automation;

■ *Facility design* – layout, size aesthetics;

■ *Location* – consumer demographics, sites, competition, site characteristics;

■ *Capacity planning* – managing queues, number of customer servers employed, demand characteristics and strategies for matching demand.

Managerial

■ *Service encounter* – service culture, motivation, selection and training, levels of employee empowerment;

■ *Quality* – measurement of levels, methods of delivery, value and expectations, service guarantees;

■ *Management of demand and matching capacity* – satrategies for coping with demand and changing capacity to match (see chapter 9);

■ *Information resources* – data collection, processing and use of information sources (including sharing with trading partners).

For a successful service operations strategy, the cluster of strategic decisions taken concerning the structural subsystems are supported by the managerial elements in order to deliver a high quality service concept. However, the reader should be aware that we are dealing with a competitive environment: the operations strategy for a product and service combination cannot be developed in isolation – the wider domain must also be considered, especially its demands for variety.

Service operations strategies can be grouped depending upon the degree to which they offer variety (that is, customized to individual needs) and the volumes of services produced:

- *Standardized service operations strategies*. These have little variety and high volume. Typical competitive priorities will be consistent quality, on time delivery and low cost. Mail and parcel delivery firms like FedEx, fast-food restaurants and cinemas will use standardized service strategies.

- *Assemble-to-order service operations strategies*. This service strategy designs operations to include processes that produce a set of standardized services and processes that are devoted to assembling standardized offerings for specific customers' needs. The assembly processes are flexible so that the correct package can be assembled for each customer with a fast response time. Internet access, mobile phones, credit cards, banking services, satellite broadcast services and some food outlets such as Café Rouge will apply these approaches.

- *Customized service operations strategies*. Designed to provide for individual needs. Low volume but customized with a high-performance design. Hairdressers, general practitioners, dentists, beauty salons, repair facilities, decorating services and high quality restaurants will all apply these strategies.

Formulating a service sector operations strategy

In general, service organizations operate in a very competitive and difficult environment. As Fitzsimmons and Fitzsimmons (2001) point out, there are several reasons for these problems:

- *Low entry barriers*. Service inventions cannot be patented; innovations are easily copied. In addition, for a competitor to enter the market the capital intensity and investment necessary is relatively low. Some barriers clearly exist in term of location (a high street or beach-front resort, for example) or through the use of specialist equipment provided by the service suppliers (specialist computer terminal ordering equipment used by a hospital supply department that is provided by the supplier creates a barrier to entry). In addition, strong customer loyalty for a particular type of service will also prevent competitors from easily entering the market.

- *Opportunities for economy of scale*. Because most services are produced and consumed simultaneously and either the service or the customer must travel to consumption point, economies of scale are often low. The opportunities for large batches or runs of services, that can be stored as inventory, are minimal. Further, the necessity for physical travel will often limit the outlet size of the service provider.

- *Erratic demand levels*. Service sales levels are often a function of the time of day or day of the week – although there are also random and seasonal elements.

- *Size and power disadvantages*. As mentioned above, many service suppliers are small scale operations (clearly, there are some exceptions such as large financial institutions and firms such as McDonald's and Marriott Hotels). The SME service, however, is often at a disadvantage when dealing with supply system partners (customers or suppliers) that are much larger in size and more powerful.

- *Product and service combination substitution*. Those offerings that tend to emphasize a higher service content can often be quickly and easily substituted using new

TIME OUT BOX II

Examples of erratic service demand can be linked to: time of day (banking during lunchtimes); day of week (hair styling on a Saturday or weekend flights); seasonality (hotel accommodation at ski resorts); and random (emergency services and telephone operator services). Steady and regular demand for certain services are less common. It may be interesting to list and compare the more stable types of service provision.

innovations and creative developments. For example, many similar service providers often exist and a visit to a particular fast-food outlet with long queues and waiting times can easily be substituted by going to another outlet. Increasingly medical checks can be performed at home using equipment that was at one time only available at the medical practitioner.

■ *Exit barriers.* As we have seen in the last section, small and medium-sized firms like Dennergate often have the flexibility and agility to move into similar markets (related diversification) or different markets altogether (unrelated diversification). Often this ability is due to low capital investment (and financial exposure) and the drive and enthusiasm of the owners or managers of the firms concerned.

For any service industry, these various barriers and difficulties have to be considered when formulating an operations strategy. This involves making a number of choices regarding the broad direction of the strategy. These choices form part of a pattern of decisions that also have various integrative elements, as we can see in Fig. 12.1. The integrative devices help provide a consistent business and operations strategy that will deliver service value.

The business decisions or choices and integrative devices in Fig. 12.1 are now covered in detail.

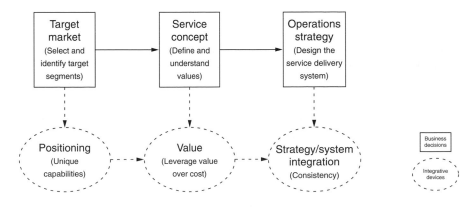

Figure 12.1 Business decisions and integrative elements

Business choices for a service strategy

The service sector operations strategy must reflect and support a number of broader business decisions in order to bring to life the service concept:

- *Target market.* Most product and service combinations will be unlikely to appeal to all people; it is impossible to satisfy everybody and a mistake to try! Careful identification and selection of target market segments is vital.
- *Service concept.* The product and service must also be carefully defined and the values or outcomes it provides well understood. The question 'what business are we in?' defines the service concept. These definitions must be well understood internally as well as externally and should be broad enough to accommodate future extensions due to diversification and changes in technology, consumption patterns and other opportunities. However, too broad a definition will leave a firm stuck in the middle and unable to properly satisfy the value demanded for any groups of customers due to lack of ability, competence and capability.
- *Operations strategy.* As part of the total operations strategy for services, important long-term decisions will need to be made about the service delivery system (how an organization prepares for and delivers service requirements). These include work force and human resource issues, organizational policies, control of quality and cost, technology, resources and value delivery, layout, technology, equipment, processes and procedures, work force levels and job descriptions and roles. The design of the delivery system should ensure maximum customer satisfaction. A well-designed delivery system (and operations strategy for that matter) will be a source of competitive advantage and difficult for competitors or new industry entrants to copy. We cover these in more detail in the next section.

Integrative elements for a service strategy

In addition to the business choices, the various integrative devices provide guidelines for planning actions at all levels to implement a service value provision that is positioned, leverages value over cost and is integrated.

- *Positioning.* As seen in chapter in chapter 3 conceptual and practical positioning is the method by which the organization can differentiate itself from its competitors. It requires a deep understanding of customer needs, the organization's capabilities and competencies, competitors' service offerings (as well as their capabilities), and the ability of the service to meet and provide value needs. Once understood, the organization can seek unique attributes that match the service offering to the value needs of the segment targeted. This uniqueness can use cost, service features, advertising and promotion, distribution channels and delivery systems *et al.* to satisfy core parts of the model service value discussed above.
- *Value/cost leverage.* A well-designed and positioned service offering provides unique benefits to customers and creates value; hopefully more value than competitors. Such uniqueness can justify premium prices for the service, which some customers are

prepared to pay, but it also adds cost to the organization. If the firm can deliver an exceptional value without driving costs equally high it leverages value over costs and enjoys higher margins (and profits) over competitors. However, like the search for the Holy Grail, this task is harder than it sounds. Various operations strategies and tactics must be used for the leverage necessary. These can include customizing certain features of the service that are highly valued and standardizing others, managing quality levels, managing demand and supply, and involving the customer, to various degrees, in the value creation.

- *Strategy/system integration*. In addition to the consistency between target market and service concept, and between service concept and operations strategy, the operations strategy must also be consistent with the delivery system to provide integration and consistency. This consistency can be achieved by carefully designing the delivery system to reflect the operations strategy and overall business strategy for the service.

We can now examine how these business decisions and integrative devices can be combined to form a service operations strategy. To do this we will use a case vignette. Unusually, the organization chosen will not be a large multi-million pound corporation, but an SME (for as we have pointed out, the vast majority of service providers in Europe, Asia and North America are small and medium-size).

We can now examine the building blocks of the operations strategy in more detail.

CASE VIGNETTE **THE RE-BAR**

The Re-Bar can be found in Bastion Square in Victoria, the capital of Vancouver Island, just off the west coast of British Columbia. This bustling and vibrant small city is, like its close neighbours Vancouver City and Seattle, famed for its innovation, creativity and new thinking – the latest trends are likely to spring from the entrepreneurial spirit found here.

The name Re-Bar is a take on the reinforcement rods used in the concrete foundations, similarly, the food served is 'reinforcing, rejuvenating and re-energizing – and we have a bar!' The concept of the Re-Bar is to provide:

> Nourishing meals that we love to prepare and serve, we plan our seasonal menus in a 'planet friendly' effort to benefit from naturally 'in season' produce. Our visions could are only realized through our customers without whom we wouldn't be able to do what we love best – being creative and making beautiful food for you ... the bar guarantees that it recycles everything that comes through the door, even the customer, our paper products are 100 per cent recycled and the water and hot drinks that are served are filtered using charcoal filters.

The Bar offers forty-seven different types of tea, thirty-six coffees, twenty-seven herbal infusions and a range of hot and cold wholefoods with 100 per cent guaranteed natural and organic ingredients. However it's the juices and power tonics that are the main

continued

continued

attraction. These come in a bewildering range of vegetable and fruit combinations – both hot and cold and as 'smoothies'. They arrive in large tall glasses that are full of a kaleidoscope of swirling colours carefully and painstakingly layered to create the effect of a delicate painting – far too good to actually drink with titles such as 'Saturn Return', 'Brand New Bag', 'Axis Shift', 'Full Metal Jacket', 'Belly Rub', and 'Liver Quiver'! Power tonics, just as beautiful, have names such as 'Soul Charge', 'Angelwater', 'Floo Fighter', 'Sinatra Mantra' and 'Rocket Scientist'. Wheatgrass drinks called 'Pharaoh's Sneakers', 'Green Heaven', 'Picassos' Tonic', and 'Astro Turf'. Fruit drinks such as 'Sun Ra' 'Amour de Cosmos', 'Atomic Glow', 'Dragon Fly', 'Cootie Bug', 'Emma Peel', and 'Hummingbird'. Yet it is not just art or a beverage. Each particular concoction serves a purpose and is a tonic for any particular ailment, for each drink can include ingredients such as bee pollen, flax seed oil, rice protein, royal jelly, aloe vera, amino acids, electrolytes, ginseng, spirulina, echinacea, ginko biloba and even hangover tonic!

The Re-Bar is a cooperative and as such strategic service decisions are made by consensus in a committee forum. We can examine this process of developing a service strategy using the business choices and integrative devices highlighted above. Business choices include.

- *Target market*. The Re-Bar is the 'in place'. Its main market segments are the young and professional, health conscious client. In addition, the tourist trade in Victoria from the US is also an important sector.
- *Service concept*. As we can see above, natural and organic ingredients, local sourced and environmentally friendly operations that will stand the strongest scrutiny.
- *Operations strategy*. Decisions and planning are required concerning the suppliers of local produce, which, when in season, must be closely coordinated for both quality and timing. Re-Bar needs high quality staff with artistic talents and who have an interest in ecology and the environment. In addition, they must be prepared to work as a team and continually learn new skills in producing the high quality drinks and meals. Such skills must also be considered when human resource policies are developed. Some of the latest catering equipment and technology is also employed behind the scenes in the back office. Demand for tables in the Re-Bar is particularly high at peak times. The staff are not keen to entertain a reservation system and so they have to be particularly adroit at ensuring a fast turnaround without giving the impression customers are being rushed – again the planning of these skills is important.

The various integrative devices for the service strategy are also interesting:

- *Positioning*. The Re-Bar seeks to position itself as being the latest concept in healthy food and drink but at the same time being environmentally friendly. There are of course other health food restaurants, but the Re-Bar have positioned themselves in such a way as to suggest that the various beverages are actually good for you and treat ailments. Instead of talking a daily vitamin pill a vitamin drink is just as good and much more fun – and a social experience!

■ *Value/cost leverage.* Despite the artistic flair and the health conscious additives, the Re-Bar admits that the contents of most of its drinks are basically high quality vegetables and fruits. Further, the clientele seem to prefer the clean yet functional, no frills atmosphere that is further evidence of being environmentally friendly. Consequently, costs are low, yet premium prices are paid for food and drink.

■ *Strategy/system integration.* The operations strategy delivers the business 'vision' of the Re-Bar. However, to achieve this, the strategy and operational systems have to be integrated. Thus, the planning and polices of the operation (above) must be translated into tactical, daily activities.

Service operations strategy building blocks

The building blocks of the service operations strategy will, for many service providers, place a strong emphasis upon system or coordination capabilities across the whole organization rather than process-based capabilities.

TIME OUT BOX III

For the service sector, why might the coordination of activities across the whole organization or network be more important than the transformation capabilities alone?

Core competencies, capabilities and processes

For many service sector operations a physical transformation will not always be a key capability. As discussed in chapter 1, we can think of product and service combinations as existing on a continuum with pure goods to one end and pure services to the other. The higher the service contribution the less important the physical transformation and the more crucial coordination-based activities across an organization and its supply system. For the Re-Bar, however, the more tangible elements of their products are also important.

1 *Process-based capabilities* (derived from the transformation activities). Here, decisions are made concerning the production of the food and drinks involved, the skill levels needed in the future, the technology, the raw materials, and the type of products that will satisfy the customer (including the presentational elements).

2 *System or coordination-based capabilities* (found across the entire operations system). The kitchen and preparation areas must coordinate activities with the order taking and delivery systems. This harmonization is vital, especially during the periods of

heavy demand. Similarly synchronization of a wide variety of inputs (raw materials and human resources) must also be carefully controlled to coincide with the production needs.

3   *Organization-based* (across the entire enterprise). Here, we can think of the distinctive competencies necessary for the Re-Bar to provide an atmosphere conducive to customers' requirements together with a fast and effective service levels. The role of information is also important. Given the positioning that the restaurant adopts in terms of environmentally-friendly and health-promoting products, patrons inevitably seek advice as to which preparation might best suit a particular condition or ailment. Staff will have to balance the need to provide a well-informed information service with the pressures for efficiency and speed of response (especially in high demand periods).

4   *Network-based* (covering the whole supply network). The integration of the whole supply system is vital for this type of operation. Decisions will need to be made concerning future supplies of local, fresh, in-season produce that is of a high quality. Thus, the sourcing of goods from a wide variety of suppliers (some regular and some at particular times of year) will be a key building block for the Re-Bar's operations strategy. Indeed, it may be necessary to form strategic alliances with a number of key vendors.

Resources

As indicated above, decisions regarding key resources will include raw materials and a properly trained and skilled workforce.

Technologies

Production and communication technology (especially with and between suppliers) is a vital element. At present the Re-Bar is seeking to establish an electronic reorder system with main suppliers of certain types of fruit and vegetables that are used all year round. This system will enable automatic replenishment as produce is used. This is a particularly important requirement for the future, as the Re-Bar intends to open five other sites in major cites in Northwest Canada and the United States – the Re-Bar could be coming to a city near you!

Key tactical activities to support a strategic positioning

From the Re-Bar case study, there are certain tactical and support activities that will be essential for a particular strategy or positioning. For example, customer service levels, creative flair and skills in preparation, hygiene and cleanliness and sourcing coordination of seasonal fruit and vegetables from local suppliers.

CONCLUSION

This chapter has demonstrated the importance of both SMEs and the services sector. We have also gone some way to rectifying a considerable omission in the academic literature, by providing a detailed consideration of their needs in terms of operations and operations strategy. Chapter 13 will now focus upon another new and developing sphere of operations: global trade and supply networks.

CASE STUDY – OPERATIONS STRATEGY IN ACTION

Swedish Medical Centre, Seattle – operations strategy: SME and service sector applications (www.swedish.org)

For more than eighty-five years, the Swedish Hospital in Seattle has been one of the top US medical centres attracting patients from around the world. As a hallmark for excellence in healthcare, the Swedish mission is to redefine excellence as being 'Not only the best place to receive care, but to be the best place to purchase care too. To become the best place to work, and practice medicine. And at every level the best organization with which to partner.'

The Swedish Hospital began with US$10,000 and a dream. Dr Nils Johanson, a young Swedish emigrant, saw the need for a first-rate non-profit hospital in the thriving port town of Seattle. He convinced ten of his fellow Swedish emigrants to buy US$1,000 bonds and in 1912 the Swedish Hospital opened in a renovated apartment building, with just twenty-four beds.

In the first years of operation, founder Johanson and President JA Soderberg paid the bills out of their own pockets. It was the beginning of a legacy of humanitarianism and stewardship that would transform the small hospital into a world renowned medical centre. Today the Swedish spans two campuses and twenty city blocks. It currently employs 4,000 people with 1,500 physicians that represent virtually every medical specialty and subspecialty, and has 860 beds. Its demand for excellence is fuelled by a commitment to continuing medical research. At any one time more than 350 treatment protocols are under investigation by Swedish physicians in dozens of specialities.

In meeting the demand for excellence, patients come to Swedish from every walk of life: premature babies and senior citizens; blue-collar workers and CEOs. They come from neighbourhoods like Kirkland and from cities as far away as London and Tokyo. Their needs are as diverse as they are. But they share one common desire: to have access to the best possible health care. Whether they come from across town or across the globe, they have access to a unique combination of resources and technologies, innovation and expertise that has made Swedish a respected international teaching hospital.

At the Swedish they perform more than 22,000 surgeries a year and it is an international leader in both volumes and outcomes. But it isn't merely the volume of cases that set it apart from the competition. It is the calibre of its surgeons, anesthesiologists, nurses and support staff and its state-of-the-art facilities and technology. In dozens of specialities, surgeons who practice at Swedish have earned a worldwide recognition for pioneering new procedures. A highly trained staff of nurses, social workers, physical and occupational therapists and the most sophisticated equipment is also currently available to support them.

The scope of services available at the hospital is remarkable and extends far beyond traditional hospital care, from accident and emergency to outpatient services to home care; from addiction recovery to pain management. Patients can use home-health services, hospice services, outpatient treatment, the eye or eating disorder centre and even a sleep disorder programme. In true Swedish tradition, they continue to partner physicians in the community in developing new initiatives and services, assuring continued access, worldwide, to state-of-the-art services.

Swedish also leads the way in developing systems to improve and reduce costs. Its innovative surgical care pathways literally guide patients through every step of the process, from pre-admission to rehabilitation. The focus is on communication and patient education to provide positive results: patients feel more in control, recover faster and have fewer complications.

Independent research conducted by the National Research Corporation in the US consistently names Swedish as one of the top hospitals in the world. But as the hospital has evolved, so has the scope of its services, that aim to recognize the vision of its founder: to be the best non-profit medical facility in the region.

The Swedish is more than just equipment and facilities, research and new techniques. It is people coming together to care for others in need – nurses, physicians, social workers, dietitians, etc. Dedicated teams of people, each defining at a personal level what excellence really means. The philosophy of Swedish is summed up by their President and CEO, Richard Peterson:

> Swedish aims to evolve through quality initiatives, through innovation and through strategic partnerships that all redefine excellence in health care. Today, however, health care providers face increasing pressures to reduce costs. At the hospital we are committed to the belief that the best way to reduce costs is to increase both quality and the variety of service.
>
> You must recognize that health care is a very personal matter. Patients are diverse and have individual and diverse needs – no two are alike. We have to satisfy these demands but within certain cost constraints – a difficult challenge. We like to think that excellence is not an end result, it is a process. It demands vision, discipline and an absolute commitment to settle for nothing but the best.

ANSWERS TO TIME OUT BOXES

Time out box I

Technologies dedicated to specific and narrow tasks will be inflexible. However, in many industries this is inescapable. For example, Dennergate must employ process technology to aid the operations task. This will include cutting, sewing, fusing and pressing equipment as well as some computer-integrated manufacturing capability to control specifications, quality levels, and general production planning. Much of this technology is specific to the task and could not, for instance, be switched to producing car engines or garbage cans. Nevertheless, Dennergate have taken steps to reduce their reliance upon single customers. They have started to use their process technology for other types of garment in different seasons. Instead of relying upon orders for women's summer tops, they now also supply cold weather and waterproof jackets for the sailing and water-sports market. Dennergate also offer a tailored men's and women's jacket service. Instead of going to a retailer, customers can choose a style, colour and fabric either online, at the company shop or from a catalogue. Their measurements are taken on site or at home and a customized jacket made. This related product diversification utilizes their process equipment throughout the year. Often, equipment can be less process specific and more flexible. PCs and other electronic equipment can be used for multiple purposes. For example, Dennergate supply a small local retail chain in Wales. The retailer provides Dennergate with data regarding sales on a regular basis. At the end of each day, each store will fax Dennergate a tear-off slip giving details of sales by stock keeping unit (i.e. style, colour and size of garment being sold). This advance information not only helps the manufacturer to plan production, it also avoids purchasing dedicated equipment to receive PoS information and utilizes existing equipment.

Time out box II

Some services are demanded with a high degree of regularity and can be planned and timetabled. These include: artistic performances with advance ticket sales, delivery of lectures at a set time of day and high quality restaurant services that have to be reserved in advance.

Time out box III

In most service operations, transformation activities essential to the service delivery will be found across the whole enterprise. These core capabilities or competencies will not be function specific and there is unlikely to be an operations department or function as such, thus coordination is often a problem that, if successfully overcome, can lead to competitive advantage.

DISCUSSION QUESTIONS, WORK ASSIGNMENTS AND EXAM QUESTIONS

1   What are the strengths and weaknesses of an SME? In what way might the SME operational environment differ from other larger organizations?
2   Why does the SME operational structure pose particular problems?
3   What are the important components of an operations strategy for many SMEs?
4   How can we model the value of a service?
5   Explain what is meant by the term a 'package of features' when discussing a service.
6   Why is the service sector a particularly difficult environment for operations?
7   What are the business choices and integrative elements needed for a service strategy?

Reader questions related to the Swedish Medical Centre case study

1 At the beginning of this chapter we described a model of service value as having six essential parts:
   - Perceived quality;
   - Intrinsic attributes;
   - Extrinsic attributes;
   - Monetary price;
   - Non-monetary price; and
   - Time.

   A service was also described as being a 'bundle' consisting of four features:
   - Supporting facilities;
   - Facilitating goods;
   - Explicit services; and
   - Implicit services.

   Using each of these elements, classify the important elements of service that the Swedish hospital offers and the necessary operational activities that will be essential in each case.

2 We can see from the case study that the Swedish provides a vast range of services, many of which have to be customized to an individual level. Bearing this in mind, what are the main operations strategy decisions necessary for the Swedish? It may be helpful to classify these as:
   - Core competencies, capabilities and processes;
   - Resources;
   - Technologies; and
   - Key tactical activities vital to support a particular strategy.

3 Does the Swedish require more than one operations strategy? If so, for what products and/or services?

4 Can these strategies be customized? If so, how?

5 Intriguingly, the Swedish CEO suggests that increasing both quality and the variety of service can cut costs. Can this be done? If so, how?

RECOMMENDED READING

Fitzsimmons J.A. and Fitzsimmons M.J. (2001) *Service Management*, 3rd edn, Chapter 4 'Service Strategy', McGraw-Hill, New York.

Chapter 13

Operations strategy

Globe trade and supply network applications

The penultimate chapter concerns the global trade and supply network applications of an operations strategy. These two areas have been deliberately chosen for their increasing popularity. As we shall see later, due to the growth in communication technology many firms are now trading on a global basis. In addition, these firms also recognize that their supply systems are of vital strategic importance, despite their inherent complexity.

LEARNING OBJECTIVES

After considering this chapter, the reader will be able to:

- Discuss the driving forces for global and international trade
- Analyse the types of international strategy
- Appreciate the importance of sourcing and procurement as an operations strategy
- Consider the advantages and disadvantages of offshore and domestic sourcing
- Consider the history and evolution of the supply network
- Understand the nature of both supply network and supply chain operations strategies

INTRODUCTION

As with the other chapters in this section, we will deal with two distinct yet interrelated elements. The importance of international and global trade has increased dramatically; consequently it is clear that many firms will wish to develop operations strategies for this purpose. In addition organizations, no matter what their size or particular sector of trade, now understand the importance of operations strategies that recognize the role of other firms in their domain – the supply network.

GLOBAL OPERATIONS STRATEGIES

Even small and medium-sized companies are now sourcing and trading on a global basis. Advanced forms of information communication technology and the Internet have made operations and the selling and buying of products and services on a worldwide basis feasible. New markets are now available in corners of the world previously unthinkable; even micro-organizations are realizing the benefits to be gained when utilizing (often through outsourcing) international resources of both labour and materials.

International competition is a complex arena for any firm. As Meredith and Shafer (2002) suggest, firms now operate in domestic, exporter and international markets at the same time. We have global firms, joint ventures, partial ownership, strategic alliances, outsourced production and services, build and assemble offshore, foreign suppliers of parts, joint ventures, even reimporting manufacturing arrangements. However, whilst global operations are often used to reduce direct costs, they also exact a price in terms of coordination and flexibility (as we shall see later).

Meredith and Shafer (2002) comment that global operational coordination consists of many elements. Accurate information provision is required in the supply chain, to minimize costs of errors as well as costs of storage and inventories. Indeed, as global coordination becomes a problematic issue, many firms will seek to establish closer sole-source arrangements with a smaller, preferred, supply base.

This growth in world trade and the extension of operational activities beyond the boundaries of the firm has clear implications for competitiveness and the dimensions of an operations strategy. Operations have a crucial role to play in international competitiveness. Strategic operations decisions are necessary regarding such issues as the responsiveness and flexibility of domestic supply compared with outsourcing to low cost, low-wage producers offshore; the appropriate locations for international facilities; the output capacity of plants; and the labour–technology trade-offs in each location. There are six primary characteristics of the transformation system that are crucial when making such decisions (these have been adapted from the work of Meredith and Shafer [2002]):

- *Efficiency or 'doing the thing right'*. Measured as output per unit of input. The problem comes in making comparisons, finding meaningful comparisons and choosing the right measures for these inputs and outputs.
- *Effectiveness or 'doing the right thing'*. Are the right sets of outputs being produced? Are we focused on the right task?
- *Capacity*. The maximum rate of output that is attainable. Here, a balance must be struck between capacity and efficiency.
- *Quality*. Are the quality levels of the output right and can they be consistently attained?
- *Response Time*. How quickly can the output be produced? Or preferably, can the output levels be set to respond to the exact nature of real time demand?
- *Flexibility*. Can the transformation system produce other, different outputs? How easily? How fast? What variety of levels of customization are possible?

Choice of operations strategy

As we shall see later, the choice of an operations strategy can reflect two important variables:

- The levels of cost reduction necessary;
- The levels of flexibility and responsiveness required.

Fig. 13.1 demonstrates the operations strategies that might be applied – depending upon the objectives of the enterprise.

The matrix in Fig. 13.1 details the two variables above. The vertical axis shows the operational cost of a particular strategy, the horizontal axis the degree of flexibility and responsiveness. The implications for each international operations strategy are critical for both trade and competitive edge. We can now look at the various types of strategy and compare their advantages and disadvantages in terms of flexibility, responsiveness and cost.

International operations strategy

Here, the domestic enterprise imports and exports goods and services from its home country to another, abroad – a strategy relying upon the granting of licences and agents abroad. In this instance, the firm operates in high cost and low responsiveness mode. It is the least

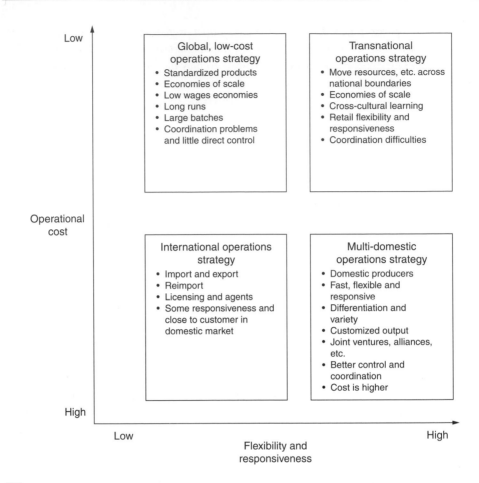

Figure 13.1 *Cost and flexibility considerations in choosing a global operations strategy Sources: adapted from Hill and Jones (1998) and Hitt et al. (1999)*

advantageous, with little local responsiveness or flexibility and little cost advantage because the transformation processes are some distance from the market. However, as an international strategy, it is sometimes the easiest to establish with little change in existing operations and risk exposure mainly taken by the licensees. These agents are, nevertheless, based in the offshore markets concerned and they will understand the local market.

Multi-domestic operations strategy

In this instance operational decisions are decentralized and taken in each particular country concerned. Organizationally, the firms involved are usually strategic business units, subsidiaries, franchises, outsourcing partners or joint ventures with suppliers. Local producers in local markets maximize response and flexibility and encourage differentiation and variety – high degrees of mass customization to accommodate local tastes are often also an option. Control and coordination are also easier using this strategy, as the firm is not just exporting a product but also managing the processes. There are, however, few cost advantages using this multi-domestic approach. The advantages and disadvantages of this type of operations strategy can also be applied to sourcing from domestic vendors rather than offshore.

Global, low cost operations strategy

Applied to standardized products and process that can be produced in bulk (often in advance of a sales season) by large manufacturers operating in low wage economies such as Asia. Economies of scale are possible due to long runs and the size of operations. Coordination is often a problem as control over the numerous offshore suppliers can be difficult; there is also a degree of instability in these arrangements. The strategy also lacks responsiveness and flexibility to demand.

Transnational operations strategy

This strategy seeks to achieve the best of both worlds. It exploits economies of scale and learning, as well as pressure for responsiveness, by recognizing that core competencies, capabilities or processes do not just reside in the domestic or home country. The strategy is transnational as it moves people, processes, material and ideas that transgress national boundaries. These firms can then pursue differentiation, low cost and response simultaneously. We can think of such firms as world companies whose country of origin is unimportant because they possess an independent network of worldwide operations. Key activities are neither centralized or decentralized; instead the resources and activities are dispersed, but specialized, so as to be both efficient and flexible (Bartlett and Ghoshal, 1992). In fact these firms are, as Toffler (1994) suggests, stateless.

In summary, global operations strategies increase the challenges and opportunities for most organizations. Many domestic firms have chosen to develop internationally for strategic reasons such as cost and supply network improvement. However, there are also problems in terms of providing sufficiently flexible and responsive operations that can provide a variety of goods. Some of these costs and benefits are now explored, as we examine in a little detail one specific operations strategy that is widely used across a number of disparate industries and sectors.

Sourcing and procurement operations strategies

Many organizations (small, medium and large) are increasingly attempting to source goods and services on a global basis. With the growth of communications technology and political events such as the enlargement of the European Union and the opening of trade links with many former Soviet Union states, procurement decisions now involve much wider geographic possibilities when dealing with suppliers from a number of countries. This particular type of operations strategy forms an important input to the organization and involves strategic decisions. We will now examine two of the most important, yet often conflicting, objectives in strategic sourcing: cost versus flexibility and response.

Organizations often make use of lower-priced goods supplied by foreign vendors. Taking advantage of low wages, such suppliers are able to undercut competitors operating in domestic markets. However, by their very nature, many of the consumer goods – clothing, footwear, food, drink, toys, furniture, electrical, electronic, household goods, etc. – and services involved have behaviours that are dynamic and complex, usually being sold in discrete seasons. Low cost, although important, may not be the only strategic purchasing criteria for either end consumer or retail buyer. In this section, we endeavour to establish, using empirical research, exactly what the advantages and disadvantages are for an operations strategy using foreign producers as opposed to domestic suppliers. Further, we examine all the various trade-offs concerned for both and analyse the true costs involved.

The role of strategic sourcing and procurement as an operations strategy

Purchasing and supply management as operations strategies have developed from adversarial, clerical transactions between supplier–customer, to strategic, co-operative, buyer–seller relationships. This has subsequently led to the rise in strategies of supply base reduction (a restructuring in the way firms do business with key suppliers in order to gain competitive advantage).

Typically, low cost seems to be the primary purchasing requirement for many organizations – with the strategic operational objective of a supplier relationship being cost reduction. Stuart and McCutcheon (2000) identify four primary mechanisms to achieve this:

- Lower production costs of the suppliers;
- Improved conformance quality (consistently meeting specifications);
- Material/location substitution;
- Lower transaction costs, including the costs of incoming materials inspections, vendor searches and evaluations, corrected supplier problems, and communications with suppliers.

But is low cost the only strategic objective? And are these strategic supply decisions made in full knowledge of all the cost/benefit trade-offs involved? We now address these and other questions.

Sourcing locations and discounts

Research conducted by the Strategic Operations Management Centre at the University of East Anglia, UK (Lowson, 2001d), analysed the operational sourcing strategies of a number of organizations divided between North American (44 per cent) and European (56 per cent). The firms involved were first asked to confirm the main locations from which they had procured goods and services over the past twelve months (it should be remembered that for most enterprises sourcing is a dynamic activity that changes from season to season). The organizations also provided an indication of the average discount (per cent lower unit cost) achieved from non-domestic, offshore sourcing operations strategies. Table 13.1 details the findings:

270

Table 13.1 *Sourcing location, percentage of goods purchased over the last 12 months by organization and discount available*

Firms and average discount	USA	UK	Europe	Central America	Asia	Africa	Other
North American	52	0	1	24	20	3	0
Average discount available (% lower cost)	–	0	5–10	20–25	20–30	10–15	–
European	3	34	24	0	36	2	1
Average discount available (% lower cost)	1–5	–	10–15	–	25–35	15–20	5–10

Clearly, the cost implications of offshore sourcing are evident. For both North America and the UK companies, discounts of between 20 per cent and 30 per cent are achievable in Asia and Central America. This demonstrates the importance that these organizations attach to low cost. However, is low cost the only objective, or do sourcing decisions take into account other factors?

Sourcing objectives

Table 13.2 details the main sourcing objectives of these operations strategies for both North American and European respondents. The participants ranked these objectives and they were divided between domestic and foreign (to include the advantages in each case).

For both sets of organizations low cost is a prime advantage in foreign sourcing; (it is interesting to note that offshore, quality ranks second for both North American and UK enterprises). Domestic sourcing decisions are less clear. Quality, response time, design and

Table 13.2 *Sourcing objectives and advantages of domestic and foreign supply*

	Domestic sourcing objectives Advantages (%)	Offshore sourcing objectives Advantages (%)
North American firms	Quality 41 Response time 30 Design 15 Flexibility 8 Innovation 3 Cost 3	Lower cost 53 Quality 27 Innovation 13 Design 5 Response time 2
European firms	Response time 22 Flexibility 20 Design 20 Innovation 15 Quality 13	Lower cost 66 Quality 32 Design 2

flexibility all score highly. It seems that cost may not be the only sourcing aspiration – other objectives can be seen, although these will clearly change from season to season.

Given that there are a number of purchasing goals involved in a procurement operations strategy, we need to establish what cost/benefit trade-offs or measures might be used when assessing the advantages of foreign versus domestic supply and when making strategic purchasing decisions. To do this it is necessary to analyse two pertinent factors: (a) the levels and types of responsiveness and flexibility available from both foreign and domestic suppliers, and (b) the hidden costs associated with foreign supply and any subsequent inflexibility.

Sourcing responsiveness and flexibility

First, to deal with the responsiveness and flexibility organizations achieve from their suppliers in various geographic regions. The respondents supplied data for the average lead times or advance ordering times necessary for goods and services supplied. Table 13.3 now looks at responsiveness by examining the advance lead time the firms had to withstand when dealing with suppliers in different locations.

It is apparent that longer lead times are required for services and goods sourced from Asia, Africa and Central America, and that this may prove problematical to all in the supply system. The next two tables investigate flexibility issues. In Table 13.4, the respondents commented on the latitude suppliers (in various regions) offered for volume and mix change once an order had been placed both *before*, and more crucially *during*, a sales season.[1]

Table 13.4 provides powerful evidence of the wider strategic sourcing debate. There are, it seems, many important issues other than just unit item cost. We need to understand the flexibility of suppliers once an initial order has been placed, in other words, once demand trends become clear. Such flexibility may be sought both in the volumes needed as well as

Table 13.3 Lead time when ordering from suppliers (by geographic region)

Sourcing regions	Average weeks lead time following order					
	6–12	12–24	24–36	36–48	48–60	60+
North America	———————→					
UK	——→					
Europe	——————————→					
Central America	———————————————→					
Asia	———————————————————————————————→					
Africa	————————————————————————————→					
Other	—————————————————————→					

1 Here, we must remember that some industries (clothing and apparel for example) operate in distinct sales seasons and orders have to be placed before the beginning of such a season. However, reorders are often needed to top up if a particular SKU is in demand (a particular style or colour or size, perhaps).

Table 13.4 *Suppliers' latitude for volume and mix change both before and during sales season (by geographic region)*

	Sourcing regions	Order volume change (% respondents)			Order mix change (% respondents)		
		None	Some	Substantial	None	Some	Substantial
Before the start of the sale season	North America	16	49	35	21	49	30
	UK	9	52	39	21	46	33
	Europe	29	43	28	37	38	25
	Central America	41	38	21	46	34	20
	Asia	66	22	12	70	19	11
	Africa	58	19	23	62	20	18
	Other	34	40	26	30	37	33
After the start of the sale season	North America	39	33	28	47	29	24
	UK	19	46	35	28	39	33
	Europe	35	38	27	41	35	24
	Central America	52	33	15	63	30	7
	Asia	70	21	8	86	12	2
	Africa	61	11	18	73	8	19
	Other	32	42	26	39	37	24

the product mix. The flexibility required by an organization from its suppliers will apply both pre- and post-season opening (it being harder to adjust to the latter despite better known demand trends). *Before* the start of the sale season there is, in general, substantial latitude for volume and mix change from domestic suppliers (i.e. suppliers to the firms in the study from North America and Europe). Whilst vendors in Central America, Asia and Africa offer little flexibility. Similarly, *during* a sale season, North American, UK and European suppliers offer much more flexibility than their Central American, Asian and African counterparts. It seems that flexibility is an important objective of strategic procurement!

Table 13.5 shows the flexibility of vendors by region *after* the sale season has been completed. In other words, their adaptability to deal with surpluses by way of returns, discounts and markdowns.

A similar pattern to that in Table 13.4 emerges. At the end of the season, domestic suppliers (UK and North American, and to a degree European) appear to be more flexible when it comes to such negotiations.

To summarize, there seems to be something of a paradox. Greater cost discounts are obviously available from foreign vendors (especially in Asia, Central America and Africa),

Table 13.5 *Suppliers' latitude to deal with surpluses after a sales season (percentage by geographic region)*

	Sourcing regions	None	Some	Substantial
After the end of the sale season	North America	24	54	22
	UK	11	70	19
	Europe	33	49	18
	Central America	50	41	9
	Asia	73	23	4
	Africa	66	34	–
	Other	40	53	7

as seen from Table 13.1. However, lower cost is not the only objective. Table 13.2 demonstrated that quality, response time, flexibility and design also have a strong role to play. Yet we see from Tables 13.4 and 13.5 that many sources of supply (Central America, Asia and Africa) fail to offer any of these advantages. Further, Table 13.1 tells us that North American organizations in this study source 47 per cent of goods over a twelve month period from such regions, and European retailers 38 per cent. From these findings, we are left to assume that the operations strategy purchasing objectives of these organizations are clearly suboptimal in nearly 50 per cent (North American) and 40 per cent (European) of cases.

Given the various advantages and disadvantages of domestic versus foreign sourcing, the next consideration must be whether they can be quantified and the various trade-offs properly assessed. We know that the unit cost of goods is often lower offshore (the main attraction) but what are the costs of inflexibility and lack of responsiveness? What is the resultant picture when these costs are compared? Is an offshore operations strategy for the supply of goods and services such an attractive option in those circumstances? It is to these questions that we now turn.

The hidden and inflexibility costs of offshore sourcing

Many of the costs of sourcing offshore can be classified as *hidden costs*. The organizations involved in this study were asked to suggest the cost categories associated with purchasing abroad, apart from the cost of the goods themselves (see Table 13.6).

It would seem that the impact of these hidden costs is not insubstantial. However, it is unclear as to whether the respondents in fact quantify these costs or compare them with the advantages of offshore sourcing (an area for future research). The firms in this study cited, in justification of the reason to import, the fact that low offshore prices allow sales at below traditional price points, while still giving attractive margins. Yet these margins may be substantially eroded when the hidden costs are quantified. In addition to the hidden costs, we also need to know what are the costs of using suppliers that are inflexible and unresponsive (*inflexibility costs*).

Table 13.6 *The hidden costs of importing*

Cost categories	Degree of importance (% respondents)
Irrevocable letters of credit charges	15
Delays at the port of entry	7
Last minute use of air freight	5
Expensive administrative travel and quality problems	11
The requirement of an early commitment to manufacturing before sales trends are clear	25
Limited ability to change mix or volume of orders shortly before or during the sales season	37

The costs of importing may well be closely linked to the type of operations sourcing strategy used. Our research indicates that many organizations utilize operations strategies for procurement that can be classified into three generic types:

1   *Offshore, low cost* – a foreign supplier produces and ships 100 per cent of the goods needed for a sale season prior to the start of that selling season. Purchasing decisions are made considerably in advance of the sale season before any demand indication is known.

2   *Combined* – a foreign supplier ships a large proportion of the goods needed prior to the start of the season. The retailer then makes a weekly replenishment order on a domestic supplier. However, PoS information is often not shared with this domestic vendor. Thus supply is often shipped from his stock-holding, built as a buffer against uncertainty. This approach is similar to vendor managed inventory (VMI), although it is suboptimal as far as the supplier (and ultimately the retailer) are concerned.

3   *Domestic, responsive and flexible* – a domestic supplier ships a proportion (for instance 40 per cent) of the goods needed prior to the start of the selling season. Thereafter, in season supply is based upon a re-estimation of actual demand using PoS data provided by the retailer and reorder using Electronic Data Interchange (EDI) to provide for a quick-turnaround supply and shipment of products that are in demand. For the retailer the strategy results in more accurate stocking that reflects demand preference, reduces inventory through faster turns, and increases retailer service metrics.

There are advantages and disadvantages associated with each of these operations strategies. Low unit cost is available offshore compared with higher priced, but more flexible and responsive, domestic suppliers that are operating according to actual demand requirements. Despite charging a higher unit cost for goods, it is possible that the latter are in fact cheaper for the retailer in the long term. It is suggested that if the costs of inflexibility could be measured properly, offshore sourcing might not be the most cost-effective strategy. Research is needed to quantify the costs of these various sourcing scenarios.

In an initial attempt to analyse the implications of the three operations sourcing strategies described, we enlisted the help of three retailers of clothing goods. Each provided detail of performance measurements for sourcing the same clothing item (men's denim jeans[2]) during a single apparel season in 2000/2001 (see Table 13.7). Retailer A sourced jeans mainly from Hong Kong during the season; Retailer B used two suppliers in the season, bulk orders from Thailand, then reorders from the UK; Retailer C used entirely domestic vendors with flexible and responsive operations.

The performance measurements supplied were for similar-sized orders and adjusted for exchange rates, etc. At this level, we are not trying to establish any direct relationship between sourcing performance and a particular supplier and/or supplier location. We do, however, suggest that there are strong reasons for a range of performance measures (over and above price alone) to be used when analysing the performance of different sourcing operations strategies. These different performance metrics demonstrate the advantages and disadvantages of each source of supply and should be used in a combination, not isolation. It is also an

Table 13.7 Retail sourcing performance measurements

Measure	Retailer C	Retailer B	Retailer A
GM/sales revenue[1]	0.47	0.46	0.59
GMROI[2]	5.30	4.40	2.50
Inventory turns[3]	6.20	5.40	1.80
Average inventory[4]	1.00	1.70	3.43
Sales revenue[5]	1.00	0.74	0.59
Service level %[6]	94.00	83.00	72.00
Lost sales %[7]	6.00	11.70	18.00
Sell through %[8]	90.40	81.90	72.90
Sold off %[9]	0.90	6.80	16.00

[1] Gross margin to sales revenue
[2] Gross margin return on investment
[3] Inventory turns per season
[4] Average inventory carried during the sale season (scaled to domestic supply = 1)
[5] Sales revenue during the season (scaled to domestic supply = 1)
[6] Service level – the percentage of times a customer finds her first choice of SKU
[7] Lost sales – the percentage of times customers find none of their first choice SKU preferences
[8] Sell through – the proportion of a season's merchandise selling at initial set price
[9] Sold-off – the percentage of unwanted units remaining after the season

Retailer A Offshore, low cost strategy. US-based specialty clothing store. European and North American outlets. No manufacturing capability. Sources mostly offshore (Asia and Central America).
Retailer B Combined strategy – using foreign and domestic sources in the same season. Independent UK retailer. 'own' or 'private' label goods, increasingly provided from Asia but reorders from UK.
Retailer C Domestic, responsive and flexible strategy. Retailer with manufacturing operation. Large European and North American operation. Sources from contract manufacturers in UK, Europe, North America, Asia and Central America.

....

2 A number of studies have established that the sale rates of denim jeans are seasonal with some large peaks and troughs – see for example King and Hunter (1996).

example of how future research might establish different types of cost measurement (including hidden costs and inflexibility costs) that should be included in any sourcing calculation.

From Table 13.7 we can see that for the three retailers involved, in all performance measures, apart from gross margin/sales, the use of domestic, responsive and flexible vendors emerged as the best sourcing strategy. We speculate that the underlying reason for the superior retail performance of goods sourced using such strategies is the realization that no forecasts are perfect – it is only during the sale season, when consumer demand is revealed, that intelligent supply decisions can be made.

The research in this section does suggest an important finding. In nearly all measures of performance, domestic, responsive and flexible sourcing is possibly far more efficient and optimal than offshore supply, despite the lower unit cost of the latter. In addition, it can be demonstrated that domestic manufacturers can charge nearly 25 per cent more per item and still prove a cheaper option for their retailer customers. This is due to their flexibility and responsiveness, and the savings they offer through avoidance of the hidden costs and inflexibility costs associated with importing (Lowson *et al.*, 1999; Hunter *et al.*, 2002). The advantages associated with speed of response and flexibility will also allow a retailer to reduce price points to below that of competitors (using offshore supply) by as much as 30 per cent, and still earn the same return as the competitor (Lowson, 1999; Gilreath *et al.*, 1995).

Some conclusions

Purchasing, procurement and sourcing has assumed strategic importance as an operations strategy for a number of firms. For many, the search for a low unit cost of goods seems to be the principal goal, with considerable discounts seemingly available offshore. We have endeavoured to establish what other objectives (apart from cost) were fundamental to the sourcing decision and whether these could in fact be ranked. It is clear that a number of other demands are involved in the procurement debate, although many were not as easily quantified as low purchase cost.

The organizations taking part in the study described the various advantages of domestic as opposed to foreign supply. Cost was far from being the only issue. The flexibility and responsiveness of suppliers was widely held to be crucial, both at an operational and strategic level. However, the degree of flexibility and response exhibited by various suppliers to the changing demand patterns, both before and after the season, varied widely, and seemed to depend upon sourcing location. We can conclude that there are substantial hidden costs involved with the use of imported goods. When one adds to these the inflexibility costs, the low cost, offshore sourcing operations strategy starts to look less attractive.

The fundamental lesson of this section revolves around the costs of import compared with local, responsive and flexible suppliers, and what performance measures are used to decide between the two. Further work is needed to establish the exact costs of importing and to assess whether or not these are actually computed by retailers when making sourcing decisions.

We have taken a first step towards developing an axiomatic framework, (widely accepted across a number of consumer industries), that demonstrates the full implications of domestic versus offshore purchasing operations strategies. Research is currently underway to develop a Total Acquisition Cost Model (TACM) that will allow the full implications of these strategic sourcing decisions to be properly analysed and assessed using all the relevant information available. In addition, such a model will also help domestic organizations to demonstrate the advantages of using their flexible and responsive services – rather than continuing the current practice of relying upon the somewhat inefficient use of low-cost, offshore sourcing.

We now turn to another operations strategy that is pervasive in modern commerce: the supply network operations strategy.

SUPPLY NETWORK OPERATIONS STRATEGY

Supply management, or more properly demand management and value stream management, has become a pervasive influence across a number of sectors. The term supply chain refers to all the value adding operational activities involved with supplying an end user with a service or product. Unfortunately, the analogy to a chain fails to do justice to the complexity of the various networks involved. It should be remembered that it is not just goods flowing through a supply system but also information, funds, paper, people, recycled and reused goods and other such items in a bidirectional channel of value that can be likened to multiple, entwined streams in the same river bed. Supply system management also encompasses other functional areas and organizations – it is in fact a cross-functional and inter-organizational discipline and capability.

The phrases supply network, supply system or even supply pipeline are perhaps a more accurate reflection of the complexity involved in this debate. However, the reader will no doubt encounter a myriad terms including supply strategy, supply chain management, value stream management, demand chains and network sourcing. We take the view that many of these expressions are synonyms and are in fact interchangeable; some being operations strategies while others are operations management activities. As a reminder, in chapter 3, by way of clarification, we proposed a genealogy (see Table 3.2, p. 55).

In this chapter, we are dealing with a particular type of operations strategy – a supply network strategy that, by its very nature, deals with the supply of goods and services, at various points or nodes in both a horizontal and vertical system – from originating supplier to final end user. This type of operations strategy can cover both the demand and supply flows between tiers of customers and tiers of suppliers, but its essence is the trading relationship between buyer and supplier in a supply network. Martin Christopher (1992) offers the following definition of a supply network:

> An interconnection of organizations which relate to each other through upstream and downstream linkages between the different processes and activities that produce value in the form of products and services to the ultimate consumer.

History and evolution of supply network and supply chain operations strategies

As discussed in chapter 2, since the early 1950s the systems approach has assumed increasing importance in various scientific disciplines. Bertalanffy (1950, 1956), one of the earliest contributors, revealed the importance of the notion of a system being open or closed to the influences of its environment. Today, these ideas pervade many subjects, not the least management, with the use of terms such as synergy, emergent property, holism and gestalt theory.[3] The importance of these developments is the fact that it is now recognized that an organization does not exist in a vacuum; its success or failure is very much dependent upon other bodies and individuals in its environment.

From these systemic concepts came the understanding that an organization performs as part of a wider group or supply system (also referred to as channel or pipeline or chain). Such a chain is only as strong as its weakest link, although it has to be said that the earlier proponents limited the theory to one vertical chain of organizations without any particular horizontal connections (Stevens, 1989).

It is difficult to be precise as to the exact origination of supply network or supply chain strategies. Possibly they grew from the disciplines of materials management and logistics, and, during the late 1970s and early 1980s, the notion of integrating functional areas within a firm to obtain synergy.

TIME OUT BOX I

What is meant by the term 'integrating'? Can different types of integration be identified?

CRITICAL REFLECTION

Integration strategies, either vertically or horizontally, will often be governed by the decision to make (produce in-house) or buy — enter the marketplace to secure products or services externally. We can examine such decisions using a discipline of micro-economics called 'the theory of the firm' that involves the allocation and distribution of resources at the organisational level. Theories of the firm attempt to understand and explain how inputs to the organization (raw material, energy, skills, etc.) are transformed into outputs (products or services), and the resultant outcome should internal changes need to be made as a reaction to the demands of the market.

It was Coase (1937) who first speculated about the 'make or buy' decision in any firm. This is the decision as to whether to use an administrative relationship (inside — make) or use a market relationship (external — buy). According to Coase, the key to this decision is the cost of the transaction. Transaction costs are not those related to the costs of material and labour, etc. They refer to the costs, often hidden, of managing and controlling the transaction as well as those associated with uncertainty and risk. Firms judge whether or not to make or buy based on minimizing the cost of the transactions involved. Such calculations provide important insights into the boundary of the firm.

continued

---

3 The debate between the reductionist application of many physical sciences and a more systemic approach has raged in the social and natural sciences for many years.

continued

Williamson (1981) further developed transaction theory. He based the theory and its analysis upon two 'behavioural assumptions' and three 'principles of organizational design'.

Behavioural assumptions:

- *Bounded rationality*. Decisions are intended to be rational. However, they fail in this objective due to factors such as limited information about the situation or a limited ability to deal with the information should it be possessed. This contrasts with many other economic models that assume logical decision-making based upon perfect knowledge.
- *Opportunism*. There is a hidden agenda behind any decisions made on behalf of the organization by individuals. Williamson called this 'self interest seeking with guile'.

Principles of organizational design:

- *Asset specificity*. Resources such as skills and equipment become specialized and will have little or no value outside their particular production context. This applies mainly to organizations such as suppliers, who will focus on one particular input to a larger product. For example, firms that produce plastic bottles and supply major soft drink manufacturers will have high degrees of asset specificity, and competition is reduced to a few specialists.
- *Externality*. Agents, or any bodies representing the firm in the marketplace, will have private goals that are often inconsistent with those of the organization.
- *Hierarchical decomposition*. This rather ugly term describes the most effective management structure. In terms of transaction costs, the advantage of carrying out transactions internally within an organization clearly depends on the efficiency with which the organization manages its activities. At the time Williamson was writing, the predominant organization form was the U-form (unitary form), whereby each function reported vertically to an executive board. As businesses grew, this structure became ill-equipped to cope with the increasing complexity of decision-making. Accordingly, more decentralized structures evolved, e.g. the M-form (multidivisional form). Thus, we see that hierarchical decomposition refers to delegation of decision making within the organization.

A transaction occurs when a good or service is transferred across a distinct and separable interface; for example, the purchase of plastic bottles by the soft drink manufacturer. When such a transaction takes place, there are costs involved – whether they be part of an implicit or explicit contractual arrangement. Any organization will try to minimize the costs of its transactions. Decisions as to whether the transaction takes place within the organization (under hierarchical governance) or in the market (under market governance) will depend on the lowest cost and will determine the boundaries of the firm.

What determines lowest cost? The behaviour of individuals has a bearing. Decision makers will have bounded rationality, especially in the marketplace, and this will increase costs. For transactions taking place within the organization, there may be more control and flexibility with reduced costs.

Similarly, opportunism e.g., individuals cheating for their own gain, may be lower internally due to control and greater information levels. Where there is asset specificity, a strong case will also exist for keeping the activities within internal control, under internal management. Uncertainty of supply and exploitation by a few suppliers can be controlled by backward integration – bringing the transaction within hierarchical governance, that is, 'make' rather than 'buy'. In addition, externality will increase costs, especially in market situations. The distribution of products is a classic example; if a manufacturer sells his products to independent retailers, and the logistics between the two is handled by a third party specialist, the lack of control and distance from the customer can result in costs greater than mere distributional efficiency.

Hierarchical decomposition is critically important, as the optimum structural efficiency of the organization will influence the transaction cost. There is little point in bringing activities in-house, under hierarchical governance, that is 'make', if the firm does not have the structure necessary to support these activities.

The theories of Williamson offer some insights into where organised boundaries are drawn, and why changes in these boundaries may occur due to alterations in demand and transactions costs. Other environmental influences can also change such decisions. The growth of the outsourcing of various non-core activities, such as logistics and distribution, to specialists, is a recent example.

According to Williamson, all things being equal, it is more efficient for an organization to use the market to carry out its transactions. Transaction cost is lower because the market offers:

- *Scale economies*. Specialist suppliers focusing on one activity such as producing plastic bottles;
- *Risk pooling*. A supplier can spread the risk over many customers;
- *Economies of scope*. A supplier with many customers can offer variety.

However, these market advantages can disappear for a number of reasons and then it may make sense to bring them in-house; the soft drink manufacturer producing his own bottles, for example.

Transaction cost theory, although it has other applications, is a useful tool in the strategic analysis of firms seeking to become more flexible and responsive. In the past, organizations tended to focus on sets of core activities, described variously as core competences or critical success factors, that were the basis of competitive advantage. Other non-core activities were outsourced. A focus upon activities and operations is not of itself sufficient in the new competitive climate; it neglects demand variety and brings about a form of tunnel vision unsuited to new demands.

Theories such as transaction cost ignore one crucial element: cost and cost efficiency may cease to be the sole determinant of success and the prime goal. Performance measures to do with quality, responsiveness, variety and flexibility may become overriding factors.

One of the earliest influences upon the integration school of thought was Porter (1985) who described an organization's value chain as being embedded within a value system comprising suppliers and buyers. The linkages within this chain or system provided the building blocks of competitive advantage. The term 'value added chain' comes from the field of microeconomics, where it is used to describe the various steps a good or service goes through from raw material to final consumption. Economists conceived these transactions as being either arm's-length relationships, or hierarchies of common ownership. Conversely, supply chain management involves partnerships that are developed between organizations performing adjacent, linear steps in the chain. The supply chain is viewed as a whole rather than a set of fragmented parts in order that activities, the basic units of competitive advantage, can be configured, confined and performed in different ways to rival chains (Porter, 1996).

Other early influences upon supply network thinking included system dynamics – in particular the amplitude of volatility upstream along the supply channel (Forrester, 1961); the integration of members into partnerships along a supply chain called a 'value added partnership' (Johnson and Lawrence, 1988); and the facilitation of data and information along the chain using information systems and information technology (McFarlan, 1984; Malone et al., 1987).

Once the importance of supply networks had been recognized, operations strategies were developed that included supply network strategies as a particular example or type (a supply chain strategy being a subclass). Within these, at a tactical level, we have key operational activities such as supply chain management. We will take a moment to examine the nature of supply network and supply chain management strategies.

Forming a supply network operations strategy

Forming and implementing adequate supply network strategies is a difficult and complex task. Most organizations are embedded in an extremely intricate and complicated network structure, and it is difficult to construct operations strategies that take into account every consideration. As with all strategies, they can only ever be partial and are in need of continuous alteration. A network operations strategy, according to Gadde and Hakansson (2001), involves three important dimensions:

- *Thinking and planning in network terms.* Activity patterns are part of resource constellations and overall network structures. Developing an operations strategy requires some appreciation of the structures and processes involved in this complexity. The thinking necessary here involves knowledge not only of the wider organization but also the network in which it is embedded. This demands understanding of spatial relationships (the network is never stable and changes constantly over time – historical influences and evolution are as important as expectations); the boundaries of the network (including the resources and relationships that are complementary, influential and crucial); and the different dimensions of efficiency.
- *The importance of network organizing.* All networks are organized webs of actors, activities and resources. This involves positioning the company in relation to others through relationship building. Strategy and structure are built simultaneously.

282

According to Lorenzoni and Baden-Fuller (1995), when the capabilities of partners are crucial for the development of the hub firm in a network, then strategy and structure must be built concurrently. The network operations strategy is as dependent upon the capability of others and the connections to these capabilities as it is to internal capabilities – Lorenzoni and Baden-Fuller argue that novel forms of strategic thinking are required. Information sharing is a crucial issue in all types of network. The firm as a knowledge unit and the firm as a communication unit are completely dependent upon functioning information flows. Part of this information exchange concerns hard data but also ideas, feelings and thoughts. However, the design of the appropriate information systems is a problematic task, and the manager must ensure a structure is designed that provides a favourable environment for interactions to form and new information to be generated.

■ *The importance of acting in networks.* Acting in networks is a reflection of network thinking and network organizing. One of the key features of networks is that actions can most often be seen as reactions to the actions undertaken by others. Therefore, strategic thinking must be in terms of a pattern of actions and reactions. Networks are never in equilibrium; there is always a state of flux. As complex adaptive systems (see chapter 10) comprehensive control and management is impossible. A network actor may influence what is going on, but the complexities of the reaction patterns are almost impossible to predict. Although the system is to a degree deterministic, that is within certain boundaries, it is non-linear and future actions cannot be predicted with any degree of accuracy as the same pattern of behaviour is never repeated. Small variances in one variable can lead to disproportionately large changes in another variable and vice versa.

Finally, we must also recognize that supply network operations strategies are as important to SMEs as to larger firms. The larger organization may form the hub of a network; the SME, however, will often exist in a mutually dependent system that links small and medium-sized firms with a range of institutional arrangements that further the well-being of the industry as a whole. These arrangements are an important means of assuring collaboration in technological development. As well as strengthening the social structure in which firms are embedded in order to encourage cooperative relations that attenuate the destructive aspects of competition.

Forming a supply chain operations strategy

A supply chain operations strategy is a subclass of the supply network strategy. It determines the nature of procurement of raw materials, transportation of materials, manufacture of product or delivery of service, and distribution (including after-service follow-up). Such a strategy is also known as a value-chain operations strategy and is usually a linear interaction between nodes (see Table 3.2, p. 55).

Supply chain or value chain management is composed of the operational or tactical activities (*genus*) and can be defined as 'Managing the entire chain of raw material supply, manufacture, assembly and distribution to the end consumer' Jones (1989).

283

Other definitions abound, but all concentrate on similar themes. Christopher (1998), for example, describes supply chain management as 'The management of upstream and downstream relationships with suppliers and customers to deliver superior consumer value at less cost to the supply chain as a whole'.

A supply chain will consist of three primary elements: structures, processes and the linkages between them:

- *Structures* – these are the organizational units within the supply chain that interact. They include a company, its suppliers, its customers, distribution channels, design and engineering centres, manufacturing and service centres.
- *Processes* – the operational activities that transform inputs into outputs. These can involve demand and supply planning, forecasting, sourcing, purchasing, manufacturing and service operations, logistics, order entry, materials management, and new product or service development.
- *Linkages* – connecting process to structure via communication, usually in the form of shared information and continuous communication.

To these we can add:

- *Cross-functional teams* – to co-ordinate the interaction between supply chain functions.
- *Cross-enterprise teams* – co-ordinating the interaction between nodes or supply chain organizations.

At a strategic level, a supply chain operations strategy involves making long-term decisions about some of the following elements (adapted from Walker and Alber, 1999):

- Coordination and integration of all supply chain activities into a seamless process within and external to the organization;
- Planning and collaboration across a distributed supply chain;
- Optimally delivering the right product to the right place at the right time.

Unfortunately, a number of practitioners and academicians from various schools of thought have tended to apply more localized interpretations of the supply chain. For example, one very narrow perspective views supply chain management (and its accompanying operations strategy) as including only those activities prior to point of manufacture. Another, although slightly wider, considers only those elements up to the last point at which a product differentiation decision is made (Jones, 1989). Clearly, both of these neglect the end consumer – a rather radical omission.

A supply chain operations strategy in its true sense encourages a much wider viewpoint of the flow of information and products in a supply setting (supply alone being merely a logistics view point). It should incorporate the notion of end consumers and the provision and coordination of activities that will provide product and service combinations that they require. Further, as the chain metaphor implies, this is achieved through management across and between company boundaries.

284

What of the benefits from supply chain management and a supply chain operations strategy? Although often difficult to quantify (this is one of the disadvantages) there are undoubted advantages. Quinn (1997) suggests that total supply chain costs represent more than half, and in some cases three-quarters, of the total operating expenses of most organizations. Ferguson (2000) reports that firms employing such approaches enjoy a 45 per cent supply system cost advantage. Lumus and Vokurka (1999) note meanwhile that firms operate with 36 per cent lower logistics costs, which translates into a 4 per cent increase in net profit margins. Other more qualitative benefits include:

- *A focus upon the end consumer*. The recognition that customers make decisions affecting the success of an industry was long overdue. In order to remain competitive every enterprise must ensure that all activities along the chain are managed in accordance with customer demand.
- *Synergy*. The achievement of optimal interaction of enterprise resources of the supply system will allow more effective and efficient operation; thus providing higher value to the end consumer but with lower cost. In theory, the benefits of synergistic operation should far outweigh those achievable by any individual firm.
- *Continuity*. Firms in a closely linked supply chain tend to build longer-term partnerships and alliances. Security amidst a turbulent environment comes from the development of such relationships and the shared expertise it brings, as well as the barriers to entry it develops.
- *Information*. Successful supply chain management operations rely heavily upon shared information. The sharing of data/information should, in theory, enrich the business process and link supply to demand more closely.
- *Cooperation*. With reduced organizational barriers, other firms can contribute their expertise into what would traditionally have been an internal function such as research and development, new product development, marketing and promotion, etc.
- *Customer access*. Potentially, using supply chain management, organizations further upstream can establish closer links to customer demand than they would normally expect.
- *Diversity*. As has been alluded to in chapter 9, many sectors are witnessing increased demand for variety, choice, uniqueness and customization. This being so, the business environment becomes more turbulent. Integration of the complete product cycle at its various stages along the supply system does have the potential to increase product customization possibilities.

As noted, the term supply chain management is synonymous with a mixed bag of concepts, theories, terms and tools that apply to more than one industry. The overall proposition is quite simple, however; it has been made unnecessarily complex by various diverse and disparate movements within different industries.

Supply chain management covers a number of activities, some of which are more value adding than others, while a supply chain strategy involves making long-term decisions concerning core operational processes, resources, technologies and certain tactical and support activities. It is suggested that the many of the terms encountered in the literature regarding the former, in fact equate to a short list of common sense axioms:

■ The organization, being an open system, exists in a wider environment and is influenced by it;
■ Organizations, as systems themselves, have inputs that they transform into outputs using a variety of energy sources;
■ For their inputs and energy sources, they nearly always rely upon other organizations, likewise for the sale or transfer of their outputs;
■ Other organizations, upon which they are reliant, are part of a wider supply system or network that contains a number of chains;
■ Products, services, information and value added activities form part of the currency of these supply networks and they are constantly generated, traded, bought and sold;
■ The more the parties in a supply network align their focus on the end customer and the necessary value adding activities, the more profitable will be the venture;
■ A common agreement is needed between the members of a supply network as to exactly what does and does not add value, and how this is to be measured;
■ Effective and open communication is essential;
■ Unlimited flows of data and information are necessary, travelling both forwards and backwards, to which each and every organization has unrestricted access;
■ If the parties in any particular supply network recognize their joint dependence, in what is a symbiotic relationship, it is a first step to improving the performance of the total entity. Should they then form closer working partnerships as a result, so much the better.
■ A commitment to continually improve the whole network activity is mandatory.

Having briefly examined the nature of supply network and supply chain operations strategies, a small digression is in order. It is important to remember that there are certain processes and cycles involved in both supply network and supply chain. For a strategy to be developed, these must be well understood; as there will be certain longer-term strategic decisions necessary concerning how the organization delivers products and services.

Supply network processes

The supply network and its component chains involve a sequence of processes and flows that take place between different nodes or stages. Chopra and Meindl (2001) suggest we can view the processes in the supply network from two perspectives.

The cycle view

The processes in a supply network are divided into a series of cycles, each acting as an interface between two successive nodes. Not every network will have clear separation between the cycles, and some can even be bypassed altogether. The structure of the industry will determine the unique profile of the cycle processes. In addition, the provision of services will also involve a different set of cycles and processes (thus we can only offer general guide-lines here). The cycle view of a network also assists in understanding the key operational processes necessary. The following process cycles can usually be identified:

- *Customer order cycle.* Usually at the customer interface and includes all the processes directly involved in receiving and filling a customer order. The customer will usually initiate the order and start the demand process. The customer order cycle can be further broken down into processes such as customer arrival, order entry, order fulfilment, and order receiving.
- *Replenishment cycle.* This will describe the interface between product provider and a first tier supplier replenishing the product. This cycle is initiated either by an order from the product provider or, more effectively, by the customer order in the first cycle. The first tier supplier is then tasked to replenish goods and services to demand at a minimum cost while providing the necessary quality and product availability. The cycle includes the processes of order trigger (either by customer or product and service provider), order entry, order fulfilment and order receiving.
- *Production and delivery cycle.* A process between producer of a good/service (a first tier supplier) and the product provider (in some cases the end consumer can directly interface with the producer). The cycle involves all the processes necessary to offer products for the replenishment cycle. The cycle will typically include order arrival (from distributor, retailers or end consumer), production scheduling (of good or service), production and shipping, receiving by service/product provider.
- *Procurement cycle.* This is the interface between the first tier supplier (or the producer of a good) and the second tier supplier to that producer. It includes all the processes necessary to ensure materials or components are available for the production cycle and the first tier supplier. The second tier supplier provides inputs to replenish the production and delivery cycle. However, this supplier is operating more precise dependent demand (see chapter 9) based upon known quantities of the final finished product or service (rather than independent demand faced by the product provider and/or the first tier supplier). The cycle processes here will be similar to those of the production and delivery cycle.

The pull/push view of supply chain processes

All processes in a supply network fall into one of two categories – push or pull – depending upon the timing of their execution relative to demand. In pull processes, execution is initi-ated in response to a customer order. Push processes are those that are executed in *anticipation* of a customer order. At time of execution of a pull process, customer demand is known and the firm is said to be reactive and operating in real time demand mode. With a push system, we are operating in advance of demand knowledge and speculating and relying upon estimates or forecasts of demand. There is usually a boundary that separates push from pull processes – the decoupling point. In other words, the decoupling point sepa-rates the part of the organization oriented towards customer orders from the part of the organization based upon forecasts.

In general the decoupling point will coincide with the main stocking point. In principle, downstream of that point (to the right in diagrammatic terms) there are no stocks, while upstream (to the left), there are stocks but usually only if economically justified. Selection of the decoupling point is a strategic operations decision and balances market requirements and lead times in the production and delivery processes. Hoekstra and Romme (1992) suggest that five different positions of the decoupling point are sufficient to describe all product-market situations in control terms:

- *Decoupling point 1 (DP1) – make and ship*. Here, DP1 is far to the right closest to the customer. Products are manufactured and distributed to stock-points that are spread out and located close to the customer.
- *Decoupling point 2 (DP2) – make to stock*. Finished products are held in stock at the end of the production process and from there are sent directly to many customers who are scattered geographically.
- *Decoupling point 3 (DP3) – assemble to order*. Only elements of the system are held in stock; the final assembly takes place on the basis of a specific order.
- *Decoupling point 4 (DP4) – make to order*. Only raw materials and components are kept in stock: each customer order is a specific project.
- *Decoupling point 5 (DP5) – purchase and make to order for a specific customer*. No stocks are held for purchasing and the whole project takes place on the basis of each individual order and the decoupling is far to the left (upstream).

Decisions about these various supply network processes (cycles, push/pull and decoupling) are an important part of the operations strategy and will have to be made for product group and the particular customers involved. This involves a balancing process between delivery time requested by the customer and the throughput time in purchasing, production and distribution processes. The shorter the lead time and the more flexible the organizations in the supply network, the further upstream (to the left) the decoupling point can be located. This involves less reliance upon forecasting (to the left of the decoupling point) and more attention to customer demand (to the right of the decoupling point).

TIME OUT BOX II

When might decisions about these processes be particularly important for an operations strategy? Are there particular types of operations strategy that would focus upon such decisions?

The role of logistics

To conclude this section a brief mention of logistics is in order, if only to again clarify some misapprehensions. We can view logistics as a particular group of operational activities (*genus*) that can either exist on its own, and/or be part of an independent logistics operations strategy (*subclass*) or be subsumed within a supply network operations strategy (*class*) – see Table 3.2, p. 55.

In the field of logistics, many of the tenets of supply chain management have been practised since the early 1960s. Drucker (1962), for example, wrote: 'Physical distribution is today's frontier in business. It is one area where managerial results of great magnitude can be achieved and is largely unexplored territory.' This view of distribution had, in fact, been identified by Borsodi (1927) some 40 years earlier:

> In the 50 years between 1870 and 1920 the cost of distributing necessities and luxuries has nearly trebled, while production costs have gone down by one-fifth . . . what we are saving in production we are losing in distribution.

And in 1988, Johnson and Lawrence suggested that advantages could be gained by:

> a set of independent companies that work closely together to manage the flow of goods and services along the entire value added chain . . . we term such arrangements 'Value adding Partnerships' (VAPs).

The early meaning of logistics was simple – it referred to the cost of having things where you want them to go, with the major components being transportation and warehousing. Later, it was realized that the term should include both the suppliers' costs, or inbound logistics, as well as the costs of storing and moving goods within the company; the internal logistics.

Thus, the total logistics cost (Christopher, 1985) could be equated to the sum of the following:

- Transportation costs – incoming, within the company, and outgoing;
- Facilities costs – warehousing, distribution centres, and handling equipment;
- Communications costs – order processing, invoicing, information systems;
- Inventory costs;
- Material handling costs;
- Packaging costs;
- Management costs.

In this regard, the US Council of Logistics definition is admirable:

> The process of planning, implementing, and controlling the efficient flow and storage of goods, services, and related information from point of origin to point of consumption for the purposes of conforming to customer requirements.

Today, supply chain management and logistics can be seen as a strategic capability (subclass) encompassing all organizational activities. In many organizations they are accorded a degree of planning and coordination necessary to ensure added value, reduced cost and the requisite customer service levels. Recently the emphases have turned towards speed and shortening product life cycles; strategic information flows; customer partnerships and relationships; cross-functionality; flow-through distribution and business processes rather than functions. Indeed, the province of supply chain management is now widely recognized as overlaid and spanning other functional hierarchies within the organization.

CONCLUSION

We have now completed the third chapter in Part III, having discussed the importance of operations strategies for global trade as well as the supply network. The final chapter brings this work up to date with a detailed review of how operations strategies can be applied in e-business settings. In addition, we also explore a more recent research proposition: the suggestion that these strategies are also methods by which to deploy and co-ordinate the wider corporate or business strategy.

CASE STUDY – OPERATIONS STRATEGY IN ACTION

Lee Cooper Jeans – operations strategy: global trade and supply network applications (www.leecooper.com)

There's more to a pair of jeans than you thought. Large manufacturers of denim jeans such as Lee Cooper and Levi Strauss source the component parts from all over the world. For example, the cotton could be grown in Benin in West Africa or the southern states of the USA. The threads are often produced in Ireland. Zip teeth are likely to be made in Japan. Brass rivets are made from Namibia copper and Australian zinc. The jeans may be sewn in Tunisia and then dyed in Italy before stone washing using pumice from a Turkish volcano. Clearly, the manufacturer does not source all these materials and is only concerned with the immediate inputs for his production system. However, when mapping a supply network we can see the huge number of activities from mother earth to consumer. This is also an example of how sourcing and procurement for many firms, even SMEs, is now a global trade – which brings much complexity with it.

ANSWERS TO TIME OUT BOXES

Time out box I

Integration describes the extent to which a firm owns the network of which it is a part. Vertical integration occurs when an organization acquires either suppliers (upstream or backward integration) or customers (downstream or forward integration). Horizontal integration takes place when an enterprise acquires a degree of ownership of another firm at the same node or point in the supply system (one manufacturer acquiring another). Integration is a strategic move to secure resources, products, or access to a market. Ownership is often not the sole reason for integration, such decisions are often taken to increase capacity and to ensure the correct network balance.

The supply system stages or nodes can be fully balanced (capacity at each stage is fully devoted to the next) or partially balanced (each stage sells part of its output to other companies or it sources goods and services from a range of firms).

Integration has a number of advantages:

■ It secures a dependable supply of goods and services (controlling sources of key materials, components or services in-house rather than trusting the vagaries of the market);

■ It helps to reduce costs (a firm may have the skills, technology or specialist processes in-house and can utilize these at a much cheaper rate than buying in such services);

■ It can improve the quality of a service or product (specialist knowledge of a product or process is kept in-house to protect a unique innovation from research and development); and,

■ It helps to build and advance knowledge of the market (ownership of certain activities helps a firm continue to understand demand and keep in touch with the value sought by customers and consumers).

The disadvantages of integration are:

■ Creation of a monopoly market (customers can be faced with little choice as prices increase and service and/or quality decline).

■ Inability to exploit economies of scale (specialist suppliers can be dedicated to a particular product or process and can gain economies of scale due to producing higher volumes and thus lower prices – Tesco Stores would not, for example, want to own egg producing facilities, it is not their core business);

■ A loss of flexibility (heavily integrated firms will be committed to particular investments in resources and technology as being the reason for the integration – they will have difficulty changing direction and offering different products and services if market forces alter).

■ Lack of innovation (new product and service flexibility can also be reduced as the firm may have heavily invested in certain activities, processes and technologies, as part of an integration move, and finds it hard, both economically and emotionally, to justify a switch in direction. In addition, they will also lack the creative input of suppliers and customers); and

■ A distraction from core capabilities (the more integrated a firm becomes, the more activities it will have to undertake – it tries to be 'all things to all people' and neglects its core competencies that are a key determinant of competitive advantage).

Time out box II

An excellent example of the fundamental significance of these factors for an operations strategy can be seen in chapter 4 (p. 80). In discussing operations strategy types, strategic postponement was introduced and examples of its employment by Benetton and the National Bicycle Company examined. When employing such a strategy, and we can also include time-based competition as being a similar approach; key decisions are required as to cycles, processes and the decoupling points necessary. For instance, Benetton will assemble some garments to order once demand preferences are better know (this allows the firm to operate to real time consumer demand rather than to forecasts of that demand).

DISCUSSION QUESTIONS, WORK ASSIGNMENTS AND EXAM QUESTIONS

1   Describe the four classifications of a global strategy. What are the key differences between them?
2   What are the advantages and disadvantages of (a) offshore sourcing and (b) domestic sourcing from responsive suppliers?
3   Give examples of the hidden and inflexibility costs involved with foreign sources of supply.
4   Discuss the main differences between a supply network and supply chain operations strategy.
5   What do we mean by the term 'transaction cost'?
6   Describe the nature of supply network processes. Why are they important?

Reader questions related to Lee Cooper Jeans case study

1   What are the main reasons for this internationalization of trade? Can the forces be classified in any way?
2   Are such trends also visible in the service sector?
3   What are the advantages and disadvantages of commerce on a global scale?

Chapter 14

Operations strategy

E-business and strategic coordination applications

This final chapter examines two new and exploratory fields. First the use of operations strategies in e-business environments, and second, how such strategies can act as methods by which to deploy or cascade the wider corporate or business strategy throughout an organization – their role as an interface between policy-making and tactical functions.

LEARNING OBJECTIVES

After considering this chapter, the reader will be able to:

- Appreciate the nature of e-business
- Discuss the commercial benefits of e-business
- Consider the approach of e-operations and an e-operations strategy
- Understand the use of an operations strategy as a method for strategic coordination

KEY TERMS

- E-business
- E-operations
- E-operations strategy
- Strategic coordination
- Continual improvement

INTRODUCTION

The final chapter ascertains the nature of e-business and e-operations. We discuss the use of an operations strategy for e-business and the advantages and disadvantages likely to occur. In addition, there is also a short review of the role of the operations strategy in the deployment and coordination of general business strategies.

E-OPERATIONS STRATEGY

E-business or e-commerce is the execution of business transactions over the Internet. E-business and e-commerce are terms used interchangeably: we can and should differentiate between them. Certain strands of the literature do attempt a distinction. Chaffey (2002) for example, considers e-commerce to be a subset of e-business using the following definitions:

- *Electronic commerce* (e-commerce). All electronically mediated information exchanges between an organization and its external stakeholders.
- *Electronic business* (e-business). All electronically mediated information exchanges, both within and organization an with external stakeholders supporting the range of business processes.

According to Chaffey, then, e-commerce involves external transactions only and is a subset of e-business. The latter being both internal and external processes and, presumably, wider than just commercial exchanges (selling and buying). E-business then, can include:

- E-commerce
- E-integration
- E-banking
- E-marketing
- E-mailing
- E-operations
- E-directories
- E-trading or e-tailing

294

- E-engineering
- E-exchanges and auctions
- E-learning
- E-gambling

For the purposes of this chapter, we will use the term 'e-business' in its widest sense.

Whatever the terminology, we must be aware that there are a range of different perspectives involved in e-business, as suggested by Kalakota and Whinston (1997):

- A communication perspective. The delivery of information, products/services or payment by electronic means.
- A business process perspective. The application of technology towards the automation of business transactions and workflows.
- A service perspective. Enabling cost cutting at the same time as increasing the speed and quality of service delivery.
- An online perspective. The buying and selling of products and information online.

Companies conducting e-business will perform some of the following operations transactions:

- Providing information across a supply network or chain;
- Negotiating contracts with customers and suppliers;
- Allowing customers to view goods and services electronically and to place orders;
- Allowing consumers to track orders;
- Filling and delivering orders to customers; and
- Receiving payment from customers.

Web sites can be used in many ways:

- As a channel to sell a product or service (like Amazon.com, which sells exclusively through the Internet).
- As a supplemental channel ('click-and-mortar' firms represent traditional retailers that have extended their market reach by adding a web site).
- Technical support (customers can solve problems regarding the products they have purchased).
- Embellish an existing service (mail services, for example, can be augmented using a web site for tracking orders or to provide further explanation, as in the case of a text book).
- Process orders (a direct connection between the service provider and the customer that cuts out any intermediate stage).
- To convey information (technical information about companies, their product or other services such as health).

Within e-business, four definitions or business models are used for distinct transaction types:

- Business-to-business (B2B). This implies that both sides are businesses, non-profit organizations or governments and quasi-governmental bodies.
- Business-to-consumer (B2C). These are e-business transactions in which buyers are individual consumers;
- Consumer-to-consumer (C2C). Here, consumers sell directly to each other by electronic classified adverts or auction sites.
- Consumer-to-business (C2B). In this category individuals sell services or goods to businesses.

Economics of e-business for e-operations

E-business can revolutionize operations management and operations strategy, due to its effective cost reduction. This is mainly achieved through improved communication and dissemination of economically valuable data and information and a consequent fall in transaction costs. E-business can also increase economic efficiencies by matching buyer and seller and facilitating the exchange of information and goods and services – a move closer to the perfect market. In addition, some of the time constraints of trading are reduced (although it has to be said that others do remain, e-fulfilment for example). The following benefits and limitations of e-business are apparent (adapted from Heizer and Render, 2001). However, these advantages do have a cost to the industry competitors concerned, as they also reduce the barriers to entry, allowing new competitors to enter at low cost.

Benefits of e-business

- 'Consumer-centric' as opposed to 'production-centric' collaborating with consumers to identify their needs and then provide tailored solutions using holistic business approaches rather than discrete functions.
- E-business allows true collaboration with customers, leading eventually to mass customization (see chapter 6) in which the customer is an active player in the design of products and services. It also allows collaboration with suppliers through the sharing of data and information.
- Interoperability not only between a firm's internal systems, but also those of its partners both inside and outside its industry (in the supply network).
- Disintermediation (cutting out the middle man) as a means to bypass channel partners to remove sales and infrastructure cost and increase speed of response.
- An enabling device for customer relationship management (CRM) that can record customers purchasing activities and preferences, problems and other information that can be used in determining individual current and future needs and values. This in turn will allow one-to-one marketing, knowledge management, e-analytics (or data mining) and better customer support.
- Improved lower-cost information flows that make buyers and sellers more knowledgeable and can drive down industry costs.
- Low industry entry cost.
- Increased information sharing.

- Increased availability, both geographically and time of day.
- Information availability expanding the market for buyers and sellers.
- Reduction in cost of creating, processing, distributing, storing and retrieving information.
- Reduction in the cost of communication.
- Richer communication flows than traditional media.
- Fast delivery of digitized products.
- Faster ordering of goods.
- Increased flexibility of locations from which service can be provided or purchase made.
- Less paper work, fewer manual processes, instant availability of information, reduced transaction costs and quicker cycle times.

Limitations of e-business

- Lack of system security, flexibility and standards
- Lack of privacy
- Insufficient band width slowing many transactions
- Back end systems for fulfilment still rely on traditional methods and are thus slow compared with front end ordering
- Integrating e-business software with existing systems and databases remains a problem
- Lack of trust in (1) unknowns at the other end of a transaction, (2) integrity of the transaction itself, and (3) electronic money that is in reality only bits and bytes.

E-operations

In operations, the term e-business brings a particular revolution that is fuelled by the Internet and business-to-business commerce. E-operations is quite simply the application of the Internet and its attendant technologies to the field of operations management. Cohen and Agrawal (2001) describe the ideal scenario, in which:

> Information, material flow, product attributes and decision making realize the full potential of e-commerce technologies. Information flows in this ideal world will be accurate, rich and instantaneous. Information, moreover, will be based on all supply [network] transactions . . . and will be visible throughout the [network]. The Internet will reduce search and price discoveries to a minimum.
>
> Goods will flow directly between supplier and end consumers, controlled by just in time shipment. In this environment the cost of changing suppliers will be zero. Products will be more customized. Companies might also be able to develop economies of scale in production by adopting automated flexible manufacturing processes.

As the authors ask, how realistic is this picture of the future? Certainly the technologies and profit incentives exist for firms to build such networks. Innovative supply chain structures now offer expanded access to e-sources of supply that can use web-based exchanges and hubs, interactive trading mechanisms and advanced optimization and matching algorithms to link customers with suppliers for individual transactions. In terms of an operations strategy, these developments require flexibility and responsiveness and, as we saw in chapter 6, necessitate the need for more than one strategy that is tailored to customer and/or product group.

We can define e-operations as:

> Electronically mediated data/information exchanges, and the information communication technology systems that support them, to facilitate the operation, enhancement, re-engineering and integration of the range of business processes, both within an organization and externally (up and downstream), necessary for efficient, effective and efficacious supply network systems.

We propose the e-operations strategy task includes: longer-term strategic decisions concerning operation, improvement, innovation and integration as well as efficacy. In other words the three dimensions of performance: *efficiency* (minimum waste – doing the thing right), *effective* (doing the right thing) and *efficacy* (producing the right result).

The context of an e-operations strategy

To understand the organizational context of e-operations and an e-operations strategy, it is useful to view the infrastructure of the modern organization as consisting of four conceptual levels:

1   The business model level, where a general, long-term business strategy is defined;
2   The operations strategy level: here decisions are made regarding the medium- to long-term operational aspects of providing certain products and services;
3   The operations management level that deals with the tactical processes necessary to implement both of the above strategies and provide products and services; and
4   The information system (IS) and information technology (IT) architecture level that defines the supporting information and technology necessary (often there might also be distinct IT and IS strategies).

The role of the operations strategy and operations management (stages 2 and 3) is to execute or implement the general business strategy and effectively use the tools and information flows from stage 4. In addition, an organization must seek to understand how to take advantage of new operational and IS/IT capabilities to better operate new and existing business models. The challenge for an operations strategy is that it has to translate and implement these business models. This involves a continual and, in some cases, ever-shortening business cycle.

An e-operations strategy is concerned with both the internal and external decisions necessary to translate the business vision. The business model subsequently developed will be a fluid collection of business activities, and each node or business activity will focus on a limited number of competencies to create value. The term business-web or b-web can be used for these types of business activity. The business models can be classified into particular types (adapted from Tapscott *et al.*, 1999):

- *Auction or marketspace models*. Marketspace business webs match buyers and sellers and provide a mechanism for negotiating price. The marketspace model handles complex exchanges between buyers and sellers using dynamic pricing. In operations terms, it is mainly a question of maintaining an information database. These models can include both B2C and B2B approaches. A good example would be Ebay.
- *Aggregator models*. These offer a variety of similar products to the marketplace. The company will position itself as a value adding intermediary between producers and customers. The main tasks will be needs matching and distribution and delivery. Operations strategies will need to consider selection, pricing and order fulfilment as delivery reliability, inventory management, cost control and online tracking and analysis will all be crucial. Amazon.com is perhaps the best example at the time of writing.
- *Alliance models*. Alliance business webs support collaboration and sharing of information between cooperating companies. These are members of a creative community that designs, creates knowledge or produces shared experience. Creative collaboration and information sharing to test new concepts are the main themes. These are the most virtual of b-webs being almost online communities; the operations role is therefore modest. America Online would be a prime example of such a community.
- *Supply network or value chain models*. Companies will use web sites to manage both customers and suppliers. These are partnered companies that help produce a highly integrated value proposition through a managed process. Products are often tailored to match customer needs. The main theme is process integration involving partner firms that share product design, transformation processes and supply network management, both up- and downstream. Operations strategy decisions will reflect the entire process using a mix of internal and outsourced operations. Operations performance will hinge upon degrees of mass customization, just in time delivery, tracking and updating. The Ford Motor Company, Dell Computers and Rank Zerox operate some of the most advanced supply network e-webs.
- *Distributive network models*. These are logistical or transportation networks that cut across all business web axes to provide essential transfer services. Delivery, reliability, speed, responsiveness, flexibility will be the main themes. United Parcel Services (UPS) and Federal Express (FedEx) are good examples.
- *Catalogue hub models*. Used to reduce the cost of placing orders to suppliers as well as the cost of goods or services themselves. Suppliers will post a catalogue of items on the hub, and buyers select and purchase electronically. Prices can be negotiated for both single and multiple purchases. The hub connects the firm potentially to many suppliers through the Internet rather than EDI.
- *Exchange models*. An electronic market for buying and selling firms. In this environment spot purchases can be made such as oil, steel, energy or any other

commodity. Hotels for example, can now use exchanges for one-stop shopping of various supplies such as linen, towels, toiletries, etc., without having to deal with individual suppliers for each one.

Impact of e-business on an operations strategy

First, e-business will have a number of revenue enhancing opportunities for an organization that will need to be considered in any operations strategy.

- *Direct sales to customers.* An e-operations strategy allows more members of the supply network an opportunity to have direct contact with the customer in channels not previously open or controlled by intermediaries (a retailer or wholesaler for example).
- *Twenty-four hour access from any location.* An e-business is accessible, in theory, twenty-four hours a day and seven days a week for the placement of orders. Unfortunately, however, unlike a retailer the goods are not always provided straight away. Similarly, geographic location is no barrier to accessing e-services.
- *Aggregating information.* Sales can be increased by offering information regarding a large selection of products and services that do not have to be held in inventory (a corresponding variety offered by a retailer would entail having large stock-holding). For an e-business there is, however, a danger in going overboard with an infinite variety that confuses the customer.
- *Personalization and customization.* The Internet offers the potential to use a customer's personal information to intelligently guide each customer's buying experience and increase sales. At a B2B level is it possible to establish customer-specific sites to personalize the buying experience.
- *Speeding up time to market.* Increased revenues are available by introducing new products much faster than using physical channels. A new product can be made available as soon as the first unit is produced.
- *Flexible pricing.* An e-business can alter prices by changing one entry in a database. Prices can be adjusted rapidly to reflect inventory and demand preferences.
- *Price and service discrimination.* Prices can also be altered to reflect the buying power of individuals. Prices can be adjusted for each micro-segment and even by individual customer – rather than having a single price for all.
- *Efficient funds transfer.* The payment collection cycle can be much shorter for an e-business – this can substantially increase revenues.
- *Shipping time and e-fulfilment.* This is still a potential revenue disadvantage for an e-business. For example, physically buying a pair of jeans allows the customer to touch and try on the goods. After payment the customer leaves with their purchase. For an e-business, shipment takes time (unless we are dealing in services and goods that can be downloaded).
- *Centralized inventory.* The ability to stock goods in one location rather than spread over numerous scattered locations allows the firm to keep substantially lower amounts by avoiding duplication.

300

- *Reduced facilities cost*. Avoiding the need for stores and other outlets in expensive prime locations.
- *Self-sourcing*. Customers can often do some of the work of the business. For example, delivery services encourage the customer to track their own deliveries online; purchasing of tickets, paying bills and setting up banking facilities online. Keen (1997) describes these advantages as the single most important feature of the Internet.
- *Job specialization and scheduling*. E-business operations strategies allow companies to centralize operations and this in turn allows greater task specialization. For service firms especially, this is a valuable benefit as it allows a high degree of customization to be retained in the front end of the service, but this is supported behind the scenes by standardized tasks and process that can utilize economies of scale through high volume transactions. The Internet alleviates the fundamental trade-off between customization and efficiency, especially when applying technology to twenty-four-hour, seven-day a week services (Chase 1978).
- *Other positive cost impacts*. Cost reduction opportunities include reduced product handling and shorter supply network, postponement of product differentiation until the order is placed, decreasing delivery cost and time with downloaded goods, reduced physical processing costs, reduced inventory costs and improved supply chain coordination from better information flows.

Drawbacks and challenges to an e-business operations strategy

- *Technology*. An e-business and its operations strategy will live or die by its technological choice. The flexibility brought by information technology will also have a price in terms of the necessary development and maintenance. Often, firms will not possess the expertise necessary in these areas and will either have to outsource or hire the human resources necessary. This can result in higher cost and loss of control. In addition, according to Moore's law, computing power doubles every 18–24 months. To keep pace, investment in new technology is both necessary and substantial.
- *Increased shipping*. Rather than delivering one shipment to a store for customers to purchase, with e-operations each individual purchase must be delivered. For tangible goods, this has high cost implications that cannot be avoided – especially if they are fragile or large.
- *Accountability/legality*. Accountability for the sale of controlled items is always a problem with the anonymity of the Internet. It is difficult to ensure that items such as liquor or prescription drugs do not fall into the wrong hands. Similar problems arise regarding copyright of music and other intellectual property.
- *Communication barriers*. Despite the customized web pages of Amazon and Dell, there is still a barrier to communication without two-way or face-to-face interaction
- *Other negative cost impacts*. Higher costs: inbound and outbound transportation costs are likely to be higher as the e-business will tend to aggregate inventory at a central location rather than at a number of geographic points; increased handling cost if customer participation is reduced (groceries for example, where some tasks are performed by the customer); and large initial investment in information infrastructure.

301

CRITICAL REFLECTION

The Internet is an extremely important new technology that has received much attention and fervour through the latter part of the twentieth and the early twenty-first centuries. But, as Michael Porter (2001) points out, it is perhaps time to take a clearer view of the Internet. A move away from the rhetoric about 'Internet industries' and 'e-business strategies', and a 'new economy' to see, according to Porter, the Internet for what it is: 'an enabling technology – a powerful set of tools that can be used wisely or unwisely in any industry and as part of almost any strategy.' Technology, and the Internet in particular, does provide better opportunities for companies to establish distinctive strategic positionings than did previous generations of information technology. However, the Internet per se will rarely be a competitive advantage.

Many e-commerce or dot.com enterprises are artificial business propped up by capital that was readily available at the time. The creation of economic value (the gap between price and cost to produce) will be the true test of their survival or failure. Sustainable competitive advantage can only be achieved by operating at lower cost, by commanding a premium price, or doing both. As we have seen earlier, cost and price advantages can be achieved in two ways. First *operational effectiveness* (doing the same things as your competitors but doing them better. Second, *strategic positioning* (doing things differently from competitors in a way that delivers a unique type of value to customers). Operational effectiveness includes, for example, better technologies, superior inputs, better trained employees, more effective management structure, etc. and is the domain of the operations strategy. Strategic positioning might include a different set of features, a different array of services or different logistical services (these aspects are mainly the focus of the wider business strategy, but will also concern an operations strategy).

The Internet can affect both operational effectiveness and strategic positioning. In the case of the former, the Internet is a powerful tool, but, according to Porter, 'simply improving operational effectiveness does not provide competitive advantage ... this can only be done by achieving and sustaining higher levels of operational effectiveness than competitors.' Best practice tends to be copied quickly! As it becomes harder to sustain operational advantages, strategic positioning becomes all the more important. This goes far beyond the pursuit of best practices (the quest of the operations strategy). It involves the highly integrated configuration of a tailored value chain – the series of primary activities required to produce and deliver a product or service (inbound logistics, operations, outbound logistics, marketing and sales and after-sales services – the first three again being the province of the operations strategy).

Thus we are left, according to this viewpoint, with the proposition that the Internet is ostensibly a powerful new technology, but in reality just another way of doing business and not a strategy in itself. It is, however, clearly an operations management resource that can, in some cases, depending upon the industry, be a strategic consideration at an operations strategy level.

OPERATIONS STRATEGIES FOR STRATEGIC COORDINATION

It is now suggested that an operations strategy may be used as a method to manage the translation of the business or corporate strategy throughout the business: an attempt to focus everyone in the organization on common goals and priorities, by translating corporate strategy into measurable objectives throughout the levels of the organization. This involves a recognition that all employees should understand the strategic plan and how it translates into goals that drive daily activities.

In this perspective, we are viewing the operations strategy as a method to cascade the higher level business strategy throughout the firm using a series of action plans as the means of achieving objectives at a particular level. These then become the target or objectives for the next level. It is a similar view to that of total quality management in adopting the idea that there are internal as well as external customers and suppliers. The operations strategy, then, acts as an interface between business strategy and operational management at a tactical level. The operations strategy translates longer-term objectives into medium term, tactical operations aspirations that can be used to plan resources, technologies, capabilities, etc. for future, day-to-day operations. It has to be said, however, that this is, to a degree, a rational, top-down and deterministic approach to strategic management. Nevertheless, the operations strategy is also the conduit by which improvement achievements can be filtered back up through the organization.

Operations strategies for continual improvement

As part of policy deployment, an operations strategy can also be used as a vehicle for continual improvement. To be effective continuous improvement must account for the needs of customers and the competencies of competitors. The object is to build on the organization's evolutionary capabilities and to bridge the gap between larger innovative, revolutionary or step changes in improvement. As an operations strategy, it must be woven into the fabric of the organization and be easily translated into everyday tactical activities.

Originating in Japan, continuous improvement is also known by the term 'Kaizen' (Imai 1986). It involves the continual improvement of everything – from equipment and procedures to skills, quality, throughput time, supplier relationships, etc. Japanese management will often use 'stretch targets' to keep momentum for change going. The coordination of continuous improvement at these levels is through the use of an operations strategy. In the service sector continuous improvement tends to be called total quality management (TQM) as a broad approach that encompasses an organization-wide continuous improvement programme in meeting customer value requirements

CONCLUSION

Chapter 14 has presented the final strategy application. Here, it was suggested that those organizations adopting elements of e-business will benefit from the adoption of an operations strategy for those particular business processes. We also, briefly, discussed the latest conceptual research suggesting an operations strategy may also prove a useful policy deployment vehicle – an interface between business strategy and tactical and daily activities. In other words, as with continuous improvement initiatives, a method by which to cascade the business strategy throughout the daily operations of the firm.

CASE STUDY – OPERATIONS STRATEGY IN ACTION

E-operations strategies in the European footwear industry – operations strategy: e-business and strategic coordination applications

The footwear industry in many western economies is under substantial threat from low wage imports flooding their markets at price points well below economic commercial viability. In order to compete and attempt to redress the balance, a number of European manufacturers (principally from Scandinavia, Portugal, the Netherlands, Italy and the UK) have developed e-business operations strategies in a mutual network between suppliers, manufacturers and retailers. These strategies are founded on an ability to provide high quality, high fashion footwear that can satisfy individual needs, much faster than the competition. Confidentiality and competitive necessity restrict full disclosure of the firms and systems involved, but a brief résumé of the strategies deployed is informative in an e-business context.

As with any fashion industry, the secret of success is to put new fashion on the shelf before your competitor and to employ fast-cycle design changes. Buyers will often tour footwear fairs, fashion shows and boutiques where inspiration may be available for a new design. New design themes can be photographed or sketched and rapidly digitized within seconds to be sent to leading designers for remodelling into products suitable for middle-priced mass markets.

Once design pictures are received, computer-aided design (CAD) systems can be used to turn the pictures into a range of 3D virtual shoes. Thereafter, e-analytics software can explore whether suitable lasts (a shoemaker's model for a shoe or boot) exist or if modifications are required, or indeed, if new lasts have to be developed. At the same time, e-procurement systems can contact suppliers, linked via an Intranet, to transmit requirements and source the necessary material. At the same time, the range of designs has been transmitted back to the buyer to modify and finalize the design from his or her perspective. Simultaneously, the customer relationship team has identified a set of volunteer customers who are known to be 'early adopters', and who will predict, quite accurately, the response to the new products. Their comments on the virtual designs entitle them to a range of discounts and other incentives. From their response, the manufacturer can decide which virtual range to develop for retail customers.

Within twenty-four hours of taking the initial pictures or sketches, a new range of designs, all in 3D, is ready for pattern engineering and pre-production work. Using a proximity manufacturing operations strategy (see chapter 4) – offering quick response, high variety and small batch sizes – prototyping, computer cutting and production can begin. The e-procurement system, via the Intranet, will collaborate with suppliers to check forward plans and inventory levels so as to schedule material and component deliveries that are in line with production and final delivery schedules.

Within days, the new range of shoes is available from retail shops and from the manufacturers sales catalogue and web site. Sales data are continually fed upstream from retail sources in order to help manufacturers, and their suppliers, to replenish any particularly strong selling lines. In addition, work has already begun with a follow-up range ready to replace them.

This form of operation does, however, require a very proactive operations strategy that is continually under review and capable of change. The advantages are nevertheless clear. Despite higher unit cost, the flexibility and response provided will offer a lifetime of service to a loyal customer (be it retailer or consumer) who will actively collaborate in the development of a manufacturer's products and services in return for complete satisfaction of their unique value needs.

DISCUSSION QUESTIONS, WORK ASSIGNMENTS AND EXAM QUESTIONS

1   Distinguish between e-business and e-commerce.
2   What are the benefits and limitations of e-business?
3   Discuss the various types of e-business model outlined earlier terms of their particular focus and advantages or disadvantages.
4   What are the main impacts of e-business on an operations strategy?
5   How can an operations strategy provide a method by which to deploy policies throughout the organization?

Reader questions related to the European footwear industry case study

1   Discuss how an e-operations strategy could be applied to other non-fashion sectors. In particular, what would be the implications for the financial services sector or for the Swedish Medical Centre (see chapter 12)?
2   Are the advantages of an e-operations strategy and using e-business always clear-cut? Many leading grocery retailers offer Internet shopping facilities. However, the retailer is required to select goods and deliver to the buyer's home (activities the consumer would traditionally perform). It would appear that this method of operation does increase the retailer's direct costs. Are there other advantages to the retailer in the longer-term?

Epilogue

Science begins with myths, and the criticism of myths.
Karl Popper, 'The Philosophy of Science'

We have now reached the conclusion of the book. It is hoped that readers have found elements of the work useful and perhaps an inspiration for further investigation. As mentioned in the very early stages, this is a new and burgeoning discipline and one very much in need of further exploratory research. Our contribution has been to offer a particular unification: a fusion of the latest, cutting-edge empirical research with the contributions of some of the leading authors in the field. At the very least, we hope the book has been, in part, challenging and thought provoking – as research is intended to be!

Of course, the author welcomes constructive academic views, thoughts and comments and can be contacted via e-mail at: Bob.Lowson@uea.ac.uk. See also www.mgt.uea.ac.uk/research/somc.

References

Abbeglen J. and Stalk G. (1985) *Kaisha: the Japanese Corporation*, Basic Books, New York.

Ahlstrom P. (1998) 'Sequences in the Implementation of Lean Production', *European Management Journal* 16, 3, 327–34.

Aldrich H.E. (1979) *Organizations and Environments*, Prentice Hall, Englewood Cliffs, NJ.

Anderson J.C., Cleveland G. and Schroder R.G. (1989) 'Operations Strategy: A Literature Review', *Journal of Operations Management* 8, 2, 133–58.

Anderson M.G. and Katz P.B. (1998) 'Strategic Sourcing', *The International Journal of Logistics Management* 9, 1, 1–13.

Ansoff H.I. (1965) *Corporation Strategy*, McGraw-Hill, New York.

Atkinson J. (1984) 'Manpower Strategies for Flexible Organizations', *Personnel Management*, August.

Baden-Fuller C., Targett D. and Hunt B. (2000) 'Outsourcing to Outmanoeuvre: Outsourcing Redefines Competitive Strategy and Structure', *European Management Journal* 18, 3, 285–95.

Barclay I., Dann Z. and Holroyd P. (2000) *New Product Development*, Butterworth-Heinemann, Oxford.

Barlett C. and Ghoshal S. (1992) *Transnational Management*, Richard B. Irwin, Homewood, IL.

Beer M., Lawrence P., Mills D. and Walton R. (1985) *Human Resources Management*, Free Press, New York.

Beer M., Spector B., Lawrence P., Mills D. and Walton R. (1984) *Managing Human Assets*, Free Press, New York.

Berggren C. (1993) 'Lean Production – The End of History?', *Work, Employment and Society* 7, 2, 163–88.

Bertalanffy L. von (1950) 'Theory of Open Systems in Physics and Biology', *Science* 111, 23–9.

Bertalanffy, L. von (1956) 'General Systems Theory', in Bertalanffy 1968.

Bertalanffy, L. von (1968) *General System Theory*, Braziller, New York.

Blackburn J.D. (ed.) (1991) *Time-Based Competition: The Next Battleground in American Manufacturing*, Business One Irwin, Homewood, IL.

Bloom B.S. and Krathwohl D.R. (1956) *Taxonomy of Learning Objectives*, Longman, London.

Borsodi R. (1927) *The Distribution Age,* Appleton & Co, New York.

Bourgeois L.J. (1980) 'Strategy and the Environment: A Conceptual Integration', *Academy of Management Review* 5, 25–39.

Bowersox D.J. and Closs D.J. (1996) *Logistical Management, the Integrated Supply Chain Process,* Macmillan, New York.

Brown S., Lamming R., Bessant J. and Jones P. (2000) *Strategic Operations Management,* Butterworth-Heinemann, Oxford.

Bryce D.J. and Useem M. (1998) 'The Impact of Corporate Outsourcing on Company Value', *European Management Journal* 16, 6, 635–43.

Burbidge J.L. (1961) 'The New Approach to Production', *Production Engineer* 40, 12, 769–84.

Burnham J.M. and Natarajan R.T. (1999) 'Logistics is a Customer-driven Strategy', *APICS – The Performance Advantage (USA)* 9, 3, 38–43.

Burns T. and Stalker G.M. (1961) *The Management of Innovation,* Tavistock, London.

Chaffey D. (2002) *E-Business and E-Commerce Management,* FT Prentice Hall, Harlow, Essex.

Chandler A. (1962) *Strategy and Structure,* MIT Press, Cambridge, MA.

Chase R.B. (1978) 'Where Does the Customer Fit in a Service Operation', *Harvard Business Review* November/December, 137–42.

Chase R.B., Aquilano N.J. and Jacobs F.R. (2001) *Operations Management for Competitive Advantage,* McGraw-Hill Irwin, Boston.

Choipra S. and Meindl P. (2001) *Supply Chain Management: Strategy, Planning, and Operations,* Prentice Hall, Englewood Cliffs, NJ.

Christopher M. (1985) *The Strategy of Distribution Management,* Butterworth-Heinemann, Oxford.

Christopher M. (1992) *Logistics and Supply Chain Management,* Financial Times, Pitman Publishing, London.

Christopher M. (1998) *Logistics and Supply Chain Management: Strategies for Reducing Cost and Improving Service,* 2nd edn, Pitman Publishing, London.

Clarke M.P. (1998) 'Virtual Logistics: An Introduction and Overview of the Concepts', *International Journal of Physical Distribution and Logistics Management* 28, 7, 56–74.

Coase R.H. (1937) 'The Nature of the Firm', *Economica NS,* 4, 386–405.

Cohen M.A. and Agrawal V. (2001) 'All Change in the Second Supply Chain Revolution', in J. Pickford (ed.) *Mastering Management 2.0,* Financial Times Prentice Hall, London.

Cohen J. and Stewart I. (1994) *The Collapse of Chaos,* Viking, New York.

Collins O.F. and Moore D.G. (1970) *The Organization Makers,* Appleton-Century-Crofts, New York.

Collis D.J. (1996) 'Organizational Capability as Source of Profit', In B. Moingeon and A. Edmondson (eds) *Organizational Learning and Competitive Advantage,* Sage, London.

Dale B.G. and Plunkett J.J. (eds) (1990) *Managing Quality,* Philip Allan, New York.

De Meyer A. (1996) *Creating the Virtual Factory,* INSEAD Research Report, Paris.

De Meyer A. (1998) 'Manufacturing Operations in Europe: Where Do We Go Next?' *European Management Journal* 16, 3, 262–71.

Drucker P. (1962) 'The Economy's Dark Continent', *Fortune* April, 136–40.

Duguay C.R., Landry S. and Pasin F. (1997) 'From Mass Production to Flexible/Agile Production', *International Journal of Operations and Production Management* 17, 12, 1183–96.

Economist, The (1999) 'The Rise of Services', 29 May.

Emery F.E. and Trist E.L. (1965) 'The Causal Texture of Organizational Environments', *Human Relations* 18, 21–32.

Feitzinger E. and Lee H.L. (1997) 'Mass Customization at Hewlett-Packard: The Power of Postponement', *Harvard Business Review* January/February, 16–22.

Ferguson B.R. (2000) 'Implementing Supply Chain Management', *Production and Inventory Management Journal* 41, 64–7.

Filippini R. (1997) 'Operations Management Research: Some Reflections on Evolution, Models and Empirical Studies in OM', *International Journal of Operations and Production Management* 17, 7, 655–71.

Fincke U. and Goffard E. (1993) 'Customizing Distribution', *The McKinsey Quarterly* 1, 115–31.

Fisher M.L. (1997) 'What is the Right Supply Chain for your Product?', *Harvard Business Review* March/April, 105–17.

Fitzsimmons J.A. and Fitzsimmons M.J. (2000) *Service Management: Operations, Strategy, and Information Technology*, McGraw-Hill Inc., New York.

Fitzsimmons J.A. and Fitzsimmons M.J. (2001) *Service Management, Service Development and Process Design*, 3rd edn, McGraw-Hill, New York.

Fombrun C., Tichy N. and Devanna M. (1984) *Strategic Human Resources Management*, John Wiley & Sons Inc., New York.

Forrester J.W. (1961) *Industrial Dynamics*, The MIT Press, Cambridge, MA.

Fralix M. and Off J. (1994) *Agile Manufacturing within a Demand Activated System*, Quick Response Proceedings, Chicago.

Fung V. (1998) 'Fast, Global, and Entrepreneurial, Supply Chain Management, Hong Kong Style', *Harvard Business Review* September/October, 102.

Gadde L.E. and Hakansson H. (2001) *Supply Network Strategies*, John Wiley and Sons, Chichester.

Garvin D.A. (1988) *Managing Quality*, Free Press, New York.

Ghemawat P. (1999) *Strategy and the Business Landscape: Text and Cases*, Addison-Wesley, New York.

Giffi C.A., Roth A.V. and Seal G.M. (1990) *Competing in World Class Markets: America's 21st Century Challenge*, Business One Irwin, Homewood, IL.

Gilmore J.H. and Pine II B.J. (1997) 'Four Faces of Mass Customization', *Harvard Business Review* January/February, 91–101.

Gilreath T.L., Reeve J.M. and Whalen Jr C.E. (1995) 'Time is Money', *Bobbin* March, 50–5.

Godfrey P.C. and Hill C.W.L. (1995) 'The Problems of Unobservables in Strategic Management Research', *Strategic Management Journal* 16, 7, 23–45.

Goldman S.L. and Nagel R.N. (1993) 'Management, Technology and Agility: The Emergence of a New Era in Manufacturing', *International Journal of Technology Management* 8, 18–38.

Grant R. (1991) 'The Resource-based Theory of Competitive Advantage: Implications for Strategy Formulation', *California Management Review* 33, 114–22.

Gunston R. and Harding P. (1986) 'Quick Response: US and UK Experiences', *Textile Outlook International* 10, 43–51.

Hadjiconstantinou E. (ed.) (1999) *Quick Response in the Supply Chain*, Springer-Verlag, Berlin.

Haksever C., Render B., Russell R.S. and Murdick R.G. (2000) *Service Management and Operations*, Prentice Hall, Englewood Cliffs, NJ.

Hall R.H. (1977) *Organizations: Structure and Process,* 2nd edn, Prentice Hall, Englewood Cliffs, NJ.

Hamel G. and Prahalad C.K. (1990) 'Strategic Intent', *Harvard Business Review* May/June, 79–92.

Harrison A. (1992) *Just in Time in Perspective*, Prentice Hall, London.

Harrison A. (1999) 'Meeting Customer Demand: The Role of Agility', *Logistics and Transport Focus* 1, 3, 45–7.

Harrison M. (1993) *Operations Management Strategy*, Financial Times Pitman Publishing, London.

Hayes R.H. (1981) 'Why Japanese Factories Work', *Harvard Business Review* July/August, 114–26.

Hayes R.H. and Wheelwright S.C. (1984) *Restoring our Competitive Edge*, John Wiley & Sons Inc., New York.

Hayes R.H., Pisano G.P. and Upton D.M. (1996) *Competing through Capabilities*, The Free Press, New York.

Hayes R.H., Wheelwright S.C. and Clark K.B. (1988) *Dynamic Manufacturing*, The Free Press, New York.

Heizer J. and Render B. (2001) *Operations Management*, 6th edn, Prentice Hall, Englewood Cliifs, NJ.

Hendry C. (1991) 'International Comparisons of Human Resources Management: Putting the Firm in the Frame', *International Journal of Human Resources Management* 2, 415–40.

Hendry C. and Pettigrew A. (1986) 'The Practice of Strategic Human Resource Management', *Personnel Review* 15, 3–8.

Heskett J.L., Sasser W.E. and Schlesinger L.A. (1997) *The Service Profit Chain*, Free Press, New York.

Hill C.W.L. and Jones G. (1998) *Strategic Management*, Houghton-Mifflin, New York.

Hill T. (2000) *Operations Management: Strategic Context and Managerial Analysis*, Macmillan Business, Basingstoke.

Hines P. (1999) 'Value Stream Management: The Next Frontier in the Supply Chain?' *Logistics and Transport Focus (UK)* 1, 3, 36–40.

Hines P. and Rich M. (1997) 'The Seven Value-Stream Mapping Tools', *International Journal of Operations and Production Management* 17, 1, 23–36.

Hines P., Holweg M. and Sullivan J. (2000) 'Waves, Beaches, Breakwaters and Rip Currents – A Three-dimensional View of Supply Chain Dynamics', *International Journal of Physical Distribution and Logistics Management* 10, 827–46.

Hitt M., Ireland R.D. and Hoskisson J. (1999) *Strategic Management,* Southwestern College Publishing, Cincinnati.

Hockstra S. and Romme J. (eds) (1992) *Integral Logistics Structures,* McGraw-Hill, Maidenhead.

Holmström J. and Hameri A. (1999) 'The Dynamics of Consumer Response', *International Journal of Operations and Production Management* 19, 10, 993–1009.

Huda F. (1992) *Kaizen: The Understanding and Application of Continuous Improvement,* Technical Communications Ltd, Letchworth.

Hum S.H. and Sim H.H. (1996) 'Time-based Competition: Literature Review and Implications for Modeling', *International Journal of Operations and Production Management* 16, 1, 75–91.

Hunter N.A. (1990) *Quick Response in Apparel Manufacturing,* The Textile Institute, Manchester, UK.

Hunter N. A., King R. and Lowson R.H. (2002) *The Textile/Clothing Pipeline and Quick Response Management,* The Textile Institute, Manchester, UK.

Imai M. (1986) *Kaizen: The Key to Japan's Competitive Success,* McGraw-Hill, New York.

Imai M. (1997) *Gemba Kaizen: A Commonsense, Low-cost Approach to Management,* McGraw-Hill, New York.

Institute of Grocery Distribution (1996) *Efficient Consumer Response,* May, IDG, London.

Istvan R. (1988) *Time-Based Competition: The New Series,* Boston Consulting Group, Boston, MA.

Johnson R. and Lawrence P.R. (1988) 'Beyond Vertical Integration – the Rise of the Value adding Partnership', *Harvard Business Review* July/August, 271–96.

Jones C. (1989) 'Supply Chain Management The Key Issues', *BPICS Control* October/November, 15, 6, 23.

Juran J.M. and Gryna F.M. (1993) *Quality Planning and Analysis,* McGraw-Hill, New York.

Kalakota R. and Whinston A. (1997) *Electronic Commerce. A Manager's Guide,* Addison-Wesley, Reading, MA.

Kanji G.K. (1990) 'Total Quality Management: The Second Industrial Revolution', *Total Quality Management* 1, 1, 3–12.

Kast E. and Rosenzweig J.E. (1973) *Contingency Views of Organization and Management,* Science Research Associates, Chicago.

Katz D. and Kahn R.L. (1978) *The Social Psychology of Organizations,* John Wiley & Sons Inc., New York.

Kay J. (1993) *Foundations of Corporate Success,* Oxford University Press, Oxford.

Keen P.G.W. (1997) *The Process Edge: Creating Value Where it Counts,* Harvard Business School Press, Boston.

Keough M. (1993) 'Buying Your Way to the Top (The Purchasing Function)', *The McKinsey Quarterly* 3, 93, 41–63.

Khandwalla P.N. (1977) *The Design of Organisations,* Harcourt Brace Jovanovich, New York.

Kidd P. (1994) *Agile Manufacturing – Forging New Frontiers,* Addison-Wesley, Reading, MA.

King, R. (2001) 'Weathering the Industry's Perfect Storm', *Bobbin,* January, 24–8.

King R.E. and Hunter N.A. (1996) 'Demand Re-estimation and Inventory Replenishment of Basic Apparel in a Specialty Retail Chain', *The Journal of the Textile Institute* 87, 1, 31–41.

King R.E. and Hunter N.A. (1997) 'Quick Response Beats Importing in Retail Sourcing Analysis', *Bobbin* 38, 7, 27–35.

Kohn J.W. and McGinnis M.A. (1999) 'Logistics Strategy: A Longitudinal Study', *Journal of Business Logistics (USA)* 18, 2, 1–14.

Kolb D.A., Rubin I.M. and McIntyre J.M. (1979) *Organisational Psychology: An Experiential Approach*, Prentice Hall, London.

Kotha S. (1996) 'From Mass Production to Mass Customization', *European Management Journal* 14, 5, 442–50.

Krajewski L.J. and Ritzman L.P. (1999) *Operations Management*, Addison-Wesley, Reading, MA.

Kurt Salmon Associates (1988) *Quick Response Implementation – Action Steps for Retailers, Manufacturers and Suppliers*, KSA, Atlanta, GA.

Kurt Salmon Associates (1993) *Efficient Consumer Response: Enhancing Consumer Value in the Grocery Industry*, Food Marketing Institute, Washington, DC.

Kurt Salmon Associates (1995) *Efficient Consumer Response*, Food Marketing Institute, Washington, DC.

La Londe B.J. and Masters J.M. (1994) 'Emerging Logistics Strategies: Blueprints for the Next Century', *International Journal of Physical Distribution and Logistics Management* 24, 7, 35–47.

Lamming R. and Cox A. (1995) *Strategic Procurement Management in the 1990s: Concepts and Cases*, The Chartered Institute of Purchasing and Supply, Stamford, UK.

Lauterborn R. (1990) 'New Marketing Litany: Four Ps Passé; C-words Take Over, *Advertising Age*, 1 October, 26.

Lawrence P.R. and Lorsch J.W. (1967) 'Differentiation and Integration in Complex Organizations', *Administrative Science Quarterly* 12, 1–47.

Lee H. (1998) 'Postponement for Mass Customization: Satisfying Customer Demands for Tailor-made Products', in J. Gattorna (ed.) *Strategic Supply Chain Management*, Gower, Aldershot, UK.

Levy D. (1994) 'Chaos Theory and Strategy: Managerial Implications', *Strategic Management Journal* 15, Summer, 167–78.

Levy S. (1992) *Artificial Life: The Quest for a New Creation*, Pantheon Books, New York.

Lilienfeld R. (1978) *The Rise of Systems Theory*, John Wiley & Sons Inc., New York.

Loch C. (1998) 'Operations Management and Reengineering', *European Management Journal* 16, 3, 306–17.

Lorenzi G. and Baden-Fuller C. (1995) 'Creating a Strategic Center to Manage a Web of Partners', *California Management Review* 37, 3, 146–63.

Lowson R.H. (1998) *Quick Response for SMEs: A Feasibility Study*, The Textile Institute, Manchester, UK.

Lowson R.H. (1999) '*The Impact of Quick Response in the Textile and Clothing Industry: Analysis and Application*', PhD Thesis, Cardiff University, UK.

Lowson R.H. (2001a) 'Customized Operational Strategies for Retailers in Fast-moving Consumer Goods Industries', *International Review of Retail, Distribution and Consumer Research* 11, 2, 201–24.

Lowson R.H. (2001b) 'Analysing the Effectiveness of European Retail Sourcing Strategies', *European Management Journal* 19, 5, 543–51.

Lowson R.H. (2001c) 'Retail Operational Strategies in Complex Supply Chains: Analysis and Application', *International Journal of Logistics Management* 12, 1, 97–111.

Lowson R.H. (2001d) 'Retail Sourcing Strategies: Are they Cost-effective', *International Journal of Logistics* 4, 3, 271–96.

Lowson R.H., King R.E. and Hunter A. (1999) *Quick Response: Managing the Supply Chain to Meet Consumer Demand*, John Wiley and Sons, Chichester.

Lumus R.R. and Vokurka R.J. (1999) 'Managing the Demand Chain through Managing the Information Flow: Capturing "Moments of Information"', *Production and Inventory Management Journal* 39, 49–58.

McFarlan F.W. (1984) '*Information Technology Changes the Way You Compete*', *Harvard Business Review* May/June.

Makridakis S., Wheelwright S.C. and Hyndman R.J. (1998) *Forecasting: Methods and Applications*, John Wiley & Sons Inc., New York.

Malone T.W., Yates J. and Benjamin R.I. (1987) 'Electronic Markets, Electronic Hierarchies', *Communications of the ACM* 30, 6, 484–97.

Marion R. (1999) *The Edge of Organisation*, Sage, Thousand Oaks, CA.

Maturana H. (1988) 'Reality: The Search for Objectivity or the Quest for a Compelling Argument', *Irish Journal of Psychology* 9, 1, 25–82.

Maturana H.R. and Varela F.J. (1980) *Autopoiesis and Cognition*, D. Reidel Publishing, Dordrecht.

Maturana H.R. and Varela F.J. (1987) *The Tree of Knowledge*, Shambhala, Boston.

Meredith J.R. and Amoaka-Gyampah K. (1990) 'The Genealogy of Operations Management', *Journal of Operations Management* 9, 2, 146–67.

Meredith J.R. and Shafer S.M. (2002) *Operations Management for MBAs*, John Wiley & Sons Inc., New York.

Miles R.H. (1980) *Macro Organizational Behaviour*, Goodyear, Santa Monica, CA.

Miller J.G. and Roth A.V. (1994) 'A taxonomy of manufacturing strategies', *Management Science* 40, 3, 285–304.

Milne, A.A. (1973) *Winnie-the-Pooh*, Methuen Children's Books, London.

Mintzberg H. (1978) 'Patterns of Strategy Formulation', *Management Science* 24, 934–48.

Mintzberg H. (1979a) 'An Emerging Strategy of Direct Research', *Administrative Science Quarterly* 24, 582–89.

Mintzberg H. (1979b) *The Structuring of Organizations*, Prentice Hall, Englewood Cliffs, NJ.

Mintzberg H. (1982) 'Tracking Strategy in the Entrepreneurial Firm', *Academy of Management Journal* 7, 465–99.

Mintzberg H. (1985) 'Of Strategies: Deliberate and Emergent', *Strategic Management Journal* 6, 257–72.

313

Mintzberg H. (1987) 'Crafting Strategy', *Harvard Business Review* July/August.

Mintzberg H. (1988) *Mintzberg on Management: Inside Our Strange World of Organizations*, Free Press, New York.

Nagel R.N. and Dove R. (1991a) *21st Century Manufacturing Enterprise Strategy*, Volume 1: *An Industry Led-View*, Agile Manufacturing Enterprise Forum in cooperation with the Iacocca Institute, Lehigh University, Bethlehem, PA.

Nagel R.N. and Dove R. (1992b) *21st Century Manufacturing Enterprise Strategy*, Volume 2: Agile Manufacturing Enterprise Forum in cooperation with the Iacocca Institute, Lehigh University, Bethlehem, PA.

Narasimhan R. and Das A. (1999) 'An Empirical Investigation of the Contribution of Strategic Sourcing to Manufacturing Flexibility and Performance', *Decision Sciences* 30, 3, 683–719.

New Shorter Oxford English Dictionary (1993) Clarendon Press, Oxford.

Oakland J.S. (1989) *Total Quality Management*, 2nd edn, Heinemann, Oxford.

Off C. (1976) *Industry and Inequality*, Edward Arnold, London.

Ohmae K. (1982) *The Mind of the Strategist: The Art of Japanese Business*, McGraw-Hill, New York.

Parasuraman A., Zeithaml V.A. and Berry L.L. (1985) 'A Conceptual Model of Service quality and its Implications for Future Research', *Journal of Marketing* 49, 4, 41–50.

Penrose E. (1959) *The Theory of the Growth of the Firm*, Basil Blackwell, Oxford.

Peteraf M.A. (1993) 'The Cornerstones of Competitive Advantage: The Resource-based View', *Strategic Management Journal* 14, 2, 37–46.

Pine II B.J., Bart V. and Boynton A.C. (1993) 'Making Mass Customisation Work', *Harvard Business Review* September/October 108–19.

Piore M.E. and Sabel C. (1984) *The Second Industrial Divide: Possibilities for Prosperity*, Basic Books, New York.

Porter M.E. (1979) 'How Competitive Forces Shape Strategy', *Harvard Business Review* March/April, 86–93.

Porter M.E. (1980) *Competitive Strategy: Techniques for Analysing Industries and Competitors*, Free Press, New York.

Porter M.E. (1985) *Competitive Advantage: Creating and Sustaining Superior Performance*, Free Press, New York.

Porter M.E. (1996) 'What is Strategy', *Harvard Business Review* November/December, 61–79.

Porter M.E. (2001) 'Strategy and the Internet', *Harvard Business Review* March/April, pp 63–78.

Pragman C.H. (1996) 'JIT II: A Purchasing Concept for Reducing Lead Times in Time-based Competition', *Business Horizons* July/August, 54–9.

Prahalad C.K. and Hamel G. (1990) 'The Core Competency of the Corporation', *Harvard Business Review* 68, 79–91.

Priesmeyer H.R. (1992) *Organizations and Chaos: Defining the Methods of Nonlinear Management*, Quorum Books, Westport, CT.

Prigonine I. (1997) *The End of Certainty*, The Free Press, New York.

Quinn F.J. (1997) 'What's the Buzz? Supply Chain Management Part I', *Logistics Management* 36, 43, 68–75.

Quinn J.B., Doorley T.L. and Paquette P.C. (1990) 'Beyond Products: Services-Based Strategy', *Harvard Business Review* March/April.

Rising E.J., Baron R. and Averill B. (1973) 'A Systems Analysis of a University Health-Service Outpatient Clinic', *Operations Research* 21, 5, September/October, 415–21.

Rovizzi L. and Thompson D. (1992) 'Fitting Company Strategy to Industry Structure: A Strategic audit of the Rise of Benetton and Stefanel', *Business Strategy Review* Autumn, 73–99.

Rumelt R.P. (1984) 'Towards a Strategic Theory of the Firm', in R. B. Lamb (ed.) *Competitive Strategic Management*, Prentice Hall, Englewood Cliffs, NJ.

Russell R.S. and Taylor B.W. (2001) *Operations Management*, Prentice Hall, Englewood Cliffs, NJ.

Safizadeh H.M., Ritzman L.P., Sharma D. and Wood C. (1996) 'An Empirical Analysis of the Product-Process Matrix', Management Science 42, 11, 1576–91.

Schonberger R.J. (1986) *World Class Manufacturing: The Lessons of Simplicity Applied*, Free Press, New York.

Selznick P. (1957) *Leadership in Administration*, Harper and Row, New York.

Sethi N.K. (1970) 'A Research Model to Study Environmental Factors in Management', *Management International Review* 10, 75–86.

Sharp D. and Hill R. (1998) Efficient Consumer Response: From Harmful Competition to Winning Collaboration in the Grocery Industry', in J. Gattorna (ed.) *Strategic Supply Chain Alignment*, Gower, Aldershot, UK.

Sherman R.J. (1998) 'Collaborative Planning, Forecasting and Replenishment', *Journal of Marketing Theory and Practice* 6, 4, 16–24 (http://www.cpfr.org).

Skinner W. (1974) 'The Focused Factory', *Harvard Business Review* May/June 113–21.

Skinner W. (1985) *Manufacturing, The Formidable Competitive Weapon*, John Wiley & Sons Inc., New York.

Skinner W. (1996) 'Three Yards and a Cloud of Dust: Industrial Management at the Century End', *Production and Operations Management* 1, 11–12.

Slack N. (1991) *The Manufacturing Advantage*, Mercury/Management Books, Didcot, UK.

Slack N. (ed.) (1999) *Encyclopedic Dictionary of Operations Management*, Blackwell Business, Oxford.

Slack N. and Lewis M. (2002) Operations Strategy, Financial Times and Prentice Hall, Harlow, UK.

Slack N., Chambers S. and Johnston R. (2001) *Operations Management*, Financial Times and Prentice Hall, Harlow, UK.

Sparrow P. and Hiltrop J.M. (1996) *European Human Resources Management in Transition*, Prentice Hall, Englewood Cliffs, NJ.

Stacey R.D., Griffin D. and Shaw P. (2000) *Complexity and Management*, Routledge, London.

Stalk G. (1988) 'Time, the Next Source of Competitive Advantage', *Harvard Business Review* July/August, 41–52.

Stalk G. and Hout T. (1990) *Competing Against Time: How Time Based Competition is Reshaping Global Markets*, The Free Press, New York.

Stalk G. Jr and Webber A.M. (1993) 'Japan's Dark Side of Time', *Harvard Business Review* July/August, 93–102.

Stevens C.G. (1989) 'Integrating the Supply Chain', *International Journal of Physical Distribution and Materials Management* 19, 8, 27–35.

Stevenson H.H. and Gumpert D.E. (1991) '*The Heart of the Enterprise*', in W.A. Sahlman and H.H. Stevenson (eds) *The Entrepreneurial Venture*, Harvard Business School, Boston.

Stewart H.M., Hope C.A. and Mühlemann A.P. (1996) 'Professional Service Quality: A Step Beyond Other Services', Third DIRASS/EIRASS International Conference on Retailing and Services Science, 22–5 June, Telfs/Buchen, Austria.

Stock G.N., Greis N.P. and Kasarda J.D. (1998) 'Logistics, Strategy and Structure: A Conceptual Framework', *International Journal of Operations and Production Management* 18, 1, 37–52.

Stuart F.I. and McCutcheon D.M. (2000) 'The Manager's Guide to Supply Chain Management', *Business Horizons* 43, 2, 35–45.

Sugimori T., Kusunoki K., Cho F. and Uchikawa S. (1977) 'Toyota Production System and Kanban System Materialization for Just in time', *International Journal of Production Research* 15, 6, 91–107.

Suri R. (1998) *Quick Response Manufacturing*, Productivity Press, Portland, OR.

Swamidass P.M. and Newell W.T. (1987) 'Manufacturing Strategy, Environmental Uncertainty and Performance: A Path Analytic Model', *Management Science* 33, 4, 509–24.

Tapscott D., Tocoll D. and Lowy A. (1999) 'The Rise of the Business Web', *Business 2.00* November, 198–204.

Teece D.J., Pisano G. and Shuen A. (1997) 'Dynamic Capabilities and Strategic Management', *Strategic Management Journal* 18, 7, 509–33.

Thompson K., Mitchell H. and Knox S. (1998) 'Organisational Buying Behaviour in Changing Times', *European Management Journal* 16, 6, 698–705.

Thompson P. and McHugh D. (1995) *Work Organisations: A Critical Introduction*, Macmillan Business Press, London.

Tichy N., Fombrun C. and Devanna M. (1982) 'Strategic Human Resources Management', *Sloan Management Review* 23, 2, 47–61.

Toffler A. (1994) 'Recipe for Intelligence', *Information Today* March, 61–3.

Treacey M. and Wiersema F. (1997) *The Discipline of Market Leaders*, Addison-Wesley, Reading, MA.

Trosiglio A. (1995) 'Managing Complexity', unpublished working paper, in D. Deutsch (1997) *The Fabric of Reality*, Penguin, New York.

Upton D.M. (1994) 'The Management of Manufacturing Flexibility', *California Management Review* Winter, 72–89.

Upton D.M. (1995) 'What Really makes Factories Flexible?' *Harvard Business Review* July/August, 72–89.

US Bureau of the Census, http://www.census.gov/prod/www/titles.html rt

316

Van Looy B., Van Dierdonck R. and Gemmel P. (1998) *Services Management,* Financial Times Pitman Publishing, London.

Vandermerwe S. and Rada J. (1988) 'Servitization of Business: Adding Value by Adding Services', *European Management Journal* 6, 4, 314–24.

Venkatraman N. and Henderson J.C. (1998) 'Real Strategies for Virtual Organizing', *Sloan Management Review* 40, 1, 33–49.

Vining A. and Globerman S. (1999) 'A Conceptual Framework for Understanding the Outsourcing Decision', *European Management Journal* 17, 6, 645–54.

Voluntary Interindustry Commerce Standards (VICS) Association (1998) *Collaborative Planning, Forecasting and Replenishment,* UICS, Arlington, VA.

Walker W.T. and Alber K.L. (1999), 'Understanding Supply Chain Management', *APICS – The Performance Advantage,* 9, 38–43.

Wernerfelt B. (1984) 'A Resource-based View of the Firm', *Strategic Management Journal* 5, 2, 171–80.

Westbrook R. and Williamson P. (1993) 'Mass Customisation: Japan's New Frontier', *European Management Journal* 11, 1, 38–45.

Whicker L. and Walton J. (1996) 'Logistics and the Virtual Enterprise', *Logistics Focus* 4/8, 2, 23–40.

Williams K., Haslam C., Williams J. and Cutler T. (1992) 'Against Lean Production', *Economy and Society* 21, 3, 321–54.

Williamson O.E. (1981) 'The Modern Corporation: Origins, Evolution, Attributes', *Journal of Economic Literature,* 41–78.

Womack J. and Jones D. (1996) *Lean Thinking,* Simon and Schuster, New York.

Womack J., Jones D. and Roos D. (1990) *The Machine that Changed the World,* Macmillan, New York.

Wood A. (1993) 'Efficient Consumer Response', *Logistics Information Management* 6, 4, 104–13.

Woodward J. (1958) *Management and Technology,* HMSO, London.

Yourcenar, M. (2000) *Memoirs of Hadrian,* trans. G. Frick, Penguin, London.

Zeithaml V.A. (1988) 'Consumer Perceptions of Price, Quality and Value: A Means-End Model and Synthesis of Evidence', *Journal of Marketing* 52, 2–22.

Zipkin P. (2001) 'The Limits of Mass Customization', *Sloan Management Review* 42, 3, 81–8.

Index